Josh McDowell's
One Year® Book of
Family Devotions

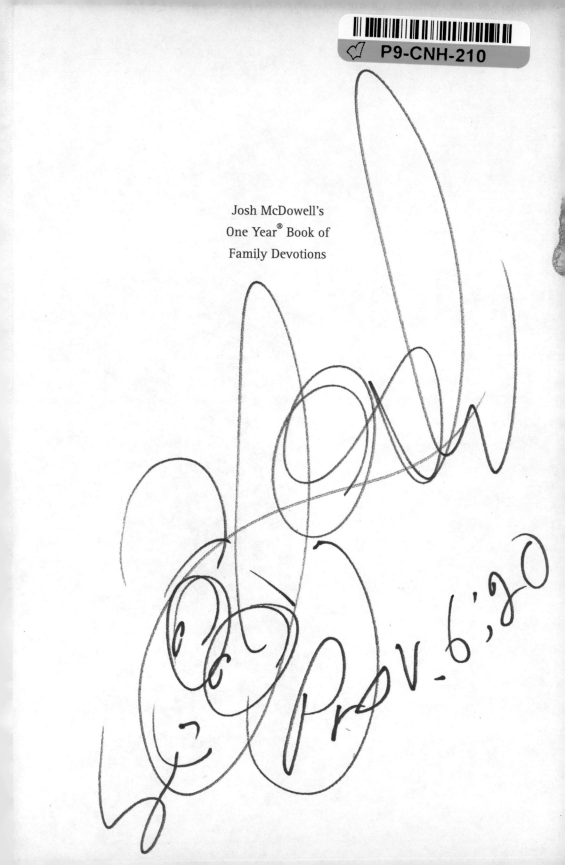

Prov. 6:20

Josh McDowell's

ONE YEAR®

BOOK OF

FAMILY DEVOTIONS

BY Bob Hostetler

Tyndale House Publishers, Inc.
WHEATON, ILLINOIS

Visit Tyndale's exciting Web site at www.tyndale.com

Edited by Betty Free and Linda Washington
Designed by Cathy Bergstrom

The One Year is a registered trademark of Tyndale House Publishers, Inc.

Library of Congress Cataloging-in-Publication Data

McDowell, Josh.
   [One year book of family devotions]
   Josh McDowell's one year book of family devotions / Bob Hostetler.
     p.   cm.
   Includes index.
   ISBN 0-8423-4302-4 (pbk. : alk. paper)
   1. Family—Prayer-books and devotions—English. 2. Devotional
calendars. I. Hostetler, Bob, [date]– . II. Title.
BV255.M394 1997   97-17460
249—dc21

Printed in the United States of America

03 02 01 00 99 98
7   6   5   4   3

CONTENTS

Using This Book

January

February

March

April

May

June

July

August

September

October

November

December

Using This Book

EVERYONE'S TALKING ABOUT values and virtues. But *Josh McDowell's One Year Book of Family Devotions* offers you a chance to do more than just talk; it is designed to help you and your family *do something* about the "crisis of truth" that threatens our culture, our churches, and our children.

This book is part of a multifaceted campaign designed to restore biblical values and views to today's families. The campaign, launched in 1994 with the publication of the book *Right from Wrong* (Word Publishing), has helped hundreds of thousands of Christians rebuild and strengthen the crumbling moral and ethical foundations of the current generation. Repeatedly, however, parents, pastors, and teachers have cried out for a tool that will help them apply the life-changing message of that campaign to the daily lives of themselves and their families.

This book is designed to help you teach biblical views of right and wrong in 366 gripping and captivating readings. Each day's reading includes a reference for a Bible reading, a verse of the day, and printed suggestions for discussion questions or activities and prayer. The main point of the day's reading is displayed in large, bold letters to help parents understand and reinforce the message. The daily stories and questions are designed for use with children of all ages, from toddlers to teenagers.

In addition, *Josh McDowell's One Year Book of Family Devotions* is designed according to a plan that will, over the course of a year, expose a family to the biblical virtues of love, honesty, justice, mercy, purity, self-control, compassion, faithfulness, generosity, respect, humility, kindness, perseverance, and patience. These godly qualities and behaviors are taught by means of a process introduced in the Right from Wrong Campaign, often called the Four Cs:

Consider the choice. In other words, the first step in making a right choice is remembering that it is God who determines what is right or wrong, not the individual, his culture, or the opinions of others.

Compare our attitudes and actions to God. The second step in making right choices is to compare a contemplated action or attitude to God, because it is his nature and character that determine what is right or wrong. Therefore, many of the daily readings are designed to help readers trace right and wrong behaviors through God's *precepts* (or commands) to godly *principles* and, finally, to the *person* of God himself.

Commit to God's ways. When we compare our attitudes and actions to God as God, we *admit* that his character and nature define right and wrong absolutely. Those attitudes and actions that are like him are right, and those attitudes and actions that are not like him are wrong. But when we commit to God's way, it means we turn from our selfish attitudes and actions and *submit* to him as Lord of our lives. It means we rely on the power of his Spirit to live out his way in us.

Count on God's protection and provision. When we humbly admit God's sovereignty and sincerely submit to his loving authority, we can begin not only to clearly see the distinctions between right and wrong, but we can also count on God's protection and provision. Living according to God's way and allowing the Holy Spirit to live through us brings many spiritual blessings, like freedom from guilt, a clear conscience, the joy of sharing Christ, and most importantly, the love and smile of God in our lives. Additionally, we enjoy many physical, emotional, psychological, and relational benefits when we are obedient to God. This doesn't mean everything will be rosy; in fact, God says that we may suffer for righteousness' sake. But God's commands were nonetheless given to protect and provide for his people (Deuteronomy 10:13; Jeremiah 32:39).

In addition to the Four Cs, *Josh McDowell's One Year Book of Family Devotions* also teaches many basic concepts of biblical morality. Some readings deal with the issues of tolerance and truth in easy-to-understand ways, while others help readers understand how to resist temptation, how to respond after making a wrong choice, and how to stand for truth. All the readings are offered with the understanding that a personal relationship with God through his Son, Jesus Christ, is fundamental to making right moral choices in life.

Finally, *Josh McDowell's One Year Book of Family Devotions* can be used in tandem with *Josh McDowell's One Year Book of Youth Devotions*. The two devotionals correspond to each other, so that a young person who is using the youth devotional will receive reinforcement and a different perspective in the daily youth readings. More on other resources to help you in the battle to keep the culture from capturing your kids is found at the back of this book.

Teaching biblical truth to each new generation is a solemn responsibility of godly parents (Deuteronomy 6:4-9). Our prayer is that these simple devotions will help you better impart godly values and views to your family.

1 Radio Daze

SOME PEOPLE THINK THAT RIGHT AND WRONG ARE OLD-FASHIONED IDEAS.

Bible Reading of the Day: Read Psalm 19:8-11.
Verse of the Day: *"[Do] what is good and right in the eyes of the Lord your God" (Deuteronomy 12:28, NIV).*

Melissa and her parents were on their way to the grocery store.

"Can we listen to that new radio station, Dad?" Melissa asked. When she saw her father shrug, she quickly turned the station.

"Ooo! That's my song, the new one from Toe Jam!" she exclaimed. She sang along: *"Ain't no wrong, Ain't no right, Ain't no reason not to love you tonight."*

"Melissa!" Dad said, surprised. "Do you know what you're singing?"

"I never pay much attention to the words. I only like this song because of the music." Melissa looked from one to the other of her parents. "What's wrong?"

"Maybe you should pay attention to the words," Mom said.

Melissa played the lyrics back in her mind. *Ain't no wrong, Ain't no right, Ain't no reason not to love you tonight.*

"OK, I see what you mean. They're saying there's nothing that's wrong or right. But *I* don't think that."

"But you still listen to the song," Mom said.

"Everybody does! My whole school talks about this group," said Melissa.

"A lot of people do think that way these days," Dad said. "They think *right* and *wrong* are old-fashioned ideas and that people have to decide right or wrong for themselves."

"But we don't think that, do we?" Melissa asked.

"It doesn't matter what *we* think," Mom answered. "It doesn't matter what I say, or what you say, or what Toe Jam says. All that matters is what God says."

"And God says some things are right and some things are wrong," Melissa said.

"Right! You know what else?" Dad said, laughing. "Even people who say there is no such thing as 'right' or 'wrong' expect you to treat them fairly. They may say, 'You have to decide what's right for you, and I have to decide what's right for me,' but if you try to cheat them in any way, they'll tell you your behavior isn't 'right!'"

"Because in their hearts they know the truth," said Mom.

Melissa nodded as if she understood. "Can I ask a question?" she asked.

"Of course, sweetheart," Mom said, smiling.

"Can we change the radio station?"

Dad answered, "I think we can arrange that."

 TO DISCUSS: Should a person listen to lyrics that go against his or her beliefs? Why or why not? How can a person know what's *right* or *wrong*?

TO PRAY: "Lord, you are the one who decides what is right or wrong. Help us to follow you."

2 How Do You Choose?

IF GOD SAYS SOMETHING IS WRONG, THEN IT'S WRONG. PERIOD.

Bible Reading of the Day: Read Joshua 24:14-15.
Verse of the Day: *"As for me and my family, we will serve the Lord"* *(Joshua 24:15).*

Mom stood in front of the vending machine at the highway rest stop. Mom, Rita, and Kim were on their way home from camp. "What kind of candy would you like, Rita?" she asked.

"I don't know," Rita said. She turned to her friend. "You choose first, Kim."

Kim crossed her arms and tapped her foot. "OK." She thought for just a moment. "I'm in the mood for a Smackaroon bar, please," she said to Rita's mom.

"A Smackaroon bar it is," Mom said as she inserted the coins and pressed the button. "Now, Rita, have you made a decision yet?"

Rita smiled and nodded. "I'll have the same thing she chose," she announced.

Mom inserted more coins and pushed the same button. Rita pulled her candy bar from the machine, and the two girls walked back to the car with Mom.

"It was interesting to watch you two girls make choices," Mom said. "You chose your candy the way a lot of people try to make right choices."

"What do you mean, Mom?" Rita asked.

"Well, some people try to make right choices the way Kim chose her candy bar. They try to decide what's right or wrong based on how they feel. For example, if they feel mad, they think it's all right to hit someone or call someone a name." Mom, Rita, and Kim got into the car, and Mom continued talking as she drove.

"Other people try to make right choices the way you chose your candy bar, Rita. They try to decide what's right or wrong depending on what everyone else is doing. If they see other people cheating or breaking the law, they think it's OK for them to do it too."

"You're right, Mom," Rita said. "I never thought of that before."

"It would be kinda dumb to choose right and wrong the way we choose a candy bar, wouldn't it?" Kim said. She and Rita exchanged smiles.

"I think so," Mom said. "Instead of making decisions based on how you feel or what other people are doing, I hope you girls will always make your choices according to what God says to do. If you do that, you won't go wrong."

"Uh, Mom," Rita called. "You just made a wrong choice."

"What's that?" Mom asked.

"You passed our house!"

 TO DO: Carry a piece of candy in your pocket or purse tomorrow to remind yourself that it's best to make your choices according to what God says to do.

TO PRAY: "Jesus, help us to honor you with our choices."

3 Do the Right Thing

WHATEVER IS LIKE GOD IS RIGHT, AND WHATEVER IS NOT LIKE GOD IS WRONG.

Bible Reading of the Day: Read Deuteronomy 32:3-4.
Verse of the Day: *"Make them pure and holy by teaching them your words of truth"* (John 17:17).

"I have to go down to the attendance office for a few minutes," Mrs. Stanford announced to the class. "I want everyone to read pages 89 through 92 while I'm gone."

As soon as their teacher disappeared, Bobby and Stan made a dash for the teacher's desk. They started playing with an object made of strings and silver balls, which clacked together in a swinging motion. It was fun to watch. Soon the desk was surrounded with almost the whole class—until one of the silver balls broke loose from the string that held it and rolled across the floor. Immediately, the students returned to their seats.

Mrs. Stanford returned to the room and noticed the damage. She began asking the students what had happened. The first girl lied; she said she didn't know. The second student said the same thing. Then the teacher asked Amy, who explained matter-of-factly what had happened.

When Amy got home after school, her mother had already heard what had happened that day. She took Amy out for ice cream, and they talked while they ate.

"Honey," Mom said, "I'm glad you told the truth today. Why would it have been wrong for you to lie?"

She thought for a moment. Then she said, "Because the Bible says it's wrong."

"Why does the Bible say it's wrong?"

"Because God said not to lie."

"Why did God say not to lie?"

"I don't know," Amy admitted.

"Because God is truth, honey. God never lies. Whatever is like him is right, and whatever is not like him is wrong. Lying is not like God. *That's* why lying is wrong."

Amy nodded and crunched into her ice-cream cone.

"It was hard for you to tell the truth in class today, wasn't it?" Mom asked.

Amy nodded. "Yeah, because I was the only one who did!"

"But you did the right thing, because you told the truth."

Amy popped the rest of the ice-cream cone into her mouth. "And that was right because it was like God," she said proudly.

"Right!" Mom said.

"Right!" Amy echoed.

 TO DISCUSS: What makes an attitude or an action right or wrong? How can you know if something is right or wrong?

TO PRAY: "Lord God, you have made us pure and holy by your words of truth. May our actions reflect your holiness and truth."

4 Freedom of Truth (Part 1)

THE TRUTH WILL SET YOU FREE.

Bible Reading of the Day: Read John 8:31-32.
Verse of the Day: *"And you will know the truth, and the truth will set you free" (John 8:32).*

Brian ran excitedly from one exhibit to another as he and his father toured the Air and Space Museum. Brian loved airplanes, helicopters, and spaceships. He had a collection of airplane toys and models. He wanted to be a pilot when he grew up.

"Brian," his dad called. "Come over here. I want you to see something."

Brian joined Dad beside the airplane the Wright brothers had flown at Kitty Hawk, North Carolina, in 1903.

"Do you know what this is?" Dad asked.

Brian made an impatient sound. "Give me a break, Dad! This is Orville and Wilbur Wright's first plane. It was the first power airplane. It flew thirty miles on its first flight."

"Hmm," Dad said, sounding impressed. "How did they know it would fly?"

"Because they did all kinds of tests, Dad. They really studied the laws of aerodynamics and all that kind of stuff."

Dad thought for a moment, then looked at Brian. "Let me ask you another question. What do you think would have happened if the Wright brothers had tried to fly without studying the laws of aerodynamics?"

"They would have crashed!"

"You mean they never would have flown? like a bird? They never would have been free to fly through the air?"

Brian looked suspiciously at his dad. "What's this all about, Dad?"

Dad smiled and shrugged. "I just wanted you to recognize how the truth can set people free, Brian. If the Wright brothers hadn't paid attention to the laws of physics, like gravity and force and velocity and all that stuff, their airplane would have never gotten off the ground. It was the truth that set them free to fly."

Dad continued, "The same thing happens in other things, too. If you or I go through life ignoring God's truth, we'll never know real freedom. We'll be imprisoned in sin. We may be enslaved by drugs, or depression, or other things.

"But if we know God's truth, and pay attention to it, and obey it, we'll be free—free from sin and free from the consequences of wrong choices. That's what Jesus meant when he said 'the truth will set you free.'"

Brian glanced at the plane again, then looked back to his father. "I see what you mean," he said thoughtfully.

TO DISCUSS: What does the phrase "the truth will set you free" mean to you? Have you been reminded of any truths today? In what ways has knowing the truth set you free? Can you give examples?

TO PRAY: "Loving God, set us free by your truth."

5 Freedom of Truth (Part 2)

THE WAY OF THE WICKED IS LIKE COMPLETE DARKNESS.

Bible Reading of the Day: Read Proverbs 4:18-19.
Verse of the Day: *"And you will know the truth, and the truth will set you free" (John 8:32).*

Dad and Brian walked through the doors of the Air and Space Museum and into the bright light of a sunny day. As they walked down the museum's stone steps, Brian asked, "Dad, you know what you were saying about how the truth sets you free?"

Dad nodded.

"Can you explain that some more?" he asked.

"Sure, Son," his dad said. "Let me ask you this. How did you feel when you woke up this morning?"

Brian shrugged. "OK, I guess. I was a little sleepy at first. . . ."

"Did your head hurt?"

"No."

"Did your mouth feel like you had swallowed a bag of cotton balls?"

"No," Brian answered.

Dad nodded. "I'm glad to hear that, Son, because those feelings are common to someone who drank too much alcohol the night before. It's called a hangover."

Brian rolled his eyes. "I'm just a kid, Dad. You wouldn't let me drink that stuff anyway."

"You're right," Dad said with a wink. "But *I'm* not a kid, and you don't see me getting drunk, do you?" Brian shook his head solemnly. "Why not?"

"Because the Bible says that it's wrong?"

"Right. But also because I know the truth will set me free. I know that if I obey God's commands not to get drunk, I'll be free from the pain of a hangover. And I'll never take the chance of hurting or killing someone by driving while I'm drunk.

"That's just one of the ways the truth sets us free, Son. Obeying God's commands makes us free in so many ways. If I obey his command not to steal, I can be free from the guilt, shame, and fear of punishment that would plague me, even if I never got caught. If I obey his command not to lie, I can avoid being trapped by my own lies, without having to tell new lies to cover up the old ones. If I obey his command to be faithful to your mom, I free myself and my family from a lot of pain and trouble."

"I bet a lot of people don't even know how free they are!" Brian said.

Dad nodded. "And a lot of people don't even know how much they're missing if they don't follow God's ways."

 TO DO: The next time you see a bright, sunny day, remember that "the way of the righteous is like the first gleam of dawn, which shines ever brighter until the full light of day" (Proverbs 4:18).

 TO PRAY: "Lord, help us live by your standards of right and wrong."

6 Change for the Better

SHOULD WE DO SOMETHING WRONG JUST BECAUSE IT'S EASY?

Bible Reading of the Day: Read Leviticus 19:11-13.
Verse of the Day: *"Do not steal. Do not lie. Do not deceive one another"*
(Leviticus 19:11, NIV).

Stacy walked home from her piano lesson with her friend Anna. The day was hot, and they were both thirsty. As they passed the corner gas station, Anna gazed at the soft-drink machine at the side of the station.

"I sure wish I had some money," she said. "A can of soda sure would taste good right now."

Stacy dug into her pocket and found enough change to buy one can. "Look, we can share a can of soda."

Anna's face brightened for a moment, but she shook her head. "No, that's OK. Thanks anyway, though."

"Are you sure?" Stacy asked.

Anna nodded.

Stacy inserted her coins, and a can thunked noisily out of the machine. As she grabbed the ice-cold can, she heard the sound of coins dropping into the change slot.

"Look, Anna!" she cried as she held the can in one hand and fished the money out of the change slot. "We have enough to buy you a can, too!"

Anna eyed the coins in her friend's hand, and the cold can of soda in her other hand. After a moment of hesitation, she shook her head.

"No," she said. "That money doesn't belong to us."

"What do you mean 'it doesn't belong to us'?" Stacy asked.

"That money belongs to the company you bought the soda from. Keeping that money would be stealing."

"But nobody's going to know," Stacy said. "What's the big deal?"

"We'd know," Anna said. "Should we do something wrong just because it's easy?"

Stacy thought for a few moments. She looked from the can in one hand to the change in the other hand. "So what are we supposed to do?"

Anna looked around and saw an employee at a cash register inside the gas station. "We'll give it to him," she said.

Stacy hesitated. She looked as if she were going to say no to her friend. Finally, she said, "OK, but only on one condition."

"What's that?" Anna asked.

"Only if you agree to share this can of soda with me."

The two girls smiled at each other and walked into the gas station.

TO DISCUSS: Why did Anna think that keeping the money was wrong? How would you have acted if you were Stacy? How would you have acted if you were Anna?

TO PRAY: "Lord, guard us from acting in ways that would dishonor you."

7 The Fear of the Lord

WE'RE NOT READY TO KNOW AND SERVE GOD UNTIL WE UNDERSTAND HOW AWESOME AND POWERFUL HE IS.

Bible Reading of the Day: Read Psalm 111.
Verse of the Day: *"The fear of the Lord is true wisdom; to forsake evil is real understanding" (Job 28:28).*

"You learn something new every day, you know that?" Brad slapped his friend, Andrew, on the back as he sat beside him in the youth group room at their church.

Andrew tossed his head to brush his hair out of his eyes and look at his friend. "You sound like my dad."

"Have you ever heard adults talk about 'the fear of God'?"

"Yeah," Andrew answered. "So?"

"Well, for the first time in my life, I think I understand what they're talking about. . . . You remember how Mr. Phillips started our first driver's ed. class last Tuesday?"

"Yeah," Andrew said with a shrug. "He gave us some speech about how we should 'be afraid, be very afraid' when we get behind the wheel of a car."

"Right! He said we should respect driving, because, while driving a car could be really good for us—getting us to school, taking us to the amusement park, stuff like that—it could also take our life or our passengers' lives away like that—" he snapped his fingers—"if we're not responsible drivers."

"Yeah," Andrew said, as if waiting for the punch line of a joke. "He said we're not ready to drive a car until we're 'afraid, very afraid.' So?"

"Well, I was reading my Bible this morning, and I came across the verse that says, 'The fear of the Lord is the beginning of wisdom.' And for the first time, I understood what the fear of God is all about. It's not being scared of him, but it's realizing that he's *God*, he has the power of life and death, and he's the judge of good and evil."

Andrew smiled and nodded with understanding.

"So," Brad finished, "just like we're not ready to drive a car until we 'fear' it, we're not ready to know and serve God until we understand how awesome and powerful he is."

"And how happy we should be that he loves us," Andrew said.

TO DO: As a family, come up with your own definition of what it means to "fear the Lord." Then hang your definition in a place where everyone will be sure to see it.

TO PRAY: "God, we are happy that you love us. Thank you for your love. Please teach us to respect your power and authority."

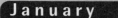

8 The Look of Love

LOVING GOD MEANS OBEYING HIS COMMANDMENTS.

Bible Reading of the Day: Read 1 John 5:1-5.
Verse of the Day: *"This is love for God: to obey his commands"*
(1 John 5:3, NIV).

"Angela!" Mom stared into Angela's bedroom with a shocked expression. "What have you done?"

Her daughter sat in the middle of her bedroom floor, smiling. "I cleaned my room!"

Mom's mouth hung open as she turned to take in the sight. Angela had picked up and dusted her room, and had even organized her closet and her desk.

"It looks beautiful," Mom said. "I can even see the floor of your closet!"

"Yup," Angela answered. "You like it?"

"I love it." Mom hesitated. "But—"

"But what?"

Mom's eyes narrowed. "Why did you do all of this?" she asked suspiciously.

Angela stood and walked to her mother. She smiled and gripped her mom in a hug. "Just because I love you," she said.

"No, really," Mom answered.

Angela loosened her hug and stood away from her mother, looking hurt. "I did it because I love you, because I knew it would make you happy," she insisted. "Don't you believe me?"

Mom hesitated only a moment, then answered, "I'm sorry, sweetheart. I do believe you. I'm just so surprised."

Angela shrugged her shoulders. "It's like that Bible verse we read together yesterday."

"Bible verse?"

"Yeah," Angela said, "about how loving God means obeying his commands."

Mom smiled, remembering the verse. "Uh-huh," she said.

"So I thought if I cleaned my room I could show my love for God *and* for you—all at the same time."

Mom nodded, and then a serious expression crossed her face. "That's wonderful, Angela! But I need to give you another commandment."

Angela stopped smiling. "What?" she asked.

Mom's face broke into a broad smile. "Thou shalt give thy mother another big hug!" she said.

 TO DISCUSS: How can you show your love for God today? How can you help others in your family to show their love for God?

TO PRAY: "Lord, we love you. Help us show our love by obeying your commands."

9 Why So Many Rules?

RULES AREN'T SUPPOSED TO MAKE YOU MISERABLE. THEY'RE FOR YOUR PROTECTION.

Bible Reading of the Day: Read Exodus 20:1-17.
Verse of the Day: *"And the Lord our God commanded us to obey all these laws and to fear him for our own prosperity and well-being, as is now the case" (Deuteronomy 6:24).*

Jason sat beside the swimming pool on the first day of summer camp. The head lifeguard explained the pool rules.

"No running in the pool area," he declared. "No diving into the shallow end. Only one person at a time is allowed on the diving board."

Jason turned to the other boys in his cabin. "This is worse than home," he whispered. "Do this, don't do that!"

"When you hear one blast on the whistle," the lifeguard continued, holding the whistle that hung from a cord around his neck, "it means I need your attention, probably to get you to stop what you're doing."

"This is the pits," Jason said, a little louder.

"Two blasts on the whistle," the lifeguard said, "means everyone stop swimming, look my way, and listen to me."

"We won't be able to have *any* fun!" Jason said.

"And three blasts on the whistle," the lifeguard concluded, "means everybody out of the pool. Any questions?"

"Yeah," Jason said. "Why so many rules? I'm sick of rules! Why can't we just have fun?"

"The rules aren't supposed to make you miserable," the lifeguard said. "They're for your protection. 'No running in the pool area'—that's to keep you from falling on the concrete and slicing your knee open. 'No diving in the shallow end'—that's to prevent you from hitting your head on the bottom of the pool and maybe paralyzing or even killing yourself. If you follow the rules, you'll be much better off. If you don't follow them, you'll end up getting hurt."

The lifeguard faced the rest of the campers. "Any other questions?"

"Yeah," Jason said, raising his hand this time. The lifeguard nodded to him. "When do we start swimming?"

The lifeguard smiled. "As soon as you finish talking!"

TO DISCUSS: Why do you think God gave so many rules? Can you think of ways his commands protect you?

TO PRAY: "Lord, help us to obey your rules, even if we think they're unfair."

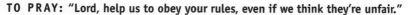

9

10 Clues to Character

GOD'S RULES SHOW HIS CHARACTER.

Bible Reading of the Day: Read Exodus 33:7–13.
Verse of the Day: *"Teach me your ways so I may know you" (Exodus 33:13, NIV).*

"You sure do have a lot of rules in your house," Ben said. He was spending the night at his friend Jeremy's house.

"Like what?" Jeremy asked, without taking his eyes from the video game he was playing.

"Like, what your mom just said," Ben answered.

"What, you mean because she said lights out when we're finished with this game?"

"Yeah. You have a *bedtime?"* Ben asked.

"Don't you?" Jeremy asked.

"No. My parents don't care what time I go to bed."

"Well, I have to go to bed so I'll get enough sleep. That way, I won't fall asleep in church tomorrow."

"That's another thing. Your parents make you go to church!" Ben said.

"I like going to church," answered Jeremy. "But even if I didn't, Mom and Dad make sure I go because we're Christians. Their rules show that they love me."

"Yeah, right!" Ben said, picking up the video control to get ready for his turn.

"Really," Jeremy said. "The rules they make show what kind of people they are. They like a clean house, so they make me keep my room clean. They're really honest themselves, so they expect me to be honest. And they love me and my sister, so they get on me if I'm mean to her, or if she's mean to me."

"You mean you have to be nice to your sister, too?"

"Yeah, even though she's a pain sometimes," Jeremy said with a shrug. "That's not all," he added.

"What? You mean it gets worse?"

Jeremy nodded. "Yeah," he said with a smile. "I have to be nice to you, too."

Ben looked at his friend with an expression of surprise, then punched Jeremy's shoulder. The boys ended up wrestling together on the floor.

 TO DISCUSS: What are the rules of your household? How do they reveal what your family is like? How do God's commandments reveal what he is like? Talk about one of God's commandments and how it reflects God's character.

TO PRAY: "Lord, may our family rules reflect your character. We want to be loving and fair in the way we treat others."

11 God Is Unique

GOD'S FIRST COMMANDMENT SHOWS HIS UNIQUENESS.

Bible Reading of the Day: Read Exodus 19:16-20; 20:1-3.
Verse of the Day: *"Let all the world look to me for salvation! For I am God; there is no other"* (Isaiah 45:22).

"Dad, what does this word mean?" Ching was studying for the regional finals of the fourth-grade spelling bee. He showed his father a flash card he had made, bearing the word *unique.*

Ching's dad removed his reading glasses and set down the newspaper he had been reading. "It means 'one of a kind,'" Dad said.

"One of a kind," Ching echoed thoughtfully.

"Yes." Dad thought for a moment, then said, "For example, bats are unique."

"Because they're blind?" Ching asked.

"Good guess, but bats really aren't blind. They have poor eyesight, but they can see," Dad said. "No, bats are unique because they are the only kind of mammal that can fly. They're unique among mammals."

"I get it," Ching said.

"Can you think of something else that's unique?" Dad asked.

Ching smiled proudly and blurted, "God!"

Dad looked surprised, then smiled back at his son. "Well, yes, I suppose you're right. God *is* unique." He paused. "In fact," he said, "God is unique in a unique way."

"What do you mean?"

"Well, a painting can be unique, but there are many paintings. Every snowflake is unique, but there are many snowflakes. Every human being is unique, but there are many other humans. Those things are all unique within their classes, within their own category."

"But there is only one God," Ching said.

"Yes, there is nothing—or no one else—in his class! He is his own category. There is no other God, no one who even comes close. That is why he tells us to worship no one but him. Because he is *unique.*"

"Unique," Ching repeated. "U-N-I-Q-U-E! That's one word I don't think I'll forget how to spell, now that I know what it means."

 TO DISCUSS: Take turns completing this statement: "God is unique because
_____." What word would you use to describe God?

TO PRAY: "God, there is no one else like you. You alone are God."

12 God Is Spirit

GOD'S SECOND COMMANDMENT SHOWS THAT HE IS SPIRIT.

Bible Reading of the Day: Read Exodus 20:4–6.

Verse of the Day: *"God is spirit, so those who worship him must worship in spirit and in truth"* *(John 4:24).*

"Bobby, what does God look like?" Kristie asked her brother.

Bobby, who was nine years old—two years older than Kristie—answered confidently, "He looks like an old man, with a long, white beard."

Kristie peered at her brother through narrow eyes. She knew Bobby sometimes made things up when he didn't know what he was talking about.

Just then, Kristie saw Mr. Peerson walking his German shepherd. He came to the fence that stood between her backyard and the sidewalk.

"Mr. Peerson, what does God look like?" she asked.

"That's a good question, Kristie," Mr. Peerson said. He tilted his head and looked to the sky. "I think God looks like a lot of things. Like a tree, or a mountain, or even like Andrew Jackson here," he said, patting his dog's head.

Kristie waved good-bye to Mr. Peerson, then walked purposefully into the house. She found her mother sitting at the desk in the room they called the "study."

"Mom," Kristie said, peering over the large desk at her mother, who was typing on the computer. "What does God look like?" She told her mother what Bobby and Mr. Peerson had said about God.

Mom motioned for Kristie to come stand beside her chair. She clicked a few buttons on the computer. "I want to show you a verse in the Bible," she said. Kristie watched as the screen filled with verses from the Bible. Her mother pointed to one of the verses. "The Bible says that God is Spirit. Do you know what that means?"

Kristie tried to think of the right answer, but finally shook her head.

"It means that God doesn't have a body. That's why in the Ten Commandments, God said we shouldn't make any images to worship, thinking that those things look like God, because God is spirit. We can't make anything that looks like him, because we can't make anything that can be everywhere at once, invisible, all around us, and even *in* us."

Kristie smiled broadly.

"Why are you smiling?" Mom asked.

"I *knew* God didn't look like Andrew Jackson," Kristie said.

Kristie's mom watched with a confused look as her daughter left the room. "Andrew Jackson?" she whispered.

TO DISCUSS: What does the phrase "God is Spirit" mean to you? How can this truth help us when we think God isn't near?

TO PRAY: "Lord, we're thankful that you can be everywhere through your Spirit."

13 God Is Holy

GOD'S THIRD COMMANDMENT REVEALS HIS HOLINESS.

Bible Reading of the Day: Read Exodus 20:7.
Verse of the Day: *"Do not use my name to swear a falsehood and so profane the name of your God. I am the Lord" (Leviticus 19:12).*

On the first day of a mountain hiking trip with Danny Franklin and Danny's father, Will suddenly lost his footing and slid several feet down the hillside. He finally checked his slide by gripping a sapling in one hand while he searched for a foothold.

When Mr. Franklin saw Will lose his footing, he immediately dropped his backpack and unwrapped a length of clothesline.

"Will! Grab the rope! I'll pull you up!" Mr. Franklin called. He flung the line to Will.

A few moments later, Will stood safely beside Danny and Mr. Franklin. He whistled and said God's name, followed by a curse word. "That was close," he said.

Mr. Franklin draped his right arm around Will's shoulders. "It sure was, Will. But will you do something for me?"

"Sure, Mr. Franklin," Will said. "What?"

"I'd appreciate it if you wouldn't use God's name like that. Saying God's name with a curse word isn't right."

"Why not?" Will asked.

"Because God said we're not to take his name in vain," Danny interrupted.

"What does that mean?" Will asked.

"It means several things," Mr. Franklin explained. "In the Ten Commandments, God forbids making a false pledge or vow using his name. But it also applies to any frivolous or profane use of his name. In fact, in Jesus' day, the Jews considered the name of God so holy that they wouldn't say it, or even spell it. Instead, they would substitute other names for it, like 'the Lord,' or 'the Holy One.'"

"But why?" Will asked.

"Because God is holy. He's so holy that even his *name* is to be respected."

"I never realized that," Will said.

Mr. Franklin stretched his arms around both boys. "You see, men, God's commandments not only tell us what we should or shouldn't do. They also show us what God is like, because his commands are rooted in his character."

"Oh," said Will. "Sort of like that little tree I was holding on to was rooted in the hillside."

"Yeah," Mr. Franklin answered with a smile. "Now if you can hold on to God's commandments like you held on to that tree, you'll do all right."

 TO DISCUSS: What are some ways that people misuse God's name? How can a person honor God's name?

 TO PRAY: "God, we want to honor your name and never use it thoughtlessly or frivolously. We want to do that by praising your name and by blessing others."

14 God Is Gracious

GOD'S FOURTH COMMANDMENT SHOWS HIS GRACE.

Bible Reading of the Day: Read Exodus 20:8-10.
Verse of the Day: *"The Sabbath was made to benefit people"*
(Mark 2:27).

"Do you know what tomorrow is?" Mom asked Luke and Hannah.

"God's Day!" the children shouted in unison.

"What's 'God's Day'?" asked Jenny, the woman who lived next door. She had dropped by to return a pair of hedge clippers that Mom had loaned to her, and Mom had invited her in for a cup of tea.

Mom smiled at her neighbor. "That's what the children call Sunday," she explained. Jenny didn't attend church, although Mom had invited her several times.

"They *like* going to church?" Jenny asked, a tone of surprise in her voice.

"Oh, yes," Mom answered. "They love Sunday school and church as much as Ben and I do," Mom said, referring to her husband. "But God's Day is more than that."

"More?" Jenny said, sipping her tea.

"God's Day is special to them because it means going to Sunday school and church. It's also special because it means their daddy doesn't go to work. He gets to spend all day with us, and it's always a very special day. Sometimes we go hiking. Sometimes we play games together. Sometimes we sit and read stories together."

"It sounds really nice," Jenny said dreamily.

"Oh, it is, Jenny," Mom answered. "You see, God commanded his people to observe the Sabbath for their own good. It shows how loving and gracious he is." Mom picked up the teapot and refilled Jenny's cup. "He didn't have to finish the work of creating the heavens and the earth in six days. He didn't rest because he was tired. He rested on the seventh day in order to establish a Sabbath for us humans. He set aside one day for us to worship him and to be refreshed and restored."

"Makes sense," Jenny said. *"My* husband hasn't taken a day off in months. I think it's really starting to take its toll on him."

Mom nodded sympathetically. "The Sabbath also reminds us that the world will go on without us, and that we don't have to do it all."

A long moment of silence passed between the two women. Finally, Jenny broke the silence. "Thank you," she said. She took a final sip of tea. "I must get some of this for myself," she said.

"Here," Mom said, standing, "let me give you a few tea bags. It's just herbal tea."

"I wasn't talking about the tea," Jenny answered.

 TO DO: This week do something special that will honor the Lord's Day and make it different from every other day this week. You might unplug the television, sing worship songs, look at family photo albums, or play board games together.

TO PRAY: "Lord, your special day is our special day too. Thank you for being a gracious God."

15 God Is Respectful

GOD'S FIFTH COMMANDMENT SHOWS THAT HE VALUES RESPECT.

Bible Reading of the Day: Read Exodus 20:12.

Verse of the Day: *"Children, obey your parents because you belong to the Lord, for this is the right thing to do" (Ephesians 6:1).*

"But your parents are never going to know!" Darren pleaded with his friend Mark. They stood together at the edge of the school parking lot. "It won't hurt anything just to drive me and Angie to the water park. Then you can take your little brother home."

Sean, Mark's eight-year-old brother, spoke up before Mark did. "I'm not little!" he retorted. "Besides, Dad won't let Mark drive that far!"

Mark shot him a silencing look, then turned back to Darren. "They let me use the car to go to school. If I want to go anywhere else, I need to check with them."

"But they're going to say no, you know they will," Darren complained. He knew that Mark's parents would never give him permission to drive the thirty miles to the water park on a school night.

Mark shrugged. "So there's no point in even asking them," he said.

"That's" what I want to hear," Darren said triumphantly. "You just drop off Angie and me, and you'll be home before your parents are."

"You're not getting it, Darren," Mark said. "I'm not taking you."

"Why not?" Darren asked, whining like a two-year-old. "There's nothing wrong with helping out a friend."

Mark sighed. "Yeah, there is, if my friend wants me to disobey my parents." He paused. "See, Darren, the Bible says to honor your father and mother. Doing something that I know they would not approve of would not be honoring them."

Anger flashed in Darren's eyes. "Oh, come on, Mark. You can't base everything you do on the Bible."

"I can try," Mark answered. "But it's not just the Bible I'm basing it on; it's God himself. See, God's commands are a reflection of what he's like."

"You're telling me God honors *his* parents?" Darren squealed.

Mark shook his head. "No, God doesn't have parents. But he respects us enough to give us the choice to do right or do wrong. He respects us enough to entrust us with his Word. And it's that part of his nature we reflect when we respect our parents."

Darren stared at his friend in silence for a moment. Finally, Darren spoke. "I guess that means you're not taking me and Angie to the water park."

"You don't have to guess," Mark answered, winking at his younger brother.

"Guess you told him!" Sean said with a grin.

 TO DISCUSS: Why should parents be honored? How have you honored your parents in the last few days? Name some practical ways to continue honoring them.

TO PRAY: "God, teach us to honor our parents and those who are like parents to us."

16 God Is the Author of Life

GOD'S SIXTH COMMANDMENT SHOWS HIM AS THE CREATOR OF LIFE.

Bible Reading of the Day: Read Genesis 4:1-10.
Verse of the Day: *"Do not murder" (Exodus 20:13).*

"Daddy! Daddy!" Krystal burst into her dad's workshop in the garage. "Have you seen Snowball?"

Dad lifted the goggles he wore to protect his eyes and looked at Krystal. Her expression was frantic. He set the goggles down on the table saw and shut it off. "She's right here, Krystal," he said, pointing to the cat curled up on the threadbare sofa behind him.

Krystal's eyes opened wider. She dashed to the couch and scooped the furry white creature into her arms.

"What's wrong?" Dad asked.

Krystal stroked the animal's soft fur. "Shane told me that Mr. Greems is putting out poison because he doesn't like people's cats coming into his yard. I just had to find Snowball and make sure she was OK."

Dad smiled and sat on the couch next to Krystal. He draped an arm around his daughter. "You really love Snowball, don't you?" he said. Krystal nodded. "You'd hate to see anything happen to her, wouldn't you?" Again Krystal nodded.

They sat in silence for a few moments. Finally, Dad took a deep breath. "You know, Krystal," he said, "the way you feel about Snowball, and how you'd be so upset if anything happened to her, well, that's only a fraction of the way God feels about all his creatures—people especially."

The cat purred in Krystal's lap as she listened to her father.

"It may be hard to imagine, but, as much as you love Snowball, our lives are even *more* precious to God—every one of us. And as much as you want to protect Snowball and preserve her life, God wants to protect and preserve all the people he's created. That's why he says we should never kill another human being—because that person's life is precious to God."

"Maybe we should have named her Precious instead of Snowball," Krystal suggested.

Dad smiled. "She's precious no matter what we call her," he said.

 TO DISCUSS: Why does God say, "Do not murder"? How does that commandment reveal God's nature? Why is it important to understand that God values human life?

TO PRAY: "God, help us to respect life just as you respect it."

17 God Is Pure and Faithful

GOD'S SEVENTH COMMANDMENT SHOWS THAT HE IS PURE AND FAITHFUL.

Bible Reading of the Day: Read Hebrews 13:4.
Verse of the Day: *"Do not commit adultery" (Exodus 20:14).*

The church was decorated with white candles and ribbons. People continued to file into the sanctuary. Terry and his family had been seated a few minutes earlier and were waiting for the wedding to start.

Terry saw his mom and dad trade wedding rings. He leaned across his sister, Anna, and tapped his mom on the arm. "Why did you do that?" he asked, pointing to the ring she held in her hand.

Mom smiled. "I'll tell you after the wedding," she whispered.

Once the crowd was seated and the ceremony started, Terry turned back to ask his mom to tell him why she had exchanged rings with his dad, but she simply smiled and shook her head when he started to speak.

Finally, when the ceremony was over, Terry squeezed by his sister before his parents could stand up. "Why did you and Dad trade rings?" he asked. He looked at his mom's hand and noticed that she wore her own ring again.

"Your father and I do that every time we attend a wedding," she said.

Dad leaned closer to his son. "I gave that ring to your mother on our wedding day, a long time ago," he said, pointing to the sparkling ring on Mom's finger. "And she gave me this ring," he said, twirling the gold band on his finger. "These rings are symbols of the vows we exchanged that day."

Terry wrinkled his nose to reflect his confusion.

Dad interlaced his fingers with Mom's and held their hands up so Terry could see both rings. "We wear these rings," Dad said, "to remind each other of our promise to love each other and to be pure and faithful to each other for the rest of our lives."

"And every time we attend a wedding," Mom said, "we repeat those promises all over again. That's why we traded rings at the beginning of the ceremony, so we could promise all over again to be faithful to each other."

"Because, you see, Son," Dad continued, "when we're pure and faithful to each other, we please God, because that's what God is like. He is pure and faithful himself. Our marriage is beautiful because it reflects the character of God."

"Oh," Terry said. "Can I ask you another question?"

Mom and Dad nodded together.

"Can we go eat now?" he said, thinking of the wedding cake. "I'm hungry."

Mom and Dad laughed, as they walked out of the sanctuary together.

 TO DO: Make a card for a couple you know who have been married for a long time. Let them know how much their faithfulness to each other has meant to you over the years.

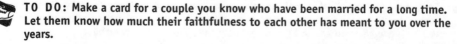 **TO PRAY:** "Lord, we praise you for your purity and for your faithfulness. Help us to reflect your character."

18 God Is Trustworthy

GOD'S EIGHTH COMMANDMENT SHOWS THAT HE IS TRUSTWORTHY.

Bible Reading of the Day: Read Ephesians 4:22–28.
Verse of the Day: *"Do not steal" (Exodus 20:15).*

"Cathy, look what I've got!" Gina called.

Gina dug into her jacket pocket. As she did so, Cathy noticed that her friend carefully looked around the school bus, as if making sure no one was watching her. Gina pulled out a pair of sunglasses.

"Those are cool!" Cathy said, excited for her friend. "I wish I had a pair like that."

"Yeah," Gina cooed, as she turned them over in her hands.

"Can I wear them?" Cathy asked.

"Just wait," Gina whispered. "I have to wait until Stacy gets off the bus."

"Why do you have to wait until Stacy . . . ?" Cathy's voice trailed off as she suddenly realized the answer to her own question. "You stole those from Stacy!"

Gina shot her friend a vicious look. "Keep it down," she hissed. "I didn't steal anything."

"Yes, you did," Cathy insisted. "Those sunglasses don't belong to you."

"They do now."

"Gina, don't do it." Cathy's tone turned pleading. "You know it's wrong."

"No, it's not." Gina looked for understanding in her friend's eyes but saw only disappointment. "Look, Stacy can have anything she wants. She's got the best clothes, the best shoes, the best everything. She won't even miss these stupid sunglasses."

"That doesn't make it right, Gina. Stealing is wrong."

"Says who?"

"Says God. 'Do not steal,' remember?"

"Give me a break!" Gina said. "This is *Stacy* we're talking about!"

"No, Gina, it's *you* we're talking about. And the same thing that makes it wrong to steal from you makes it wrong to steal from Stacy—because it's not the way God is. It's not the way God wants *us* to be."

Gina rolled her eyes, but Cathy continued. "God tells us not to steal because *he's* totally honest and trustworthy, and he wants us to be like him. You may think you're cool if you wear those sunglasses, but God thinks it'd be cool to give them back." She paused. "And I do too."

Gina stared at Cathy for a few moments. Finally, she reached into her pocket. "I guess you know what you can get me for my birthday, don't you?" she said.

 TO DO: *Good Housekeeping* magazine has what is known as the "Good Housekeeping Seal" for products. By this seal, people know that a product is trustworthy. Have each family member make his or her own trustworthy "seal." What symbol will you use? What phrase will you say to let others know that you are trustworthy?

TO PRAY: "Lord, we want to be honest just as you are honest."

19 God Is True

GOD'S NINTH COMMANDMENT SHOWS THAT HE IS TRUE.

Bible Reading of the Day: Read Proverbs 12:17–22.

Verse of the Day: *"Do not testify falsely against your neighbor"* (Exodus 20:16).

All heads in Hannah's classroom turned and watched as a student entered the room and handed Mrs. Busby a piece of paper. The teacher read the note, then stood.

"I want you all to work quietly at your desks for a few minutes," Hannah's teacher announced. "I'll only be gone for a minute or two."

As soon as the teacher left, Hannah's friend Amy dashed to the classroom window. "Hannah!" she whispered, furiously waving a hand. "Come here."

Hannah tried to ignore her, but Amy wouldn't be quiet. Finally, Hannah got up from her seat and stood beside Amy at the window.

"Look," Amy said. "There's Bobby Myers. He said he thinks you're pretty cool."

"Is that all you wanted? To show me Bobby Myers?" Hannah turned from the window and returned to her seat just as Mrs. Busby entered the room.

Amy still stood at the window. She tried to dash into her seat, but she was too late. Mrs. Busby had seen her.

"Amy," Mrs. Busby said, "I'll expect to see you after school." The teacher turned to face the rest of the class. "Did anyone else leave his or her seat?"

The room fell silent, and after a few moments, Hannah's hand crept into the air.

"Anyone else?" Mrs. Busby scanned the room, but no other hands were raised. "Then I'll expect to see *you* after school, too," she said, nodding toward Hannah.

After class, Amy and Hannah walked to their next class together.

"Sorry I got you in trouble," Amy said.

Hannah shrugged. "It was my fault, too."

"You shouldn't have said anything," Amy said.

"That would have been lying, though," Hannah answered.

"Just to keep your mouth shut?"

Hannah nodded. "I've been learning that the reason lying is wrong is because it's not like God. He tells us not to tell lies because he always tells the truth."

"So that's why you told the truth today?" Amy asked. "Even though it got you in trouble?"

"I didn't like getting in trouble with Mrs. Busby," Hannah answered. "But I *did* like doing the right thing."

Amy studied her friend's face. "What do you know," she said. "Bobby Myers is right for once." She smiled. "You *are* pretty cool."

 TO DISCUSS: How does the ninth commandment reveal God's nature? Are there other ways a person can lie?

 TO PRAY: "Lord, protect us from any sinful desires to lie."

20 God Is Enough

GOD'S TENTH COMMANDMENT SHOWS THAT HE VALUES CONTENTMENT.

Bible Reading of the Day: Read Exodus 20:17.
Verse of the Day: *"Godliness with contentment is great gain"* (1 Timothy 6:6, NIV).

Randy and his dad watched the special news bulletin that had interrupted their favorite television show. The newscaster reported the arrest of three teenagers who had beaten a classmate to death with a baseball bat after the classmate refused to give up a jacket. When the report ended, Dad turned the volume down.

"What do you think about what those three teenagers did?" Dad asked.

Randy shrugged. His dad asked him that kind of question all the time. "It was wrong," he answered.

"*Why* was it wrong?"

"Well," Randy said, as if the answer were obvious, "because killing is wrong." Then Randy added, "And killing is wrong because God said 'Do not kill.' And God said 'Do not kill' because he values life."

Dad smiled broadly. "Wow!" he said. "I'm impressed. Now I have another question," Dad said. "Those three teenagers did something wrong before they even started to beat up that boy, before they took his jacket. In fact, their first sin led to all the others. Do you know what that was?"

Randy fell silent for a few moments, but finally he shook his head at his father.

"What's the last of the Ten Commandments?" Dad asked.

Randy thought for a moment, then answered, "'Do not covet.'"

Dad nodded, but said nothing. Suddenly, Randy's eyes grew wide.

"I know!" he said. "The thing that started it all was when those guys coveted the other guy's jacket!"

"Exactly," Dad said. "Their first sin was coveting. . . ."

"God said 'Do not covet.'"

"But *why* did God say that?" Dad asked, pressing further.

Randy thought for a minute. Finally he shook his head. "I don't know."

"God said not to covet because he wants us to be content," Dad said. "The Bible says, 'Godliness with contentment is great gain.' God values contentment because he is never discontent. He has everything he needs—because he *is* everything he needs. And he wants us to be content with him and with all he gives us." Dad paused. "Before I turn the volume up on the TV, why don't we pray for God to help us both become less covetous and more like him?"

Randy smiled and nodded thoughtfully.

 TO DISCUSS: What does it mean to covet? Why do people covet? Why do you think God doesn't want people to covet? Can you trust God and still covet? Why or why not?

TO PRAY: "Lord, protect us from wanting what others have. May we be content with what you have given us."

21 Snake Eyes

NOT MY RULES. NOT YOUR RULES. THE RULES.

Bible Reading of the Day: Read Genesis 3:1-7.

Verse of the Day: *"Do not add to or subtract from these commands I am giving you from the Lord your God. Just obey them" (Deuteronomy 4:2).*

"You can't tell *me* what's right or wrong!" Chris stood on Jamie's porch, his hands balled into fists at his side. The two boys had been playing a board game when suddenly Chris had decided that he should get to roll the dice again because he had rolled "snake eyes"—two ones.

When Jamie protested that there was no such rule, Chris got mad and threw the game pieces all over the porch.

"You can't make up your own rules," Jamie said calmly.

"I can if I want to," Chris answered.

"But there's no sense playing the game if you can change the rules any time you feel like it," said Jamie.

"You just don't want me to win," Chris countered. "You're just afraid I'll beat you."

"That's not true, Chris," Jamie said. "But when you sit down to play a game with somebody, you don't make up your own rules. You follow the rules that have already been set."

"By who?" Chris answered. "By you?"

"No, by the person who made the game. That's who set the rules. See?" Jamie held up the booklet that came with the game. "Not my rules. Not your rules. *The* rules."

Chris frowned and shuffled his feet.

"Why don't we start over," Jamie suggested, "and I'll try not to beat you *too* badly."

Chris's eyes narrowed into slits. "Oh yeah?" He snatched the rules booklet from Jamie. "We'll see who beats who."

 TO DISCUSS: Was Jamie right to object to Chris's made-up rules? What happens when we try to ignore God's rules and make up rules of our own?

TO PRAY: "Lord, we want to be fair and live by your rules."

22 Knowing the Holy One

KNOWING GOD IS ONE OF THE KEYS TO DOING THE RIGHT THING.

Bible Reading of the Day: Read Proverbs 9:10-12.
Verse of the Day: *"Fear of the Lord is the beginning of wisdom.*
Knowledge of the Holy One results in understanding" (Proverbs 9:10).

Maria and her friend Holly stayed in the auditorium after the school assembly. They waited in line to talk to the speaker, a man who had delivered a message about resisting drugs and refusing to use violence to try to solve problems. His message was often funny, sometimes sad, and sprinkled with frequent impressions of famous people.

When they finally reached the front of the line, Maria shook the speaker's hand and said excitedly, "I loved it when you talked like Elvis Presley!"

"Thank you. Thank you very much," the speaker said with a crooked smile.

Maria and Holly giggled. "How do you make yourself sound so much like those famous people?" Maria asked.

"Well, I work at it. Like, with Elvis, I've watched certain parts of his movies and concerts over and over on videotape, until I know how he walked, how he talked, how he did everything. The more I know a person, the easier it is to act like him."

Later that afternoon, as Maria and Holly walked home from school, Maria said, "Remember what the speaker said about studying the people he wanted to imitate? That's kind of what we've been studying in Sunday school. As Christians, we want to do the right things, right?"

"Right," said Holly.

"But sometimes we don't know what the right thing is, right?"

"Right," Holly said.

"Right. But we know that if something is like God, then it's right, right?"

"Right," Holly answered.

"Right. Because God is perfect and holy and righteous and all those other things. And," she continued, "if a thing is not like God, then it's wrong, right? So if we act like God, then we'll be doing the right thing, right?"

"Right."

"And I know how we do that. The speaker today said, 'The more I know a person, the easier it is to act like him.'"

"Right," said Holly, a little slower this time, as she thought about what her friend was saying.

"So one of the keys to doing the right thing is to *know* God. The more we know him, the easier it will be to do the right thing." She paused. "Right?"

Holly nodded her head and smiled at her friend. "Right!" she said.

TO DISCUSS: How can a person "know" God? Do you "know" God? How do you know?

TO PRAY: "Father God, we want to know you better so we can please you more."

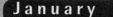

23 Through the Maze

GOD CAN SEE THE DIRECTION WE NEED TO GO IN MUCH BETTER THAN WE CAN.

Bible Reading of the Day: Read Psalm 25:4-9.

Verse of the Day: *"Whether you turn to the right or to the left, your ears will hear a voice behind you, saying, 'This is the way; walk in it'"* *(Isaiah 30:21, NIV).*

Dawn and Kara were visiting a small amusement park with their mother. While Mom went to get ice cream, Kara entered a maze of intersecting paths and tunnels that wound through high walls and confusing intersections.

The maze was sunk into a pit, so Dawn could stand by a railing and watch Kara as she tried dead end after dead end. Finally, Dawn could stand it no more, and she waved to her sister from her vantage point above the pit.

"Kara! Kara! Look up here!" she cried.

Kara stopped in the middle of the maze and looked up beyond the walls. She finally recognized her sister waving at her from above.

Dawn cupped her hands around her mouth. "I'll tell you where to go!" she shouted.

"No!" Kara shouted back. "I want to do it myself."

"But you're going the wrong way."

"I don't care," Kara insisted. "Don't tell me what to do."

Soon, Mom joined her at the railing above the maze.

"She's so stubborn," Dawn complained.

"What do you mean?" Mom asked as she handed a melting ice-cream cone to Dawn, who began licking the dripping ice cream off the sides of the cone.

Dawn pointed to her sister's confused meanderings through the maze. "She can't see where she's going. But I can see everything from up here."

"Well, why don't you tell her how to get through the maze?"

"I tried to," Dawn said, "but she doesn't want me to tell her where to go."

"I think I know how you can convince her to take your direction," Mom said.

"How?" Dawn asked.

Mom held up the other ice-cream cone. "Try telling her that her ice cream is melting."

TO DISCUSS: What was Dawn able to see that Kara could not see? What is God able to see that we can't see? What promise does today's reading give to people who need direction?

TO PRAY: "Lord, you can see what we can't see. Help us to trust the directions you give us."

24 Holding to the Truth

IF YOU WANT TO KNOW IF SOMETHING IS RIGHT, COMPARE IT TO GOD.

Bible Reading of the Day: Read Ephesians 4:14–15.
Verse of the Day: *"We will hold to the truth in love, becoming more and more in every way like Christ" (Ephesians 4:15).*

"I'm so confused!" Julie stomped her foot and crossed her arms.

"What's wrong?" Mom asked.

"I don't know who to believe anymore," Julie explained. "You tell me it's wrong to lie and stuff like that."

Mom nodded. "Go on," she said.

"Well, Andrea says sometimes a lie is OK. She says sometimes her parents even ask her to lie."

"Oh?" Mom asked.

"Well, sometimes when Andrea answers the phone and her parents don't want to talk, they'll tell her to say that they're not home."

"I can see how that might be confusing to you," Mom said.

"It sure is!" Julie said. "I don't know who to believe!"

Mom said, "We've talked about this kind of thing before, Julie. We've talked about how we can figure out what's right and what's wrong. Do you remember?"

Julie hesitated.

"If you really want to know if something's right or not, what do you do?"

Julie thought for a moment, then her eyes brightened. "I remember! I'm supposed to compare it to God!"

"Right!" Mom said. "And you compare it to God's rules first. Has God given us any commands about lying?"

"Uh-huh," Julie said. "He said not to lie."

"You're right. He gave many commands saying we should not lie or deceive one another but always tell the truth, right?"

Julie nodded.

"After we consider God's rules, then we identify the truth behind the rule, right?"

"Yeah," Julie agreed. "The truth is, God likes honesty, right?"

Mom nodded. "And why does he like honesty?"

Julie screwed up her face. "Because he's honest?"

"Right! See, God is honest and true. *That's* why honesty is right. It's not right because I say so. It's right because of who God is."

Julie smiled. "I remember now," she said proudly.

 TO DISCUSS: What three steps did Julie's mom teach her for figuring out if something is right or wrong? How can you "hold to the truth in love" today and tomorrow?

 TO PRAY: "Lord, we believe that honesty is right, because you are honest. Help us to be like you: honest and true."

25 Led by the Spirit

KNOWING THE RIGHT THING IS ONLY THE FIRST STEP. DOING IT IS ANOTHER.

Bible Reading of the Day: Read Galatians 5:13-16.
Verse of the Day: *"I advise you to live according to your new life in the Holy Spirit. Then you won't be doing what your sinful nature craves"* *(Galatians 5:16)*.

"Strike three!"

The umpire raised his right hand in the air, and Kasey banged her bat on home plate. Then she turned and walked back to the bench, her shoulders slumped and her face a picture of dejection.

"What happened, Kasey?" the coach asked. "You never even swung at a pitch."

"I know what to do, Coach," Kasey said. "I do it in practice all the time."

"I know," the coach said. "I know you can hit the ball."

"But I get up to the plate during a game and I can't do what I want. I know what to do: 'Keep your eye on the ball.' 'Keep your elbow up.' 'Nice level swing.' I just can't seem to do it."

That evening, Kasey told her Grandpa about her problem.

"Boy, that sounds familiar!" he said.

"You had the same problem?"

"Not with baseball, no," Grandpa said. "But it's not so different. See, my problem—like most people's—is with doing the right thing. I know what the right thing is. 'Honor your father and mother,' 'Do not lie,' 'Do not steal,' 'Do not covet.' But *knowing* the right thing is only the first step. *Doing* it is another thing entirely."

"So when did you learn to do the right thing?" Kasey asked.

"Never. Nope, never. My sinful nature doesn't want to do the right thing. The only way I've ever found it possible to do the right thing is by living my life according to the Spirit. That means committing myself early, every day, to his control, and then trying to stay in step with him all day long."

"Committing yourself early . . . ," Kasey whispered.

"Yeah, just like in hitting. Your problem may be that you wait too long to commit yourself. By the time the ball gets to the plate, it's too late to swing."

"Hmm . . . ," Kasey muttered.

"And don't forget to take a little step in the right direction as you commit yourself."

"Are you talking about baseball now, or about doing the right thing?"

Grandpa smiled. "Both," he said.

 TO DISCUSS: What does it mean to "live in the Holy Spirit"? How can you begin today to commit yourself early, every day, to his control? How can you stay in step with him all day long?

 TO PRAY: "Holy Spirit, thank you for guiding us. We want to stay in step with you each day."

26 God's Protection

GOD'S COMMANDS PROTECT US.

Bible Reading of the Day: Read Psalm 119:1-6.

Verse of the Day: *"I will never forget your commandments, for you have used them to restore my joy and health" (Psalm 119:93).*

Rain pelted the ground as Cindy and her father walked from their car to the mall entrance. While others all around them raced back and forth in the rain, trying to reach their destination before they got soaked, Cindy and her father were shielded by the large umbrella they had brought with them from home. As they walked to the entrance, holding hands, Cindy looked at her father.

"Daddy, what happened to Tommy Blevins?" she asked. Tommy lived down the street from Cindy's family. "Mommy said he's in the hospital."

"Yes," her father answered as they arrived at the entrance. He shook the rain from the umbrella and began folding it up. "Tommy was in an accident and got hurt very bad."

"Why?" Cindy asked.

"Why?" her father echoed. "Well, he went out drinking with some friends and had too much to drink. Then he tried to drive home while he was drunk."

Cindy thought for a few moments as they entered the mall. Finally, she asked, "Did God make that happen to punish Tommy?"

"No," her father said slowly. "No, I don't think so, Cindy. But Tommy wouldn't be in the hospital if he had obeyed God's warnings about getting drunk."

"So God *is* punishing him," Cindy said, "because he got drunk."

Cindy's father stopped walking and turned to face his daughter. He held the folded umbrella in his hands as if he were about to open it.

"It's like this umbrella, Cindy," he said. "We didn't get wet on our way into the mall today, did we? Why not?"

"Because the umbrella kept us dry," she answered.

"Right. As long as we stayed under the umbrella, we were protected from the rain." He paused, then continued. "What would have happened if you had decided to jump out from under the umbrella on the way into the mall?"

"I would have gotten wet, Daddy," Cindy said, as if the answer were too easy.

"Right. Well, God's commands are like this umbrella, Cindy. If we obey his commands, we will be protected from many terrible things. But if we ignore God's commands, it's like stepping out from under an umbrella during a rainstorm. We're no longer protected."

 TO DO: Gather together all the umbrellas in the house and place them at strategic points where they'll be seen frequently (hallway, kitchen, etc.) to remind all in the family that God's commands shelter and protect them.

TO PRAY: "Lord, thank you for protecting us through your commandments."

27 Accepting the Truth

WHEN WE'RE WRONG, WE CAN STILL PLEASE GOD BY ADMITTING WE'RE WRONG, AND ASKING FOR HIS FORGIVENESS.

Bible Reading of the Day: Read 1 John 1:8-10.

Verse of the Day: *"If we confess our sins to him, he is faithful and just to forgive us and to cleanse us from every wrong" (1 John 1:9).*

Kaneesha heard the siren before her dad did. She turned around and looked out the car's rear window. "Daddy," she said, "I think that policeman's following you!"

Dad looked in the rearview mirror and then glanced quickly at his speedometer. "Oh, no," he groaned. He checked the rearview mirror again before pulling over to the side of the road.

"Are you in trouble, Daddy?" Kaneesha asked.

Dad didn't answer Kaneesha right away. He just sighed, pulled his wallet out of his pocket, and got his driver's license out.

"Are you going to get arrested, Daddy?" Kaneesha asked.

Dad finally answered his daughter. "No, Kaneesha. The policeman's not going to arrest me. But he'll probably give me a ticket."

A police officer walked up to Dad's window. "Do you know how fast you were going, sir?" he asked.

Dad nodded and said, "Yes, sir, I do. I was going too fast."

The officer nodded. "I'll need to see your license, registration, and insurance card." Once he was handed the items, he took them back to his car.

Kaneesha turned around and watched the police officer. "What's he doing now, Daddy?" she asked.

"He's writing me a ticket."

"What's a ticket?"

Dad thought for a moment. "Well, Kaneesha, it's a way of punishing people for doing the wrong thing. I was going too fast back there. So he has to write a ticket that tells me how much money I have to pay as punishment for breaking the law."

Kaneesha wrinkled her forehead. "You could have told the policeman you didn't really go that fast."

"But that would be lying," Dad said. He turned in his seat to face Kaneesha. "God wants us to do the right thing, because it makes him happy when we act like him."

"It makes him sad when we do the wrong thing, doesn't it, Daddy?"

"That's right, Kaneesha. But even when we do the wrong thing, we can still make him happy by admitting we're wrong and asking for his forgiveness."

"Sometimes," Kaneesha said, just as the police officer appeared at the window "even daddies can be wrong."

 TO DISCUSS: Why is it important to admit to something we've done wrong? How is forgiveness related to God's faithfulness?

 TO PRAY: Take this opportunity to bring anything you have done wrong to the Lord. Ask for his forgiveness.

28 Mistake at the Lake

THERE'S A DIFFERENCE BETWEEN A MISTAKE AND A WRONG CHOICE.

Bible Reading of the Day: Read 1 Corinthians 10:23-24.
Verse of the Day: *"Don't think only of your own good. Think of other Christians and what is best for them"* (1 Corinthians 10:24).

"Oh, Crystal!" Shayna ran into the family's vacation bungalow by Lake Mohawk, her cheeks streaming with tears.

"What's the matter, girl?" her older sister asked. Crystal was a sophomore in college; Shayna had just started junior high.

"It was awful, just awful!" She flopped onto the couch and buried her face in her hands.

"What was awful?" Crystal sat down beside her little sister and put a hand on Shayna's knee.

"I feel so bad!" Shayna struggled to control her tears while her sister waited patiently. "I saw Gary Emerson at the beach today. He was there with his mother and brother."

Crystal handed her sister a tissue and waited while she wiped the tears from her eyes.

"We talked for a few minutes and then I said, 'Where's your dad?' I made some smart crack like, 'He's probably working on that stupid car of his, isn't he?'"

Shayna stopped and blew her nose. "Gary got real red, and then he said, 'No, Dad's not here. He died a few months ago.'" She looked at her sister with a pain-filled expression. "He looked so sad, Crystal. How could I do something so . . . so awful?"

Crystal waited a few moments, then gripped both her sister's hands in her hands. "Shayna," she said, "did you mean to hurt Gary?"

Shayna shook her head.

"Of course not," Crystal said. "You made a mistake, Shay. An honest mistake. You didn't do anything wrong. There's a difference between a mistake and a sin."

"But I feel so bad!" Shayna cried.

"Sure you do, Shay. You feel sorrow for what Gary's feeling. But you don't need to feel guilty or ashamed about what you did. You can be sorry even when you did nothing wrong."

Shayna wiped her eyes again and fell silent for a few moments. Finally, she stood and walked to the door.

"Where are you going now?" Crystal asked.

"I'm going to visit Gary's family. I want to tell Gary I'm sorry about his dad."

 TO DISCUSS: What's the difference between a mistake and a sin? Can a mistake sometimes be a sin? Give some examples.

 TO PRAY: "Lord, help us not to feel guilty when we make mistakes. Remind us to come to you when we sin."

29 "I Had to Lie!"

CHOOSING TO DO THE RIGHT THING IS BETTER IN THE LONG RUN.

Bible Reading of the Day: Read 1 Peter 2:22-23.
Verse of the Day: *"Remember that the temptations that come into your life are no different from what others experience. And God is faithful. He will keep the temptation from becoming so strong that you can't stand up against it. When you are tempted, he will show you a way out so that you will not give in to it"* (1 Corinthians 10:13).

"But Dad, I *had* to lie!"

Jessica looked miserable as she sat in the front seat of the car her father drove.

"If I had told the truth, I would have gotten my best friend in trouble!" She wiped her tears with the back of her hand. "Katie asked me to tell her mom that somebody stole her coin purse. That way she wouldn't have to tell her mom that she'd lost her money again. . . . Her mother screams at her so loudly."

Her father nodded his understanding. The loud arguments at the Ramsey's home were legendary around the neighborhood. Both of Katie's parents had bad tempers. Jessica had once heard her parents talking about that.

"So you lied," he said.

Jessica nodded and looked ashamed. "I just didn't want her to get in trouble."

"And Katie's mom accused you of stealing money from Katie," Dad said.

Jessica nodded again as her eyes welled up with tears. "I couldn't get my best friend in trouble."

Dad drew a deep breath and steered the car into the driveway of their home. He turned the engine off, but neither he nor Jessica made a move to get out of the car.

"Do you really think you had to lie?" Dad asked.

Jessica was silent for a few moments. Finally, she said, "I guess I didn't *have* to lie. I could have told Mrs. Ramsey the truth. But I would have felt bad if something had happened to Katie."

"I understand that," Dad said. "It can be hard to tell the truth sometimes, especially when we might get embarrassed or punished for doing so. Or when the truth might hurt a friend. But we should do what's right even when it's not easy. Doing the right thing may be hard sometimes, but it is better in the long run."

"I guess," Jessica agreed.

Dad hugged her. "Think you and Katie are ready to tell her mom the truth now? I'll go with you to talk to Katie's mom."

Jessica sighed. "OK."

 TO DISCUSS: Have you ever felt like you had to lie? Describe what happened. Usually, when we feel as though we have no choice but to lie, the truth is, we just don't like our choices. How can you respond the next time you find the truth difficult to tell?

 TO PRAY: "Lord, there are times when we're tempted to lie. Help us not to give in to temptation."

30 The Temple of God

IF THERE'S NOTHING WRONG WITH WHAT YOU'RE DOING, WHY DO YOU HAVE TO HIDE IT?

Bible Reading of the Day: Read 1 Corinthians 6:19-20.
Verse of the Day: *"God bought you with a high price. So you must honor God with your body"* *(1 Corinthians 6:20).*

Mitchell and Andy walked home from school together.

"Hey, Andy, wanna see something?" Mitchell asked.

"What?" Andy answered.

"Just follow me," Mitchell said.

"Mitchell, wait!" Andy said, as his friend turned down a side street. "I'm supposed to go straight home."

"It'll just take a minute! Come on."

Andy hesitated a moment, then turned the corner and caught up with his friend. "Mitchell," he said, "what are you doing?"

"You'll see."

After a few moments, Mitchell stopped. He pointed down the street to a man in the parking lot of a vacant gas station and pulled a five-dollar bill out of his pocket.

Andy looked at the man, then at Mitchell's money. Suddenly, he realized what Mitchell had in mind. "Are you crazy?" he asked his friend. "That man's selling drugs!"

"No kidding," Mitchell said, rolling his eyes. "Nick told me about him."

"No way!" Andy said. He turned and started walking in the other direction.

"Go ahead, Andy. Go on home to your mother!" Mitchell sneered.

"I will!" Andy called over his shoulder. Then he stopped and turned back around. "Mitch, come on," he pleaded. "You shouldn't be doing this."

"Why? Because *you* say so," Mitchell said, "or because your mommy says 'Just Say No'?"

"No, not because of me *or* my mom. Because of God."

"What's God got to do with it?"

"He's the one who decides if something's wrong," Andy said. "Something's right if it's like God, and it's wrong if it's not like him."

"You're really getting on my nerves, you know that?" Mitchell countered.

"OK," Andy said. "But just answer me one question: If there's nothing wrong with what you're doing, why do you have to hide it from your parents?"

"They wouldn't understand."

"Neither do I, Mitchell." Andy turned and walked straight home.

 TO DISCUSS: How can we honor God with our bodies? How can a person respond when friends try to lead him or her into making a wrong choice?

 TO PRAY: "Loving Lord, thank you for your willingness to protect us from people and things that would harm us."

31 In the Long Run

DOING WHAT'S RIGHT USUALLY PAYS OFF IN THE END.

Bible Reading of the Day: Read Psalm 1.
Verse of the Day: *"Whoever pursues godliness and unfailing love will find life, godliness, and honor"* *(Proverbs 21:21).*

"It's so unfair!" Gina said, as she stormed through the front door, slamming it behind her.

"What's up, Sis?" her brother Grant asked.

"Angie and I found a wallet today at King's Mountain," she answered, referring to the amusement park she had gone to that day with her friend's family. "It had a lot of money in it, like fifty dollars."

"Didn't you count it?" Grant asked.

"Angie did. She wanted to keep it, but I told her the honest thing to do would be to turn it in, since the money didn't really belong to us."

Grant smiled, looking amazed. "Wow! Good for you, Sis."

"Yeah, but then we turned it in, and the man who claimed it didn't even leave us a reward. And now, to top it all off, Angie's not even talking to me. She says we should have kept it like she wanted to in the first place."

Grant shrugged. "That's too bad, Sis. But you did the right thing."

"Then why is everything going wrong? I almost wish I had kept the money like Angie said. I'd be a lot richer, and my best friend wouldn't be mad at me."

"You can't always expect to be rewarded for doing the right thing," Grant said.

"Why not?" Gina asked.

Grant shrugged again. "It just doesn't work that way. Sometimes doing the right thing can be a real pain, at least in the short run. Like once, I was late for a test at school because I overslept, and I could have made up some excuse, but I didn't! I just told the truth, and the teacher wouldn't let me take the test. I had to take a 'zero' on the test and had to work really hard to get the grade I wanted in that class. But the next time I had that teacher for a class, he let me do some really cool stuff because he trusted me. Doing what's right usually pays off in the end."

Gina rolled her eyes, but nodded her head. "I sure wish the 'end' would hurry up and get here," she said.

TO DO: Wear your watch on the opposite wrist or turn the clocks in your house upside down today to remind yourself that, while it may be difficult in the short run, doing what's right usually pays off in the long run (and, of course, in eternity).

TO PRAY: "Lord, sometimes serving you seems hard, especially when we think about suffering in the here and now. Help us to take our eyes off our own wants and desires and focus on you."

1 Truth Has a Name

TRUTH HAS A NAME—JESUS.

Bible Reading of the Day: Read John 18:36-38.
Verse of the Day: *"Jesus told him, 'I am the way, the truth, and the life. No one can come to the Father except through me'" (John 14:6).*

Rusty turned around and looked at his parents, who sat on the couch behind him. His mom had just paused the movie they were watching, using the remote control to the VCR.

"What's wrong?" he asked. "What did you do that for?"

"Did you hear what that lawyer just said?" Mom asked.

Rusty looked puzzled. "Yeah," he answered.

Dad leaned forward on the couch. "What did he say?"

The puzzled look on Rusty's face deepened. "I don't know. I don't remember now."

"He asked the jury, 'What is truth?'" Mom said.

"Oh yeah," Rusty said. "Now I remember."

"He's not the first to ask that question, you know," Dad said.

Rusty said nothing, but his face wore an expression of curiosity.

"A long time ago, a Roman governor named Pontius Pilate asked the same question," Dad said.

"You mean the guy in the Bible?" Rusty asked.

Mom and Dad both nodded.

"You know what's sad, though?" Mom asked. "At the very moment that he asked that question, the truth stood right in front of his eyes. When Pilate asked 'What is truth?' he was staring into the face of Jesus, who had already revealed himself as 'the way, the *truth*, and the life.'"

Dad shrugged. "A lot of people make the same mistake today—like that lawyer in the movie. They say they're looking for truth, but they look everywhere but the one place it can be found—in Jesus."

"They don't understand," Mom said, "that truth has a name. It's not just an idea or a concept, it's a person. Jesus is the truth."

"That's why having Jesus in your life can help you understand the truth, because *he is the truth!*" Dad added.

Rusty nodded. "There's just one thing I want to know," he said. His parents nodded together, ready to answer his question. "Can we finish watching the movie?"

Mom and Dad looked at each other, smiled, and Mom pointed the remote control at the VCR.

TO DISCUSS: What does "the truth" mean to you? How can knowing Jesus as your Savior help you to understand the truth?

TO PRAY: "Lord, we acknowledge that you are the way, the truth, and the life."

2 Cassie's Job

IF YOU DON'T DO WHAT GOD SAYS, YOU'RE NOT CHANGING THE RULES—
YOU'RE BREAKING THEM.

Bible Reading of the Day: Read James 4:11-12.
Verse of the Day: *"You are not a judge who can decide whether the law is right or wrong. Your job is to obey it" (James 4:11).*

Cassie held the red rubber kickball in her hands as she and her friend Melanie prepared to gather some of the other kids together for a game. Melanie nodded toward Heather Adams, their classmate who was playing on the monkey bars.

"She thinks she's so smart," Melanie snarled.

"Why?" Cassie asked. "Why do you say that?"

"Because," Melanie said, as if Cassie should already know the answer, "she's Mrs. Browning's favorite. Everybody knows that. And besides, she didn't invite me to her birthday party last week."

"Yeah, so?" Cassie answered. "She didn't invite me, either. What's the big deal?"

"Well, I've never liked her since she called me fat in the third grade."

"You're still mad at her about that?" Cassie asked.

"She called *you* stupid," Melanie said.

Cassie shrugged. "I know. But I forgave her for that. You should too."

"I don't have to forgive her," Melanie insisted.

"God says we should forgive each other. He tells us to love one another."

"Yeah, well, it's different with me and Heather. I don't have to love her. Not after what she did."

Cassie shook her head. "You're not the one who makes up the rules. You can't just say, 'I don't have to love *her* because she did this or did that.' God tells us to love each other. If you don't do that, you're not *changing* the rules—you're *breaking* them!"

"Well, didn't she break the rules when she called me fat?" Melanie asked.

"Yeah," Cassie said, hesitating for a moment. "I guess so. But it's not our job to worry about whether she broke the rules or not. It's our job to do what God says ourselves, right?"

Melanie didn't answer.

"Right, Melanie?" Cassie repeated.

Melanie rolled her eyes. "I guess so." She sighed. "So what am I supposed to do?"

"Well, you can stop talking about Heather behind her back." Cassie tossed her friend the kickball. "And you can go ask her if she wants to play kickball with us."

"OK," Melanie answered. She started to walk toward Heather. After a few steps, she stopped and turned around. "Will you come with me?"

Cassie smiled and jogged a few steps to walk beside her friend.

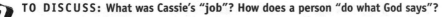

TO DISCUSS: What was Cassie's "job"? How does a person "do what God says"?

TO PRAY: "Holy Spirit, we worship you. We want to obey you. May your kingdom come. May your will be done."

3 Fair Play

DO FOR OTHERS ONLY WHAT YOU WOULD WANT THEM TO DO FOR YOU.

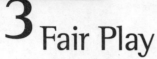

Bible Reading of the Day: Read Matthew 7:12.

Verse of the Day: *"Do for others what you would like them to do for you"* (Matthew 7:12).

"That's not fair!" shouted Jason.

Jason and Kyle were playing *Morph's Revenge,* a one-player video game. They had agreed to take turns every fifteen minutes until it was time to go.

"I can't quit now," Kyle explained without taking his eyes off the television screen. He weaved and bobbed with the motion on the screen as Morph, the video character, dodged fireballs and low-flying vultures.

"But it's my turn!" Jason whined.

"But I'm gonna break my record," Kyle said. "If I stop now, I'll lose the whole game!"

"If you keep playing, I won't get my turn," Jason said.

"I have to make it to the next level," Kyle said. "Then I can save it."

"Mom!" Jason cried. He ran upstairs and found their mom. He explained the situation to her, ending with, "He's not playing fair!"

Mom went downstairs. "Pause the game, Kyle," she said. He pressed a button and the screen froze in place. "Kyle, I thought you two decided to take turns," she said.

"We did, Mom," he said. "But I didn't know I was going to have such a good game. I'm about to get to a level I've never been to before."

"But that's not fair!" Jason shouted.

"Do you think it's fair to change the rules just because you're having a good game?"

"But once I get there I can save it and let Jason play!"

"That doesn't answer my question," Mom said. "Do you think it's fair to change the rules on Jason?"

"No, ma'am," Kyle answered.

"It sounds to me like you're trying to decide what's fair and what's not fair on your own, aren't you?" Mom asked. "But who decides what's fair?"

"You do," Kyle answered.

Mom laughed. "No!" she answered quickly. "No, honey, *I* don't decide—God does. He decides what's right and what's wrong. And God's Word says to do for others only what you would want them to do for you. *That's* how God defines what's fair."

"So that means I should let Jason play now, right?"

"What do you think?" Mom asked.

Kyle didn't answer his mother. He simply handed the video controller to his brother. "Sorry, Jason," he said.

TO DISCUSS: How can we show by our actions that we want to treat others fairly? Why is fairness important?

TO PRAY: Take turns completing the following prayer: "God, help me to do what you say is right and treat others fairly by _____."

4 In the Halls of Justice

WE VALUE JUSTICE AND FAIRNESS BECAUSE GOD, OUR CREATOR, IS A JUST GOD.

Bible Reading of the Day: Read Deuteronomy 32:3-4.
Verse of the Day: *"He has showed you, O man, what is good. And what does the Lord require of you? To act justly and to love mercy and to walk humbly with your God" (Micah 6:8, NIV).*

"Where are we going, Dad?" Kelly asked.

"You'll see," Dad answered. He and Kelly walked side by side up the marble steps of a large building. The halls of the building were dim and quiet. Dad pressed his finger against his lips to signal Kelly to be quiet as he opened a large wooden door and motioned for Kelly to go in.

She entered a wide courtroom with a judge's bench at the front. Some people sat in wooden chairs, whispering to each other, while others walked in and out of the room.

Soon a man spoke in a loud voice and told everyone to stand. The judge, wearing a black robe, entered and sat in the chair behind the bench and smacked the desk with her gavel. For the next thirty minutes or so, Dad and Kelly watched as the judge heard three different cases. The people who won the cases left smiling, and the people who lost left with sad or angry expressions. After the third case ended, Dad nudged Kelly. They walked out of the courtroom.

"So," Dad said, as they walked down the hallway toward the exit, "what do you think about what you saw this morning?"

"That was neat," Kelly answered. "I'd never been in a real courtroom before."

"I know. I wanted you to see how important justice is," Dad said as he led Kelly back to the car. As he pulled the car out of the parking lot and into traffic, he continued. "You see, Kelly, everybody wants to be treated fairly. That's why we have courts and judges and laws. But *why* is it right to be fair?"

Kelly thought for a moment. "Because . . . ," she started. Her face wrinkled as she concentrated harder. Finally, she shook her head. "I don't know, Daddy."

"I didn't either, until just recently. I knew being fair and just toward other people was right, but I didn't know why." He paused. "The reason we value justice and fairness is because God, our creator, is a just God. Everything he does is just and fair. And because he is just, it's always right for us to be just."

"I didn't know that, Dad," Kelly said. "I don't know if I can remember it."

Dad smiled. "Oh, don't worry too much about that, Kelly. Part of my job is to keep reminding you."

 TO DISCUSS: How does today's Bible reading (Deuteronomy 32:3-4) describe God? What do those words say about how *we* should act?

TO PRAY: "Lord, teach us to be fair just as you are fair."

5 A Break in the Game

GOD VALUES JUSTICE BECAUSE GOD IS JUST.

Bible Reading of the Day: Read Isaiah 45:21-25.
Verse of the Day: *"There is no other God but me—a just God and a Savior—no, not one!" (Isaiah 45:21).*

Philip sat on the family room couch with his dad watching the Braves play the Cubs on TV. A huge bowl of nacho chips and a smaller bowl of salsa dip were set on the couch cushion between them. Suddenly, Philip jumped up from the couch, nearly upsetting the chips and salsa.

"No way!" he cried. "Did you see that call?" he yelled, pointing to the television screen. "There was no way he was out!" Philip's face flushed crimson as he jumped up and down in the middle of the floor as if *he'd* been called out at home.

A few moments later, when Philip had calmed down, Dad asked Philip if he realized why he'd gotten so mad. He shook his head.

Dad shrugged. "You thought the umpire made the wrong call, didn't you?"

"He did!" Philip answered. "The catcher never tagged the runner."

"So what?" Dad said. Suddenly it dawned on Philip what Dad was getting at.

"It's not fair, that's what," Philip answered.

"But why is it not fair?"

Philip, who had recently had many similar discussions with his dad, cocked his head and replied slowly, "Because God has commanded us to be fair." He hesitated. "Right?"

Dad nodded. "That's right. The Bible says, 'Give everyone what you owe him,' and somewhere in Colossians it says, 'Masters, provide your slaves with what is right and fair,' and of course, 'Do for others what you would have them do for you.' Plus, God commanded his people to treat foreigners fairly, to provide for orphans and widows—even to return stray animals to their owners."

"OK," Philip said, enjoying the "game" of trying to discern right and wrong, a game he and his father had played many times before. "And the principle behind all those precepts is the principle of justice, of being fair."

"Right!" Dad said. "And all those precepts God issued show that God values justice—"

"And God values justice," Philip continued, "because God is just himself."

"Absolutely!" Dad declared. He slapped Philip on the shoulder, and they returned their attention to the TV screen, the baseball game, and the chips and salsa between them on the couch.

 TO DISCUSS: Why does God value justice? What evidence in your life leads you to believe that? What other biblical commands can you think of that require us to act justly or to treat others fairly?

 TO PRAY: "Lord, you are a just God. We want to be people of justice. We want to treat others the way you would want us to treat them."

6 The Rest of the Story

KNOWING RIGHT FROM WRONG IS ONLY PART OF THE PICTURE. WE MUST STILL CHOOSE TO DO THE RIGHT THING.

Bible Reading of the Day: Read Proverbs 21:2-3.
Verse of the Day: *"The Lord is more pleased when we do what is just and right than when we give him sacrifices" (Proverbs 21:3).*

Asit heard the whistle as he climbed out of the swimming pool. He glanced up to the lifeguard chair, where his big brother, Ravi, sat.

Ravi beckoned to his little brother. "Asit," Ravi said, leaning over in his chair as he talked, "how did you get back on the diving board so quickly?"

Asit shrugged. "I told Robbie to let me ahead of him because I wanted to go again," Asit said.

"Asit, that wasn't fair."

"I know."

"Then why did you do it?"

"I don't know." Asit thought for a moment before answering. "I guess I just didn't *want* to be fair. I wanted another turn."

"Well, don't do it again, or I'll make you sit out for a while, OK?"

Asit frowned. "OK," he answered after a pause. He walked back to the diving-board steps and joined the end of the long line.

Ravi was shocked at his brother's behavior. He and Asit had both been learning about right and wrong in Sunday school and in youth group at church. He felt confident that Asit knew the wrongness of his actions. But he'd done wrong anyway.

After further thought, Ravi realized he shouldn't be so surprised. *Knowing right from wrong isn't enough,* he thought. *Even when we know right from wrong we can still choose to do the wrong thing. Asit and I both need to make a commitment to choose God's way.*

"Lord," he whispered, "I commit to your way. I commit to acting fairly when I'm faced with the chance to do something unfair. Help me be a good example to Asit. Please help us both to not just *know* what's right but to *choose* what's right too."

Ravi suddenly noticed Kristie, one of the other lifeguards, standing beside his chair. He felt suddenly embarrassed as she asked, "Who are you talking to?"

"I was . . ." Ravi realized he was about to make something up about how he was just talking to himself, but the lie seemed to stick in his throat. He'd just finished asking God to help him choose to do the right thing. He didn't know God would answer his prayer so quickly. "I was . . . I was praying," he said finally.

"I thought so," Kristie said with a smile. "That's really cool."

"Thanks," Ravi said, directing his comment as much to God as to Kristie.

TO DISCUSS: Should a person make a commitment to being fair to others? Why? How can a person show by his or her actions that he or she has made this commitment?

TO PRAY: "God, we have no right to judge others since we're sinners ourselves. Help us not to look for the sin in others but to look for opportunities to be fair."

7 Fruits of Fairness

ACTING JUSTLY PROTECTS FROM DISHONOR AND PROVIDES FOR HONOR.

Bible Reading of the Day: Read Psalm 112:1-8.
Verse of the Day: *"All goes well for those who are generous, who lend freely and conduct their business fairly" (Psalm 112:5).*

Mom burst in the door, dropping her briefcase on the kitchen table. "I'm home!" she called.

Dad kissed her as she entered the living room, and Marcus and JoEllen hugged her.

"I've got some great news for you all," Mom announced as she peeled Marcus and JoEllen off her legs. "I was promoted today! You're looking at the new human resources *director!*"

"What's that mean, Mommy?" Marcus asked.

Mom sat on the edge of the wingbacked chair beside the couch where she could talk to Marcus and JoEllen at eye level. "Well, it means I'll make a little more money. But mostly it means I'll have more responsibilities."

"Why?" JoEllen asked.

Mom winked at her seven-year-old daughter. "That's a good question."

"Because your mommy did a good job," Dad said.

Mom turned to her husband. "Actually, they said the deciding factor was that several employees told my boss that I'd never treated any of them unfairly."

"That's great, sweetheart," Dad said. "I'm proud of you." He hugged her and then turned to his children. "And I want you two to realize that Mom was given her new position because she tries very hard to treat people fairly."

Dad sat on the couch and drew the children onto his lap. "See, let's pretend that Mom was the kind of person who always tries to play favorites, treats one person different from another, and tries to take credit for other people's work. Do you think she would have gotten this promotion?"

"No!" JoEllen said firmly. Marcus shook his head.

"You're right. Because treating people unfairly doesn't just hurt them, it can hurt you, too."

"It can make people not like you," JoEllen offered.

"That's true," Dad said. "But because Mom treats people fairly, she's been given the honor of a new, more important position."

Marcus got up from his dad's lap and crawled into Mom's.

"But you know what will always be my most important position?" Mom asked. "Being your mommy."

TO DISCUSS: Review today's Bible reading. See if you can identify all the benefits and blessings that belong to those "who delight in doing what [God] commands."

TO PRAY: "Lord, we need your help to delight in doing what you command. Thank you for the direction that you provide."

8 Ready for Revenge?

ACTING JUSTLY PROTECTS US FROM REVENGE AND PROMOTES PEACE.

Bible Reading of the Day: Read 1 Peter 3:8-11.
Verse of the Day: *"Don't retaliate when people say unkind things about you. Instead, pay them back with a blessing" (1 Peter 3:9).*

Renee drew her fist back and prepared to slug Sara. She straddled Sara, who lay on her back on the school playground, her fingers entwined in Renee's hair.

"Stop that right now, you two!" Mrs. Knight peeled the girls apart and stood them up, one at the end of each arm. "What's the meaning of this?"

"She started it!" Sara said. "She charged me a dollar for a candy bar!"

"What?" the teacher said, her face showing her confusion.

Sara rolled her eyes and sighed. "Renee was selling candy bars to raise money for the class," she explained. "So I came to buy one—" Sara glared at Renee—"and she told me they were a dollar. So I bought one."

Mrs. Knight nodded. "I still don't see what started the fight."

"After I ate my candy bar, I found out they were really only fifty cents—she just charged me a dollar to be mean."

"I see," Mrs. Knight said, glancing from Sara to Renee. "So you decided to get even."
Sara nodded.

"Well, I'd say you both made some pretty poor decisions." She turned to Renee. "Renee, if you had treated Sara fairly, this wouldn't have happened. When you treat people unfairly, you shouldn't be too surprised if they get mad and try to get even." She paused. "As it is, you not only owe Sara fifty cents, you're going to have to stay after school for a few days."

Mrs. Knight turned to Sara. "And Sara, you may have been treated unfairly, but you were wrong to start a fight with Renee. You'll be staying after school, too. And I'll have to have a talk with your parents and Renee's parents."

Mrs. Knight continued. "I think you can both figure out how you should have handled this differently," she suggested.

"I should have charged Sara what I charged everyone else," Renee said. "I'm sorry, Sara."

"I'm sorry too, Renee. . . . And I should have told you," Sara said to Mrs. Knight, "instead of starting a fight."

"Very good," Mrs. Knight said. She placed a hand on each girl's shoulder. "I don't know about you two, but I'm in the mood for a candy bar."

"Not me!" Sara answered.

"Me, neither!" Renee said.

 TO DISCUSS: How could Renee have protected herself by choosing to do what was right? How can acting justly protect you from revenge? How might acting justly provide for more peaceful relationships with other people?

 TO PRAY: "Lord, we desire peaceful relationships with others. When people treat us unfairly, help us not to take revenge. Instead, lead us to honor you by our actions."

9 That's Not Fair!

ACTING JUSTLY PROTECTS US FROM GUILT AND PROVIDES US WITH CLEAR CONSCIENCES.

Bible Reading of the Day: Read Proverbs 2:6–11.

Verse of the Day: *"[God] grants a treasure of good sense to the godly. He is their shield, protecting those who walk with integrity"* (Proverbs 2:7).

"It's your turn to do the dishes!" Joel protested to his older sister.

"Look," Kathy said, "Evan's going to be here any minute to pick me up for our date. I don't have time to do them."

"Well, I'm not going to do them!"

"Yes, you are! When Mom and Dad are gone, I'm in charge. If you don't do them, they'll be mad at *you*, not me."

"But that's not fair!" Joel's angry tone had turned to a whine.

The doorbell rang.

"I don't have time to argue," Kathy said over her shoulder as she walked toward the front door. "Just do the dishes!"

Kathy cast one last look into the kitchen as she closed the door behind her. She saw her brother standing beside the sink, an angry look on his face.

He makes such a big deal out of everything, she told herself as she got into Evan's car. *It's not like he can't do the dishes to help me out just this once. I've done lots of things for him.*

Kathy and Evan didn't talk much on the drive to the movie theater. Her mind was still on her little brother's frustrated form in front of the kitchen sink, which was piled high with dishes. *He's right, it's not fair,* she thought. *I should have done the dishes instead of talking to Brittany on the phone after dinner.* She began to feel guilty, but shrugged it off. *I'll apologize to him later.*

She said nothing to Evan as they got in line to buy tickets at the theater. She still couldn't shake her feelings of guilt over the way she'd treated Joel. Finally, she couldn't stand it anymore.

"Wait," she said just as they arrived at the ticket counter. "I need to go home." She quickly explained the situation to him and was relieved that he seemed to understand.

As soon as she arrived home, Kathy announced to a shocked Joel that she was going to do the dishes. "And," Kathy added, "I'll do the dishes tomorrow night, too."

"Wow!" Joel said. "How about doing my homework, too?"

"Don't push your luck," Kathy said, as she pointed the sink sprayer in her brother's direction.

 TO DISCUSS: Have you ever felt guilty for treating someone unjustly? How can treating others fairly "fill you with joy"? How can acting justly give you a clear conscience?

 **TO PRAY:** "Help us, Lord, to value others by our just actions."

10 The Absolute Truth

ABSOLUTE TRUTH IS TRUE FOR ALL PEOPLE, FOR ALL PLACES, AND FOR ALL TIME.

Bible Reading of the Day: Read Philippians 4:8.
Verse of the Day: *"Fix your thoughts on what is true"* (Philippians 4:8).

Sean looked at his father. "Daddy, who was the greatest hockey player ever?"

Dad shrugged. "Some people would say Wayne Gretzky. Others might say Gordie Howe."

Sean looked puzzled. "Does anybody know for sure?"

"People have different opinions about those things," Dad said.

"Oh," Sean said. He sounded disappointed as he started to walk away.

"Wait," Dad said. He motioned for Sean to come back. "That's the way it is with some things. Some people think one thing and some people think another thing, and no one is necessarily right or wrong. They just have different opinions."

Sean nodded.

"But some things are *absolute* truths. That means they are true for all people, for all places, and for all time. For example, Sean, we have a rule in our family that you're not allowed to ride your bike in the street, right?"

"Yup," Sean answered.

"But that's not an absolute truth because it's not true for all people."

"Yeah," Sean answered immediately. "Nick's allowed to ride in the street," he said, referring to his older brother.

Dad nodded. "Is it true for all places?"

Sean shook his head. "I can ride my bike on the sidewalk."

Dad smiled. "You're right; that rule is not true for all places. And it's not true for all time, either, because when you get older, Mom and I will let you ride in the street just like we let Nick ride there now." He paused. "So even though you would be doing wrong if you disobeyed us and rode your bike in the street, that rule isn't an *absolute* truth. But Mom and I have also taught you that it's wrong to lie, right?"

Sean nodded.

"Is it true for all people?" Dad asked.

"Yes," Sean answered slowly. "Everybody should tell the truth."

Dad nodded. "Is it true for all places and for all times?"

Sean nodded.

"I'll never be 'old enough' to lie!"

"That's the difference between opinions or rules and absolute truth—absolute truth is true for all people, for all places, and for all time."

"Even for Nick?" Sean asked.

Dad smiled. "Even for Nick."

TO DISCUSS: Which of the following are true for all people, for all places, and for all time: "Do not steal," "No right turn on red," "Love your neighbor," "Do not murder," "Eat all your vegetables"? Why?

TO PRAY: "God, help us to remember what is true for all times and for all people."

11 Tough Love

YOU DON'T DECIDE WHAT'S RIGHT OR WRONG—GOD DOES.

Bible Reading of the Day: Read Matthew 5:43-45.
Verse of the Day: *"Love your enemies! Do good to them!" (Luke 6:35).*

Stefanie and Julia whispered to each other near the fish pond at the Sunday-school picnic. They watched and waited as Jasmine stopped by the shallow, rock-lined pool to watch the goldfish swim in the clear water.

The two girls strolled closer and closer to Jasmine. Finally, Stefanie pretended to trip, and fell against Jasmine, pushing her into the water. Jasmine landed face first in the pool, splashing and spluttering loudly as she struggled back to her feet.

"You did that on purpose!" she screamed.

Stefanie didn't answer her because, like everyone else in the class, she was laughing too hard. Suddenly, however, she felt a hand grip her elbow, and her Sunday-school teacher whirled her around.

"Stefanie and Julia," Miss Penny said, "go wait for me inside, please."

Stefanie and Julia waited at Miss Penny's kitchen table. The teacher passed through the room with a sobbing, wet Jasmine and returned a few minutes later.

"Jasmine's getting changed," she said. "I want you both to know I saw what happened, and I'm very disappointed in you both. That was a hateful thing to do."

Julia started to cry, but Stefanie spoke up. "She would have done the same thing to us!" she said. "Isn't that right, Julia?" Her friend nodded through her tears. "Jasmine's always being mean to me and Julia."

"So," Miss Penny asked, "you're saying that what you did was OK because you did it to Jasmine?"

"Well, yeah," Stefanie answered. *"She's* mean to *us."*

"I want you girls to listen to what you're saying. You're saying that *you* decided it would be all right to act hatefully toward Jasmine. But since when do *you* get to decide what's right or what's wrong?"

"But, Miss Penny, you should hear the things she says about us!" Stefanie whined.

Miss Penny shrugged. "That may be true, but that doesn't change the facts. Fact one: *You* don't decide what's right or wrong, God does. Right?" The girls nodded sullenly. "And fact two: God says 'love your neighbor.' He even says 'love your enemies.' So what does that say about what you did to Jasmine?"

"It was wrong," Julia said, speaking up for the first time.

"What else?" Miss Penny asked.

"We need to go apologize to Jasmine," Stefanie answered.

"That's a fact!" Miss Penny said.

 TO DISCUSS: Do you ever try to decide right and wrong yourself, instead of accepting what God has revealed on the subject? Why or why not? Who is your "neighbor"? What can you do today to love your "neighbor" and an "enemy"?

TO PRAY: "Lord, help us to do what you say is right and avoid what you say is wrong."

12 God Is Love

GOD WANTS US TO LOVE EACH OTHER.

Bible Reading of the Day: Read Matthew 22:34-40.
Verse of the Day: *"God is love" (1 John 4:8).*

"Your little *brother's* going to come?" Rachel said in a shocked tone.

"Yeah," Nicki said with a shrug. "Why not?"

"Well, we're going to ditch him once we get to the mall, aren't we?"

"No, we're not going to ditch him," Nicki answered. "He's my brother!"

Rachel stared at Nicki as if her friend had just sprouted a second head.

"Get in the car," Nicki said. "I've got to pick him up at home, then we can get going to the mall."

As Nicki drove, Rachel talked. "Why would you want your little brother to come with us?"

"Because he's my brother. And he's fun to be around."

Rachel's face still registered shock. "I *hate* my brother and he hates me," she said.

"You should love each other." Nicki protested.

"There's something wrong with you," Rachel said.

"No," Nicki argued, her tone still friendly, "I'm OK. I'm just worried about *you,* girl! You know it's wrong to hate your brother, Rachel."

"Why?" Rachel's tone was defiant. She crossed her arms on her chest.

"Well," Nicki said, hesitating only a moment. "Because the Bible says we should love each other. Jesus said we should love our neighbors as we love ourselves."

"Joey's not my neighbor!"

"Sure he is," Nicki said. "He lives in the bedroom right next to yours!" She pulled the car into the driveway of her house and honked.

"So I should love Joey just because the Bible says so."

"Well, yeah," Nicki said. "But also because when you love, you're being like God. The Bible says, 'God is love.' See, Rachel, the fact that God commands us to love each other shows us that God values love. And he values love because *he* is a loving God. Love is right because God is love."

Nicki's brother, crawled into the back seat and closed the door behind him.

"Hi, Nicki. Hi, Rachel," he said. "You sure you don't mind me going to the mall with you?"

"We're sure," Nicki answered. She smiled at Rachel. "Aren't we?"

Rachel stared straight ahead without acknowledging Nicki's question, but she couldn't completely suppress the smile that crept across her lips.

TO DISCUSS: Take turns completing one of the following statements: "I show love for God when I _____." "I show love for my neighbor when I _____." "I show love for my family when I _____." Discuss your reasons for completing the sentences the way that you did.

TO PRAY: "God, please love others through me."

13 Mister Crump

WE NEED TO MAKE A COMMITMENT TO ACT IN LOVE, EVEN WHEN IT'S HARD TO LOVE.

Bible Reading of the Day: Read 1 John 4:7-11.
Verse of the Day: *"Dear friends, let us continue to love one another, for love comes from God"* (1 John 4:7).

"That man is impossible!" Dad thundered as he slammed the kitchen door behind him.

"Dear," Mom said with concern, "is something wrong?"

"Yes, something's wrong!" Dad bellowed. "It's that George Crump again!"

"He's a hard man to love, isn't he?" Mom said quietly, casting a worried glance toward the family room, where the children were watching television. She didn't want them to overhear their father complaining about Mr. Crump again.

"Hard?" Dad echoed. "He's impossible! He speaks against everything I suggest in the church board meetings!"

"Alex, can you keep your voice down, please?" Mom said. "The children are watching television in the family room."

"I've *had* it with him. The next time he opposes me or criticizes me, I'll—"

Mom held her hands in the air in a gesture intended to soothe her husband. "Please hold it down," she said.

"Hold it down! How can you ask me to hold it down?"

"Because I'm afraid they might hear their father doing what he tells them not to do."

"What?" he said loudly. Then he repeated it, softer this time. "What?"

"You've been telling the children that it's wrong to act spitefully because God is love. And you've been trying to help them see the need to act in love, even when it's hard, right?" She waited until she saw him nod before continuing. "And remember, the other night, you tried to help them see how hard it must have been for God to love *us,* and yet he gave his only Son for us?"

Dad sighed wearily. "And I told them that, if God could love us when it was that hard, we could certainly love others, even when it's hard."

Mom nodded.

"Well," Dad said, "it sure is hard to love George Crump. But I guess I need to practice what I preach."

Mom smiled.

Dad embraced her, then closed his eyes. "Father," he began to pray, "forgive me for my unloving attitude toward George Crump. I sure do need your help to love him, but I commit to doing that right now. Amen."

"Amen," his wife repeated.

 TO DISCUSS: Can you think of any times when it might have been hard for others to love you? During those times, who loved you anyway? Mom? Dad? God?

 TO PRAY: Do you need to make a commitment to love someone? If so, take a few moments to speak the prayer Dad prayed above, changing it or adding to it as necessary.

14 Double the Fun

LOVE MAKES YOU HAPPY TWICE—WHEN YOU GIVE IT, AND WHEN YOU RECEIVE IT BACK.

Bible Reading of the Day: Read 2 Peter 1:5-8.
Verse of the Day: *"Make every effort to apply the benefits of these promises to your life" (2 Peter 1:5).*

Tina raced in the front door. "Mom!" she yelled. "Look at all the valentines I got at school today!" She dumped the contents of her backpack onto the table.

Mom smiled. "That's wonderful, Tina," she said.

"I'm going to keep them forever!" Tina announced.

"Will you show them to me?" Mom said as she dried her hands on a towel.

Mom sat at the table and listened attentively as Tina showed her all the valentine greetings she had brought home from school. Tina chattered happily, identifying which cards were the biggest, the fanciest, and the funniest.

"Did your teacher explain to you what Valentine's Day is about?" Mom asked when Tina finished showing her the cards.

Tina flashed her mother a puzzled look. "What do you mean?"

"Well, do you know that Valentine's Day is named after a Christian who lived a long time ago?"

"No," Tina said.

"That's right," Mom said. "One story says that Valentine was so loved by children that, when he was put in prison for refusing to worship false gods, the children all came to visit him and passed him notes through the bars of his cell window. Some people think that's how the custom of exchanging valentines got started."

"I really like that story, Mommy," Tina said. "I'm going to try to remember it."

"Good," Mom said. "But do you know what I'd like you to remember even more?"

Tina shook her head.

"I'd like you to remember that love makes you happy twice—when you give it, and when you receive it back . . . just like giving and receiving valentines."

"I gave a lot of valentines today!" Tina said.

"I know," Mom answered. "And that was fun, wasn't it? That's the way love is. And that's one of the reasons God wants us to love each other—because love makes us so much happier than being angry, or hating, or not liking each other."

Tina suddenly jumped up from her chair and started to dash out of the room.

"Wait a minute!" Mom said. "Where are you going?"

"I'm going to look for some more valentines so I can give some more love away!" Tina answered.

 TO DO: If you have any valentine cards left over, make it a family project to send valentines with personal greetings to prisoners in a nearby jail or prison or to residents in a retirement home. Or, instead of giving valentine cards to each other, you could give cards to another family or bake them a batch of cookies.

 TO PRAY: "Lord, help us to be alert to ways we can give our love away as a family."

15 Love: It Does a Body Good

LOVING ATTITUDES AND ACTIONS DON'T JUST BENEFIT OTHERS, THEY BENEFIT US.

Bible Reading of the Day: Read 1 Corinthians 13:4-7.
Verse of the Day: *"Let love be your highest goal"* (1 Corinthians 14:1).

The doctor shook his head as he finished giving Dad a physical examination.

"What's wrong, Doctor?" Dad asked, buttoning his shirt.

"Nothing!" the doctor answered, smiling. "I wish *I* had your blood pressure!"

Dad laughed. "Well, that's good news."

"You bet it is," the doctor answered. "I was talking to my brother-in-law yesterday. Now *he's* a walking time bomb." He shook his head sadly. "Sky-high blood pressure. High cholesterol count. Plus, he's developing an ulcer."

"Isn't there something you can do for him?" Dad asked.

The doctor shrugged. "He takes medication," he explained, "but that will accomplish very little unless he changes his life."

"What do you mean?" Dad asked.

The doctor sighed. "He had a fight with his brother fifteen years ago. They haven't spoken two words to each other since, but his resentment and hatred for his brother are eating him alive. The effects of his hatred for his brother are literally killing him."

Dad nodded. "I can believe that," he said. "I think that's part of the reason God wants us to love each other, because he knows how destructive hate can be, and how helpful and healthy love can be."

The doctor fingered the stethoscope that hung around his neck. "You know, I think you're right. I watch people spend thousands of dollars on medical treatment to help them combat stress. If they'd just be more like you, they might save money *and* make themselves healthier at the same time!"

"They don't need to be more like me, Doc," Dad said. "They need to be more like God: loving and forgiving. But you're right. Loving attitudes and actions don't just benefit others, they benefit *us*. That's all part of God's amazing wisdom. When he says 'Love one another,' he says it for our own good. Following his commands can help us avoid all sorts of unpleasant things."

The doctor nodded thoughtfully.

"Of course," Dad said, smiling slyly, "if everybody followed God's commands to love each other, you might not get so much business."

The doctor laughed. "That would be just fine with me! I could use the extra time to work on my golf game!"

"I know," Dad said, smiling broadly. "I've seen you play."

 TO DISCUSS: Booker T. Washington once said, "I will not let any man reduce my soul to the level of hatred." What do you think he meant by that? What can you do today and in the future to enjoy the benefits of following God's commands to love each other?

 TO PRAY: "Lord, help us to never let any man reduce our soul to the level of hatred. Instead, help us to show love, even when it's hard to love."

16 Love in Action

WE SHOW BY OUR ACTIONS THAT WE ARE LIVING IN TRUTH.

Bible Reading of the Day: Read 1 John 3:18-20.
Verse of the Day: *"Dear friends, let us continue to love one another, for love comes from God"* (1 John 4:7).

Mallory noticed the woman's dirty fingernails as she dropped a bread roll onto the plate and handed it to her. *Doesn't she ever take a bath?* she thought, staring at the woman's matted hair.

The woman took the plate from Mallory and shuffled away without looking up. Mallory glanced at the next person in line at the homeless shelter Mallory's family visited once a month. The gray-haired woman smiled at her, revealing a mouth with only a few teeth.

"Her name's Clara," the woman said. "Her husband died a few months ago. She hasn't been the same since."

Mallory quickly shifted her gaze and reached for another bread roll. She placed it on the plate of chicken, mashed potatoes, and gravy that her brother gave her and handed it to the woman.

The woman smiled. "Thank you," she said. "God bless you."

Mallory blushed. This woman seemed different from many of the others at the shelter, who took their food and shuffled off without a word. She wasn't dirty. *Except for her missing teeth and worn clothes, she seems—well, normal,* Mallory thought. Watching her walk away, Mallory felt embarrassed as she recalled her earlier complaints to her parents about going to the shelter. Her parents had gently insisted that she go, and Mallory had been grumpy ever since.

Mallory's gaze once again found the woman with the missing teeth. She sat beside Clara and began to butter her roll. Then she cut Clara's chicken, gently placing the fork in Clara's hand when she was done.

Mallory left her place in the food line and took a seat next to the woman. "Are you related to Clara or something?" she asked.

"No," the woman answered. She looked curious.

"I saw what you did for her. I mean, cutting her meat for her and everything."

The woman shrugged. "I just want her to know that God loves her, and so do I. I tell her that often, but I think I say it a lot better in my actions. But why am I telling you? I bet that's why you come here—to show God's love to people like me."

Mallory's face showed her surprise. "Yeah," she answered. "That's why I come here." She smiled at the woman, determined not to forget that again.

 TO DO: Take a few moments to plan a family "project" intended to show God's love to someone outside your family. You might bake cookies for a shut-in, take the family pet to visit nursing-home patients, baby-sit for a single parent, or shovel snow for an elderly couple.

TO PRAY: "Lord, we're fortunate to have what you've given us. Show us ways we can share ourselves and our blessings with others."

17 Seat Belts

GOD'S COMMANDS ARE LIKE SEAT BELTS. THEY ARE INTENDED FOR OUR OWN GOOD, TO KEEP US SAFE.

> **Bible Reading of the Day: Read Deuteronomy 6:20-24.**
> Verse of the Day: *"The Lord our God commanded us to obey all these laws and to fear him for our own prosperity and well-being, as is now the case" (Deuteronomy 6:24).*

"OK, kids!" Mom shouted from the bottom of the stairs. "It's time to go! Everybody in the car!"

Keshawn ran downstairs with Randy, who had spent the night so they could leave bright and early for their day at Water World. They raced to the car and jumped into the back seat. Keshawn's mom and sister, Raviana, occupied the front seats.

Mom turned around in her seat and smiled at the boys. "Ready to go?"

Keshawn snapped his seat belt into place. "Ready!" he declared.

Randy saw Keshawn fasten his seat belt but made no move to follow his example.

"All right, then," Mom said. She glanced at Randy. "I think we're all set as soon as you fasten your seat belt, Randy."

Randy rolled his eyes. "My parents don't make me wear seat belts."

"Oh, I see," Mom said. "Do you need help?"

"No," Randy said, defiance in his voice. "I can do it myself." He gripped the two belts and connected them.

As Mom turned the car out of the driveway and onto the road, Randy turned to Keshawn. "Why do you have to wear seat belts?" he asked.

Keshawn shrugged. "We've just always done it," he answered. "We don't even think about it anymore. Besides, it's the law."

"It's stupid," Randy announced.

"No, it's not," Keshawn said.

"It's so uncomfortable."

"Maybe at first. But once you get used to it, you don't even realize you're wearing a seat belt."

"I don't see why your parents make you wear it, though." Randy's expression made it clear that he thought Keshawn's parents were too strict, even mean.

Keshawn laughed. "They make us wear seat belts for our own good. They know that if we ever got into an accident, wearing a seat belt could save our lives!" He shook his head at his friend, who still seemed annoyed. "You think they do it just to be mean?"

Randy didn't answer. He rolled his eyes, as if he knew he'd lost the argument.

Keshawn punched his friend lightly on the shoulder. "I didn't think so!" he said, laughing.

 TO DISCUSS: How are God's commands like seat belts in a car? How can you "put on" God's commands like you would a seat belt?

 TO PRAY: "Lord, thank you for the protection of your Word. Help us to value your rules."

18 Fun in the Sun

FOLLOWING CHRIST CAN BE A LOT OF FUN.

Bible Reading of the Day: Read Hebrews 11:24-25.

Verse of the Day: *"I have told you this so that you will be filled with my joy. Yes, your joy will overflow!" (John 15:11).*

Nate lost control of his icy sled and rolled down the hill, laughing and shouting.

"This is great!" he said to his friend, Ted. "When you called me this morning to ask me to go sledding, I thought you were crazy. Here it is, not a single snowflake on the ground and the temperature in the forties. This was a great idea, man!"

Ted laughed as he gripped a rope that was frozen into a fifty-pound block of ice. He lugged the block back up the grassy hill.

"Where did you come up with this idea?" Nate asked.

Ted shrugged. "My church youth group does it almost every year. It's easy. You just buy a block of ice, freeze a circle of rope into it, and you're in business!"

"This is so great!" Nate repeated. "You don't even need cold weather or snow!"

"So," Ted said, turning to face Nate at the top of the hill, "you having fun?"

"Absolutely!" Nate said.

"I seem to remember you saying once that you didn't think Christians ever had fun," Ted said, smiling broadly. "You said anybody who doesn't drink or go to wild parties had to have a totally boring life."

Nate looked a little sheepish. "I said that?"

"I said that?" Ted echoed sarcastically. "The next time you think God wants to spoil our fun or steal our joy, just remember today."

Nate hesitated. "But don't you ever wish you could do the things I do?"

Ted shook his head. "I know you have fun sometimes when you go out partying, but the fun doesn't last too long, does it? And it can have some pretty rotten consequences, can't it?"

Nate shrugged. "I guess," he said.

"I'll admit that sometimes it's not easy to do the right thing," Ted said, "but believe me, man, following Christ can be a lot of fun. He didn't come to spoil all our fun—he came so we could *have* fun!"

"All right," Nate said, holding up his hands, "I give up."

"So does that mean you're ready to become a Christian?" Ted asked.

"I don't know about that," Nate said.

Ted studied his friend thoughtfully, then said, "Well—just so you know—when you *are* ready to become a Christian you'll know what fun really is!" Ted said. He flung himself onto the ice slab and hurtled toward the bottom of the hill.

 TO DO: Plan something fun to do as a family to remind each other (and perhaps some of your non-Christian friends) that following Christ can be a lot of fun.

 TO PRAY: "Lord, thank you for the joy of being in your family. Help us to spread that joy to others."

19 Roots and Fruits (Part 1)

PEOPLE DO WRONG THINGS BECAUSE EVERYBODY HAS A SINFUL NATURE.

Bible Reading of the Day: Read Romans 5:12-17.
Verse of the Day: *"What a difference between our sin and God's generous gift of forgiveness" (Romans 5:15).*

Grandpa shifted the tractor into gear. Heather sat on her grandpa's lap, laughing as the tractor lurched forward. She craned her neck to look behind her grandpa to watch a tree stump, attached to the tractor by a giant chain, being ripped out of the ground.

A few moments later, Grandpa turned the tractor off, and he and Heather climbed down from the tractor to inspect the stump and the hole it had left in the field. Grandpa started to unwind the chain from around the stump.

"Grandpa," Heather asked, "why couldn't Jonathan come with us today?" Jonathan was Heather's older brother. He and Heather usually helped Grandpa together.

"Well, Heather," Grandpa answered, "Jonathan has to stay in his room today because he did something wrong. I thought you knew that."

Heather nodded. She knew Jonathan had been caught taking money from their mom's purse, but she was still puzzled. "Grandpa," she said, "why do people do bad things even when they know they're wrong?"

Grandpa finally freed the chain from the stump. He straightened and began gathering the chain in his gloved hands. "That's a good question," he said. He thought for a few moments before answering. "People do wrong things because everybody has a sinful nature. Ever since the first man and woman sinned by disobeying God, we've all been born with a sinful nature. That means that people find it *natural* to do what's wrong.

"Some people give in to pressure from friends," he continued. "Some people do wrong things because they've developed bad habits that they find hard to break. But all of us make wrong choices because it seems easy to us." He turned to the tree stump. "You see that?" he said, pointing to the tangle of roots that had been pulled out of the ground. "That ol' tree is like us. Those roots went deep into the ground beneath the tree, just like our sinful nature. We have the roots of sin inside us, and we make choices every day—we can make right choices or we can make wrong choices. We can trust God and follow his way, or we can make the mistake of giving in to our sinful nature. God never takes the choice away from us. And sometimes people make wrong choices instead of doing the right thing."

"We don't have to do wrong, though, do we Grandpa?" Heather asked.

"No," Grandpa answered. "We don't. And I hope you'll *always* remember that."

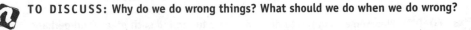 **TO DISCUSS:** Why do we do wrong things? What should we do when we do wrong?

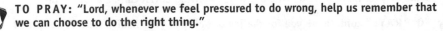 **TO PRAY:** "Lord, whenever we feel pressured to do wrong, help us remember that we can choose to do the right thing."

20 Roots and Fruits (Part 2)

MAKING RIGHT CHOICES IS THE FRUIT THAT COMES OUT OF OUR LIVES WHEN WE TRUST GOD.

Bible Reading of the Day: Read Romans 5:18-21.
Verse of the Day: *"Christ's one act of righteousness makes all people right in God's sight and gives them life" (Romans 5:18).*

"What are we going to do with that stump now, Grandpa?" Heather asked. She had just watched her grandpa pull an old stump and its roots out of the ground with his tractor.

Grandpa said, "We'll just bring some kerosene and kindling back from the barn and burn it right where it sits."

He gripped Heather under her arms and hoisted her up to the tractor seat. Then he vaulted up after her and sat her back down in his lap. "Like I told you, Heather, that ol' stump is like our sinful nature," he reminded his granddaughter, "and that sinful nature is what keeps us from choosing to do right all the time, right?"

Heather nodded.

"Do you think you could have pulled that stump out of the ground all by yourself?" Grandpa asked.

Heather's eyes widened. She shook her head.

Grandpa smiled. "Do you think *I* could have pulled that stump out of the ground by myself?"

Heather hesitated a moment, then answered quietly, "No."

Grandpa let out a good-natured laugh. "Don't worry, Heather, that doesn't hurt my feelings. You're right. That mess of roots is stronger than both of us put together."

"But you pulled it out with the tractor!" Heather said triumphantly.

"Exactly right!" Grandpa said. "It took something a lot stronger than me—" he patted the tractor's large metal fender—"to overcome those roots. It's the same way with doing right, Heather. Neither one of us—not even both of us put together—can overcome our sinful nature. We can only make right choices by relying on God's strength and trust him to make us good."

Grandpa rubbed his chin. "Come to think of it," he said, "making right choices is the fruit that comes out of our lives when we trust God."

Heather pivoted on her grandfather's lap. "Was that tree an apple tree?" she asked, pointing to the stump they had pulled out of the ground.

"No," Grandpa said. "That's a hickory. It did bear fruit, though."

"What kind of fruit?" Heather asked.

"Nuts," Grandpa answered, "just like you!" Grandpa started the tractor's engine with one hand and tickled his granddaughter with the other as they laughed together all the way back to the barn.

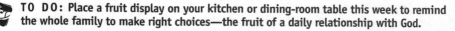

 TO DO: Place a fruit display on your kitchen or dining-room table this week to remind the whole family to make right choices—the fruit of a daily relationship with God.

TO PRAY: "Lord, we want to live fruitful lives. Help us to trust you."

21 Molly's Moment of Truth

SHOW MERCY AND KINDNESS TO ONE ANOTHER.

Bible Reading of the Day: Read Zechariah 7:9-10.
Verse of the Day: *"Show mercy and kindness to one another"*
(Zechariah 7:9).

Molly knew something was wrong as soon as she walked into the classroom. The teacher was not in the room, and a cluster of children huddled around a desk in the middle of the room. As she approached the group, she heard the voice of Tammy, one of the most popular girls in the school.

"Why don't you say something, Gayle?" Tammy said.

"Yeah," another voice chimed in. "Tammy called you a big fat whale. Aren't you going to do something?"

Molly squeezed into the crowd to get a look at the girl they were taunting. Gayle was a misfit. She didn't really have any friends, and sometimes she did weird things.

Gayle sat at her desk with her face buried in her folded arms. She hadn't said anything since Molly had entered the room. Molly secretly wished the teacher would come back into the room and stop the mistreatment. But there was no sign of the teacher.

"Gayle," Tammy called, poking her finger in Gayle's face. "Gayle the whale!"

Molly felt sorry for Gayle. *But if I say something,* she thought, *Tammy might get mad at me. She might even stop being my friend.*

Suddenly the whole group of children started chanting, "Gayle the whale!" over and over again.

It's not like I'm doing anything wrong, Molly figured. *It wouldn't be so wrong just to stay out of it, would it?* Immediately, however, she knew she was wrong. Her job was to follow what God said was right. And what her friends were doing was wrong.

Finally, Molly couldn't take it anymore. "Stop!" she yelled. "Everybody stop it!"

The girls looked at her like she'd just sprouted a second head.

"Let's leave Gayle alone," she said. She flashed a pleading look at Tammy.

"What's wrong with you?" Tammy asked.

"Nothing," Molly said with a shrug. Gayle slowly lifted her head and looked at Molly with tearful eyes. Molly smiled at her, then looked back at Tammy, worried about what her friend might do.

Tammy clucked her tongue and whirled around. "Oh, fine," she said. She went back to her desk. The crowd of girls also took their seats, leaving Molly and Gayle.

Gayle wiped her eyes with the sleeve of her blouse. "Thanks," she said, quietly.

Molly shrugged. She had known all along it would have been wrong to join in her friends' cruelty, but now she *really* knew she had made the right choice.

TO DISCUSS: What do you think Molly would have done if she had tried to decide right and wrong all by herself, instead of following what she knew God said was right?

TO PRAY: "Lord, we need your help to do what's right. Thank you for showing us ways to do the right thing."

22 Kevin's Complaint

MERCY IS RIGHT BECAUSE GOD IS MERCIFUL.

> Bible Reading of the Day: Read Micah 7:16-18.
> Verse of the Day: *"The Lord has already told you what is good, and this is what he requires: to do what is right, to love mercy, and to walk humbly with your God"* (Micah 6:8).

Kevin flopped onto the front seat of the minivan and closed the door behind him. He threw his glove on the floor.

"How was the game, or shouldn't I ask?" Dad said. He had dropped Kevin off at the Little League game about two hours earlier.

"Terrible," Kevin groaned. "We lost! Our team stinks!"

Dad groaned. "That's too bad, Son. I'm sorry to hear that. And I'm sorry I couldn't stay to see it."

"You didn't miss anything! The coach wouldn't let me play that much."

"What was the score?" Dad asked. He could see tears in Kevin's eyes.

"Ten to zero!" Kevin growled. "The other team kept calling our team losers every time they scored a run."

They drove in silence for a few minutes. Finally, Dad glanced over at Kevin, who was glaring out the window. "Makes you mad, doesn't it?"

Kevin nodded and continued to stare out the window.

"Do you know *why* it makes you mad?"

Kevin flashed a puzzled glance at his dad. "Sure. We lost."

"I know you're disappointed, Kev. I think you're upset because that team showed no mercy when they were winning. Right?"

Kevin's face relaxed. "Yeah," he said.

"So you think not showing mercy is wrong. And showing mercy is right."

"Well, yeah," Kevin said, as if anyone should understand that.

"Why?" Dad asked. Kevin's answer was a blank look. "I'll tell you why," Dad continued. "God commanded us to be merciful because he values mercy. His commands show what kind of attitude and behavior he values. The Bible says he delights in showing mercy. Mercy is right because it reflects God's nature and character. And refusing to show mercy is wrong because it's not like God."

Kevin nodded thoughtfully.

"That other team may have won, but they're the losers when it comes to sportsmanship." Dad put his arm around Kevin's shoulder. "You up for some ice cream?"

"Yeah!" Kevin said, looking as if he felt better already.

TO DISCUSS: Why do you think God "delights in showing mercy"? How does a person's actions reflect a delight in showing mercy?

TO PRAY: "God, you are a God of mercy. Help us to value mercy as you do, and help us to delight in showing mercy as you do."

23 Lee Lets Go

KNOWING THE TRUTH DOESN'T GUARANTEE THAT YOU WILL CHOOSE THE TRUTH.

Bible Reading of the Day: Read Luke 6:36-38.
Verse of the Day: *"Be merciful, just as your Father is merciful"*
(Luke 6:36, NIV).

Lee bounced a beach ball on the floor between her legs as she sat in front of the television watching cartoons.

Lee's baby-sitter, Mrs. Hastings, came into the room and sat beside her, groaning as she crossed her legs. "Your little sister's trying to put a puzzle together," she said. "I thought you might like to help her."

"No," Lee said.

Mrs. Hastings frowned. "You've forgiven your sister for breaking your keyboard, haven't you?"

Lee shrugged. "I don't know."

"I see," Mrs. Hastings said. She reached into her pocket and pulled out a dollar bill. "Let's play a little game, Lee. I'm going to hold this dollar bill like this." She stretched the dollar bill tight between her hands and held them out in front of her. "Now, I want you to hold that beach ball with both hands."

Lee squeezed the ball tightly between both palms.

"Now," Mrs. Hastings said. "I'll give you this money if you can take hold of both ends of this dollar bill while you hold tightly onto that beach ball. OK?"

Lee looked at her hands, then at the dollar bill. She moved her hands—and the beach ball—closer to the money.

"I can't," Lee said.

Mrs. Hastings nodded. "What if you let go of the beach ball? Could you grab both ends of the dollar bill then?"

Lee dropped the beach ball onto the floor and reached out for the dollar bill. She gripped both ends of the money, and Mrs. Hastings gripped both of Lee's hands. She held Lee's hands as she spoke. "You see, you couldn't grab the money if you held onto the ball. And you won't be able to fully receive forgiveness for the wrong things you do unless you let go of your unforgiving feelings toward your sister."

Mrs. Hastings released Lee's hands and let her take the money. "You know it's right to forgive your sister, don't you, Lee?"

Lee nodded.

"But even though you know what's right, you haven't been doing it, have you?"

Lee shook her head. She watched Mrs. Hastings walk out of the room, then turned toward the television. But suddenly, she didn't feel like watching cartoons anymore. She was in the mood to put a puzzle together.

 TO DISCUSS: How is forgiveness related to mercy? Do you ever have trouble forgiving others? Do you need to express forgiveness to anyone?

TO PRAY: "Lord, we need your help to forgive others. Help us to cling to forgiveness rather than to bitterness."

24 A Lesson in Truth

MERCY BLESSES THE PERSON WHO GIVES AND THE PERSON WHO RECEIVES.

Bible Reading of the Day: Read Matthew 5:1-7.

Verse of the Day: *"God blesses those who are merciful, for they will be shown mercy" (Matthew 5:7).*

Courtney was hardly in the door when she smiled at her mom and said, "Guess what we learned in school today, Mom!"

"What?" Mom asked.

"Truth!"

"Is that right?" Mom said. "And what truth did you learn about?"

"Sojourner Truth!" Courtney answered. "Get it?"

Mom chuckled. "I get it," she said. "Tell me what you learned about her."

Courtney took off her coat and mittens. "She was a really neat lady, Mom. She was a slave when she was a kid. Then she got free and started trying to help other people escape slavery." Courtney stuffed her mittens into her coat sleeves and hung them together in the hall closet. "She, like, worked really hard finding homes and jobs for people who escaped from slavery."

Mom nodded. "Do you think she was a religious person?"

Courtney's brow wrinkled. "I don't know. They didn't tell us that."

"Well, she was," Mom said. "She had a deep faith in God. She was convinced that God had called her to speak out against slavery. She believed that one of the ways people could best show their love for God was by being loving and merciful toward other people."

"Wow," Courtney said. "I didn't know that. I'm going to put that in the report I have to write."

"Let me ask you one more question," Mom said.

"OK," Courtney said.

"Do you think Sojourner Truth was worse off because she showed so much mercy to so many people?"

Courtney looked at her mom as if her mom's question was crazy. "No way!" she said. "She's famous now! She was even famous back then. She got to visit Abraham Lincoln in the White House, and a lot of people really looked up to her."

"So you think that showing mercy to others earned her more respect and love than she would have had otherwise?"

"Yeah," Courtney said. "Easy. We probably would have never heard of her if she hadn't been such a neat person."

"I think you're right," Mom said with a wink. "I think you're absolutely right."

 TO DISCUSS: The Bible says that "God blesses those who are merciful." How was Sojourner Truth blessed? How are people today blessed for being merciful? Name examples of people you know of who were blessed for being merciful.

TO PRAY: "Lord, show us ways to be merciful to others."

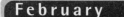

25 The Triumph of Mercy

MERCY BRINGS BENEFITS.

Bible Reading of the Day: Read James 2:12-13.
Verse of the Day: *"Mercy triumphs over judgment!"* (James 2:13, NIV).

Felipe heard the commotion coming from the kitchen of the fast-food restaurant where he worked after school and on weekends. He left his position at the cash register and walked toward the banging and shouting.

As he arrived at the scene, he saw Brett pointing a finger and shouting at Paul. (Paul was a mentally handicapped adult who had worked part time at the restaurant for several years.) At Paul's feet lay a split plastic mustard container.

"You moron!" Brett was saying when Felipe arrived. He pointed at the mop in Paul's hand. "Why don't you watch where you're going with that thing?"

Felipe looked from Brett to Paul. Paul's lower lip was quivering; the man was about to burst into tears. Felipe turned to Brett.

"Tell you what," he suggested. "How about taking over for me at the counter? I'll handle this."

"No problem," Brett answered. "Good luck with *him.*"

Felipe spoke gently to Paul. "Why don't you and I clean this up together?" he said. Paul offered the mop to Felipe, but Felipe shook his head. "You're a lot better at mopping than I am. I think you should do that part." He looked around as if he were going to tell a secret. "I always get the floor too wet."

Paul flashed a nervous smile then, and they started working together. Felipe scooped up the spilled mustard with a rubber dustpan, and Paul mopped. They had the floor cleaned in just a few minutes.

A few days later, Felipe was helping the restaurant manager stock shelves in the storeroom. When he tried to build a stack of boxes too high, the entire stack tumbled to the ground. Two boxes of wrapped drinking straws spilled onto the floor.

Felipe saw an angry look cross his boss's face. He expected an angry response from the man. However, after a moment of hesitation, the boss shook his head.

"You know, Felipe," he said seriously, "a few days ago, I would have yelled at you for what just happened. But I saw how you handled that situation with Paul and Brett the other day." He saw the look of surprise on Felipe's face. "I was watching from the back entrance," he explained. "Anyway, if that unkind Brett had been the one to spill all those straws, I would have given it to him. But since it's you . . ." He smiled. "You're a lot better at picking up straws than I am. I think you should do that part."

Felipe immediately recognized the echo of what he had told Paul a few days ago. He laughed and began picking up the straws he had spilled.

 TO DISCUSS: How did Felipe's act of mercy toward Paul benefit Paul? How did it benefit Felipe himself? How can you be more alert to opportunities to show mercy to others this week?

 TO PRAY: "Lord, thank you for the mercy you show us each day. Open our eyes to the people around us who need to be shown mercy."

26 What's in a Name?

FOLLOWING GOD'S COMMAND TO SHOW MERCY TO OTHERS CAN PROVIDE THE
BLESSING OF A GOOD REPUTATION.

Bible Reading of the Day: Read Proverbs 3:1-4.
Verse of the Day: *"Choose a good reputation over great riches, for being
held in high esteem is better than having silver or gold" (Proverbs 22:1).*

Valerie and Jasmine sat silently in the school principal's office. The principal, Mrs.
Sheldon, looked at them sternly.

"Now, ladies," Mrs. Sheldon said, "I understand we have a small problem."

"We didn't do it," Valerie insisted. "Honest, Mrs. Sheldon."

The principal crossed her arms and leaned against her desk, facing the girls. "Why
don't you start by telling me how all this got started?"

"Somebody put Vaseline on Kelly Porter's crutches during lunch period," Jasmine
said softly, referring to a girl who had a broken leg. "She slipped and fell when she
tried to walk on them."

"It wasn't us," Valerie said. "Kelly just blamed us."

"Why would she blame you if you didn't do it?" the principal asked. She noticed
that Valerie had to suppress a smile at Kelly's misfortune, but Jasmine seemed truly
sorry for their classmate.

"I don't know," Valerie said with a shrug.

"We were sitting behind Kelly," Jasmine offered.

"But we didn't do it," Valerie repeated.

"Is Kelly OK?" Jasmine asked.

Mrs. Sheldon uncrossed her arms and gripped the edges of the desk she leaned
against. "I think so," she said. "She apparently has quite a gash on her forehead, but
I think she's hurt more on the *inside* than on the outside."

Jasmine nodded. "I would be, too."

"We really didn't do it, Mrs. Sheldon," Valerie said.

Mrs. Sheldon sighed loudly. "I believe you," she said. She tapped her fingers on
the edge of the desk. "But I want you to know *why* I believe you." She turned to
Jasmine. "I believe you because I've never seen you treat anyone cruelly. Quite the
opposite, in fact. I've seen you act kindly to other students, even when you thought
no one was watching. *That's* why I believe your story, ladies."

Jasmine looked shyly at the principal. "Thank you, Mrs. Sheldon," she said softly.

"You're welcome," Mrs. Sheldon answered. She stood. "Now, if you'll excuse me,
I have to go check on Kelly to see how she's doing."

"Mrs. Sheldon?" Jasmine said as she and Valerie stood. "Can we come, too?"

Mrs. Sheldon smiled. "That would be nice," she said.

**TO DISCUSS: How might showing mercy to others produce a good reputation? What
might be the benefits of such a reputation?**

**TO PRAY: "Lord, we choose the good reputation that comes from showing mercy
to others. Thank you for your kindness to us."**

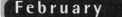
27 The Right Change

RIGHT CHOICES AREN'T ALWAYS REWARDED IN THIS LIFE.

Bible Reading of the Day: Read 1 Samuel 26:1-11.
Verse of the Day: *"The Lord gives his own reward for doing good and for being loyal"* (1 Samuel 26:23).

"I can't believe it!" Nathan said, as he entered the house that afternoon.

Mom looked up from her crossword puzzle. "What's wrong?" she asked.

"Amber forgot her lunch money last week at school, so I gave her some money," he explained. He set his backpack on the kitchen table.

"Yeah, so?" Mom asked.

"Well, today she stood behind me in line at the soda machine. I put my money in and nothing happened. So I figured it was broken or something and I turned around to Amber and told her the machine ate my money."

Mom nodded.

"She said, 'I'll try it anyway,'" Nathan continued. "So she started to put her money in and the machine started giving her change right away. She pressed the button, got a can of soda, and then started counting her change. It turns out she got a can of soda for five cents!"

"And she didn't offer to pay you back the money you lost," Mom said.

"No!" Nathan said. "She just smiled and walked away, leaving me without a soda."

Mom shook her head. "You're right," she said. "That does seem pretty thoughtless. But that doesn't change the fact that you did the right thing by helping her when she forgot her lunch money. It just points out that right choices aren't always rewarded—at least not in this life." She placed a hand on Nathan's shoulder. "But don't let that stop you from making right choices the next time. Whether they're rewarded or not, they're still the best way to go."

TO DISCUSS: Even though David spared Saul's life in the wilderness of Ziph, David continued to live in exile until Saul's death. Do you think David regretted showing mercy to Saul? Why or why not? Have you always been rewarded for showing mercy? Have you ever regretted showing mercy?

TO PRAY: "Lord, help us to be merciful, even when people treat us unfairly."

28 If in Doubt, Leave It Out

IF YOU THINK SOMETHING'S WRONG AND YOU GO AHEAD AND DO IT ANYWAY,
THAT WOULD BE SIN.

Bible Reading of the Day: Read Romans 14:23.
Verse of the Day: *"Anyone who believes that something he wants to do is wrong shouldn't do it" (Romans 14:23, TSLB).*

"Aunt Helen," Shadayva asked, "can I ask you a question?"

Aunt Helen smiled and nodded. She and Shadayva sat side by side at the bus stop. They had spent Saturday morning at church, packing bag lunches to be delivered to needy people. "You can ask me whatever you want, child," Aunt Helen said.

Shadayva hesitated for a moment. "Is it a sin," she asked, speaking slowly and thoughtfully, "if you're not sure something is wrong, but you do it anyway?"

"I don't know," Aunt Helen said. "It may be, and it may not be. It isn't necessarily a sin to do something that you don't know is right or wrong. You can't know everything, and nobody expects you to. Why, sometimes your ol' Aunt Helen doesn't even know exactly what to do. Of course, if you think it's wrong and you go ahead and do it anyway, that would be sin." She studied Shadayva's face. "Why do you ask, child?"

Shadayva shrugged. She swung her legs beneath her as she sat on the wooden bench. "Tamera—she's one of my friends—asked me to do her a favor."

"What kind of favor?" Aunt Helen asked.

"She wanted me to show her my homework so she could see how I did the hard problems."

"Did you give her your homework?"

Shadayva shook her head. "Not yet."

"Do you think she wants to copy your homework?"

Shadayva shrugged. "I don't know."

"So you're wondering if it would be wrong to let Tamera see your homework," Aunt Helen said.

"Yes, ma'am," Shadayva answered.

Aunt Helen shifted on the hard wooden bench. She draped her arm around Shadayva's shoulders and pulled her closer. "Well, child, when you have doubts about whether something is right or wrong, the best thing to do is nothing."

"Nothing?"

"That's right," Aunt Helen said. "You should try to make sure what you want to do is right *before* you do it. If you're not sure, then don't do anything until you can pray about it, and read your Bible, and ask your mother and father."

"Or my Aunt Helen," Shadayva added.

Aunt Helen smiled and hugged her niece. "Or your Aunt Helen," she said.

 TO DO: Have a "Do Nothing Contest." See who can sit for the longest period of time without moving, twitching, speaking, or laughing. The winner's prize: nothing!

 TO PRAY: "Lord, help us *remember* to do right *before* we take a step in any direction."

29 A Good Call

SOMETIMES PEOPLE MAKE THINGS WORSE BY TURNING A SIMPLE MISTAKE INTO A WRONG CHOICE.

Bible Reading of the Day: Read Proverbs 19:2-3.
Verse of the Day: *"Do not let your mouth lead you into sin"*
(Ecclesiastes 5:6, NIV).

Eddie dropped back to throw a pass. Tad stood five or six feet away, counting to five, while Eddie's teammate, Greg, raced toward the goal line—the line between Eddie's front yard and the neighbor's property. Suddenly, Tad shouted, *"Five-*Mississippi!" and lunged toward Eddie.

Eddie saw Greg's pursuer, Tad's teammate, slip on the grass and fall to the ground. Greg was wide open. Eddie dodged Tad's grasp, planted his feet, and hurled the miniature football toward Greg with all his might.

Eddie watched the ball sail through the air toward Greg, who sped to meet it. The two teammates realized at the same time, however, that the ball would sail beyond the end zone. Greg's legs pumped in a burst of speed as he raced to catch up with the ball, but Eddie could see that the pass would never be caught. He watched it sail past Greg and smash through the corner window of the neighbors' house.

Eddie's three friends dashed in different directions, leaving Eddie standing alone.

A moment or two later, Eddie's neighbor appeared and walked toward Eddie with the little football in his hands.

"Your football?" the neighbor asked.

"No," Eddie answered without thinking. "I saw the guys that did it, though," he added. "I've seen them around, but I don't know their names."

"I see," the neighbor answered. "Well, then . . ." He hesitated. "If you, uh, find out who did it, let me know."

"Sure," Eddie said.

The neighbor started to walk back to his house, then turned around to face Eddie again. He turned the football around in his hands. "You know," he said, "sometimes people make things worse by turning a simple mistake into a lie. Throwing this football through my window was just a mistake." He shrugged. "But running away—or lying about it—that's not just a mistake. That's wrong." He headed back toward his house.

"Wait," Eddie called.

The man stopped and turned around.

Eddie sighed. "I broke your window," he said. "I'll pay for it."

The neighbor tossed Eddie the football. "Good call," the man said. "Maybe you can get those three other guys to pitch in. *"If* you can find out where they live!"

TO DISCUSS: Was the broken window a simple mistake or a wrong choice? Have you ever made things worse by turning a simple mistake into a wrong choice? Describe what happened.

TO PRAY: "Lord, help us to live according to your Word. When we make mistakes, help us correct our errors, if we can. When we sin, help us to confess what we've done wrong and turn from that sin in the future."

1 Dangerous Minds

A MIND THAT IS CLOSED TO THE TRUTH IS A DANGEROUS MIND.

Bible Reading of the Day: Read Ephesians 4:17-23.

Verse of the Day: *"Since you have heard all about him and have learned the truth that is in Jesus, throw off your old evil nature and your former way of life"* (Ephesians 4:21-22).

Sonya got out of the truck and followed her dad up the sidewalk. He ran his own heating and cooling business. She rode with him while he made several stops to check people's furnaces.

"Dad," Sonya said as they walked, "I didn't get very far talking to Jerri." Jerri was one of Sonya's classmates, a girl she had invited to church. "She says we all have to worship our own god and find our own version of truth."

Dad nodded as they climbed the steps of the house and rang the doorbell. The door was opened immediately, and an elderly man let Dad and Sonya in.

Dad took one step inside the door, then turned to his daughter. "Sonya, wait for me in the truck." Then he turned to the man without closing the door behind him. "The first thing I need to do is open every window in the house," he told the man. "Then I'll take a look at your problem."

Sonya hesitated, then turned and walked back to the truck. About a half hour later, Dad returned to the truck and climbed in.

"I'm sorry to make you wait in the truck," Dad said. "But as soon as I stepped into that house, I smelled propane. Propane is a gas, and it can be very dangerous, especially in closed spaces. I didn't want to put you in any danger."

"Is everything OK now?" Sonya asked.

Dad nodded. "Everything's fine. We opened all the windows, and I fixed the leak. I'm glad they recognized the problem, because they were living in a very dangerous situation."

"That's how I feel about Jerri," Sonya said, returning to their earlier conversation. "I feel like she really needs God, but she won't listen to anything I say."

Dad smiled. "Just keep trying," he said. "But it does sound like she's closed her mind to the truth—at least for the time being. And a closed mind can be as dangerous as a closed house, if it's got the wrong stuff inside it."

"I'm still praying for her," Sonya said.

"That's good," Dad said. "Just pray that God will help her to open her mind to the truth. A mind can only be opened from the inside. Only God can do that."

"I hope he does," Sonya said.

"Me too," Dad added.

 TO DO: Make plans to share your faith with someone who doesn't know Jesus. Talk over ways to be sensitive to that person and faithful to God.

TO PRAY: "Father, thank you for revealing the truth to us through your Son, Jesus. Help us to know the truth, and to live it and share it with others."

2 Controlled or Controlling?

SELF-CONTROL MEANS LEARNING HOW TO CONTROL YOUR TEMPER AND YOUR DESIRES.

Bible Reading of the Day: Read Ephesians 4:24–27.
Verse of the Day: *"Don't sin by letting anger gain control over you.*
Think about it overnight and remain silent" (Psalm 4:4).

Lori's shrill scream pierced the air as she stomped her feet and crossed her arms defiantly. She stood beside the grocery-store vending machines. "I want some candy!"

"No," Mom said firmly. "Now you stop this temper tantrum right now, young lady."

"You can't make me!" Lori answered.

Mom's face flushed red, but she did not shout. "Stop. Stop right now. I'm going to take your hand and I'm going to walk you to the car. We'll talk about this in the car."

Lori didn't argue. A few moments later, they sat in the car. Mom turned to Lori. "What did you think you were doing, young lady?"

"I wanted some candy," Lori said, as if Mom should understand.

"I understand that," Mom answered, "but it was wrong for you to throw a temper tantrum like that."

"But I wanted some candy." Lori's voice had softened to a pleading whine.

"I know," Mom said. "It's not wrong to want candy, but when you lost your temper and started shouting at me in the store, that's what was wrong."

"It was?" Lori said. "Why?"

"Well, because," Mom began, then paused. She had to think for a moment. "Because it's disrespectful to me, and God says to honor your father and mother. . . ."

"Oh," Lori said.

"But also because . . . when you throw a temper tantrum like that, you're not showing very much self-control, and God wants you to learn self-control."

"What's self-control?" Lori asked.

Mom sighed loudly. Sometimes it was hard to answer her daughter's questions. "Self-control is, well, it's controlling yourself. It's learning how to control your temper, your desires, and things like that."

"Like when you wanted to yell at me in the store, but you didn't?" Lori asked.

Mom's eyes widened into an expression of surprise. "Well, yes," she said. "I guess so. Like that."

"Oh, OK," Lori said. "Now I understand."

 TO DISCUSS: Which do you think is better, to control your anger or to let your anger control you? Today's Scripture says that losing control of your anger is sinful. Do you ever have a problem controlling your anger? How can you keep from doing wrong by letting anger gain control over you?

 TO PRAY: "Father God, help us to be God-controlled, rather than anger-controlled."

3 Only God Can Decide

ONLY GOD CAN DECIDE WHAT'S RIGHT AND WRONG.

Bible Reading of the Day: Read Ephesians 4:28-32.
Verse of the Day: *"Get rid of all bitterness, rage, anger, harsh words, and slander, as well as all types of malicious behavior" (Ephesians 4:31).*

"Get outta my face!" Brandon shouted. He shoved Lyle against the wall, called him a few names, and stormed off the basketball court.

Everyone stopped and watched Brandon leave the playground. The friendly basketball game between Brandon's junior-high youth group and a youth group from another church came to an uncomfortable halt.

Paul, Brandon's youth pastor, turned to the rest of the group. "I'll be back," he said. "You guys can keep playing."

Paul found Brandon alone on a bench at a bus stop down the street. Paul sat beside him.

"I'm not sorry," Brandon said. "I didn't do nothing wrong."

Paul said nothing for a long time. A bus stopped in front of them, and the driver opened the door, but Paul smiled and waved him on.

"I'm not going to apologize," Brandon said, "'cause I didn't do nothing wrong."

"Says who?" Paul asked.

"Says me," Brandon said. "I'm old enough to decide what's right and wrong!"

"Well, Brandon, I'm a lot older than you, and I'm not old enough to decide what's right and wrong."

Brandon's eyes narrowed. He suspected a trap. "You're not?"

"No," Paul answered. "Because you have to be eternal to do that. Only God can decide what's right and wrong. If you think you have the right to make that decision, you're trying to take something that belongs to God."

"Like what?"

"Like the authority to decide what's right and wrong, that's what. That belongs to God, and it sounds to me like you're trying to take it away from him."

"I didn't mean it like that," Brandon said, softening.

"Good," Paul said. "Because when you say it's OK to lose control like you did on that basketball court, you're taking something that belongs to God. You can't call it right when God has called it wrong."

Brandon's head sagged as he kicked his feet under the bench. "You're going to make me apologize, aren't you?"

Paul shook his head. "No. I have a feeling you're going to do it without me making you."

 TO DO: Have everyone, including the adults in your family, take turns completing this statement: "I'm _____ years old, and I'll never be old enough to decide right and wrong; only God can do that."

 TO PRAY: Make the "Verse of the Day" your prayer. If there is something in particular that you need to "get rid of," ask the Lord for his help in doing so.

4 Following God's Example

GOD VALUES SELF-CONTROL.

Bible Reading of the Day: Read Ephesians 5:1-4.
Verse of the Day: *"Follow God's example in everything you do, because you are his dear children" (Ephesians 5:1).*

"You mean you've *never* said a cuss word?" Jackie's eyes widened in disbelief as she rode to volleyball practice with April. They sat together in the back seat of the van that April's dad drove.

April shrugged and shook her head.

"I can't believe that," Jackie said. "I mean, everybody cusses sometimes."

"Not everybody," April said. "Nobody in my family uses bad language."

"Why not? I mean, there's nothing wrong with it," Jackie said. "God just said 'Do not misuse my name' or something like that. He didn't say we can't cuss."

"Well, yeah, but . . ."

"If we don't say his name when we cuss, it's not bad," Jackie concluded.

April didn't know what to say. She was sure Jackie was wrong, but she wasn't sure why. That night, she told her dad what Jackie had said and asked him if he agreed.

"Well," he said, "Jackie's half right. The third commandment says not to misuse God's name. But that doesn't mean it's OK to say anything we want as long as we don't use God's name."

"I didn't think so," April said.

"The Bible says to let no unwholesome talk come out of our mouths. That includes obscene or profane language, cruel insults, and dirty jokes."

"I knew it!" April said in a voice of triumph.

"But wait a minute," Dad said. "Do you know why that kind of talk is wrong?"

April shrugged as if the answer were easy. "Because God said not to do it!"

Dad nodded. "Yes, but why did God say not to do it?"

April's face clouded with confusion. She answered, "I don't know."

"It has to do with purity and self-control. God wants us to be self-controlled because he values self-control. Do you know why he values self-control?"

April thought, then threw up her arms in exasperation. "I don't know, Dad!"

"Because he is self-controlled himself, April. God doesn't just control the universe. He's in perfect control of himself. He never gets carried away. He never loses control. He never says anything obscene, or coarse, or foolish. . . . And he wants us to imitate his self-control."

"Can you write all this down so I can remember to tell Jackie?" April asked.

Dad smiled. "Oh, I think you'll do just fine, April."

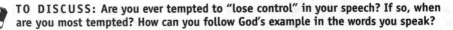

TO DISCUSS: Are you ever tempted to "lose control" in your speech? If so, when are you most tempted? How can you follow God's example in the words you speak?

TO PRAY: "Father, help us to have self-control in what we say and do."

5 The Right Stuff

GOD WANTS US TO BE SELF-CONTROLLED. HE WANTS OUR BEHAVIOR TO SHOW THAT WE WORSHIP HIM, NOT OUR OWN DESIRES.

Bible Reading of the Day: Read Ephesians 5:5-9.

Verse of the Day: *"For though your hearts were once full of darkness, now you are full of light from the Lord, and your behavior should show it!" (Ephesians 5:8).*

"Cole got in trouble today," Yvonne told her father on the way home. Cole sat in the desk next to her at school.

"Again?" Dad asked. "What did he do this time?"

"He stole Gina's watch, then told everybody it was his."

Dad shook his head but said nothing. It seemed as though his daughter came home from school every day with a different tale about Cole's conduct. They drove for a few blocks in silence.

Yvonne finally broke the silence. "Daddy?" she said. "Cole told me he didn't do anything wrong. He said that Gina's parents are rich, and she could get a new watch every day if she wanted."

Dad nodded. "Hmm," he said. He thought for a moment. "It sounds to me like Cole didn't just want to take Gina's watch—he wanted to take God's place as well."

"What do you mean, Daddy?"

Dad shrugged. "You see, sugar, God has already said that being greedy and taking things that don't belong to you are wrong. But some people, instead of worshiping God and accepting what he says about right and wrong, decide that *they* should be able to make up their own rules. So they try to do God's job for him. But when they do that, they show that they are worshiping the things they want instead of God. Getting those things is more important to them than doing what God says. Instead of controlling their desires, they're controlled *by* their desires."

"I'm not like that, am I, Daddy?"

"We've all been like that sometimes, Yvonne. But God wants to help us be self-controlled. He wants our behavior to show that we worship him, not our own desires."

"It's not wrong to want things, is it, Daddy?"

"No, no," Dad answered. "Not at all. But it's wrong when the things we want—and the ways we try to get them—make us disobey God."

"It's not wrong for me to want an ice-cream cone right now, is it, Daddy?" Yvonne asked, her eyes bright and pleading.

Dad smiled and shook his head at Yvonne's clever manipulation of the conversation. He reached out a hand and started tickling his daughter.

TO DISCUSS: Does your behavior show that you worship God? If not, why not? If so, how? Do you control your desires, or are you controlled by your desires?

TO PRAY: "God, thank you that, though our hearts were once full of darkness, we are now full of light from the Lord. Help us to show by our actions that we love and worship you. May we do only what is good and right and true."

6 The Wrong Stuff

SOME THINGS ARE WRONG BECAUSE THEY HINDER SELF-CONTROL.

Bible Reading of the Day: Read Ephesians 5:10-13, 18.
Verse of the Day: *"Therefore, prepare your minds for action; be self-controlled; set your hope fully on the grace to be given you when Jesus Christ is revealed" (1 Peter 1:13, NIV).*

"What's the matter with you?" Brian asked.

Brian, Todd, and Mike sat around on the bed and chairs in Brian's bedroom. Brian's parents weren't home, and he had invited his friends over for a little "fun." Brian had just pulled a large bottle from behind the books on his bookcase. He had unscrewed the cap and offered it to his buddies. Todd had shaken his head.

"You didn't say anything about drinking," Todd said. He tried not to let his shock—and fear—show on his face.

Brian shrugged. "What's the big deal? Nobody's gonna know."

"I-I-I don't know, Brian," Mike said.

"Look, guys," Brian said, his temper making his voice rise. "Your mommy and daddy aren't gonna find out."

"That's not the point," Todd said.

"Well then, what *is* the point?" Brian asked.

"It's wrong," Todd answered. "That's the point."

"Oh, don't be such a nerd. There's nothing wrong with having a little fun." Brian looked from Todd's face to Mike's face. "I can't believe you guys. Even *Jesus* drank a little wine, you know. So what's wrong with this?" He pointed the bottle toward his friends again.

"Well, for one, if we have to sneak around and do it behind our parents' backs, that should tell you something, shouldn't it?" Mike answered.

"And it's not about that stuff," Todd added. "It's about self-control. Whether Jesus drank wine or not, the Bible says not to *'be drunk* with wine.'"

"We're not gonna get drunk!" Brian shouted.

"How do you know?" Todd countered. "The only way to make sure—"

"No, wait a minute," Mike interrupted, sounding for the first time as though he agreed with Brian. "Brian's got a point."

"What?" Todd said.

"He's got a point. We're not going to get drunk," Mike said.

"Finally! Somebody's making sense," Brian said.

"Because we're leaving," Mike said. He left the room. Todd followed Mike out.

 TO DISCUSS: The Bible has many commands and warnings to avoid drunkenness (Proverbs 20:1; 23:20, 29-35; Romans 13:13; Galatians 5:21; Ephesians 5:18). Do you think a person can get drunk and obey God's command to "be self-controlled" (1 Peter 1:13) at the same time? Why or why not?

 TO PRAY: "Lord, prepare our minds for action. Help us to be self-controlled."

7 Mission: Control

WE CAN ONLY BE SELF-CONTROLLED IF WE ARE TRULY GOD-CONTROLLED.

Bible Reading of the Day: Read Proverbs 16:32; Ephesians 5:15-17.
Verse of the Day: *"Let the Holy Spirit fill and control you"*
(Ephesians 5:18).

Soo Lin walked with her grandmother through the mall. They paused at a soft-drink machine to allow Soo Lin to make a purchase. When she turned to join her grandmother, she lost her grip on all but one of her shopping bags. Suddenly, the can of soda slipped out of her hands and rolled toward the machine.

Soo Lin stomped her foot and threw the remaining bag onto the floor. The sudden sound of breaking glass stopped her fit of temper.

"What was that?" she asked, her voice suddenly soft.

"I think it was the figurine we just bought," Grandmother answered.

"Oh no!" Soo Lin cried as she inspected the bag. She soon discovered that her grandmother was right. The beautiful angel figurine was broken.

Soo Lin picked up the bags. "I'm sorry, Grandmother," she said.

Grandmother stooped slowly to pick up Soo Lin's can of soda.

"You let your temper get the best of you, didn't you?" Grandmother said.

Soo Lin nodded as she took the can. "I've tried to control it like we've talked about, Grandmother, but then something like this happens." She paused. "How do you control your temper?"

"I don't," Grandmother said with a smile. Soo Lin flashed her a confused look. Grandmother pointed to the soda can. "You're not going to open that yet, are you?"

Soo Lin shook her head. "Oh, no," she said. "It would spray all over the place if I did."

"And what would come out?"

Soo Lin looked confused. She turned the can over in her hands and shrugged as if the answer were obvious. "It would spray cola all over the place."

"Right. Because that's what the can is filled with, right?" She waited for Soo Lin to nod, then continued. "It's the same with self-control. I cannot make good things come out of my life. But since God's Spirit fills me, he controls me—if I let him."

"But I am a Christian, too," Soo Lin said.

"Yes. So the way to control your temper is to let the Spirit, who *fills* you, *control* you, by submitting to him each day and asking him to make the most of every opportunity for doing good."

"So *self*-control is really *God*-control," Soo Lin said.

Grandmother studied Soo Lin thoughtfully. "I had not thought of that," she said. "But you are right. We can only be self-controlled if we are truly God-controlled."

 TO DISCUSS: How can a person be "God-controlled"? Why is that necessary?

TO PRAY: "Lord, we desire to be 'God-controlled' in our actions and thoughts. Thank you for the Holy Spirit, who fills our lives with good things."

8 "I Want It Now!"

ONE OF THE MARKS OF SELF-CONTROL IS THE ABILITY TO DELAY GRATIFICATION.

Bible Reading of the Day: Read 1 Thessalonians 5:6-11.
Verse of the Day: *"Since we belong to the day, let us be self-controlled, putting on faith and love as a breastplate, and the hope of salvation as a helmet"* (1 Thessalonians 5:8, NIV).

"I want it *now!*"

Cathy stared at the toddler in the supermarket. The little boy stomped his feet and screamed at his mother, demanding a cookie.

Cathy shook her head. "That kid sure was spoiled," she whispered to her mom.

Mom smiled and nodded, but said nothing until they went down another aisle. "Have you saved enough money yet for your class trip next month?"

Cathy thought about the overnight trip to Washington, D. C. She had to raise part of the expenses herself. "No," she answered. "I haven't really saved anything yet."

Mom nodded. She had known the answer to the question before she asked.

Cathy sighed. "I just keep seeing things I want. I forget I'm supposed to be saving for my trip."

Mom stopped pushing the cart and stood still. "I know, dear," she said. "A lot of us have that problem . . . just like the little boy over in the next aisle."

"What do you mean?" Cathy asked.

"Well," Mom said, "that little boy threw a temper tantrum because he didn't want to wait for a cookie. He wanted it *now*. In other words, he had a self-control problem because he couldn't delay gratification."

"Huh?" Cathy said.

"Let me ask you this: If I gave you a choice between a candy bar right now or *two* candy bars tomorrow, which would you choose?"

Cathy answered immediately. "I'd take the candy bar now."

"Right. A lot of people would, even though they could get twice as many candy bars by waiting just one day. We have trouble putting off pleasure, even if it benefits us in the long run."

"That's why I'm having trouble saving," Cathy admitted.

"I know," Mom said. "But not being able to delay gratification can have serious consequences. It often keeps us from doing the right or responsible thing. So often it's much easier to choose wrong because that will bring immediate gratification. The right choice is much better, but it may take longer for it to pay off. But," Mom added, "making the right choice is like making a deposit in your savings account. You may not see its benefits right away, but someday you'll be very glad it's there."

TO DISCUSS: What was Cathy's problem? How can she solve it? How do you show self-control in this area?

TO PRAY: "Lord, help us learn how to delay getting what we want so we can practice self-control more and more."

9 Lessons in Self-Control

EXERCISE SELF-CONTROL TO BE WORTHY OF RESPECT AND TO LIVE WISELY.

Bible Reading of the Day: Read Titus 2:1-6.
Verse of the Day: *"A person without self-control is as defenseless as a city with broken-down walls" (Proverbs 25:28).*

"Mom, Dad, do I *have* to take piano lessons?" Curt asked. It was time for his weekly piano lesson, and he would have preferred to do almost anything else.

"Well, Curt," Mom said, "why don't you want to take piano lessons?"

"Because," Curt answered, "piano lessons are boring."

Dad joined the conversation. "They're not as boring as they used to be, are they?"

"Well, no," Curt said, "but they're still boring."

"But you like playing the piano," Mom countered.

"I like *playing* the piano, but I don't like taking lessons."

"But taking lessons is how you got to the point where you are now, where you can sit down and play almost anything you want," Mom said.

Curt sighed. "I know," he admitted.

"In fact," Dad said, "piano lessons are a good example of the way self-control and self-discipline can benefit us. You probably don't remember your first lessons, but we do." He exchanged smiles with his wife. "You had to play the same three notes over and over again."

"But now you can sit down and play some of the songs you hear on the radio and songs we sing in church," Mom added. "And you like being able to do that, don't you?"

"Yeah, but—" Curt started.

"The enjoyment you get out of playing the piano *now* is a direct result of the lessons you've taken. If you had chosen immediate gratification when you first started lessons, you'd be able to play 'Chopsticks' now, but that's about it. But you delayed some things you wanted to do—like watching TV or playing outside—and chose to practice instead. As a result, you get pleasure out of playing now."

"OK, OK, I get the message," Curt said. He acted annoyed, but he had to stifle a smile.

"Do you?" Dad said. "What's the message?"

Curt rolled his eyes as he answered, in a singsong voice, "Piano lessons are good for me."

"Not just piano lessons," Mom answered, "but any time you exercise self-control and self-discipline, you're adding to your abilities and accomplishments."

"OK," Curt said. "I think I'm going to go play the piano for a while now, OK?"

"Really?" Mom said in an excited voice. "Dad and I must really be convincing, eh?"

"No," Curt answered teasingly. "I just want to get some peace and quiet!"

 TO DISCUSS: What are the areas in which you find self-discipline hardest to maintain? How can exercising self-control add to your abilities and accomplishments?

TO PRAY: Take turns praying, "God, please help me to develop more self-control, especially in the areas of my life where I am weakest."

March

10 Blind Rage

SELF-CONTROL CAN PROMOTE THE RESPECT OF OTHERS.

Bible Reading of the Day: Read 2 Peter 1:6–11.
Verse of the Day: *"We should live in this evil world with self-control, right conduct, and devotion to God" (Titus 2:12).*

The chorus director slammed his hand down on top of the piano.

"No, no, no, no, *no!*" he shouted. "What's the matter with you kids? Don't you know anything?! You're all flat, flat, flat! . . . Amber, you've been off-key for the past half hour! . . . I ought to make you all stay after school until you learn this music!"

"He can't do that, can he?" Jennifer whispered to Adam, who sat next to her. Adam shook his head.

"Why does he get so mad?" Jennifer whispered to Adam.

Adam shrugged. "He acts that way all the time. That's why nobody wants to be in the chorus anymore," he whispered. "I even went out for drums last fall because I didn't want to take him again."

"I didn't know you played drums," Jennifer said.

"I don't," Adam answered. "That's why I'm here," he said, as the chorus director started throwing pages of music around the classroom.

Later that night, Jennifer told her older brother about the chorus director's outburst.

"Yeah," he said, "he gets more outta control every year."

"Why do they let him keep teaching?" Jennifer asked.

Her brother shrugged. "I don't know. I've heard rumors that he won't be around much longer. A lot of parents have complained."

"You mean he could lose his job?" she asked.

"Sure," he answered.

"He's lost a lot of the students' respect because of the way he goes off, screaming and throwing things, and stuff like that."

"That's what he was doing today," Jennifer said.

"Yeah," her brother said, "it's too bad. He's really a pretty good teacher. He just can't control his temper."

TO DISCUSS: How did the students feel about the chorus director? Would the chorus director have been better off if he had shown more self-control? Why or why not? Can you think of someone you admire for his or her self-control?

TO PRAY: "Lord, when we're tempted to lose control, remind us that our self-control can win the respect of others."

11 Don't Be Devoured

SELF-CONTROL PROTECTS US FROM HARM AND PROVIDES FOR OUR ENJOYMENT OF LIFE.

Bible Reading of the Day: Read 1 Peter 5:8-11.
Verse of the Day: *"Be self-controlled and alert. Your enemy the devil prowls around like a roaring lion looking for someone to devour"* (1 Peter 5:8, NIV).

"She looks terrible!" Rachel said. She sat on the couch, watching a television report of the arrest of a famous music star.

"Who looks terrible?" Josh, her little brother, asked.

She pointed at the television. "That's Tawny Morrison, the lead singer of Toe Jam."

"Where are the police taking her?" Josh asked.

"She was in a car wreck," Rachel explained, "and they found out that she was on drugs, so they arrested her. I can't believe how terrible she looks. I would be so humiliated." Then Rachel got an idea. She and her family had been talking a lot about right and wrong. She pointed the remote control at the television and turned the volume down. Then she turned to Josh.

"See how Tawny Morrison looks there?" she asked, pointing at the singer's disheveled image on the screen. Josh nodded. "She doesn't look very happy, does she?"

Josh shook his head.

"See, Josh, Tawny Morrison is a really good singer, and she's really pretty," Rachel started.

"She looks ugly now," Josh interjected.

Rachel tried not to smile. "Yeah, she does in that picture. But that's what can happen when we don't pay attention to God's commands. See, Tawny Morrison would probably never go out of the house looking like that—"

"She's a mess," Josh said, starting to enjoy the conversation.

"Yeah, and she messed up her car and got herself in trouble, and might even have hurt somebody—all because she got messed up on drugs."

"I don't *ever* want to use drugs," Josh said seriously.

"Good, Joshie," she said. "But it's not just drugs. People can lose control and get messed up a lot of ways—with drugs, alcohol, food, lots of things. That's why God wants us to be self-controlled. Because it'll protect us from stuff like that."

Josh crawled up onto the couch and said, "Can I ask you a question?"

"Sure," Rachel said proudly, pleased that her brother wanted to know more.

"Can we watch cartoons now?" Josh asked.

 TO DISCUSS: The lack of self-control can lead to all types of overindulgence and excesses. Obedience to God's commands to "be self-controlled" can not only protect us from those excesses, but also provide greater enjoyment of such things as recreation, music, art, food, health, and so on. How has self-control protected you in the past? How can self-control protect you and provide for you in the future?

 TO PRAY: "Loving God, thank you for protecting us from overindulgence. Help us to be watchful when temptation comes."

March

12 The Moral Compass

THE BIBLE IS A COMPASS THAT POINTS TO GOD.

Bible Reading of the Day: Read Psalm 119:101-105.
Verse of the Day: *"Your word is a lamp for my feet and a light for my path" (Psalm 119:105).*

Amber and Ashley accompanied Dad on their monthly hike in the canyon near their house. They loved the rock formations and wildlife of the desert area around their home. Dad had just bought a new hiking stick and had been looking forward to taking it along on this hike.

They had walked for almost an hour when Dad stopped and rested on a rock. He took a drink of water from the plastic bottle that hung from his belt. Amber and Ashley drank from their water bottles, too. After a few restful moments, Dad nudged Ashley, who sat next to him on the rock.

"I want to show you something," he said. He unscrewed the top of his walking stick to reveal a compass with a glass face.

"Wow!" Ashley said. "What is it?"

"It's a compass," Amber answered in a disgusted tone. Ashley was four years younger than she was.

"What's it for?" Ashley asked.

"It tells us which direction to go," Dad said. He held the stick between his two daughters. "The needle always points north, so if we get turned around in the canyons we can always find our way home."

"Are we lost, Daddy?" Ashley asked.

"No," Dad answered, smiling. "But I showed it to you because I wanted to tell you about another compass, a compass that doesn't show the difference between north and south but between right and wrong."

Both girls listened carefully as Dad continued. "You see, girls, people can get turned around in life—just like we can get turned around in the canyon—and sometimes they forget which way is right and which way is wrong."

"But you don't, do you, Dad?" Amber suggested.

"Oh, yes, I do," Dad answered. "But I always know where to get the right direction." He paused. "From the Bible." He tapped the compass on the end of his walking stick. "Just like this compass always shows me the right direction because it always points north, the Bible shows me the right direction because it points to God."

Dad screwed the top back on his walking stick and stood.

"It's good to have a compass, isn't it, Daddy?" Ashley asked.

"Yes, Ashley, it sure is," Dad answered. "It sure is."

TO DISCUSS: How is the Bible like a compass? How is the Bible like a lamp? How does the Bible teach us right from wrong?

TO PRAY: "Lord, thank you for the Bible, which points to you. Help us to hide your Word in our heart, so that we won't purposely sin against you."

72

13 The Pleasures of God

GOD WANTS TO BRING GOOD THINGS INTO OUR LIVES.

Bible Reading of the Day: Read Jeremiah 32:38-41.
Verse of the Day: *"I will rejoice in doing good to them" (Jeremiah 32:41).*

Willie ran to the pet store window and pressed his face against the glass. He wasn't tall enough to reach over the glass divider and pet one of the puppies, but he watched them with fascination.

An older boy walked up beside him and nudged him in the back. "Watch this," he said, with a mischievous grin. He pulled a long string of red licorice from his bag and dangled it over the glass. The puppies leaped for the red string, but the boy never let them catch it.

When the boy left, Willie's dad crouched beside his son. They watched the puppies together for a few minutes.

Finally, Dad spoke. "That boy wasn't very nice, was he?"

Willie shook his head. "He was mean."

Dad glanced at Willie, then looked at the puppies. "You know, Willie . . . a lot of people think that God is like that boy."

Willie's head whipped around to look at his dad. His eyes registered shock.

"It's true," Dad said, nodding reassuringly. "Some people think God treats us like that boy treated those puppies. They think he just gives us his commands to tease us and make us miserable. They think he just wants to keep us from having fun."

Willie's eyes remained wide. "But he's not that way, is he, Daddy?"

"No, Willie, he's not," Dad answered. "Not at all. In fact, you know what makes God happy? You know what he thinks is fun?"

Willie shook his head. He had never thought of God having fun before.

Dad placed his hand atop Willie's head. "Seeing *us* have fun," he said. "God says in the Bible, 'I rejoice in doing good to people.'" He paused and pointed at the puppies in the glass bin. "It would really make you happy to be allowed to pet one of those puppies right now, and cuddle it, and play with it, right?"

Willie nodded.

"In a way, that's how God feels. He never wants to hurt us or tease us. He always wants to show love to us. That's why he created us. That's why he gave his commands to us. That's why he sent Jesus for us."

"Daddy," Willie said, in a voice so solemn it was almost a whisper. "Can I pet one?"

Dad smiled. He reached into the bin, lifted out a squirming, panting pup, and plopped it into Willie's arms.

 TO DO: Be a "secret saint" to someone in your family today. Buy him or her a treat and put it on his or her pillow. Attach a note with Jeremiah 32:41 written on it. Or make up a coupon promising your help in some way.

 TO PRAY: "Gracious God, you allow us to have fun in so many ways. Thank you for reminding us that you seek to bring only good things to our lives."

14 Truth and Tolerance

WE SHOULD RESPECT OTHERS' RIGHTS. THAT DOESN'T MEAN WE MUST AGREE THAT OTHERS' VIEWS ARE RIGHT.

Bible Reading of the Day: Read Isaiah 5:20-21.
Verse of the Day: *"Woe to those who call evil good and good evil"* *(Isaiah 5:20, NIV).*

Dad walked into the kitchen. His daughter Danielle sat at the kitchen table doing homework. He sat in the chair beside her and waited for her to finish the arithmetic problem she was working on. When she looked up, he spoke.

"Danielle," he said, "your mom told me you got into a little trouble at school today."

Danielle nodded and shrugged. "I wore my 'Jesus Loves the Little Children' T-shirt. My teacher said I shouldn't wear that shirt."

"Why not?" Dad asked, his voice soft.

She shrugged. "She started talking about how we should get along with each other, and that there might be some kids in class that didn't believe in Jesus, and that I shouldn't make them feel bad by wearing that T-shirt."

Dad's face took on a worried expression. "How would that make them feel bad?" he asked.

Danielle wrinkled her forehead as she tried to think. "I don't know," she said. "I think . . ." she said, pausing and then starting again. "I think Mrs. Hammond thinks we should . . . we should respect everybody else and let them believe what they want."

Dad nodded. He smiled. "That's good. I think you should respect everybody else and let them believe what they want."

"You do?" Danielle's voice sounded surprised.

"Absolutely," Dad said. "Mrs. Hammond and your classmates all have a right to their opinion; but that's not the same as saying their opinion is right."

"It's not?" Danielle asked.

"No," Dad said. He pointed to Danielle's arithmetic book. "I have the right to believe that two plus two equals five, but that doesn't make it right, does it?"

"No," Danielle said seriously. "Two plus two is four."

"Right!" Dad said, smiling. "And right is right, and true is true, no matter what anyone else says. Your classmates have the right to believe anything they want, and you should respect that right. But that doesn't mean you have to agree with them or act as if they're right."

"Because Jesus really does love all the children of the world, whether they know it or not," Danielle said.

Dad's smile grew even bigger. "That's right!"

TO DISCUSS: What's the difference between respecting a person's rights and saying that what he or she says, believes, or does *is* right? How can you respect others' rights and still obey Jesus? What do you think Danielle and her family should do about her 'Jesus Loves the Little Children' T-shirt?

TO PRAY: "Lord, may our lives be 'slogans' of praise to you that others can read."

15 Fixed on Jesus

IF WE JUST KEEP OUR EYES ON JESUS, THINGS TEND TO GET STRAIGHTENED OUT.

Bible Reading of the Day: Read Hebrews 12:1-2.
Verse of the Day: *"We do this by keeping our eyes on Jesus, on whom our faith depends from start to finish"* *(Hebrews 12:2).*

"How do you get it so straight?"

Shelly's Uncle Mike was letting her help with the plowing and planting on his farm. During the plowing, she noticed that when she steered the tractor, the row turned out crooked. But when Uncle Mike drove, the row looked as straight as a ribbon on a Christmas gift.

Uncle Mike shrugged. "Simple," he answered. He pointed to the row of fence posts that stretched across the opposite end of the field. "I just pick out one of those fence posts and stare straight at it the whole time."

"You don't look around at all?" Shelly asked.

Her uncle shook his head. "Don't need to. I can see everything around me just fine in my peripheral vision. But I keep my eyes fastened on the fence and never take 'em away."

Late that afternoon, Shelly and Uncle Mike returned to the house for dinner. While Mike washed off the day's dirt and sweat, Shelly told her aunt Cindy what she had learned.

Cindy nodded and faced Shelly with a smile. "You know, Shelly, what your uncle said about plowing sounds pretty much like how we should do everything."

A look of confusion crossed Shelly's face. She lived in the city, and she couldn't imagine how staring at fence posts in order to plow and plant straight would work back home. "What do you mean?" she asked.

Aunt Cindy inhaled deeply before speaking. "A lot of people," she said, "get confused in life and wonder what's right or wrong, and they end up making a mess of things. But if we just keep our eyes on Jesus, things tend to get straightened out, because he's totally righteous and true."

Shelly nodded. "I see what you mean. . . . I probably should have taken time to pray this morning before I went out in the field with Uncle Mike. That would have helped me keep my eyes on Jesus today, huh?"

"It would have helped," Aunt Cindy said. She winked at her niece. "It wouldn't hurt Uncle Mike to wait sometimes, you know."

"It wouldn't hurt me to wait for what?" Uncle Mike asked as he entered the room.

"Supper!" his wife answered. She exchanged smiles with Shelly and left to prepare the evening meal.

TO DISCUSS: Why wasn't Shelly able to plow straight? How can we keep our eyes on Jesus?

TO PRAY: "Lord, help us to keep our eyes on you every day to find strength, direction, and wisdom through you."

16 Keep Yourself Pure

IN HIS HEART HE KNEW HE DIDN'T WANT TO CHOOSE WHAT WAS RIGHT.

Bible Reading of the Day: Read 1 Timothy 5:22-25.
Verse of the Day: *"Even children are known by the way they act, whether their conduct is pure and right"* (Proverbs 20:11).

Kendall sat in the back of the school bus, surrounded by his friends Greg, Michael, and Jeremy. Kendall looked out the window for a few moments, and when he turned around, he noticed that his friends were hunched together in the aisle between the seats.

Kendall peered over Jeremy's back and saw what they were looking at. Jeremy had pulled a magazine out of his book bag and was showing it to the other guys. Kendall knew what they were looking at even before he saw the pictures of women who were not fully dressed.

Jeremy turned slightly in his seat to make room for Kendall. "Here," he said with a leer, "take a look at this!"

Kendall froze. He knew what they were doing was wrong. But he wanted to look at the pictures with his friends. And he was afraid that if he didn't join them, they might make fun of him.

I could just take a quick look at the pictures, he reasoned. *That wouldn't hurt anything. Besides, it's not like it's my magazine or anything.*

Jeremy and the others hadn't noticed Kendall's indecision. Jeremy turned the page and pointed the magazine in Kendall's direction. "Pretty cool, huh?" he asked.

It wouldn't be so wrong, Kendall figured, *just this once.* But then he knew immediately that he was making excuses. He was trying to excuse something that he knew was wrong. He was trying to call it right, but in his heart he knew better. He just didn't want to choose what he knew was right, because his friends might make fun of him.

Kendall groaned. "You guys can look at that stuff if you want," he said as he shrugged. "Just don't show it to me, OK?"

He turned his face toward the bus window. He expected the teasing to start any second. But it didn't.

He waited a few moments, then sneaked a glance at his friends. None of them paid any attention to him.

Kendall turned his face back to the bus window and let out a sigh of relief that momentarily clouded the surface of the glass. He allowed himself a slight smile and rubbed the fogged window with the tip of his sleeve.

 TO DISCUSS: Purity means staying "clean" in thought, word, and deed. Have you ever had to make a decision like the one Kendall made? Describe it. How easy/hard was it to make the decision?

 TO PRAY: "Lord, keep us clean in thought, word, and deed."

17 Pure Indeed

GOD COMMANDS US TO BE PURE, BECAUSE HE IS PURE.

Bible Reading of the Day: Read 1 John 3:1-3.
Verse of the Day: *"I want you to understand what really matters, so that you may live pure and blameless lives until Christ returns" (Philippians 1:10).*

"I just don't see what the big deal is!" Dave said. "They're just words. I don't mean anything by them."

Rita shook her head. "How can you say that, Dave? You're a Christian." Rita had told Dave she couldn't believe the language she'd heard him use in the school cafeteria. Dave and Rita had been friends since first grade, and their families attended the same church.

"Yeah, but everybody talks that way," he said.

"Christians?" Rita asked.

Dave shrugged. "Look, they're just words. There's nothing wrong with them."

"How can you say that?" Rita asked again. "How can you let such impure things come out of your mouth and then say there's nothing wrong with it?"

"They're just words," Dave said in an exasperated tone.

"They're filthy words," Rita pressed. "Come on, Dave, you go to the same Sunday-school class as I do. You know that God commands us to be pure. He commands us to be blameless and pure."

"Yeah, but . . ."

"But nothing! You know as well as I do that the reason God commands purity is because he values purity. And the reason he values purity is because he is pure! Remember what Mr. Franklin told us?" she said, referring to their Sunday-school teacher. "Remember, he told us all about the regulations God gave for the tabernacle and the temple, and how they were supposed to use pure gold and pure incense, and not mix linen and wool, and all that stuff that was supposed to show them that God was pure and that he wanted—"

"OK, OK!" Dave said, holding up his hands in a gesture of surrender. "I'll stop using those words, if it makes you happy."

"It doesn't matter if it makes *me* happy," Rita said. "But it'll make God happy. *He's* the one who wants you to be pure."

"All right," Dave said. "But answer a question for me, OK?"

Dave's request surprised Rita. "What?"

"How can you talk so long without taking a breath?"

Rita saw the traces of a mischievous smile on Dave's face. "Practice," she said.

 TO DISCUSS: Take turns naming ways that you can be pure in thought, word, and deed.

TO PRAY: "Lord, we want our words to be as pure as the incense that was offered up in your temple. Help us to live pure and blameless lives."

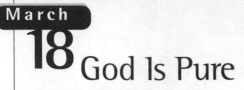

GOD IS SO PURE, HE CAN'T EVEN LOOK AT EVIL.

Bible Reading of the Day: **Read Habakkuk 1:12–13.**
Verse of the Day: *"Your eyes are too pure to look on evil; you cannot tolerate wrong" (Habakkuk 1:13, NIV).*

Robbie and his mom stood in the aisle of the small grocery store near their apartment. He noticed his mother's habit of reading the label on each package she took off the shelf.

"Why do you do that, Mommy?" Robbie asked.

"Oh," Mom said, looking at a packet of sliced cheese, "I do it to see what's in the package."

"But can't you tell just from looking at it?" Robbie asked.

"Well, yes," she said, "I can tell this is cheese. But I want to see what's in the cheese."

"You mean it's not just cheese?"

"No, not exactly," Mom answered. She hesitated for a moment before she began her explanation. "Some kinds of food have a lot of other things—like chemicals and preservatives—added to them." She dropped the cheese into the shopping cart, took a few steps down the aisle, and then stopped. "There are very few things in this world today that are pure, Robbie." She swept her hand to indicate the shelves filled with various containers of food. "The cereal we eat has added sugar, the vegetables have added preservatives, and the canned fruit even has artificial coloring in it."

"So none of it's real?" Robbie asked.

"Oh, it's real," Mom said with a chuckle. "But it's not *pure.* 'Pure' means that there's nothing dirty or . . ." she hesitated, ". . . or foreign in it. And, like I said, Robbie, very little in this world is pure. And if a thing is pure, it is usually much more valuable." She steered the cart into the next aisle as they talked. "Can you think of anything that's pure?"

Robbie shook his head.

"That's OK, I'll tell you. God is pure."

Robbie cocked his head as if he were absorbing this information.

"That's right. God is pure. Everything about him is pure. In fact, the Bible says that God is so pure, he can't even *look* at things that are impure."

Robbie's eyes widened. "Does that mean God can't see this cheese?"

Mom laughed. "No, Robbie," she said. "But it does mean that he can't stand to look at sin. That's why he sent Jesus to die for us, so that he can make us pure in God's sight."

 TO DO: Check your cabinets and refrigerator. How many "pure" items do you have? Why is purity in the products we buy important? Write Habakkuk 1:13 on a card and attach it to your refrigerator or cabinet to remind you of the importance of purity.

 TO PRAY: "God, whenever we're tempted to think impure thoughts or to add impurities to our life, remind us that we can choose to be pure as you are pure."

19 Purity Pills

GOD WANTS US TO BE PURE BECAUSE HE KNOWS THAT IMPURITY CAN CAUSE SUFFERING.

Bible Reading of the Day: Read 1 Thessalonians 4:3-7.
Verse of the Day: *"God has called us to be holy, not to live impure lives"* *(1 Thessalonians 4:7).*

Lisa groaned as she pulled her backpack off her shoulders. She had just begun a three-day backpacking trip with her father. The first three miles of the trip had taken them over two hours on foot. In the first hour, she had emptied her water bottle, which had been full when they began.

She pulled the bottle out of its pocket in her backpack and trudged through the green growth toward the stream that ran alongside the path. She dipped the plastic bottle into the current and pulled it out nearly full, dripping with cool, clear water. She lifted the bottle to her mouth.

"Wait," her dad said before she took a drink. Dad held out his hand. "Dissolve these in the water before you drink it." He dropped two green pills into her palm.

"What's this?" she asked.

"Those will purify the water," Dad explained.

"What for?"

Dad pointed to the stream. "I know that water looks as clean as could be," he said, "but unfortunately there are germs and impurities in there that could make you very sick. Those pills will make the water safe to drink."

He sat on the bank of the stream and filled his own water bottle. Then he dropped two pellets into his bottle and began shaking it. Lisa did the same, then flashed a smile.

"Thanks, Dad," she said.

"You're welcome," he answered. "I'd hate to see you get sick. You can really suffer if you drink bad water."

They sat together for a few moments, resting and drinking. Then Dad said, "Come to think of it, Lisa, that's why God wants us to be pure in what we do, in what we say, and in the things we think about. Because he knows that impurities can cause suffering."

She looked at him with a look of curiosity.

"Impure water can make you sick here," he said, patting his stomach. "Impure thoughts or deeds or words can make you sick here." He placed his hand on his chest. "In your heart and in your soul."

Lisa leaned over to refill her water bottle from the stream. "I need some more of those 'purity pills,' Dad."

Dad laughed and reached in his pocket.

TO DO: If you have an empty medicine bottle, you could fill it with "purity pills." Write the "Verse of the Day" on several small slips of paper. Roll up each slip and place it in the bottle. "Prescribe" one of the slips for each family member.

TO PRAY: "Lord, we believe that impure thoughts, words, and deeds can make our hearts sick. Help us to take a daily dose of your Word as our 'purity pills.'"

20 Prescription for Purity

WE CAN KEEP OURSELVES PURE BY READING GOD'S WORD AND DOING WHAT HE SAYS.

Bible Reading of the Day: Read Psalm 119:1-9.

Verse of the Day: *"How can a young person stay pure? By obeying your word and following its rules" (Psalm 119:9).*

Lisa put the water bottle in her backpack and swung the pack into the air and onto her shoulders. She was ready by the time her dad returned to the path from the creek.

"I see you don't need any help," he said. He shouldered his pack in one fluid motion, and they continued their hike to that night's campsite.

"Dad?" Lisa asked. "When we were talking down by the creek, you said that impure thoughts and deeds can make you sick in your heart and soul."

Dad nodded.

"What did you mean?"

Dad thought for a few moments before answering. Finally, he said, "Imagine that you heard me talking one day when I didn't know you were listening, and I was using foul language. How would that make you feel?"

"Awful," Lisa answered.

"It would make me feel awful, too," Dad answered, "in here." He tapped his heart. "I would feel guilty and ashamed because of my impure conduct." They walked in silence for a few moments. Then Dad continued. "How about this—suppose I started taking drugs. Do you think those drugs I put into my body would be good for me?"

"No," Lisa answered. "You could get addicted."

"You're right. And if I got addicted, I might do things to hurt myself and others. Impurity is not only wrong, it's almost always harmful, too."

"A lot of people do that stuff, though," Lisa said.

Dad nodded. "That's true. But they don't have to. They could be pure; they just choose not to."

They walked a while longer in silence. The path was easier now. After a few minutes, Lisa broke the silence.

"I'm glad you don't do drugs or use bad language, Daddy."

Dad smiled. "I'm glad none of us do. You know, the Bible says we can keep ourselves pure by reading God's Word and doing what he says. If we do that, we'll be a lot better off."

 TO DISCUSS: How can impure conduct be harmful? How can God's Word help a person stay pure?

TO PRAY: Using your own words, take turns reading out loud a verse from today's Bible reading, making the words of that verse your prayer. For example: "Lord, I know that people of integrity, who follow your Word, are happy. I want to be a person of integrity."

21 Futile Things

WRONG CHOICES GET YOU INTO TROUBLE ONE WAY OR ANOTHER.

Bible Reading of the Day: Read 1 Samuel 12:20-24.
Verse of the Day: *"Serve the Lord with all your heart. And you must not turn aside, for then you would go after futile things which can not profit or deliver, because they are futile" (1 Samuel 12:20-21, NASB).*

Peter jumped out of his chair the moment he saw his father enter the principal's office. "Hi, Dad," he said nervously.

Dad greeted Peter, shook the principal's hand, and then sat on the chair next to Peter. He listened as the principal explained the reason for the meeting. Peter had been telling off-color stories and jokes to his classmates. The principal explained that Peter's behavior was, of course, unacceptable and would need to stop. Dad agreed.

Neither Peter nor Dad spoke until they were out of the school and in the car. Dad inserted the key into the ignition but didn't start the car. Instead, he turned and faced Peter. His face was serious, but not angry.

"Peter," he said, "why would you say such things to your classmates?"

Peter seemed to shrink in his seat. He shrugged. "I don't know," he said. He waited for his father to speak, but silence filled the car. Finally, he said, "I guess I just wanted everybody to like me."

A few moments passed before Dad asked, "Did it work?"

Peter flashed his father a look of confusion.

Dad repeated the question. "Did it work? Did telling dirty jokes and stories make everybody like you?"

Peter shook his head. "No," he said. "It just got me in trouble."

Dad nodded. "What you did was wrong, Son, and I want you to realize that. But I also want you to realize that sin never gives you what you want. You may think that telling bad stories will make you popular, or taking drugs will make you cool, or using bad language will make you feel grown up, but it never works out that way. Because sin can't deliver what it promises. It just gets you into trouble, one way or the other."

Peter nodded.

"Sin will not only disappoint you, Son, it will betray you. It's much better to obey God and do what he says, because he doesn't want to disappoint you. He wants to do good things for you." Dad turned to start the car.

"I'm sorry, Dad," Peter said.

Dad nodded. "I'm glad you are, Peter, and I forgive you."

"Does that mean I'm not going to get punished?" Peter asked, looking hopeful.

Dad smiled and shook his head. "Nice try, Son," he said. "Nice try."

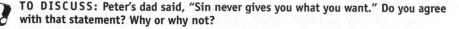

TO DISCUSS: Peter's dad said, "Sin never gives you what you want." Do you agree with that statement? Why or why not?

TO PRAY: "Lord, help us to serve you with all of our heart."

22 Better than Sunflowers

WHEN WE HAVE GOD'S SPIRIT LIVING INSIDE US, HE MAKES FRUIT GROW IN OUR LIVES THAT WE CAN'T PRODUCE OURSELVES.

Bible Reading of the Day: Read Galatians 5:19-23.

Verse of the Day: *"When the Holy Spirit controls our lives, he will produce this kind of fruit in us: love, joy, peace, patience, kindness, goodness, faithfulness, gentleness, and self-control" (Galatians 5:22-23).*

Jaran and his mom were waiting in line at the bank. While they waited, Jaran popped two sunflower seeds into his mouth and worked his teeth and tongue around to crack the hard husks of the seeds.

"Mommy," he said, sucking the salt off the seeds, "are these real sunflower seeds?"

Mom nodded. "Why, yes, they're real," she answered. "Why do you ask?"

"If they're real sunflower seeds, then why don't sunflowers grow in my tummy when I eat them?"

Mom laughed. "Well, Jaran, I think they need soil and sunshine to grow. You haven't been eating dirt or swallowing sunshine lately, have you?"

Jaran's eyes widened, and he shook his head seriously.

Mom smiled. "Well then, I don't think you have to worry about any sunflowers growing in your tummy."

Jaran nodded, seemingly satisfied.

"It would be kind of funny," Mom added, "if seeds could grow in people's tummies, wouldn't it?" she asked, prompting a smile from Jaran. "Just think, people might be walking around with apple trees growing out their ears, and tomatoes popping out of their mouths!"

Jaran and Mom both got the giggles then, and the other people in the bank started giving them funny looks.

A few moments later, as they walked out of the bank together, a serious expression came over Mom's face, and she said, "You know, Jaran, even though we'll never have apples coming out our ears, we can have another kind of fruit growing in our lives. When we have God's Spirit living inside us, he will make things grow in our lives that we can't produce ourselves."

"Like sunflowers?"

"No," Mom answered. "Like love, joy, peace, patience, and other good things. We can't make those good things happen in our lives, any more than we can make sunflowers grow in our tummies. But when God's Spirit lives in us, he makes those things grow inside us."

"That's better than sunflowers," Jaran announced happily.

"Yeah," Mom agreed, laughing. "Sunflowers might tickle your tonsils too much!"

 TO DO: The "Verse of the Day" for the next nine days will be Galatians 5:22-23. Try to memorize it by the end of the month. You might write the words on a piece of paper and post it someplace where your family will be likely to see it.

 TO PRAY: "Lord, thank you for producing fruit in our life that is much better than anything sin has to offer."

23 One Commandment

IF YOU LOVE OTHERS ALL THE TIME, YOU'LL DO WHAT'S RIGHT ALL THE TIME.

Bible Reading of the Day: Read Romans 13:8-10.
Verse of the Day: *"When the Holy Spirit controls our lives, he will produce this kind of fruit in us: love, joy, peace, patience, kindness, goodness, faithfulness, gentleness, and self-control" (Galatians 5:22-23).*

"I don't see how you can remember all those commandments," Cassandra told her best friend, Josie.

The two girls were doing their homework together in the school library.

"What do you mean?" Josie asked. She and Cassandra had had many conversations about God and Jesus. Josie was a Christian, but her friend Cassandra had just started going to church with her.

"You know," Cassandra said. "All those 'Don't do this' and 'Don't do thats.' How do you keep 'em straight?"

"I don't know," Josie answered. "It's not like that. . . ." Her voice trailed off, and her gaze searched around the library table. Finally, her eyes fastened on her math book. "It's like this," she said. "How much is one plus one?"

Cassandra's eyes narrowed as if she were expecting a trick. "Two," she said.

"How much is two plus two?"

Cassandra's expression became more confused. "Four," she said, "but I don't see—"

"How much is three plus three?"

"Six," she answered. "Why?"

"How do you remember all that?" Josie asked, a twinkle in her eye.

"I just know it. But that's different," Cassandra protested. "That's just arithmetic."

"You're right," Josie said, "it is different. But not the way you think. God's commandments are even easier to understand than addition and subtraction, because you really only have to remember one thing."

Josie reached for her paperback Bible. She thumbed through the pages, then stopped. "Here. It says, 'If you love your neighbor, you will fulfill all the requirements of God's law.'" She pointed to the page. "See?"

Cassandra read the words, her lips moving slowly and silently as she read. "What's that mean?" she asked.

"It means, the one commandment to remember is to love others. If you do that all the time, you'll do what's right all the time."

Cassandra shrugged. "I can remember that," she said.

 TO DO: The Israelites used to wear *phylacteries,* which were small leather boxes in which they kept some of God's commandments. You can make a variation of a phylactery, using yarn and cardboard, for each family member to wear on his or her wrist. Write the "Verse of the Day" on a small piece of paper and stick it in each phylactery.

TO PRAY: "Loving Father, thank you for loving us. Help us to love others through your Holy Spirit living in us."

24 The Joy of the Lord

JOY, LIKE ALL GOOD THINGS, COMES FROM GOD.

Bible Reading of the Day: Read Nehemiah 8:1-3, 9-10.
Verse of the Day: *"When the Holy Spirit controls our lives, he will produce this kind of fruit in us: love, joy, peace, patience, kindness, goodness, faithfulness, gentleness, and self-control" (Galatians 5:22-23).*

"All right!" Billy shouted.

He and Peggy flashed excited grins at each other. Mom and Dad had just announced that they were short on money until payday, so they would have to "make do" until then. And, since there weren't many groceries in the house, they would have to use what they had; that meant they would be having pancakes for dinner.

Mom and Dad were surprised at their children's reaction to the news. "What are you so happy about?"

"We get to have breakfast for dinner!" Peggy said.

"Yeah," Billy agreed. "It'll be fun!"

Mom laughed. "Well, I certainly wasn't expecting that kind of reaction." She turned to her husband. "Were you?"

Dad's face was more serious, but his expression was happy. "No, I wasn't. I think you and I have a thing or two to learn from our kids."

"You have something to learn from *us?"* Peggy asked with amazement.

"Yes," Dad said. He crouched down and took the children into his arms. "Your mother and I have been sad lately because we don't always have the money we need to buy things, even things like groceries." He exchanged a meaningful glance with Mom. "But you two have reminded us that joy doesn't depend on our circumstances."

"What do you mean, Daddy?" Billy asked.

Mom knelt on the floor beside her husband and children and wrapped her arms around all three. "What he means is, you two are grateful for the simplest things, and we love that about you. You don't need a fancy house or a steak dinner to make you happy, because you know how to be joyful."

"Oh, that's easy, Mom," Peggy said.

"Yes, it is, in a way," Mom said. "Because joy comes from God. Your father and I just needed to remember that we can rejoice even when we have to eat pancakes for dinner."

"I *like* pancakes!" Billy said.

"So do we," Dad said, hugging his family. "So do we."

TO DISCUSS: What do you think the Bible means when it says, "The joy of the Lord is your strength?" Have you been joyful or grouchy or sad lately? Do you need to be more joyful? How can you let God produce joy in your life this week?

TO PRAY: "Holy Lord, thank you for the joy of your presence in our lives."

25 Living in Peace

PEACE IS A GODLY VIRTUE, A FRUIT OF THE SPIRIT.

Bible Reading of the Day: Read Colossians 3:12-15.
Verse of the Day: *"When the Holy Spirit controls our lives, he will produce this kind of fruit in us: love, joy, peace, patience, kindness, goodness, faithfulness, gentleness, and self-control" (Galatians 5:22-23).*

"You just don't understand!" Isaac told his foster mother, Rhonda. He crossed his arms on his chest and glared stubbornly at the wall.

"Well," Rhonda answered calmly, "why don't you help me to understand?"

Isaac shrugged. "You don't know what it's like to go to that school," he said. "The only way to get respect is to show everybody that you're bad, that nobody better mess with you."

"So now that you've gotten into three fights in the past two weeks and have been suspended twice, everybody knows that you're bad, right?"

"Right," Isaac said, nodding confidently. "It's the only way to keep people from dissin' me."

"So why do you still get into fights?" Rhonda asked sweetly.

Isaac stopped nodding. He peered suspiciously at Rhonda. "What do you mean?"

"If getting into fights gets you the respect you want, then you should have everybody's respect by now, right? But fighting isn't getting you respect. It's just getting you into trouble." She paused and leaned forward until her face was just inches from Isaac's face. "Isn't it?"

"What am I supposed to do, then?" Isaac asked.

"You won't like the answer. It's too hard. I don't think you're tough enough."

"What?" Isaac said. "I'm tough enough."

"It takes more strength and courage than you've got. It takes *God's strength* to live in peace. That means you'll have to pray a lot, and ask God to help you every day. I just don't know if you're ready for that."

Isaac looked defiant. Yet he knew that his foster mother was different. She didn't use bad language. She always got along with the people in the building. Even crabby, old Mrs. Williams, who did nothing but complain.

Once he had seen Rhonda step between two men who were arguing in the hall. Isaac had been afraid she would get hurt, or that the men would tell her to back off. But they had actually listened to Rhonda. They seemed to respect her words of peace.

That's the kind of respect I want, he thought.

Isaac's expression softened suddenly. He locked gazes for a long time with his foster mother. "I think I am," he said in a soft, but strong, voice.

TO DISCUSS: What does it mean to "live in peace"? Is your life peaceful? If not, what has to change for it to be filled with the "peace of Christ"?

TO PRAY: "Teach us, Lord, to live in peace with others. May we be filled with the peace of Christ."

26 Reel Wisdom

PATIENCE IS A VIRTUE. THAT MEANS IT'S A GOOD THING, SOMETHING GOD WANTS
US TO HAVE.

Bible Reading of the Day: Read Ephesians 3:20–4:2.
Verse of the Day: *"When the Holy Spirit controls our lives, he will
produce this kind of fruit in us: love, joy, peace, patience, kindness,
goodness, faithfulness, gentleness, and self-control" (Galatians 5:22-23).*

Dan sat on the creek bank beside his grandmother as the rising sun peeked over the trees.
Between them sat a large tackle box. Both of them held a fishing pole.

"When are they going to start biting?" Dan asked.

Grandma moved nothing but her lips as she answered. "Soon enough," she said.

Dan tried to sit still, but it was too hard. He did everything he saw his grandmother
do. When she checked her bait, or put fresh bait on her hook, he did the same.

Finally, Dan couldn't stand it anymore. He found a couple of rocks and propped
his rod between them so he didn't have to hold it. Then he started climbing trees.
Before long, he started chasing squirrels and birds, but never caught up to one. Every
once in a while, he would come back to his fishing rod to make sure it hadn't fallen
into the water.

Suddenly Dan heard his grandmother laughing. He ran to the creek and arrived
just as she reeled in the biggest, most colorful fish he had ever seen.

"Look what I caught!" she said.

"No fair!" Dan whined. He looked in the large bucket by her feet and saw two
other fish just like the one she had just reeled in. "Why haven't I caught any?"

Grandma smiled at her companion. She released the hook from the fish's mouth
and slid it into the water-filled bucket with the others. "Fishing takes patience, Danny,"
she said. "Like a lot of things in life."

"I have patience," Dan said.

"Yes," she said, "sometimes you do. But I took you fishing with me because . . .
well, because I wanted to spend time with you, but also because I'd like to see you
learn to be more patient."

"Why?" Dan asked.

Grandma inhaled deeply. "Because patience is a virtue. That means it's a good
thing, something God wants us to have." She thought for a moment, then picked up
Dan's fishing rod and reeled in the line. "You see, Danny, patience doesn't just make
you a better fisherman. It will make you a better person."

"OK, Grandma," he said. "I'll be patient, as long as I don't have to wait too long!"
He sneaked a look at Grandma and was pleased to see a look of surprise on her face.
"Just kidding, Grandma," he said.

 **TO DISCUSS: Have you been impatient with anyone or anything this week?
Describe what happened.**

 **TO PRAY: "Lord, patience is a hard virtue to cultivate. Help us not to think about
how it grows in our lives. Help us to trust that it *will* grow."**

27 Backyard Kindness

KINDNESS IS RIGHT, EVEN WHEN IT'S HARD TO BE KIND.

> **Bible Reading of the Day: Read Jeremiah 31:3.**
> Verse of the Day: *"When the Holy Spirit controls our lives, he will produce this kind of fruit in us: love, joy, peace, patience, kindness, goodness, faithfulness, gentleness, and self-control" (Galatians 5:22-23).*

Heather wrestled her two lambs, Snowfall and Sunshine, into their pen in the backyard and then latched the gate. She was raising the two lambs as a 4-H project for the county fair in August. She took them for a walk every night to keep them healthy. She dusted off her hands and stomped toward the house. Her mom met her on the back porch.

"Ooh!" Heather said. "That Snowfall!"

"What's wrong?" Mom asked as they walked into the kitchen together.

"She's so stubborn!" Heather said. She flopped onto a chair at the kitchen table. Mom sat down next to her. "When I turn her back toward the pen, she starts twisting her leash and trying to get away from me."

"That's a pretty smart little lamb," Mom said.

"Huh?!" Heather responded. "Not really! If she were smart, she'd know she's just gonna get hit."

"Heather!" Mom scolded. "You hit her?"

"I had to, Mom! She's so stubborn. I got frustrated with her. So, I swatted her."

"Honey, you know better. You shouldn't be cruel to her. She's one of God's creatures. And more important, you're one of God's children."

"What's that supposed to mean?" Heather asked.

"Honey, God wants us to become more and more like him. Because he's kind, we should be kind too."

"But what difference does it make? She's just a lamb!"

"That's not the point. Whether she's a lamb or a puppy or a colt, the important thing is not what *she's* like, but what *you're* like. And when you act kindly toward animals *or* people you're acting like God. You're reflecting his nature."

Heather's form seemed to deflate slightly, like a balloon with a slow leak. "I'm kind to Sunshine," she said weakly.

Mom smiled. "It's easy to be kind to someone like Sunshine because she's so sweet. But kindness is right, even when it's hard, because kindness is like God."

"OK," Heather said softly. She jumped up and headed to the door. "Just one more question," she said.

"What's that?" Mom asked.

"How do you apologize to a lamb?"

 TO DISCUSS: Why should a person show kindness? What are some ways you can show kindness?

 TO PRAY: "Heavenly Father, when we show kindness, we're acting like you. Help us show kindness this week."

28 Oh, My Goodness!

GOODNESS HAS BEEN DEFINED AS "VIRTUE EQUIPPED AT EVERY POINT."
—WILLIAM BARCLAY

Bible Reading of the Day: Read Romans 15:13-16.
Verse of the Day: *"When the Holy Spirit controls our lives, he will produce this kind of fruit in us: love, joy, peace, patience, kindness, goodness, faithfulness, gentleness, and self-control" (Galatians 5:22-23).*

Tyler watched as his grandfather carefully searched the living room.

"Are you looking for something, Papa?" he asked, using the family name for his grandfather. Papa answered that he couldn't find the remote control for the television.

"I'll find it for you," Tyler answered. In a few moments, Tyler located the remote control and handed it proudly to his grandfather.

Sometime later, Tyler sat at the kitchen table, coloring, as his father prepared dinner. Dad spilled a few drops of milk on the floor, and Tyler jumped up from his seat, grabbed a paper towel, and announced, "I'll wipe it up for you, Daddy."

Later that evening, Tyler crawled onto his dad's lap as his father was reading a thick book. He carefully removed his dad's glasses.

"You look tired, Daddy," he said. He rubbed his dad's temples as he had seen his mother do.

Dad closed his eyes and submitted to Tyler's efforts for a few moments, then opened his eyes.

"Tyler," he said, "you are terrific."

Tyler beamed with pride and satisfaction.

"All day long, you've been so helpful and thoughtful and . . . and full of goodness."

"I have?" Tyler said. He loved being praised by his dad.

"I hope you'll be able to hold on to that goodness as you get older," Dad said. "It's a wonderful quality to have."

Tyler rested his head on his dad's chest.

Dad continued, "The Bible says that Jesus helps us to show goodness to others. Do you know what *goodness* means?"

Tyler didn't answer. Dad shifted in his seat and looked at Tyler's face. His son was asleep.

"I think you do," Dad said, smiling. "It must be tiring to show so much goodness," he said as he carefully stood and carried Tyler up to bed.

 TO DO: Write a list of ways to show goodness to others. Then come up with a list of people to whom you can show goodness. Then discuss the William Barclay quote. Would you define *goodness* that way? Why?

 TO PRAY: "Loving God and Father, please help us each to show your goodness to others."

29 Old Faithful

FAITHFULNESS IS A VALUABLE PART OF ANY GOOD RELATIONSHIP.

Bible Reading of the Day: Read 2 Chronicles 29:1-2; 31:20-21.
Verse of the Day: *"When the Holy Spirit controls our lives, he will produce this kind of fruit in us: love, joy, peace, patience, kindness, goodness, faithfulness, gentleness, and self-control" (Galatians 5:22-23).*

"Wow!" cried Annette. "Look at that!"

She and her family stood beside a road in Yellowstone National Park in Wyoming and watched a plume of boiling water shoot one hundred feet into the air. The sight was spectacular.

Annette's dad read from a pamphlet they had received at the entrance to the park. "It says here that Old Faithful is one of many geysers in Yellowstone National Park," he said. He looked up from the pamphlet to watch the display.

"That was so cool!" Annette shouted excitedly when the eruption was over. "Will it do it again?"

"Absolutely," Dad answered. "The pamphlet said it does that many times every day. But we can't stay to watch it. There are other things to see, too."

They got back in the car and headed toward Yellowstone Lake.

"What was the name of that geyser?" Annette asked.

"Old Faithful," Mom said.

"Old Faithful?" Annette echoed. "Why is it called that?"

"Because it erupts every hour or two, like clockwork. You can count on it. That's why it's such a popular tourist attraction, because of its faithfulness."

"Old Faithful," Annette repeated.

They drove in silence for a few moments, until Mom turned to face Annette.

"That's one of the things I value most about your father," she said. "His faithfulness. I've always been able to trust him and count on him. He's always been faithful—to God, to his friends, and to me. And I've always been faithful to him. That kind of faithfulness in a marriage is becoming more and more rare these days, but faithfulness is a valuable part of any good relationship. It's something I want to see you develop more and more as you grow up."

Annette and her mother faced each other thoughtfully.

"Maybe we should start calling *Dad* 'Old Faithful,'" Annette suggested.

"Hey, watch it!" Dad said, suddenly joining the conversation. "Are you saying I'm an old show-off?"

Annette started laughing. Soon the rest of the family joined in.

 TO DISCUSS: Have you been faithful to your friends? to God? to others? Do you need to work on "doing what [is] good and right and faithful before the Lord" (2 Chronicles 31:20, NIV)? How can you let God produce faithfulness in your life this week?

 TO PRAY: "Lord, help us to do what's good and right and faithful before you."

GENTLENESS MEANS BEING CONSIDERATE OF OTHERS.

Bible Reading of the Day: Read Philippians 4:5-7.
Verse of the Day: *"When the Holy Spirit controls our lives, he will produce this kind of fruit in us: love, joy, peace, patience, kindness, goodness, faithfulness, gentleness, and self-control" (Galatians 5:22-23).*

Ben lined up at the starting line for the last race of the day at his class picnic. He had been in several races but had not won any of the events all day. He was determined to win this race. He eyed the finish line and prepared for the signal.

At last, Mr. Morrison shouted, "Go!" and Ben started running.

He and Todd Weston were in the lead. Ben panted toward the finish line. Suddenly, Todd let out a pained cry and dropped to the ground in a heap.

It all happened so fast. Ben saw Todd crumple to the ground. Ben quickly turned back toward Todd, who lay flat on his back, his face twisted with pain.

Ben knelt beside Todd and placed his hand gently on Todd's shoulder. "What's wrong?" he asked. "What happened?"

"It hurts!" Todd said through gritted teeth.

Mr. Morrison and other adults soon arrived. When more people arrived, Ben stepped back from the crowd and watched as Todd was helped to a car and taken away.

Ben felt a hand on his shoulder and heard his father's voice. "I think he'll be all right," Dad said. "It looks like he pulled a muscle. That can be pretty painful, but it's not serious."

Ben nodded. His dad walked beside him toward the picnic tables.

"I was proud of you today, Ben," Dad said.

Ben looked at his father's face, then dropped his gaze to the ground. "I didn't win anything."

"Yes, you did," Dad answered. "You won my respect. I've never been more proud than when I saw you stop running and help your friend."

Ben said nothing, but lifted his gaze to his dad's face again.

"You showed me two things today," Dad said. "You showed maturity in putting Todd's pain ahead of your race. That kind of thoughtfulness and gentleness is rare."

They arrived at their picnic table. Dad sat down and fished in the ice chest for a can of soda.

"You said I showed you two things," Ben said. "What was the other thing?"

Dad answered, "Oh, yeah. You showed me more speed than I thought you had." He smiled broadly. "You would have won that race."

Ben smiled back at his father. "Yeah," he said. "I would have, wouldn't I?"

TO DO: Reward gentleness over the next few days by placing a feather or a flower by the dinner plate of a family member who has exhibited gentleness.

TO PRAY: "Lord, remind us to be gentle in the way that we treat others."

31 Spirit Song

WHEN THE HOLY SPIRIT CONTROLS OUR LIFE, HE PRODUCES SELF-CONTROL.

Bible Reading of the Day: Read Galatians 5:22-25.
Verse of the Day: *"When the Holy Spirit controls our lives, he will produce this kind of fruit in us: love, joy, peace, patience, kindness, goodness, faithfulness, gentleness, and self-control" (Galatians 5:22-23).*

Joe and Lisa watched the scene together with amazement.

A man stood on a small stage in the middle of the mall. He held the leash of a German shepherd, which sat erect on the man's left side. The man held up a dog biscuit and showed it to the crowd. Then he balanced the biscuit on the dog's nose. Biscuit and dog remained motionless. Finally, the man barked a command. In one swift motion, the dog flipped the biscuit and caught it in his mouth.

"Cool!" said Lisa. "Did you see that?"

"Yeah," Joe answered. They started walking again toward the music store. "I know some *people* who can't sit still as long as that dog did!" Joe said.

Lisa smiled. "Yeah, like *you!* You probably can't balance a dog biscuit on your nose, either."

Joe laughed. "Depends on how hungry I am!"

They fell silent for a few moments as they walked through the crowded mall.

"I do wish I had more self-control," Joe said seriously.

"Like what?" Lisa asked.

"Like everything," he said. "Like eating, like doing my homework, like getting along with my parents. Maybe I should go to that guy's obedience school."

Lisa thought for a few moments. "You don't need obedience school," she said. "You just need the fruit of the Spirit."

"The what?" Joe said.

"The fruit of the Spirit. Remember that verse in the Bible that talks about the fruit of the Spirit? Self-control is one of them." She shrugged. "You just need to let God's Spirit control you, and then *he'll* produce the self-control you need."

"How do I do that?" Joe asked.

"You just . . ." Lisa paused. "You know how a song gets in your head, and you find yourself singing it even when you're not thinking about it? It's sorta the same thing. Only instead of playing a CD every morning, you pray and ask God to control you throughout that day. You sorta listen to the Spirit's song. Then he'll produce fruit in you even when you're not thinking about it."

Joe nodded with understanding. "Tell you what," he said. "I changed my mind. I don't need to buy a new CD today. Let's go find the Christian bookstore instead."

 TO DISCUSS: In what area of your life do you need to exercise self-control? How can you let God produce self-control in your life this week? What "fruit" has the Holy Spirit produced in your family members' lives during the past week?

 TO PRAY: Pray about those areas in which you need self-control. Then thank God for answers to prayer.

April Fool

SOMETIMES PEOPLE SAY THEY'RE KIDDING WHEN THEY'RE REALLY LYING.

Bible Reading of the Day: Read Acts 4:36–5:5.

Verse of the Day: *"Just as damaging as a mad man shooting a lethal weapon is someone who lies to a friend and then says, 'I was only joking'"* *(Proverbs 26:18-19).*

"Daddy, look! A shooting star!" Carrie pointed to the sky as she walked beside her father on the way to the drugstore.

Dad craned his neck in the direction she pointed and saw nothing. When he turned back to Carrie, she was smiling.

"April fool!" she said with a giggle.

"Oh, you caught me," he answered. "I should have known. You always squint your eyes when you're not telling the truth."

"I do?" Carrie asked, opening her eyes wide and looking worried.

"April fool!" Dad said, causing Carrie to start giggling again. He picked her up and swung her around in his arms.

"Daddy, why do we play 'April Fool'?" Carrie asked when he set her back on her feet.

Dad cocked his head to one side. "I don't know, Carrie. It's just a custom, I guess. On April first, people try to fool each other. But I don't know how it got started."

"Is it OK to lie on April Fool's Day?"

Dad shook his head. "No," he answered. "It's never OK to lie."

They reached the end of the city block and waited for the "Walk" light.

"It's OK to joke and kid around, like we do on April Fool's Day," Dad continued, "but it's not OK to lie."

The "Don't Walk" light changed, but neither Carrie nor Dad noticed.

"You see, Carrie, God doesn't mind us having fun. He likes it when we laugh and play. But he doesn't want us to make an excuse for lying by saying, 'Oh, it was just a joke,' or 'I was going to tell the truth later.' He knows the difference between kidding and lying."

"What *is* the difference, Daddy?"

Dad hesitated. "Kidding is meant to make a person smile or laugh. But *lying* is meant to deceive someone, to make that person believe something that isn't true."

Carrie nodded seriously. "Sometimes people say they're kidding when they're really lying."

Dad raised his eyebrows. Sometimes he was surprised at how wise his young daughter seemed. "You're right. And *that's* no lie!"

Carrie smiled and glanced at the walk light just as it changed to read, "Don't Walk."

 TO DISCUSS: What is the difference between kidding and lying? Is it OK to change the facts when you're "telling a story" to make it funnier or more interesting? Why or why not? Is it OK to play pranks or practical jokes? Why or why not?

TO PRAY: "Lord, help us to avoid deceiving others."

2 Shoestring Choices

YOU NEED TO TRAIN YOURSELF TO KNOW RIGHT FROM WRONG AND TO DO THE RIGHT THING.

Bible Reading of the Day: Read Hebrews 5:12-14.
Verse of the Day: *"The wise look ahead to see what is coming, but fools deceive themselves" (Proverbs 14:8).*

"Sarah, you know better than that!"

Sarah's older sister, Meghan, had just caught Sarah in a lie. Sarah had wanted to go to the store with Meghan and her friends. When Meghan had asked Sarah if her homework was done, Sarah had immediately answered yes. But when they had returned home, Sarah dug out her math book, and tried frantically to finish her homework. Meghan caught her scribbling math problems.

"I know," Sarah answered, "but I didn't even think about it. I just wanted to go to the store with you. I knew you wouldn't let me if you knew I had homework, and—"

"Sarah," Meghan said, "you know that lying is wrong, and you know *why* it's wrong."

Sarah rolled her eyes. "Yeah, but come on, Meghan, you don't expect me to stop and think about every little decision I make!"

"I sure do," Meghan answered.

"Come on, Meghan! Get real!" Sarah protested. "You expect me to stop and think about every little choice and commit to doing the right thing? I'd never have time for anything else!"

"How long did it take you to tie your shoes this morning?" Meghan asked.

"I don't know, five seconds, ten seconds. Why?"

"Did you stop and think about how to tie your shoes?"

"No," Sarah answered. "I just did it."

"Exactly! When you were younger, though, you had to stop and think about every step in tying your shoes. But now you *know* how to tie your shoes. It's the same way with right and wrong, Sarah. You need to train yourself to know right from wrong and to do the right thing. The more you train yourself now, the more automatic it'll be later on."

Sarah stared at her shoestrings. Meghan was right. She remembered trying to learn to tie her shoes—it seemed like it took her forever to get it right. Now she never even thought about it, she just did it.

"OK," Sarah said. "I guess you're right." She sighed. "I'm sorry. I'll try to do better."

Meghan smiled. "You're forgiven. Now," she said, "need any help with that homework?"

 TO DO: The next time you tie your shoes, ask for God's help in recognizing the difference between right and wrong. Then make plans to continue studying the Bible together as a family. This study time can help "train" you to automatically do what is right.

 TO PRAY: "Lord, we want to be quick about obeying you. Thank you for increasing our 'spiritual' reflexes."

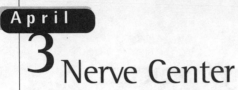

3 Nerve Center

YOUR CONSCIENCE IS A PART OF YOUR SOUL THAT IS SENSITIVE TO RIGHT AND WRONG.

Bible Reading of the Day: Read Acts 24:10–16.
Verse of the Day: *"I always try to maintain a clear conscience before God and everyone else"* *(Acts 24:16).*

"Mom, what's a 'conscience'?" Luan dropped his notebook onto the counter of the small grocery store run by his family.

His mother looked up from her work. "Aren't you even going to give your mother a kiss or say, 'Hello, Mom,' before you start asking me questions?" she asked.

Luan leaned across the counter and kissed her. "OK," he said, as if he had fulfilled a difficult obligation, "now tell me. What's a 'conscience'?"

"Why do you ask me that? Is it homework?"

"It's a vocabulary word," he answered.

Mom nodded slowly. After a few moments she pointed to the freezer in the corner of the store. "Please get me a Popsicle from the freezer," she said. "Any flavor will do."

Luan sighed as he went to do as his mother asked.

"Also, bring me a cup of coffee from the back room!" she called across three aisles of groceries. Luan disappeared into the back room. He reappeared a few moments later with the Popsicle and a cup of coffee. He started to set the items on the counter.

"No," Mom said. "Hold them in your hands and tell me what your hands feel."

Luan looked puzzled, but he answered, "This hand is freezing," he said, nodding at the hand holding the Popsicle, "and this one is warm from the coffee."

"How do your hands feel the sensations of cold and hot?"

Luan shrugged. "I don't know."

"Yes, you do. You learned it in school. You have nerves in your hands and in your fingers. Those nerves send messages to your brain, telling you what is cold or hot."

"Oh yeah," Luan said. "I remember."

"Your conscience is like those nerves. It is a part of your soul that is sensitive to right and wrong. It's a feeling inside you that reminds you to do right things and to resist doing wrong things. It sends messages to your spirit," she said, tapping Luan's chest above his heart with the tip of her index finger, "telling you right from wrong. Your conscience is that part of you that feels dirty when you choose wrong and clean when you choose right. *That,*" she concluded, "is what your conscience is."

"Oh," Luan said. He set the coffee cup down on the counter and extended the Popsicle toward his mother.

"*That,*" she said, indicating the Popsicle in Luan's hand, "is for you. This," she said, smiling and picking up the coffee cup, "is for me."

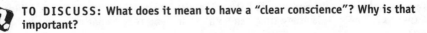

TO DISCUSS: What does it mean to have a "clear conscience"? Why is that important?

TO PRAY: "Lord, thank you for giving each of us a conscience. May we keep our consciences clear before you and everyone else."

4 The Dull Conscience

THE CONSCIENCE IS NOT LIKE A KNIFE, WHICH DULLS WITH USE, BUT LIKE THE BRAIN, WHICH SHARPENS WITH USE.

Bible Reading of the Day: Read Titus 1:15–2:1.

Verse of the Day: *"Everything is pure to those whose hearts are pure. But nothing is pure to those who are corrupt and unbelieving, because their minds and consciences are defiled" (Titus 1:15).*

"Deneen," Dad asked his daughter, "would you cut up those tomatoes for our sandwiches?" He nodded toward two bright red tomatoes on the kitchen counter.

"Sure, I guess," Deneen answered with a shrug. She drew a knife out of the drawer below the counter.

"What's wrong?" Dad asked. "You seem a little down."

She shrugged again. "Oh, I don't know." She paused. "I just don't understand some people."

"Why do you say that?"

She started slicing the tomatoes. "It's James," she said, referring to one of her classmates. "I don't see how he can do the things he does and still sleep at night."

"What do you mean?" Dad asked.

"Oh, he can be so mean and nasty sometimes." Deneen's motions with the knife became more vigorous. "You'd think his conscience would bother him."

"Hey!" Dad said. "Be careful with that knife! I don't want any finger sandwiches for lunch!" Deneen smiled at him and slowed her motions. He continued. "Well, honey, sometimes a person begins making bad choices and keeps making those kinds of choices; if he keeps disobeying God like that, eventually his conscience will become dull or distorted to the point where it doesn't work like it's supposed to. I think the Bible calls it a 'defiled' conscience."

"That sure sounds like James," Deneen said. She finished slicing the tomatoes and laid the knife on the counter.

"That may or may not be what's going on with him," Dad said. He picked up the knife and turned it around several times in his hand. "But, you see, Deneen, the conscience isn't like a knife, which gets dull as you use it. It's more like . . ." His forehead wrinkled for a moment as he thought. "It's more like your brain," he said, tapping his forehead, "which gets sharper the more you use it."

"I sure wish James would start using *his* conscience more," Deneen said.

"Well," Dad answered, "no matter what James does, I hope you'll always keep your mind—and conscience—as sharp as possible."

TO DISCUSS: How can we keep our consciences "sharp"?

TO PRAY: "Lord, we want to keep our consciences sharp. Thank you for your reminders to confess any wrong thoughts and actions."

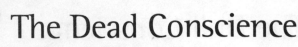
5 The Dead Conscience

IT'S POSSIBLE FOR A PERSON'S CONSCIENCE TO DIE.

Bible Reading of the Day: Read 1 Timothy 4:1-5.
Verse of the Day: *"I always try to maintain a clear conscience before God and everyone else" (Acts 24:16).*

"What are we watching tonight?" Rusty asked.

Rusty's family observed a "family night" every Monday evening. Usually they would play games, go bike riding, or read to each other. Once a month, however, Rusty's parents planned a "TV night," when they would watch a video of a program Mom or Dad had taped earlier that month for the purpose of teaching Rusty and his younger brother, Jeff, something important.

"Your mother taped a news program last week," Dad said.

"News?" Jeff whined. "Do we have to watch it?"

"It's not just news," Mom said as she slipped the tape into the VCR. She turned to face the two boys. "It's an interview with a man who has murdered over twenty people."

"You're going to let us watch that?" Rusty said, sounding excited.

Mom nodded. "Yes, and I'll tell you why as we go along."

Mom pressed "Play" and started the videotape. The family watched the interview of a former gangster. The man wore a wig and false beard to conceal his identity. He talked easily about the murders he had committed. Occasionally Mom or Dad would pause the tape to ask Rusty and Jeff questions, like "Do you think what he did was wrong?" and *"Why* was it wrong?"

Mom stopped the tape and asked the boys if they had any questions.

"How could he kill somebody," Rusty asked, "and say it was OK?"

"He didn't act like it bothered him at all," Jeff said.

Dad nodded. "He talked about killing people as if it were no big deal."

"Yeah, but how can he kill so many people and not care?" Rusty asked.

Dad picked up a Bible and read verses one and two from the fourth chapter of First Timothy. "The Bible says that for a person's conscience—the part of the person that makes it clear what's right or wrong—can die. It may be that the man you just watched felt guilty the first time he killed somebody. But he didn't stop. He kept killing. The second and third times, he probably didn't feel as bad as he did the first time. After awhile, as he kept ignoring his conscience, it may have just shriveled up and died."

There was silence in the room until Mom spoke a few minutes later. "That's one reason we want you boys to always listen to your conscience and obey God."

Rusty and Jeff looked at each other, then looked with wide eyes at their parents. "Don't worry," Rusty said. "We will!"

 TO DISCUSS: How can a person's conscience "die"? How can you keep your conscience "alive"?

TO PRAY: "God, help us to listen to our conscience, and to obey you, with the help of your Holy Spirit."

6 Old Enough to Know

CHOOSE WHAT'S RIGHT AND REJECT WHAT'S WRONG.

Bible Reading of the Day: Read Isaiah 7:13-16.
Verse of the Day: *"This is what the Lord says: Do what is just and right"* *(Jeremiah 22:3, NIV).*

Cody held his baby cousin, Alissa. The tiny infant cooed happily. "She's a good baby," he told his proud Uncle Dan.

Suddenly, however, Alissa's tiny hand gripped Cody's glasses and yanked them off his face. Before he had time to react, she released them and they flipped onto the floor, bending the frames and shattering one of the lenses.

Cody's face registered surprise, and he swiped at Alissa's hand as if to slap it. "Bad girl," he said.

Uncle Dan bent over, picked up Cody's glasses, and handed them to him. "We'll get those fixed," he said softly, "but you don't need to hit Alissa. She doesn't know what she did."

"She doesn't?" Cody said. He still held Alissa.

Uncle Dan smiled. "Her fingers just happened to close around your glasses, Cody. She has no idea that she just cost me a lot of money!"

"But if *I* did something like that," Cody countered, "I'd get in trouble."

Uncle Dan nodded and chuckled softly. "You're right, you would, because you're older than Alissa. You're old enough to know better."

Cody handed the baby back to her father.

"You see," Uncle Dan continued as he took Alissa into his arms, "babies aren't old enough to know right from wrong. But when they get a little older, they begin to understand that some things are right and some things are wrong."

"How?" Cody asked.

Uncle Dan thought. "Some of it is instinctive, because we're all made in the image of God. No one has to tell a two year old that it's unfair for another child to take a toy away from her. But it's a parent's job to add to that basic knowledge about right and wrong. A parent can help even a young child begin to choose what's right and stay away from what's wrong."

"Alissa didn't mean to break my glasses," Cody said, as if he'd just thought of the idea, "because she's too young to know she shouldn't do that."

"Right," Uncle Dan said. He winked. "But if she does it when she's your age, I'll have to have a talk with her."

"Right," Cody said. "Because then she'll be old enough to know better. Like me!"

TO DISCUSS: What does the phrase "old enough to know better" mean? When is a person "old enough to know better"? What is a child "old enough to know" by age 2? 3? 4? 7? 9? What spiritual truths are we "old enough to know" at any age?

TO PRAY: "Lord, those of us who are 'old enough to know better' still need your help to know the difference between right and wrong. Thank you for providing that help."

7 Committed

IT JUST SHOWS WHAT YOU CAN DO WHEN YOU'RE COMMITTED TO SOMETHING.

Bible ReaSding of the Day: Read Deuteronomy 6:4–9.
Verse of the Day: *"Guard my teachings as your most precious possession" (Proverbs 7:2).*

Jacqui shot the ball. It ascended in a high arc and swished cleanly through the basket.

"Nice job!" Coach Matthews said.

"Thanks," said Jacqui. "I've been practicing."

"It shows," the coach answered. "You're not the same player you were last year."

Jacqui smiled. "I practiced every day after school and on the weekends." She paused and tried to read the coach's clipboard upside down. "So, did I make the team?"

Coach Matthews raised her eyebrows. "The team roster will be posted Friday."

That Friday, Mom met Jacqui at school and went with her to the gymnasium. The team members' names were posted on the door. "I can't look," Jacqui told her mom. "Am I on the list?"

Mom looked at the list and then answered with a shout. "Yes! Jacqui, you made the team!" Jacqui screamed with happiness, and a few moments later, she and her mom were walking to the bus stop from school.

"I'm proud of you, Jacqui," Mom told her beaming daughter. "You worked hard for this."

"Coach said she could tell I was more committed to basketball this year," Jacqui said.

"You were," Mom agreed, "and it paid off." A bus pulled to the curb in front of them, but it was not their bus; Mom and Jacqui let it pass. "It just shows what you can do when you're committed to something."

Mother and daughter waited in silence for a few moments, while Jacqui continued to bask in her success.

Then Mom spoke again. "Just think," she said dreamily, "what might happen if you were as committed to following God's commandments as you were to making the basketball team. It, uh, might mean spending time in prayer and Bible reading every day before shooting baskets, and maybe memorizing a verse of Scripture while you practice. But I think that would pay off even more than practicing your slobbering."

Jacqui laughed. "I think you mean 'dribbling,' not 'slobbering'!" she said.

Mom started laughing too. "I said the wrong thing, didn't I?"

"No," Jacqui said. She stopped laughing, but still smiled. "You said the right thing."

 TO DO: Play "memory-verse basketball" as a family. If you don't have a basketball or hoop, you can use a wastebasket and paper wads. Take turns shooting baskets. Each time a person makes a basket, he or she must recite the "Verse of the Day"—Proverbs 7:2—aloud. The first person to make five baskets must recite the verse from memory or start over. The first player to make five baskets and recite the verse perfectly wins!

TO PRAY: "Lord, your Word is our prized possession. Help us to guard your Word by hiding it in our hearts."

8 True Wisdom

WISDOM MEANS KNOWING THE DIFFERENCE BETWEEN RIGHT AND WRONG.

Bible Reading of the Day: Read 1 Kings 3:5-10.
Verse of the Day: *"Give me an understanding mind so that I can . . . know the difference between right and wrong"* (1 Kings 3:9).

Dad helped Chet buckle his seat belt and then pulled a small stack of index cards from his pocket. A flight attendant walked by and peered down each row of seats to be sure every passenger was safely buckled into his or her seat.

Dad thumbed through the index cards. On each card was a short question or statement he had written down over the past several weeks. Because he traveled a lot, he didn't always get to spend a lot of time with his son and two daughters, so he had adopted the habit of writing important questions down to discuss with his children. Then, when he was riding in the car, standing in line at the grocery store, or just watching a sitcom with his family, he could easily begin a meaningful conversation with one or more of his children.

Some of the questions were simple, like "Who's your best friend?" or "Name one thing God likes." Others required thought, like the question he chose to ask Chet once the plane was in the air.

Dad turned in his seat and faced his son with a curious expression. "Can I ask you a question, Chet?" When the boy nodded, Dad continued. "What is wisdom?"

Chet had gotten used to his dad asking such questions out of the blue, but he wasn't prepared for this one. "I don't know," he answered.

"Who do you think is the wisest person who ever lived?" Dad asked.

Chet thought for a moment, then, remembering a Sunday-school lesson of long ago, answered, "King Solomon! He asked God for wisdom, and God made him the wisest man of all."

Dad nodded and smiled. "That's right," Dad said. "But do you know what I think? I think Solomon was already pretty wise."

Chet's faced reflected confusion.

"When Solomon asked for wisdom," Dad explained, "he said something like, 'Give me understanding so I can govern your people well and *know the difference between right and wrong.*' Solomon already knew that a big part of wisdom is knowing the difference between right and wrong."

"And he knew he needed God's help to know right from wrong," Chet said.

Dad patted his son's shoulder. "Sounds like Solomon's not the only wise person around here," he said.

 TO DISCUSS: How is "wisdom" different from, or similar to, "intelligence"?

 TO PRAY: Take turns praying your own version of Solomon's prayer. For example: "Lord, give me an understanding mind so that I can know the difference between right and wrong."

True to the Original

FAITHFUL MEANS TO BE "TRUE TO THE ORIGINAL."

Bible Reading of the Day: Read Deuteronomy 7:6-9.
Verse of the Day: *"Stay true to what is right"* (1 Timothy 4:16).

Curtis and Sharee left the Theater in the Park behind their parents. They had just watched a movie of a famous play by William Shakespeare.

"Did you two like the movie?" Mom asked Curtis and Sharee.

Curtis shrugged. Sharee, who was a few years older than her brother, nodded. "It was pretty good," she said.

"Did *you* like it?" Mom asked Dad.

"Definitely," Dad answered. "The acting was excellent, and it was a pretty faithful adaptation, don't you think?"

"If you say so," Mom admitted cheerfully.

"What do you mean, it was a 'faithful adaptation'?" Sharee asked.

Dad seemed pleased by Sharee's question.

"Well, it was originally a play, not a movie, but the movie script stayed pretty close to what Shakespeare wrote."

"Oh," Sharee muttered.

"In a way," Mom said, "that's what *faithful* means—'to be true to the original.'"

Sharee looked questioningly at Mom.

Mom continued. "A play is 'faithful' when it stays true to what the author wrote. A husband is 'faithful' when he stays true to the vows he made when he got married. And a Christian is 'faithful' when he or she stays true to the commandments God gave in his Word. So, being faithful is being true to the original."

Sharee's eyes brightened. "Oh," she said, "OK. I understand now."

"Do you understand, Curtis?" Dad asked.

Curtis looked at Dad like he'd just been awakened from sleep. "Uh, yeah," he answered.

"Do you know what we were talking about?" Mom asked.

"No," Curtis said slowly.

"But you said you understood," Dad reminded him.

"I understand," Curtis said, "that I should have been paying attention!"

"Well," Dad said, with a chuckle, "I can agree with you on that!"

TO DISCUSS: Today's Scripture reading says that God is faithful. For the Christian, being faithful means not only obeying God's commands but also being true to his *nature,* because he himself is faithful. Is your behavior "true to the original"— namely, true to God's nature?

TO PRAY: "Lord, we want to be 'true to the original' in our words and actions. Help us to reflect your faithfulness."

10 Man's Best Friend

FAITHFULNESS IS A GODLY VIRTUE.

Bible Reading of the Day: Read Hebrews 3:1-6.
Verse of the Day: *"Dear friend, you are faithful in what you are doing"*
(3 John 5, NIV).

Penny jumped and whirled around as she heard the yelp of her little dog, Buster.

"Oh," she cried, "I'm so sorry, Buster!" She had unknowingly stepped on the schnauzer's tail, and he had cried out in pain. She knelt down and scooped Buster into her arms just as her mother entered the room.

"What happened?" Mom asked.

Penny explained what she had done and kissed Buster on the top of the head. His tail whacked against her side as he wagged his tail in forgiveness.

"I think he forgives you," Mom said.

"Yes," Penny said, rubbing her hand over Buster's head. "He's a good dog."

"Man's best friend," Mom said as she patted the dog on the head.

"What?" Penny asked.

"Oh, you've never heard that expression?" Mom's eyebrows registered her surprise. "Dogs are called 'man's best friend,'" she explained.

"Why?" Penny asked.

"Well," Mom said, hesitating, "I don't know. I suppose it's because they're so . . . so faithful."

Penny tilted her head as if she still didn't understand.

"Take Buster, for example," Mom said. "Even though you stepped on his tail and hurt him, he's ready to forgive you immediately. He just wants to be your friend. And he's always your friend, no matter what happens."

"Yeah," Penny said, "he is, isn't he?"

"That's faithfulness. And faithfulness is a good thing to have."

"That's why he's 'man's best friend,' isn't it? He's my best friend too," Penny said, scruffing the fur on Buster's head. The dog wagged his appreciation.

Mom nodded. "You see, people naturally value faithfulness, even in dogs, because faithfulness is a good thing."

"It's too bad people aren't as faithful as Buster," Penny said.

Mom smiled. She reached over and patted her daughter on the back. "Some are," she answered.

TO DISCUSS: What is faithfulness? Can you name any people who display faithfulness to God? to others? to you?

TO PRAY: "Holy God, you're the only one who is always faithful to us. We value faithfulness because you are faithful."

11 Be Faithful

GOD COMMANDS US TO BE FAITHFUL.

Bible Reading of the Day: Read Revelation 2:8-10.
Verse of the Day: *"Remain faithful even when facing death, and I will give you the crown of life" (Revelation 2:10).*

Joel and Vanessa stood beside their grandmother's bedside. Grandma had been in the hospital for almost two weeks. They both knew that Grandma was dying; their parents had explained that she would be going to heaven soon.

"I don't want her to die." Vanessa whispered to Joel.

"Me neither," Joel said.

Suddenly, Joel and Vanessa's dad stood behind them. He wrapped his arms around them, and they buried their heads in his chest and cried.

Dad waited for a long time while his children cried, then knelt beside them and spoke. "Joel, Vanessa," he said, "I know you're sad that your grandma is dying, and that's OK. But you can be happy, too."

The children said nothing, but looked at Dad with searching eyes.

"You can be happy because your grandmother is going to heaven. She has loved God since she was just a little girl, and she's been faithful to him all these years."

Joel and Vanessa nodded. They remembered going to church with their grandmother, even in the worst weather. They remembered her reading her Bible every morning at the kitchen table. And they even knew that she had been writing letters to prisoners and invalids for as long as they could remember.

"You know who's waiting for her in heaven?" Dad asked. He had tears in his eyes.

"God?" Vanessa whispered.

"That's right," Dad answered, "the God she has loved all these years is waiting in heaven, along with the people she's loved, like your grandpa. And you know what God's going to give her when she gets there?"

Joel and Vanessa shook their heads.

"He's got a crown with your grandma's name on it! He's going to give it to her as a reward for her faithfulness to him."

"A crown?" Joel said.

Dad nodded. The children turned then and looked at Grandma's sleeping form on the hospital bed, as if expecting to see her gray hair covered with a crown.

"You know what else?" Dad said. "God has a crown for you, too."

"He does?" Joel said.

"Yes," Dad answered, "if you're faithful to him, just like your grandma has been."

 TO DISCUSS: God commands us to be faithful and promises to reward those who are. What do you think being faithful to God means? How can you be faithful to him today?

 TO PRAY: "Heavenly Father, there are many people who have been faithful to you and to us. We want to thank you for their lives right now." Pause to pray silently for the faithful people in your life.

12 A Faithful Friend

GOD COMMANDS US TO BE FAITHFUL BECAUSE HE VALUES FAITHFULNESS.

Bible Reading of the Day: Read Proverbs 3:1-8.
Verse of the Day: *"Many will say they are loyal friends, but who can find one who is really faithful?" (Proverbs 20:6).*

"Man, he makes me so mad!" Corey glared at his former friend, who walked away from the restaurant counter where he worked.

"What's up with you?" Ken asked. Ken was a year older than Corey, but they'd become good friends since Corey had started working at Mama Mia's Pizza.

Corey nodded in the direction of his former friend. "It's him. He and I used to be friends."

"Used to be?" Ken asked.

"Yeah," Corey answered sulkily. He thought for a moment. "It's like, he's your friend when you've got something he wants, but if you ever really need him, he's got something better to do."

Ken nodded. "I think I know what you mean."

"I mean, we used to do all kinds of things together, but once, when Mr. Jacobs, the history teacher, told us after a big test that our answers had been almost identical, *he* said, 'Well, Mr. Jacobs, I thought Corey was looking at my paper an awful lot, but I couldn't very well turn him in, could I? After all, he's my friend!'"

"You copied off his test paper?" Ken asked.

"No!" Corey answered angrily. *"He copied off of mine!"*

"So he betrayed you," Ken said.

Corey nodded.

"He's not a very faithful friend," Ken said.

Corey blew a short burst of air out of his mouth. "You got that right!"

"And you think faithfulness, or loyalty, or whatever you call it, is pretty important."

"Well, yeah," Corey said. "Don't you?"

Ken nodded. "Sure," he said. "But it doesn't really matter so much what I think. What matters is what God thinks. *He* commands us to be faithful, because he values faithfulness. That's why most of us know that faithfulness is a good thing, an important thing—because it's a godly value."

Corey shook his head and smiled. "You sure do talk a lot about God."

Ken smiled. "Does it bother you?"

"No," Corey said. He smiled back. "I kind of like it."

TO DISCUSS: What does *loyalty* mean to you? To whom are you loyal? From whom do you expect loyalty? How do you feel when someone you trust isn't loyal to you?

TO PRAY: Take turns praying something like, "God, please help me to value faithfulness. Teach me to be faithful to all my friends."

13 Faithful Like God

GOD VALUES FAITHFULNESS BECAUSE HE IS FAITHFUL.

Bible Reading of the Day: Read Psalm 33:1-4.
Verse of the Day: *"For the word of the Lord is right and true; he is faithful in all he does" (Psalm 33:4, NIV).*

Trevor had laughed so hard that he thought his sides would split open. He had dreaded attending his parents' twenty-fifth anniversary party, thinking it would be boring, but it had turned out to be a lot of fun.

His Uncle Don had told hilarious stories about Trevor's parents when they had first started dating as teenagers, and several others had contributed funny incidents that had happened throughout their marriage. Finally, Trevor's Aunt Diane, who wasn't really an aunt but was a close friend of the family, stood up to say something to Trevor's mom and dad.

"I want to thank you both," Diane said, with tears in her eyes, "for twenty-five years of faithfulness to each other." The laughter in the room quieted, but the smiles remained. "Every marriage has tough times," she continued, "but I've never seen either of you look at another man or woman the way that you look at each other.

"In a day and age that seems to glorify sex and excuse unfaithfulness, you two have been shining examples of God's desire for all of us." She hesitated, as if she were unsure of what to say next, but then she continued in a stronger voice than before. "Not only that, but through your faithfulness to each other, you've not only shown us what love looks like . . . you've shown us what God looks like."

Trevor's eyes filled with tears. He had always loved and obeyed his parents, but tonight he was gaining a new respect for them.

"The Bible tells us," Diane said, "that God is a faithful God. In fact, it even says that he can't be anything other than faithful, because faithfulness is a part of his nature. For twenty-five years," she said, nodding at Trevor's mom and dad, "you two have reflected his faithfulness by being faithful to each other."

Trevor looked around the room and saw that nearly everyone's eyes were filled with tears, like his own.

Diane blinked back her own tears and then, looking suddenly embarrassed, muttered a quick "Thank you" and sat down.

Everyone in the room remained silent and motionless for a few moments. Then Trevor got up from his chair, walked over to his mom and dad, and hugged them both.

 TO DISCUSS: Why does God command us to be faithful? Why does God value faithfulness? Why is faithfulness (to our friends, to our spouses, to God) right?

TO PRAY: "Lord God, keep us faithful to you and to the people in our lives."

14 Faithfulness Provides (Part 1)

FAITHFULNESS TO GOD BRINGS REWARD.

Bible Reading of the Day: Read Matthew 25:14-23.
Verse of the Day: *"The Lord rewards every man for his righteousness and faithfulness"* (1 Samuel 26:23, NIV).

Marita's mother watched her from the front porch. Marita rode her tricycle down the sidewalk in front of her house, stopped at the fire hydrant down the street, then turned around and rode back. When she turned her tricycle into the driveway of her own house, her mother came down the steps and walked over to her.

"I'm so proud of you," Mom said.

Marita wrinkled her nose the way she always did when she asked a question or didn't understand something. "Why?" she asked.

"Because you always turn around at the fire hydrant," Mom answered.

"You told me I could only ride that far," Marita said.

Mom nodded. "That's right. And you've never forgotten or tried to disobey Mommy when I wasn't looking."

Marita shook her head solemnly.

"You know what?" Mom said, then continued. "Since you've been so good about turning around at the fire hydrant, I think you're big enough to go a little farther." She craned her neck to look down the street. "From now on, you can go all the way to that telephone pole with the big orange stripe on it," she said, pointing.

Marita looked down the street, then looked back at her mother with wide eyes. "I can?" she said.

"Yes," Mom said. "Just remember to be careful."

"I will!" Marita answered excitedly. She turned her tricycle back toward the sidewalk. "I'm going to go try it right now!" she called to Mom as her legs furiously pumped the pedals.

 TO DISCUSS: Why did Marita's mom decide to let Marita have more responsibility? Do you think God also rewards us if we are faithful to him? If so, how?

 TO PRAY: "Lord, we know you reward those who are faithful. Help us to be like the faithful servants in the parable. Show us what we need to do to faithfully use the talents and abilities you have given us."

15 Faithfulness Protects (Part 1)

FAITHFULNESS TO GOD PROTECTS US FROM DISHONOR AND DISAPPOINTMENT.

Bible Reading of the Day: Read Matthew 25:14-30.
Verse of the Day: *"Fear of the Lord gives life, security, and protection from harm" (Proverbs 19:23).*

"Come on, man, it's going to be the coolest party of the year!"

Hong faced his buddy, Derek, and shook his head. "There's no way my parents would let me go to one of Greg's parties, especially if they knew Greg's parents weren't going to be there."

"They don't have to know," Derek said in a pleading voice.

"You want me to go without asking my parents?"

"You just said they'd never let you go if you asked them," Derek said.

"No," Hong insisted. "Besides, you know what Greg's parties are like—beer and drugs and stuff. You know I'm a Christian. I don't do that kind of stuff."

Derek rolled his eyes. "Look, you don't have to do any of that stuff. You can just go and listen to the music and hang out with me." He held out his hands in a pleading gesture. "If you don't go, I won't have anyone to hang with."

Hong shook his head again. "I'm sorry, Derek," he said. "I'd be disobeying God and my parents if I went. I'm not going, and I don't think you should go, either."

Derek did go to the party, however, and Hong learned at school the next day that the party had become so noisy and unruly that the police had shown up at Greg's front door. When the police found out that Greg's parents weren't home, they hauled Greg and most of the guests to the police station. The police didn't put anyone in jail, but they kept everyone—including Derek—at the police station until their parents came to pick them up.

"You were right, man," Derek told Hong. "I should never have gone to that party. I'm in so much trouble now; my parents will never let me out of their sight for the rest of my life."

Hong shrugged. He felt sorry for his friend, but he still had to stifle a smile. He realized that his decision to stay faithful to God had saved him a lot of embarrassment and grief.

TO DISCUSS: Do you think Derek was happy that he went to the party? Why or why not? Do you think Hong was happy that he didn't disobey God or his parents? Why or why not? How did Hong's faithfulness to God protect him? Do you think it's good to be faithful to God? Do you think it's good to be faithful to your parents?

TO PRAY: "Thank you, Lord, for the security and protection that faithfulness to your Word brings."

16 Faithfulness Protects (Part 2)

FAITHFULNESS TO ONE'S HUSBAND OR WIFE PROTECTS A PERSON FROM HEARTBREAK.

Bible Reading of the Day: Read Proverbs 31:10-11, 28-29.
Verse of the Day: *"To the faithful you show yourself faithful"* (Psalm 18:25).

Brian sat alone in his room, crying. Suddenly he heard a knock, and the door opened a crack.

"Can I come in?" his father asked.

Brian answered with a nod. He hurriedly wiped his eyes with his shirt sleeve.

Dad sat next to Brian on the bed. They sat in silence for several moments before Dad spoke. "I just got off the phone with Justin's dad," he said. Brian nodded and sniffed quietly. "Is that why you're crying?" Dad asked.

Brian nodded again. He and Justin were best friends. He didn't want Justin to move. But if his parents divorced, Justin might have to move if his mom did.

"Why do they have to get divorced?" Brian asked, trying hard to control his trembling voice.

"They don't have to," Dad answered, "but that's the choice they've made."

"But why?"

Dad sighed loudly and stared at his hands. "Probably a lot of reasons, some of which we just can't understand," he answered. "But I do know that somewhere along the line Justin's mom and dad stopped being faithful to each other."

Brian's eyes narrowed. "What do you mean?"

Dad looked at Brian. He inhaled deeply and cleared his throat. "You see, Brian, when a man or a woman starts thinking about, and treating other people, in ways that should be reserved for a husband or wife, it can do terrible damage to a marriage. That's what happened to Justin's parents."

"But it's not fair to Justin," Brian said.

"You're right," Dad answered. "That's one of the reasons God wants husbands and wives to be faithful to each other—because faithfulness can save us a lot of heartache. I know that Justin's dad wishes now that he'd understood that a long time ago."

"I don't ever want you and Mom to break up," Brian said.

"Neither do I, Brian," Dad answered. "I don't want to go through what Justin's parents are going through right now, and I don't want you to have to go through the kind of hurt Justin is feeling. So I plan to be faithful to your mother, just like I promised at our wedding."

"Good," Brian said. His mood seemed to lighten slightly. "Can I call Justin?"

Dad nodded and said, "He could probably use a good friend right now."

TO DO: Think of ways to show your appreciation for the faithfulness of your family members. Make cards for each other, or make a special meal to share together.

TO PRAY: "Lord, the faithfulness evident in our relationships is a blessing. Help us to never take it for granted."

17 Faithfulness Provides (Part 2)

FAITHFULNESS TO FRIENDS PROVIDES FOR STRONG, REWARDING RELATIONSHIPS.

Bible Reading of the Day: Read Proverbs 17:17; 18:24; 27:10, 17.
Verse of the Day: *"There are 'friends' who destroy each other, but a real friend sticks closer than a brother"* (Proverbs 18:24).

Hannah set her food tray on the table next to Becky's in the school cafeteria. Becky smiled at her friend, reached into her brown lunch bag, and pulled out a banana. She held it in front of Hannah.

"Thanks," Hannah said. She took the banana out of Becky's hand and, in one smooth motion, snatched the apple off her lunch tray and set it in front of Becky.

Everett, who was sitting opposite Hannah and Becky, wrinkled his forehead at the girls' behavior. "What's that all about?" he asked.

"What?" Becky asked.

"The fruit thing," he said.

"Oh, that," Becky said, realizing that he had noticed their trade. She shrugged. "It's nothing."

"The school cafeteria only has apples for lunch," Hannah explained, smiling at Everett through a mouthful of braces. "I can't eat apples because of my braces, so Becky packs a banana every day in her lunch, and we trade."

"Every day?" Everett asked.

Becky shrugged again. "Just about," she said.

Everett shook his head and looked at Becky. "You pack a banana in your lunch every day just for Hannah?"

"Sure," Becky answered. "We do all kinds of stuff for each other. We've been friends since second grade."

"When I had the measles in second grade," Hannah said, "Becky came to my house every day. Mom wouldn't let her in because she was afraid Becky would catch the measles too. But Becky still came every day to bring me something and to ask how I was doing."

Becky turned to Hannah, momentarily forgetting Everett. "And remember when I broke my wrist?" She faced Everett again. "I couldn't write with the cast on, so Hannah wrote out all my homework for me, for like four or five weeks!"

Everett rolled his eyes. "OK, OK," he said. "I get the picture. You guys are, like, Superfriends."

Hannah and Becky laughed. Becky shook her head. "No, we're not," she said. "We just know we can count on each other, right?"

"Right!" Hannah agreed.

 TO DISCUSS: What do you think it means to be faithful to your friends? How can faithfulness to your friends provide for you and protect you? Are you a faithful friend? Do you have any faithful friends?

 TO PRAY: "Teach us, Lord, to be truly faithful to our friends and our family."

18 God Remains Faithful

BEING FAITHFUL ISN'T JUST WHAT GOD DOES; IT'S PART OF WHO HE IS.

Bible Reading of the Day: Read 2 Timothy 2:8-13.

Verse of the Day: *"If we are faithless, He remains faithful; for He cannot deny Himself" (2 Timothy 2:13, NASB).*

Tim's mouth hung open as he petted the thick striped fur of the tiger cub. "He's so soft," he said, "and cuddly."

The woman who held the cub wore the badge of the city zoo. She was showing Tim and the other members of his home-school co-op the "infant care unit" of the zoo where she worked.

"Can I hold him?" Tim asked.

The woman smiled, nodded, and gingerly transferred the cub to Tim's cradled arms.

"This is so cool," Tim said. "Could I, like, keep one of these as a pet?" he asked the woman.

She shook her head. "I'm afraid not. You see," she said, speaking loud enough for the others to hear too, "that cuddly little cub is still a wild animal. And in this state, people aren't allowed to keep tigers or lions or bears as pets."

"Why not?" Tim asked.

"Well, no matter how cuddly he is right now, he'll soon be an adult tiger. And no matter how well you train him, he'll always be dangerous, because it's part of his nature. He can't change his nature. He can't be anything other than a wild tiger."

Later that day, as Tim and six other home-schooled kids ate lunch in one of the zoo's picnic areas, one of the mothers sat down beside Tim with an open Bible.

"I wanted to show you something," she said. "You remember what that zookeeper told you about the tiger, how it would always be a wild animal because it could never change its nature?"

Tim nodded.

"Well, that reminded me of a Bible verse." She pointed to 2 Timothy 2:13. "The Bible says that faithfulness is a part of God's nature. No matter what *we* do—whether we're faithful or unfaithful—*he* will always be faithful, because he cannot deny himself. Being faithful isn't just what God does; it's part of who he is."

Tim read the verse from the book that shared his name.

"Now, tell me something, Tim," the woman said. "Does that make you want to obey God or disobey him?"

"It makes me want to obey him," Tim said with a shrug. "Because I know he'll always be faithful to me, I want to be faithful to him."

"Me too," the woman said. "Me too."

TO DISCUSS: What is Paul's "testimony" of faithfulness, according to 2 Timothy 2:8-13? What is your "testimony"?

TO PRAY: Take turns thanking God for his faithfulness, perhaps using the words of 2 Timothy 2:13: "Thank you, Lord, that even if we are faithless, you remain faithful."

19 The Road to Gladness

PEOPLE WHO LOVE WHAT'S GOOD AND HATE WHAT'S WRONG TEND TO BE MORE SATISFIED WITH LIFE.

Bible Reading of the Day: Read Psalm 45:1-7.

Verse of the Day: *"You love what is good and hate what is wrong. Therefore God, your God, has given you more gladness than anyone else"* (Psalm 45:7, TLB).

Dad pointed out the car window to the high fences and stone towers of the prison they were passing on their way to a farm auction miles away from their home in the city.

"Look," he told his daughters, Pam and Stephanie, who sat in the back seat.

"What's that?" Pam asked.

"It's a prison," Stephanie answered her younger sister's question, the tone of her voice implying, *Don't you know anything?*

The sight of the prison made Dad think of something. "Hey, girls," he said, "who do you think has more fun in life: people who love God and try to do right, or people who like to do wrong?"

"That's easy," Stephanie said, still gazing at the high prison fence topped with razor wire. "People who like to do right."

"Why?" Dad asked.

"Because they don't have to go to prison," Stephanie answered.

"What about people who don't get caught doing wrong? They don't go to prison. Do you think they're happier than people who do right?"

Stephanie thought about that. "I guess so," she said, although she hated to admit it.

"Uh-uh," Pam disagreed. She thought of a boy in her class at school. "Jimmy Masters is always doing bad things, and he gets away with it all the time."

"Do you think that makes him happy?" Dad asked.

Pam shook her head vigorously, causing her ponytail to flap back and forth behind her head. "He's never happy. He doesn't like anybody, and nobody likes him."

"Do you think he'd be happier if he tried doing right?" Dad asked.

"Maybe," Pam answered with a cheerful shrug. "He wouldn't be so mean all the time, and he might make friends with someone."

Dad smiled. "You know what, Pammy? I think you're right. I think that's one of the reasons God wants us to do right. People who love what's good and hate what's wrong tend to be happier and more satisfied, because they experience the blessings that come from doing good—the way God intended in the first place."

 TO DISCUSS: Who do *you* think has more fun and happiness in life: people who love God and try to do right, or people who like to do wrong? Explain your answer.

 TO PRAY: "Lord, we want to love what is good and hate what is wrong. That way, we'll experience the satisfaction that you promise."

20 The Facts of Life

THE LINE BETWEEN GOOD AND EVIL RUNS DOWN THE MIDDLE OF EACH ONE OF US.

Bible Reading of the Day: Read Romans 7:21-25.
Verse of the Day: *"Every child of God defeats this evil world by trusting Christ to give the victory"* (1 John 5:4).

Janet leaned her head close to her friend Vicki as they sat on Janet's front porch watching cars go by. "Michael Mallon was bad again in school," she said.

"What did he do this time?" Vicki asked.

"He called the teacher a bad name," she answered.

Vicki's eyes widened. "He is *so* bad!" she said. "Why is he so bad?"

Janet shrugged. "I don't know. He's just a bad boy."

Suddenly, they heard the door behind them open. Janet's mom came out and sat beside them. "I heard you talking about Michael Mallon," she said. "So he got in trouble again, did he?"

Janet and Vicki nodded their heads in unison, as though they were both controlled by the same puppeteer.

Mom watched the cars for a few moments, too. Then she said, "So you think Michael's a bad boy?"

"Uh-huh," Janet answered, nodding her head vigorously. "He's *always* getting into trouble."

Mom smiled. She inhaled deeply. "You know, girls, sometimes I start thinking that the world is divided into two kinds of people: good people and bad people. The good people make right choices and the bad people make wrong choices."

Janet and Vicki looked at Mom and listened.

"But you know what happens when I start trying to figure out who the good people are and who the bad people are?"

The girls shook their heads.

"I remember that *I* make wrong choices, too."

Janet's and Vicki's eyes grew big and round, and they looked at each other.

Mom pulled Janet onto her lap, scooted next to Vicki, and wrapped her arm around her daughter's friend. "The world isn't made up of good people and bad people," she explained. "We're all sinners. We all make wrong choices. We all need God's forgiveness, and we all need God's help to make right choices."

Janet laid her head on Mom's shoulder. "I'm glad God helps us make right choices."

"I am, too," Mom said, "because if he didn't, I'd *always* be getting into trouble!" Mom flashed a silly smile at the girls, and they all started laughing together.

 TO DISCUSS: How does God help us make right choices? Why should a person admit when he or she has done wrong?

 TO PRAY: "Lord, thank you for your forgiveness. Thank you, also, for helping us to make right choices."

21 Living in Harmony

HOW WONDERFUL IT IS, HOW PLEASANT, WHEN BROTHERS LIVE TOGETHER
IN HARMONY!

> Bible Reading of the Day: Read Psalm 133
> Verse of the Day: *"How wonderful it is, how pleasant, when brothers
> live together in harmony!" (Psalm 133:1).*

Mom heard Rakesh and his sister, Kalpana, shouting at each other from the next room.

"Here, now, what's the matter?" Mom asked as she entered the room and quieted her children, who had been working quietly together on a jigsaw puzzle until just a few moments earlier.

"I found the puzzle piece I was looking for, and *he* says he found it first!" Kalpana protested.

"I *did* find it first," Rakesh countered. "It was right there," he said, pointing to an empty spot on the table.

"You two know better than to fight like this," Mom said. "Let's try to finish the puzzle *together*," she suggested. "I'll help."

Twenty minutes later, the puzzle was finished. Mom, Rakesh, and Kalpana smiled at each other. The puzzle formed a multicolored scene of mountains, sky, and clouds.

"Isn't that pretty?" Mom said. Rakesh and Kalpana nodded, smiling.

Suddenly, a thought occurred to Mom. "You know what this puzzle reminds me of?" Rakesh shook his head. Kalpana asked, "What?"

Mom pointed at the beautiful scene they had formed from a hundred different pieces. "It reminds me of us."

"It does?" Rakesh asked. He didn't see how the scenic picture could remind his mother of them.

"Yes, it does," Mom answered. "Do you remember what a mess all those different puzzle pieces made when they were spread out all over the table?" The children nodded. "And now, see how all those pieces form a beautiful picture? Well, that's just like us. When you two fight, it's not very beautiful, is it?"

"No," Kalpana answered.

"But when you're nice to each other and work together, it can be even more beautiful than a picture!"

Kalpana and Rakesh smiled at each other.

"I have an idea!" Rakesh said. Mom and Kalpana listened. "Why don't we keep the puzzle on the table until Daddy gets home, so he can see how beautiful we are!"

Mom laughed. "All right," she said. "I think that's a great idea."

 TO DISCUSS: What do people need to do in order to "live together in harmony"? What part does compromise play in "living together in harmony"? What can you do today to encourage "living together in harmony"?

TO PRAY: "Lord, we want your harmony in our lives. Thank you for teaching us to live peaceably with each other."

22 One Plus One Equals One

GOD COMMANDS UNITY IN MARRIAGE.

Bible Reading of the Day: Read Mark 10:1–9.

Verse of the Day: *"Therefore what God has joined together, let man not separate" (Mark 10:9, NIV).*

"Anniversary Sunday" had arrived at Fox Lake Bible Church!

One Sunday every year, Julie's church hosted a gigantic celebration of marriage. In the morning worship service, a large cake was carried into the sanctuary, and the pastor introduced all the married couples in the congregation, telling how long they had been married. Then everybody sang "Happy Anniversary" to all the husbands and wives in the church. Some couples had only been married a few months, and others had been married for a long time. One man and woman had been married sixty-eight years!

"That was neat," Julie said, as she left church with her parents.

"It was, wasn't it?" Julie's mom said.

"Yeah," Julie continued. "I couldn't believe how long some of those people have been married."

"I think it's wonderful," Mom said. "And God thinks it's wonderful, too, because he commands unity in marriage."

"What do you mean?" Julie asked.

"Well, you heard what the pastor said in his sermon," Mom said. "Jesus said that since God has joined a husband and wife together, no one should separate them."

"Yeah, but a lot of couples do split up," Julie said. A couple of her friends' families came to mind.

Mom nodded. "That's true. But when God joins a man and a woman together in marriage, he unites them in a way that only God can do. That's why it's so sad—and often so destructive—when a marriage breaks up. It's like tearing a single person in two, because in marriage, God adds two people together and makes them one."

"One plus one equals one? It sounds like God's math isn't so good."

Mom laughed. "Oh, no," she said. "Take it from me. God's math is good. Very good!"

 TO DO: Using a magic marker, make an index card with the equation "1 + 1 = 1" and place it in a prominent place all this week (such as folded, tent-style, on the dinner table or on the refrigerator door) to remind everyone in the family that God commands unity in marriage.

TO PRAY: "Lord, marriage is such a wonderful union. It can't be maintained without you, however. Help us to be unified as you would have us to be."

23 Russell's New Tune

GOD COMMANDS UNITY IN THE CHURCH.

Bible Reading of the Day: Read 1 Corinthians 1:10-17.
Verse of the Day: *"Finally, all of you, live in harmony with one another"* *(1 Peter 3:8, NIV).*

"What are we doing here?" Russell asked as his Dad pulled the car into a parking lot of a strange church. He sat in the back seat, next to his brother, James.

"We're going to worship here today," Dad answered.

"What for?" Russell asked. "What's wrong with our church?"

"Nothing's wrong with our church," Mom answered. "But we want you to understand that 'our' pastor, 'our' church, and 'our' style of worship are not all there is to the church."

"OK," Russell said. "I believe you. Now can we go?"

Dad exchanged smiles with Mom. "Give it a chance, Russell," Dad said. "These people are our Christian brothers and sisters too."

"But I don't know anybody here."

"You will," Mom answered.

Russell and James both appeared nervous as they entered the unfamiliar church, but a smiling man greeted them at the door, and soon after they were seated in the sanctuary the service began. It was like no church service Russell had ever been a part of. For most of the service, he stared wide-eyed around him, wondering what was going to happen next.

Russell and his family stayed longer than they usually did after church and met a lot of new friends. On the way to the car, Russell said, "That was really cool. I like this church."

Mom raised her eyebrows and cast a sidelong glance in Russell's direction. "Well, you've certainly changed your tune!"

Russell shrugged. "It was cool," he repeated.

"I'm glad you think so, Son," Dad said. "Because God is pleased when his people are united. We may not all worship in the same building, or even in the same style, but God wants us to act like the brothers and sisters he has made us."

Russell nodded and got into the car. As his father pulled the car out of the parking lot, Russell gazed back at the church building he had entered with such reluctance. "Hey, Dad," he said. "I wouldn't mind coming back to this church sometime."

Dad winked at his wife. "Neither would I, Russell."

"Neither would I," Mom added.

 TO DO: If you can, make plans to visit a church that worships the Lord in a different place or style than you're accustomed to. See the visit as a way of affirming your unity with all true Christian believers.

TO PRAY: Take time to pray for the different church families within your area and across the country.

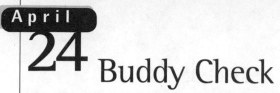

April 24 Buddy Check

GOD COMMANDS UNITY AMONG ALL PEOPLE.

Bible Reading of the Day: Read Romans 12:9–16.
Verse of the Day: *"Live in harmony with each other" (Romans 12:16).*

Jamal's teacher had paired him with Sean for the school field trip to the natural history museum. Their teacher, Mrs. Hoffmeier, required everyone to stay with a "buddy" so no one would separate from the group and get lost. But Sean had made it clear he didn't want to be Jamal's "buddy."

"Look," Jamal told Sean, "we have to stay together or we'll get in trouble."

"I'm not spending all day with you," Sean said, adding to his angry words a comment about Jamal being different.

Jamal was stunned by Sean's words, and his first instinct was to be angry. He managed to control his anger, however, and tried to reason with his classmate. "Look, Sean," he said, "let's just give it a try and—"

Sean slammed his fist into Jamal's stomach just as Mrs. Hoffmeier arrived on the scene. She saw the stunned look on Jamal's face as Sean's punch caught him by surprise. In a flash, she separated the two boys and hauled Sean back to the school bus to sit alone as punishment.

Jamal's first reaction was to gloat. *It serves him right,* he thought. Quickly, though, another thought came to him, and he approached Mrs. Hoffmeier with a plan. She seemed reluctant at first, but she finally agreed to Jamal's plan.

Moments later, Jamal appeared on the school bus with a small game he had borrowed from another classmate.

"What are you doing here?" Sean asked.

Jamal smiled. He began setting up the game. "Mrs. Hoffmeier said we could play a game while you're being punished."

Sean stared at Jamal in disbelief. "I'm here because I punched you."

"I know." Jamal finished setting up the game. "You go first."

"Are you crazy?" Sean said. "You could be with the rest of the class looking at dinosaurs and junk."

"I know," Jamal said.

Sean shook his head. "I can't believe you."

"Neither can I," Jamal said, smiling. "You want to go first?"

The two boys stared silently at each other for a long time. Finally, Sean's expression softened. He let out a sigh. "No," he said. "You go first."

Jamal smiled and started the game.

 TO DISCUSS: People often feel separated from each other by such things as race and nationality. How do you think God feels about that? How can you try to live in harmony with all people?

 TO PRAY: "Jesus, help us to reach out to people who are different from us. Help us to love them as you love us."

April 25

The Lord Is One

GOD VALUES UNITY BECAUSE HE IS A TRINITY, YET ALSO A UNITY.

Bible Reading of the Day: Read John 17:1-11, 20-21.
Verse of the Day: *"Hear, O Israel: The Lord our God, the Lord is one"*
(Deuteronomy 6:4, NIV).

Mom and Randy climbed the steps of Randy's friend Josh's house. The two boys had made plans to spend the afternoon together, and Mom was dropping Randy off.

"What's that?" Randy asked, pointing to a silver object beside the door frame.

Mom, who had been reaching for the doorbell, stopped before ringing. She looked at the cylinder. "Oh," she said, "that's called a *mezuzah.*"

"A what?"

"A mezuzah," Mom repeated. "Jewish families put it on their doorposts to remind them of their devotion to God and his Word."

"What's inside it?" Randy asked.

Mom's head tilted. "Little pieces of paper, I think," she said, "with Scripture verses on them. One of the verses is Deuteronomy 6:4, the one that says, 'Hear, O Israel: The Lord our God, the Lord is one.'"

"What's that mean?" Randy asked.

"Well, you're just full of questions today, aren't you?" Mom said. She glanced at the door, hoping that Josh's parents weren't just standing on the other side, waiting for her to ring the doorbell. "Well," she said, pondering just how much detail to provide, "in the time of Moses, all the nations around Israel worshiped many, many gods. Moses announced that Israel worshiped one God, and only him."

"But Jesus is God, too," Randy said.

"Yes," Mom said. "As Christians, we know that God is a *Trinity,* and that the Father, Son, and Holy Spirit are all God."

"But they're not three gods, are they?" Randy said.

"No," Mom answered. "That's something only God can fully understand. God is Father, Son, and Holy Spirit, yet he is *one.* In fact, his unity is an example to us, because he wants us to reflect his unity. He wants us to be unified, not divided, and to live in harmony with other people, even those who are different from us."

"Uh, Mom?" Randy said.

"Yes?" she answered, wondering to herself when his questions would stop.

"I don't think you have to ring the doorbell."

Mom turned and saw Randy's friend Josh standing in the open doorway, waiting politely for them to finish their conversation.

TO DISCUSS: How can we reflect God's unity?

TO PRAY: Pray for your family, using the words of Jesus' prayer for his disciples: "Father, I pray that our family may be unified, as you and your Son, Jesus, are."

26 The World Will Believe

GOD'S STANDARD OF UNITY PROVIDES AN EFFECTIVE TESTIMONY TO THE WORLD.

Bible Reading of the Day: Read John 17:13-22.

Verse of the Day: *"My prayer for all of them is that they will be one, just as you and I are one, Father—that just as you are in me and I am in you, so they will be in us, and the world will believe you sent me" (John 17:21).*

Bonnie and Wayne left youth group together and waited in the church foyer for Bonnie's dad to pick them up. Bonnie had invited her friend Wayne for a special fun night at youth group, but when one of the girls had revealed during prayer time that her unmarried sister had gotten pregnant, the whole group stopped what they had planned and surrounded the girl in prayer.

"I hope you're not too upset that things didn't go like we planned tonight," Bonnie told Wayne.

"I can't believe you guys," Wayne said. "You just stopped everything you were doing because Bridget was worried about her sister."

"Yeah?" Bonnie said.

"I don't know. . . . It's just not like any group I've ever been a part of. I mean, nobody complained that the fun night wasn't so fun."

Bonnie twirled a few strands of her hair between her fingers as she thought. "You're right," she said softly. "It's just . . . well, we couldn't play games and stuff with Bridget hurting like she was."

Wayne shrugged. "I know," he said, "it just wasn't what I expected."

"I'm really sorry," Bonnie said. "I hope it wasn't *too* boring for you."

"No, it's not that. It's just . . ." He hesitated. "I thought it was neat."

"You did?" Bonnie said, a note of surprise creeping into her voice.

Wayne nodded. "I've never thought much about religion. But when everybody was praying for Bridget, I was thinking, 'Wow, these guys are for real.'"

Bonnie smiled.

"It was like everybody there was thinking the same thing, and nobody was thinking of himself. That's pretty cool."

"Yeah, I guess it is," Bonnie said, hoping she didn't sound too nervous. "It sort of makes you want to find out what it's like to be a Christian, doesn't it?"

Wayne didn't answer immediately. Finally, however, he broke the silence. "Yeah," he said, as if surprised by his own answer. "It does."

Bonnie took a deep breath and prayed that her dad would be a little late picking them up.

TO DO: Think of ways your family can show appreciation for some of the members of your church family. Then put those plans into action.

TO PRAY: If you have a bulletin from your church handy, take turns praying for the various ministries of your church. Pray that the members of your church will be unified.

27 Peace Be with You

GOD'S STANDARD OF UNITY PROVIDES FOR PEACE.

Bible Reading of the Day: Read 2 Corinthians 13:7-9, 11.
Verse of the Day: *"Rejoice. Change your ways. Encourage each other. Live in harmony and peace. Then the God of love and peace will be with you" (2 Corinthians 13:11).*

"I'm not talking to Maggie," Beth declared. Her face was a mask of gloom.

"Why not?" her sister, Shannon, asked.

"She invited Katie to spend the night last Saturday instead of me," Beth answered.

Shannon's expression showed her confusion. "We weren't even home last weekend!" she said. "We were at Uncle Mike's."

"I know, but Maggie didn't know that! She still could have asked me."

"Oh, give me a break, Beth! You're not even around Saturday night, and you get mad at your best friend because she spent time with *another* friend?"

"That's not the point!" Beth protested.

"What *is* the point?" Shannon asked.

"The point is . . . well, it's just that she never even asked me!" Beth whined.

"But Maggie's *always* asking you over. And it seems like she's always coming over here."

"Well, that's all over now," Beth said. "I'm not talking to her."

"Are you saying Maggie's not allowed to have any friends except you?" Shannon asked, her voice rising in exasperation.

"No," Beth said. She crossed her arms defiantly. The two sisters stared at each other in silence for a few moments.

"Is that what you've been upset about all week?" Shannon asked, in a softer tone.

Beth nodded. It seemed like she'd spent every waking moment brooding about Maggie.

"Don't you see what your attitude is doing to you?" Shannon asked. "You're miserable! You probably spend every waking moment fuming over Maggie."

"How did you know tha—?" Beth started to say, then stopped herself. "No, I don't!" she said.

Shannon sighed. "You're just hurting yourself, Beth. You and Maggie are *friends*. And when you start acting like a friend and stop this childish act of yours, you'll be able to have some peace."

Beth's mouth hung open. Her sister was right. She *did* miss being with Maggie. She hadn't known a moment's peace since she stopped talking to her. She looked sheepishly at Shannon and sighed. "I hate it when you're right," she said.

 TO DISCUSS: How does God's standard of unity provide for peace? Be as specific as you can. What other blessings do you think unity brings?

TO PRAY: "Lord, thank you for the blessings of unity."

28 God's Spiritual Vitamins

GOD'S STANDARD OF UNITY ENCOURAGES SPIRITUAL MATURITY.

Bible Reading of the Day: Read Ephesians 4:3-7, 11-13.
Verse of the Day: *"Always keep yourselves united in the Holy Spirit, and bind yourselves together with peace" (Ephesians 4:3).*

"How's the homework coming?" Dad asked.

"Pretty good, Dad," Melinda said. "I'm doing a report for history." She squinted her eyes at her dad the way she always did when she wasn't wearing her glasses. "Did you know that sailors in the British navy used to get really sick on long sea voyages until some doctor told them to start taking fruit and stuff along with them?"

"Is that so?" Dad said, trying not to smile at his daughter's enthusiasm.

"Yeah," Melinda went on. "See, they were getting scurvy because they would be at sea for months and months without any fresh vegetables or fruit, so they wouldn't get any vitamin C. They'd start to get really weak, and their teeth would fall out."

"I get the idea," Dad said.

"But when they started taking lime juice and oranges and lemons on their ships, they stopped getting scurvy."

Later that evening, Melinda and her family read from the Bible after dinner. While Mom brought a carton of milk and a plate of brownies to the table, Dad asked Melinda to read from the last chapter of Second Corinthians. When she was finished, he said, "Those verses remind me of your report, Melinda."

"They do?" Melinda couldn't see any connection.

"Sure, they do," Dad said. "You told me how sailors used to get sick on ocean voyages because they didn't get enough vitamin C, right?" He waited until he saw Melinda nod. "Well, the same thing can happen to us spiritually."

"It can?" Melinda said.

Dad nodded. "You see, Melinda, just as God put vitamin C in oranges, and vitamin K in potatoes, and vitamin B in milk, he gives many different gifts to his people, who are supposed to exercise those gifts in the church. If we don't exercise our gifts—or if we separate ourselves from other Christians—we'll end up with a kind of spiritual scurvy."

"That's why the unity we've been talking about in our devotions is so important," Mom added. "Because unity with other Christians helps us become spiritually healthy and mature."

Melinda nodded. "That reminds me," she said. "Would you please pass the brownies and the vitamin B?"

They all laughed for a moment, and Mom passed the milk to Melinda.

TO DISCUSS: How do you think unity with other Christians can help you become mature and fully grown in the Lord? Be as specific as you can.

TO PRAY: "Lord, we need a shot of your spiritual vitamins. Remind us that regular times with you can keep us spiritually healthy."

29 Copycat Christianity

DON'T COPY THE BEHAVIOR AND CUSTOMS OF THIS WORLD. INSTEAD, LET GOD
TRANSFORM YOU INTO A NEW PERSON.

Bible Reading of the Day: Read Romans 12:1–2.
Verse of the Day: *"Don't copy the behavior and customs of this world, but let God transform you into a new person by changing the way you think" (Romans 12:2).*

"Mommmmm!" Ellen whined as she stomped out of the house and into the garden, "make him stop!"

"Make who stop?" Mom asked without looking up, as she carefully spread a layer of mulch around the row of tiny bushes that lined the walk.

"Evan!" Ellen said. "He's being a copycat."

"I am *not!*" Evan yelled from somewhere inside the house.

Mom stifled a chuckle as she asked, "What's he doing, dear?"

"He won't leave me alone. If I start playing with my dolls, *he* wants to play with them. If I want to watch cartoons, *he* has to watch cartoons."

"What's wrong with that?" Mom asked. "Your little brother likes you!"

"Mommmmm," Ellen said, still in a whining tone. "He's driving me crazy."

Mom wiped her face with the side of her gloved hand. A smudge appeared on the side of her nose. "All right," she said. "Ask Evan to come see me."

Ellen skipped toward the house to deliver the news to her brother. Mom shook her head slightly as she watched her go. Suddenly, a thought occurred to her.

Sometimes we play copycats as Christians, she thought, remembering the verse that says not to copy the behavior of the world. *We see people speeding on the interstate and think we should go just as fast. We see manners disappearing and don't want to feel weird, so we act just as rude as other people. We see our neighbors chasing after money and material things, and we think we have to keep up with them.*

She pressed her lips together in an expression of determination. "Lord," she prayed, "help me not to be a copycat Christian. Help me to copy *you* instead of the world around me."

Just then, little Evan appeared at her side.

"Mommy," he said shyly. "Did you want me?"

"Yes," Mom answered emphatically. "I wanted to ask you if you would play copycat with me."

Evan's eyes opened wide. "Really?" he said.

"Really," she answered. She handed him a handful of mulch. "I want you to copy everything I do, OK?"

"OK!" Evan said, as he happily mimicked every movement his mother made.

 TO DO: Play "shadow," the child's game in which you repeat everything another person at the table does or says. The winner is the person who can play the longest without smiling or laughing.

TO PRAY: "Lord, please help us to focus on you whenever we're tempted to copy the behavior of the world."

30 Practice Makes Perfect

IF WE PRACTICE RIGHTEOUSNESS IN OUR FAMILIES, WE'LL BE IN BETTER SHAPE
TO MAKE RIGHT CHOICES IN THE WORLD.

Bible Reading of the Day: Read 1 Timothy 5:1-4.
Verse of the Day: *"Treat younger men as brothers, older women
as mothers, and younger women as sisters, with absolute purity"*
(1 Timothy 5:1-2, NIV).

"Hey!" Nolan said, interrupting his parents' conversation at the dinner table. "Pass the gravy."

Dad stopped talking to Mom, but he did not reach for the gravy boat on the table near his plate. "I'm sorry," Dad said to his son. "What did you say?"

"I said, 'Pass the gravy,'" Nolan repeated.

"That's what I thought you said, but I was hoping I was wrong," Dad said. "Didn't you notice that your mother and I were talking?"

"Well, yeah," Nolan admitted.

"You interrupted us," Mom said.

"Sorry," Nolan said, stressing the second syllable. "Now can I have the gravy?"

Mom shook her head. "Whatever happened to saying 'please'?"

"OK," Nolan said, *"please* can I have the gravy?" He rolled his eyes. "It's not like we're out in a restaurant or anything."

"If we were in a restaurant, would you use better manners?" Dad asked.

"Well, yeah," Nolan said. "Or, like, if I was at somebody else's house for dinner."

"I see," Dad said. "Nolan, I think Mom and I owe you an apology."

Mom and Nolan both looked at Dad with surprise.

Dad's expression was serious. "I mean it. It seems that we have given you the impression that respectful behavior is something you reserve for people outside your own family, that you only need to use manners when you're around other people."

"Well, *sheesh,* Dad, you don't expect me to be all proper and everything around here, do you?" Nolan asked, waving a hand to indicate their modest surroundings.

"Actually," Dad answered, "yes, I do. You see, this is where you should *practice* righteousness. This safe and supportive environment is the perfect place to learn to do good and make right choices. Just like a football player or figure skater practices day after day to get in shape for the Super Bowl or the Olympics, you have a place to practice doing right so that when you're in a pressure situation at school or in the neighborhood, you'll be in better shape to make the right choice."

"OK, Dad, you're right," Nolan said.

Dad smiled. "Do you have any questions?"

"Yeah, Dad," Nolan answered. "May I *please* have some gravy?"

TO DISCUSS: Do you need to practice making right choices? In what area? How can your family help you get better at making the right choice?

TO PRAY: "Holy Spirit, help us to treat younger men as brothers, older women as mothers, and younger women as sisters, with absolute purity."

1 Truth Is Unchanging

TRUTH DOESN'T CHANGE.

Bible Reading of the Day: Read Isaiah 40:3-8.
Verse of the Day: *"Make them pure and holy by teaching them your words of truth" (John 17:17).*

"Hey, Mom, guess what we learned in school today?" Victor took off his raincoat and dropped it on the floor inside the back door.

Mom placed her hands on her hips and frowned playfully at her son. "Hang your coat up first, young man, and then you can tell me."

Victor did what his mother said, then turned and ran into her open arms.

"Now," Mom said, picking up Victor and holding him in her arms. "What did you learn in school today?"

"Did you know that people used to think the world was flat?" Victor said.

"Did they?" Mom said, dropping her mouth open in an expression of shock.

Victor nodded. "Yup!" he said.

"If it's not flat," Mom said, walking through the kitchen and dining room, and into the front room of the house, "what shape is it?"

"It's round," Victor said. "You know that."

"You're right," Mom admitted. They sat down in a chair next to a freestanding globe in the corner of the front room. "But all those years that people *thought* the world was flat, was it flat or was it round?"

Victor thought for a moment before answering firmly, "Round."

Mom nodded. "That's right, Victor. You see, what people *thought* didn't change what was *true,* did it?"

"No," Victor answered.

"Hmm," Mom said, nodding her head in thought. "So during all those years that people thought the world was flat, the *truth* didn't change, did it?"

Victor shook his head.

"Let me ask you one more question, Victor, before you go outside to play." Mom combed his hair with her fingers. "Some people say the Word of God isn't true." She paused. "What do you think about that?"

Victor pondered his mom's question for a long minute before answering. "What they *think* doesn't matter, does it, Mommy?" Victor answered.

"You're right, Victor," Mom said. "Because truth doesn't change." She stood, and set Victor's feet on the floor. "But I want *you* to change—into your play clothes."

"OK," Victor said, as he ran up the stairs to change out of his school clothes.

 TO DISCUSS: What are some of the things that change? What things never change?

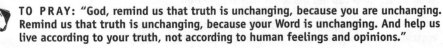 **TO PRAY:** "God, remind us that truth is unchanging, because you are unchanging. Remind us that truth is unchanging, because your Word is unchanging. And help us live according to your truth, not according to human feelings and opinions."

2 The Truth Lens

KNOWING THAT GOD HAS DECIDED WHAT'S RIGHT OR WRONG CAN MAKE OUR
CHOICES CLEARER AND EASIER.

Bible Reading of the Day: Read Matthew 6:22-23.
Verse of the Day: *"But the way of the wicked is like complete darkness.
Those who follow it have no idea what they are stumbling over"*
(Proverbs 4:19).

Margie and Liz were such close friends that their teacher called them "The Twins." They
were the same height. Their hair was cut in similar styles. They even wore glasses with
identical frames. And sometimes they finished each other's sentences.

As Margie boarded the school bus with Liz, bound for an overnight school field
trip to a nature camp, she said, "This is going to be so . . ."

"Cool!" Liz said. The girls looked at each other and burst out laughing.

At the nature camp with the rest of their class, Liz and Margie scouted out the
cabin where they would be sleeping and settled into adjoining cots. The next morning,
they started laughing together as soon as their feet hit the floor. By noon, however,
both girls complained of bad headaches. They had become crabby, criticizing everything from the food to the weather. And each girl found it hard to concentrate on what
she was supposed to be studying.

"This is the *third* time today I've had to clean my glasses," Liz complained.

"Don't you hate that?" Margie said. "I usually have to clean my glasses a lot,
but . . ."

"You haven't cleaned them at all today," Liz said.

Suddenly, the girls looked at each other. Their eyes widened and their mouths
dropped open. They took their glasses off and made a fumbling exchange.

The girls started giggling again. They each had put on the other's glasses that
morning and had worn the wrong glasses all day!

"This is *so* much better," Liz said.

"I know," Margie agreed. "I bet that's why we've been having headaches. . . ."

"And feeling so crummy," Liz added. She moved the food around on her plate.
They'd only been at the nature camp one night, and Liz was already longing for good
old *school food!*

"I can't believe something as dumb as wearing the wrong glasses can mess things
up so much," Liz said.

"Yeah," Margie said. "It's like it affected everything."

"I should have known something was wrong right away, though," Liz said.

"Why?" Margie asked.

"Because our breakfast didn't look totally disgusting!" Liz answered, laughing.

 **TO DISCUSS: What did wearing the wrong glasses do to Margie and Liz? How
do you think God's Word makes our choices clearer?**

 **TO PRAY: "Lord, when we don't know what choice to make, help us remember
to submit each choice to you."**

3 Nothing but the Truth

GOD WANTS US TO TELL THE TRUTH, THE WHOLE TRUTH, AND NOTHING BUT THE TRUTH.

Bible Reading of the Day: Read 1 Kings 22:10, 12–23.
Verse of the Day: *"I, the Lord, speak only what is true and right"* (Isaiah 45:19).

"Travis! Tricia!" Dad called. "Come here, quick!"

Tricia turned the corner from the kitchen to the living room, while her twin brother Travis galloped down the stairs from his bedroom.

"What's wrong?" Tricia asked her father.

"Nothing's wrong," Dad said. "I just wanted you guys to see this." He pointed the remote control at the television and turned up the volume. A courtroom scene filled the screen, and a small transparent logo in the corner of the screen read, "Trial TV." A woman in her mid-thirties placed her hand on a Bible as the court clerk asked, "Do you promise to tell the truth, the whole truth, and nothing but the truth, so help you God?"

The woman answered, "I do," and took her seat beside the judge's high, wood-paneled bench.

Dad pointed the remote at the screen and turned down the volume again.

"Did you hear what that man said?" Dad asked the twins.

"Uh-huh," Travis said with a nod. "He asked her to tell the truth, the whole truth, and nothing but the truth."

Dad nodded back at Travis. "That's right. Why? Why didn't he just say, 'Do you promise to tell the truth?'"

The twins stared blankly at Dad for a few moments. Finally, Tricia spoke.

"Because a person could tell the truth without telling the whole truth," she offered. "Like, if me and Travis each stole twenty dollars from Mom's purse and you asked us about it, I could say, 'Travis stole from Mom's purse,' and not tell you that I did too. That would be the truth, but not the *whole* truth."

"That's exactly right," Dad said.

"Or," Travis interjected, "I could say, 'Yes, I took money from Mom's purse, but I only took a dollar' when I really took twenty dollars. The first part would be the truth, but I'd be adding a lie to it, so I wouldn't be telling 'nothing but the truth.'"

"Right again," Dad said. "You two are pretty smart. Now, let me ask you one more question: Which do you think God wants us to do—tell the truth, the whole truth, or nothing but the truth?"

"That's easy, Dad," Travis said. "He wants us to do all three!"

"Yeah, because he's a God of truth, right, Dad?" Tricia said.

Dad nodded and smiled at his twins. *"That's* the truth!"

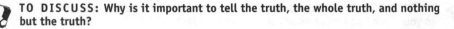 **TO DISCUSS:** Why is it important to tell the truth, the whole truth, and nothing but the truth?

 TO PRAY: "Lord, we need your courage to tell the truth, the whole truth, and nothing but the truth."

4 Yours, Mine, and Ours?

IT DOESN'T MATTER WHETHER *YOU* THINK IT'S WRONG OR NOT. ALL THAT MATTERS IS, "WHAT DOES *GOD* THINK?"

> Bible Reading of the Day: Read Psalm 32:1-8.
> Verse of the Day: *"The Lord says, 'I will guide you along the best pathway for your life. I will advise you and watch over you'"* (Psalm 32:8).

"Lin, wait 'til you see the awesome programs I installed on my computer last night!" Tara told her friend. "There's this one screensaver that's so cool! It's got flying castles and jousting knights and all kinds of stuff."

"Oh yeah, I've heard of that," Lin answered.

"Why don't you come over after school?" Tara suggested.

Lin agreed and showed up at Tara's house after she had finished her homework. The two girls sat down side by side at Tara's computer.

"I brought all kinds of cool stuff home from Mom's office yesterday," Tara said. "She worked late, so I went through and copied anything I thought I could use."

Lin smiled weakly and nodded at her friend. Tara clicked through a dozen programs, showing her friend an assortment of new games, graphics, and utilities.

"You know that's not freeware, don't you?" Lin said.

"Yeah," Tara answered, her tone implying, *What's the problem?*

"You're really not supposed to copy that stuff from other people's computers, you know. They *bought* those programs."

"Yeah, but what's the big deal? I would never buy all this stuff, so I figure it's not like I'm stealing or anything."

"If it's not like stealing," Lin said softly, "what's it like?"

Tara's face wore an offended expression. "Look, I think as long as I don't sell the stuff to other people, I'm not doing anything wrong. I'm just using it on my computer." She stared at her friend, who looked unconvinced. "I wouldn't use this stuff if I had to buy it, so I don't think I'm doing anything wrong."

"It doesn't matter whether *you* think it's wrong or not," Lin said. "All that matters is, 'What does *God* think?'"

Tara broke away from Lin's gaze and stared at the computer monitor. A comical green dragon ran screaming from a handsome prince in glistening armor. She realized she'd been justifying and excusing her actions instead of submitting them to God's standards of honesty. She let out a long sigh.

"Oh, all right," she said. She started clicking and deleting programs, including the screensaver she liked so much.

 TO DISCUSS: Was Tara wrong to "borrow" the computer software? What other kinds of "borrowing" do people engage in? For example, is dubbing a rented videotape wrong? What about cassettes and CDs? How does a person know when he or she has crossed the line from "borrowing" to "stealing"?

 TO PRAY: "Father God, sometimes we're tempted to steal or justify the times when we 'borrow' things wrongfully. Help us to be honest in our actions."

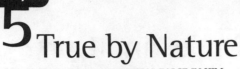

5 True by Nature

GOD IS TRUE. THERE IS NOTHING FALSE IN HIM.

Bible Reading of the Day: Read John 7:28-30.
Verse of the Day: *[Jesus replied,] "Those the Father speaks to, who learn the truth from him, will be attracted to me" (John 6:45, TLB).*

Abby's mom heard a loud crash and dashed into the family room, where Abby had been playing. She discovered Abby standing alone by the window, her hands clasped behind her back. The window behind Abby had shattered, and Mom cleverly detected the cause of the broken window—the end of the broomstick that still poked through the broken pane.

"Abby," Mom said sternly, "you broke the window, didn't you?"

"No, ma'am," Abby said, her voice and her face as sweet as candy.

Mom propped her hands on her hips. "Now, Abby, I'm not angry at you because of the broken window, but I want you to tell me the truth. You broke the window, didn't you?"

Abby shook her head. "No, ma'am," she answered.

Mom sighed and held out her hand to Abby. Abby took her mom's hand and they walked together into the kitchen. Mom lifted Abby to a sitting position on the kitchen counter so they could talk "eye to eye."

"Abby," Mom said, "do you remember what God says about being truthful?"

Abby nodded, her eyes wide. "He says not to tell lies," she answered.

"That's right. And do you remember *why* he says not to tell lies?"

Abby wrinkled her brow. "Because," she said softly, "he never tells lies."

Mom smiled. "*Very* good. And do you remember why God never tells lies?"

Abby rolled her eyes upward, as if she were watching a fly on the ceiling.

"Can I help you remember?" Mom asked.

Abby nodded, her gaze still on the ceiling.

"God doesn't want us to lie because he is true, Abby. Everything about God is true. And because he is always true, he wants us to tell the truth. When we tell the truth, we show each other what God looks like. That's what he likes."

Abby licked her lips. "I didn't mean to break the window, Mommy," she said. "I was playing with the broomstick, and I turned around and the window broke."

"I know," Mom said. She picked Abby up off the counter and whirled around the kitchen with her in her arms.

"Are you happy that I broke the window, Mommy?" Abby asked.

Mom stopped spinning. "No," she answered, smiling. "But I'm very happy that you told the truth."

 TO DISCUSS: Why does God want us to be truthful? What does telling the truth accomplish in us?

TO PRAY: "Lord, we want to be truthful because you are truthful. We want to value truthfulness because you value it."

6 Skating on Thin Ice

IT CAN BE HARD TO BE HONEST, BUT IT'S BETTER IN THE LONG RUN.

Bible Reading of the Day: Read Psalm 1.

Verse of the Day: *"For the Lord watches over the path of the godly, but the path of the wicked leads to destruction" (Psalm 1:6).*

Joe, Nick, and Daniel headed off the ice-skating rink. They were among the last to leave the rink, and only a few girls were around, gathered together at the other end of the building. As they took off their skates and put on their shoes, the boys talked about the evening.

"It sure was fun learning to skate backwards," Joe said. "Thanks for teaching me, Daniel."

"No problem," Daniel answered. "Once you get the hang of it, you can really have fun."

"Hey, look over there." Nick pointed to a bench nearby. He looked around. "Someone left their skates. Those look sweet!"

He leaped up from the bench and picked up the abandoned skates. "These are size 12," he said. "What size do you guys wear?"

"That's my size," Daniel said. "They sure beat these old blades I have. Here, put them in my bag, and I'll carry my skates out over my shoulder."

"Uh, I don't think so," said Joe. "Those belong to someone. It would be wrong to take them." The other boys looked at Joe with disbelief in their eyes. "What if you left something like that behind?" Joe reasoned. "You'd want it back. I think we ought to turn them in to the office."

"Joe, you're a real drag sometimes." Daniel had the skates in his bag. "What are you worried about? No one is gonna find out. And anyway, you're not the one taking them; I am. So butt out!"

"If you're too good to hang with us," Nick said with sarcasm, "maybe you just ought to find some other friends."

"If you're going to keep those, I'd better," Joe answered. "Because when I tell the rink office what you've done, and they call the police, my parents won't let me hang with you anymore."

"OK, then, Mr. Goody-goody!" Daniel threw the skates at Joe, hitting him in the chest. "Turn them in, then, I don't care. Just don't expect to go anywhere with me again." He and Nick walked away.

Joe sat on the bench alone, feeling mad and sad at the same time. He felt like he'd just lost something. But he felt like he had managed to hold on to something else.

 TO DISCUSS: What do you think Joe lost? What do you think he held on to? Do you think it was easy for Joe to be honest? Why or why not? Should we be honest even when it's hard? Why or why not?

 TO PRAY: *"When our friends reject us for doing what's right, remind us, Lord, that you will never reject us."*

7 The Best Policy

HONESTY ATTRACTS THE TRUST AND RESPECT OF OTHER PEOPLE.

Bible Reading of the Day: Read 1 Samuel 12:1-5.

Verse of the Day: *"Good people are guided by their honesty; treacherous people are destroyed by their dishonesty" (Proverbs 11:3).*

"Who's going to keep score?" Darlene asked.

Darlene and a few of her friends had gathered for a slumber party at Darlene's house, and they were preparing to play one of their favorite games, a fast-paced game involving a lot of shouting and screaming.

"I will!" Carrie offered, waving her hand in the air like an anxious student.

"Yeah, right," someone said. "You cheated the last time! . . . How about Ronette?"

Several voices spoke at once, objecting to Ronette's nomination.

"OK, OK, if you insist," said another girl, *"I'll* keep score."

"Oh, please!" Carrie protested. "If *I* can't be trusted, *you* can't, either!"

"What's that supposed to mean?"

"Remember the time we let you umpire in kickball?" Carrie said. "You called *everybody* safe!"

The other girl smiled wickedly. "Only if they were on my team," she answered.

"Come on," Darlene interrupted. "Just choose somebody."

"OK," Ronette offered, "I say we let Darlene keep score!"

"Yeah," Carrie agreed, turning to Darlene. "You keep score." She looked at all the other girls in the room, and her gaze was met with nods.

"I don't want to keep score," Darlene whined.

"You have to," Ronette said, handing Darlene a pencil and a pad of paper. "You're the only one in this room who won't cheat like crazy! In fact, I've never seen you cheat at anything."

"Yeah," Carrie said, laughing. She jabbed Darlene in the side with her elbow. "Just keep your eyes on Ronette," she said in a mock whisper.

"I'll try," Darlene answered, "but it won't be easy." She leaned toward Carrie and spoke in a mock whisper of her own. "Because I'll have to watch you, too!"

TO DISCUSS: What kind of "reputation" do you have among your friends? How do you know?

TO PRAY: "God, help us always remember that honesty truly is the best policy."

8 Good Gifts

GOD IS THE GIVER OF EVERYTHING THAT'S GOOD.

Bible Reading of the Day: Read James 1:13-18.
Verse of the Day: *"The Lord will indeed give what is good"* (Psalm 85:12, NIV).

"Can I open it, Mom? Can I?" Steven begged, jumping up and down beside the big box that had just been delivered. Steven's birthday dinner with his family was scheduled for that evening. He hoped that the package had something to do with that.

"No," Mom answered softly. "I think we'll wait until tonight to open it."

The rest of the afternoon passed slowly for Steven. He tried to watch television and even rode his bicycle in the driveway for a while, but he couldn't get his mind off the big box that he would open that night.

Finally, the time came, and Mom called him in for dinner. He went inside and saw that his mother had decorated the dining room with streamers and balloons!

"Can I open it now, Mom?" he asked.

"Not until after dinner," she said. "But I *will* tell you your Aunt Kate sent it."

That did it! "Aunt Kate!" Steven cried, and he started jumping up and down. "Aunt Kate sends the best birthday presents in the world!"

Steven made it through dinner and survived the long wait before Mom and Dad let him open his presents. Sure enough, Aunt Kate's gift—a set of interconnecting building blocks—was his favorite.

That night, as Steven's mom and dad tucked him into bed, Mom asked him if he had enjoyed his birthday.

"Oh, yes!" he said happily. "Especially Aunt Kate's present!"

"Aunt Kate loves you very much," Mom explained. "That's why she always remembers your birthday. But did you know that there's someone who gives even better gifts than Aunt Kate?"

Steven's eyes narrowed in suspicion. "You're making that up!" he said.

Mom smiled. "No, I'm not. God gives better gifts. The Bible says that *all* good gifts come from him."

"You mean even my connecting blocks come from God?" Steven asked.

"In a way," Mom said slowly. "Aunt Kate gave those blocks to you." She hesitated for a moment. "But who gave Aunt Kate to you?"

Steven's mouth dropped in an expression of realization. "God!" he said.

"That's right," Mom said. "And Aunt Kate is just one of God's many good gifts to us, right?"

"Right!" Steven said.

 TO DISCUSS: Spend a few minutes taking turns listing God's good and perfect gifts to you. Brainstorm ways to praise God for those good gifts.

 TO PRAY: "God, you're the giver of everything that's good. Thank you for your faithfulness to us."

9 Follow the Directions

WHEN WE KNOW WE'RE GOING THE WRONG WAY, WE MUST AGREE THAT OUR WAY IS WRONG AND TURN AROUND.

Bible Reading of the Day: Read 1 Timothy 6:11-14.
Verse of the Day: *"Follow what is right and good"* (1 Timothy 6:11).

"The man said to turn right back there, Daddy," Kirsten said.

"I heard what the man said," Dad answered coolly without turning around.

Kirsten and her family had gotten lost while on their way to a wedding. After driving aimlessly for a while, Dad had finally pulled to the curb and asked directions of a man on the sidewalk.

The man had offered a few sentences of careful directions. Dad had followed them for a little while, but soon stopped.

"Why aren't you going the way the man said, Daddy?" Kirsten asked.

"I think I know where I am now," he answered.

Mom glanced at Dad with an expression of uncertainty but said nothing.

After what seemed a long time, Dad pulled to the curb again and shouted to a person on the sidewalk. When the man turned around, Dad, Mom, and Kirsten recognized him as the man who had given him directions before. Dad stuttered in embarrassment as he asked the man to repeat his directions.

On the way home from the wedding, Dad asked Mom to drive, then climbed into the back seat with Kirsten. "My stubbornness made us late to the wedding, didn't it?" Dad asked.

Kirsten reluctantly nodded.

"I already apologized to Mom," he said, "and she agreed that I should talk to you, too." Dad took a deep breath. "Kirsten, I feel silly about what I did, but that's no big deal. But sometimes we do the same thing with God's directions, and the results can be a lot worse than being late to a wedding."

"God's directions?" Kirsten asked.

Dad nodded. "You see, Kirsten, God has explained to us in his Word how we should act and which way we should go. But sometimes—like I did tonight—we ignore God's directions and go our own way, thinking we know more than he does."

"But we don't, do we, Daddy?"

"No," Dad answered. "So, when we know we're going a different direction from the way God has commanded, we need to turn around. We can ask God's forgiveness for going the wrong way and let him help us to go the right way."

Kirsten's mind seemed to be elsewhere. "That man must have thought we were crazy, Daddy," she said.

Dad laughed. "No," he answered, reaching out to tickle his daughter. "Just me."

TO DO: Tack a road map to your family bulletin board or refrigerator to remind everyone in the family to follow God's directions today.

TO PRAY: "Lord, you promise to direct our paths. We need to follow your directions, even when we think we already know where we're going."

10 The Likeness of God

THE BETTER WE KNOW GOD, THE EASIER IT IS TO KNOW RIGHT FROM WRONG.

Bible Reading of the Day: Read 2 Corinthians 3:17-18.
Verse of the Day: *"As the Spirit of the Lord works within us, we become more and more like him and reflect his glory even more"* *(2 Corinthians 3:18).*

Sandy and Barb compared the pictures they had bought at the amusement park.

"I don't think mine looks like me at all," Barb said. She and Sandy had paid twenty dollars apiece for the chalk portraits, and Barb was disappointed with the result.

"It looks *sort of* like you," Sandy offered.

"Well, yeah," Barb said, rolling her eyes, "it's got dark hair, brown eyes, and a big nose, just like I do. But it doesn't look like me."

"You're right," Sandy finally admitted. "But I can't figure out why not."

"Maybe the eyes are too far apart," Barb suggested.

"Or too close together."

"Anyway," Barb said, studying the picture, "it's just not right."

"Yeah," Sandy agreed. "It's just not right."

Suddenly, the two girls looked at each other and burst out laughing. They had both remembered the talk their youth pastor had given to the youth group two nights earlier. "When you're faced with a tough choice," he had said, "take a good look at what you're thinking about doing and evaluate your choice by comparing it to God. If it's like God, then it's right. If it's not like God, it's just not right."

The youth pastor had said that last phrase—"If it's not like God, it's just not right"—so many times during his talk that the youth group had started saying it with him.

"Wait a minute," Sandy said, placing a hand on Barb's arm. "This is sort of what Pastor Jim was talking about." She pointed at Barb's portrait. "To someone who doesn't know you, that might look like a pretty good drawing."

"Yeah," Barb said.

"But I *know* you, so I know this doesn't really look like you."

"Right," Barb said. "And like Pastor Jim was saying, the better we know God and the closer we get to him, the easier it is to really know what's right or wrong."

Sandy nodded. "Just like I know *that's* just not right," she said, pointing to Barb's portrait.

The two friends laughed. "Let's go get a piece of pizza," Barb said.

 TO DISCUSS: According to Pastor Jim's talk in the story above, how can we know if something we're thinking about doing is right or wrong? How can you get better at making right choices?

 TO PRAY: "Lord, teach us to reflect your image more and more through our actions and our words."

11 The Unchanging God

DON'T RELY ON YOUR OWN SHIFTING OPINIONS AND IDEAS; INSTEAD RELY ON THE UNCHANGING GOD.

Bible Reading of the Day: Read Daniel 4:34-35.
Verse of the Day: *"Jesus Christ is the same yesterday, today, and forever"* *(Hebrews 13:8)*.

Tamara stomped up the sidewalk, past her mother who knelt beside the flower garden, and burst through the front door of the house.

Mom left her gardening and followed Tamara into the house. "What's the matter with you, girl?" Mom asked, sitting on the couch next to her daughter.

Tamara, who had struggled to control her emotions all the way home from school, now burst into tears. "It's Miss Johnson!" Tamara wailed, referring to her teacher. She wiped the big tears from her face. "I asked her last week if Janine and I could work together on our schoolwork sometimes because of her learning disability, and she said yes." She sniffed. "We're supposed to do our schoolwork by ourselves, usually."

Mom nodded, encouraging Tamara to go on.

"Well, today, when I moved my desk next to Janine's to help her with her work, Miss Johnson yelled at me and told me to put my desk back where it belonged!"

"Did you explain—?" Mom started to ask, but Tamara nodded her head.

"Yes!" she said. "I tried to remind her about what she said last week, but she said she never said any such thing!"

Mom draped her arm around Tamara and pulled her close. "Don't you worry, honey," Mom said. "I'll give Miss Johnson a call. I'm sure we can work this out."

"It's just not right," Tamara said after a pause. "First she told me it was OK, then she acted like I'd broken a law or something."

Mom patted Tamara's shoulder. "I know," she said.

"It's just not fair," Tamara said.

Mom nodded. "Well, Miss Johnson might have misunderstood you, or you might have misunderstood her, or she might have forgotten," she said. She paused for a few moments before continuing. "That's why God didn't put us people in charge of saying what's right and what's wrong—because we're always changing our minds and forgetting things.

"But *God*—well, now, he's a different story. He doesn't forget. He doesn't change his mind or change the rules. That's why I want you to always rely on him and what he says is right or wrong, not on what you think or what your friends think or what anybody else thinks. OK?"

Tamara smiled and lifted her books off the couch. "OK, Mom," she said.

 TO DISCUSS: Think about a time when someone's change of mind hurt your plans or your feelings. How did that make you feel about that person's trustworthiness?

 TO PRAY: "Eternal God, we are often changing. Our attitudes change, our moods change, our beliefs change. But you are unchanging. Help us not to rely on our own shifting opinions and ideas for moral guidance but to look to you and to your Word."

12 Bad Company

DON'T TEAM UP WITH THOSE WHO ARE UNBELIEVERS.

Bible Reading of the Day: Read 2 Corinthians 6:14–7:1.

Verse of the Day: *"Do not be misled: 'Bad company corrupts good character'"* (1 Corinthians 15:33, NIV).

"Don't yell at me, Dad!" Mason said as he got into the car. He had called his dad to pick him up, giving him only the address on the phone. He knew his father would be upset when he arrived at a dark street corner in front of a liquor store in a bad neighborhood. He explained, as his father turned the car toward home, that he had been riding in a car with some friends. The other guys in the car had decided to try to buy some alcohol. When Mason heard what they were planning, he had first tried to talk them out of it, then insisted that they let him out of the car if they were going to go through with it.

"I didn't do anything wrong, Dad," he explained defensively. "I didn't want any part of what they were planning."

"You did the right thing by calling me, Son," Dad said. "I'm proud of you for that. But what were you doing with those boys in the first place?"

Mason shrugged. "They're just some friends."

"What are you doing with friends like that?" Dad asked.

"They're not close friends or anything," Mason answered. "We just hang together sometimes."

Dad drove for a few moments before speaking. "Do you remember," he said after awhile, "when we used to go to our Scout outings together? Remember all those three-legged races we ran together?"

Mason cast a questioning look at his father. "Sure," he said.

"That was fun, wasn't it?"

Mason shrugged, relieved that his dad had apparently changed the subject. "Sure."

Dad chuckled. "We sure fell down a lot." He exchanged glances with Mason, who smiled. "We never did get the knack of it. Probably because my legs were so long compared to yours." Dad wasn't looking at Mason anymore. He just kept talking. "We were kind of mismatched—like you and those friends. You made a good decision to not participate in what they had planned, Mason. You're a Christian; they're not. You're trying to listen to God; they're listening to the Tempter's voice."

"But shouldn't I—shouldn't I try to witness to them?" Mason asked.

"Sure," Dad said. "But don't run any three-legged races with them. They're not running in the same direction that you are."

TO DO: If weather permits, run a three-legged race as a family today (either against each other or to see which team—mom/dad, mom/daughter, dad/son—can record the best time) as a reminder not to "team up" with unwise and ungodly companions. Or light a candle during your prayer time today or tomorrow to remind you that light has no "fellowship" with darkness.

TO PRAY: "Lord, we need your help to remember not to have fellowship with darkness. Help us to be wise rather than foolish."

13 A Clear Conscience

A CLEAR CONSCIENCE IS A JOY TO THE SOUL.

Bible Reading of the Day: Read 2 Corinthians 7:2-7.
Verse of the Day: *"Cling tightly to your faith in Christ, and always keep your conscience clear"* (1 Timothy 1:19).

A whole week had passed, but Christine had not forgotten.

She had been playing at her friend Kayleen's house. Kayleen had just gotten a new play set with houses and cars and people. When it was time to go home, Christine had carefully slipped one of Kayleen's play pieces into her pocket.

Now, a week later, Christine felt bad about taking the play piece and wanted to take it back to Kayleen's house. But she didn't know where the piece was. She had checked her pockets, and it wasn't there. She had even picked up all the toys in her bedroom, and it wasn't there. She had tried to just forget about it, but she couldn't stop thinking about the piece and wishing she could return it.

Finally, what she had done bothered her so much that she ran, crying, to her mother.

"Mommy, I did something bad, and now I'm sorry, but I can't make it better!" she said.

Mom knelt on the floor beside Christine and asked her what she had done. Christine explained, admitting that she had taken Kayleen's play piece, and adding that she had lost it.

"I see," Mom said seriously. "What you did was wrong, Christine. Do you know that?"

Christine nodded.

"But I'm very happy that you told me," Mom said. "I have something to show you." Mom stood, took Christine's hand, and led her to the laundry room. She picked up the missing play piece from one of the laundry-room shelves. "I found this in the laundry, but I knew it wasn't yours. So I decided to keep it here until I found out who it belonged to."

Christine threw her arms around her mom's neck in a tight hug. "Thank you, Mommy!" she said. "Can I take it back to Kayleen now?"

Mom nodded. "Be sure you ask her forgiveness for taking it. You'll feel much better then."

"Oh, I already do, Mommy!" Christine said as she dashed out of the house with the play piece in her hand.

TO DISCUSS: Could we as a family have written Paul's words that say, "We have not done wrong to anyone"? Can we claim, "We have not led anyone astray"? Can we say, "We have not taken advantage of anyone"?

TO PRAY: "Lord, help us to keep our consciences clear."

14 The Right Response

TRUE REPENTANCE WILL INVOLVE AN ADMISSION OF GUILT, AN APOLOGY, AND AN EAGERNESS TO MAKE AMENDS.

Bible Reading of the Day: Read 2 Corinthians 7:8-11.

Verse of the Day: *"Now turn from your sins and turn to God, so you can be cleansed of your sins"* (Acts 3:19).

Alex couldn't stand to see the look in his mother's eyes.

He and his little sister, Annie, had been arguing. Alex had gotten angry and had punched Annie hard, knocking her down. Annie's cries had brought Mom running into the playroom, asking what had happened. Alex had admitted what he had done and had even said, "I'm sorry."

"She just makes me so mad," Alex said.

His mom picked up Annie and cradled the crying girl in her arms. She cast a woeful look at Alex as she carried Annie out of the room.

"I didn't hit her *that* hard," Alex explained lamely, following his mother and sister.

Mom still said nothing. Her eyes looked sad.

"What do you want me to say?" Alex asked. "I said I'm sorry."

"Just saying 'I'm sorry' isn't true repentance, Alex," Mom said.

Alex dropped his gaze. He and Mom had discussed this before. "OK," he said, though his voice still held a stubborn edge. "I was wrong."

Mom still said nothing.

Alex sighed. He touched his sister on the arm. "Annie," he said, his voice softer now. "I'm sorry. I was wrong. Will you forgive me?"

Annie's only reply was a quiet sniff. Mom lowered Annie to the floor.

Alex knelt in front of his little sister. He raised his eyes to his mom's face and thought he detected a slight expression of approval. "I mean it, Annie. I'm sorry. If you'll forgive me, I'll show you how sorry I am." He held out his hand.

Annie sniffed again and took Alex's hand. They walked together into the playroom.

 TO DISCUSS: Do you think it's enough to say "I'm sorry" to God or to someone else you've wronged? What is the right way to respond when you do something wrong? According to today's Bible reading, what other things (in addition to an apology) should godly sorrow produce in us?

TO PRAY: "Lord, when we mistreat someone, give us the courage to say, 'I'm sorry' and to make things right between ourselves and the person we've hurt."

15 Rules Make Sense

RULES MAKE SENSE—WHEN YOU UNDERSTAND THEM.

Bible Reading of the Day: Read Deuteronomy 11:1, 26-28.
Verse of the Day: *"Make me walk along the path of your commands, for that is where my happiness is found"* (Psalm 119:35).

Katie had never lived near a pond before.

As soon as Katie and her family had moved into their new house, Mom and Dad had talked to Katie and her brothers about Blueberry Pond. "Nobody is to go to the pond without a grown-up because it can be very dangerous there," Dad had said.

But one day, Katie's new best friend, Sarah, said, "Let's play at Blueberry Pond. I'll show you where the big old turtle lives!"

"I can't go to the pond without a grown-up," Katie said.

"That's dumb," Sarah said. "We won't go near the water at all. Are you scared?"

"No," Katie said. Suddenly her parents' rule seemed silly. "OK," she said slowly, "but don't ever tell my mom."

Sarah showed Katie the turtle's home. They skipped stones. Then they saw a car coming. Katie's parents got out of the car and called, "Katie, you come here!"

Katie leaped up and walked to her parents, her heart beating wildly. "I'm sorry," she said. "I'm sorry!"

Mom and Dad both frowned in disappointment at Katie, but after a moment they took Katie's hand and led her to the edge of the pond.

"Katie," Dad said, "do you know why Mom and I made the rule that you can't come to the pond without a grown-up?"

Katie thought for a moment. "Because you don't think I'm big enough?"

"No," Dad answered. "We made the rule to protect you."

"You did?"

Dad nodded. "Your mother and I love you very much, and the rules we make are for your own good. You see, when I was about your age, I disobeyed my parents and went to a pond by myself. I slipped on the muddy bank and fell in. The pond was very deep, and I didn't know how to swim. I thought I was going to drown."

Katie saw Dad's lip quiver.

"Katie," Mom said, "disobeying is serious. It almost caused your dad to drown when he was a little boy. We never want that to happen to you."

"Me, neither," Katie said, her eyes welling with tears. "I'm sorry I disobeyed. Rules are good, aren't they, Daddy?"

Mom and Dad hugged Katie tightly. "Yes, they are," Dad answered. "Especially when they're made by someone who loves you very much."

TO DISCUSS: Why wasn't Katie allowed to go to the pond without a grown-up? God makes rules to protect his children too. What is one of God's rules that you remember? How do God's rules keep us safe?

TO PRAY: "Lord, make us walk along the path of your commands, for that is where our happiness is found."

16 True and Not True

EVERY MAN BELIEVES THAT TRUTH EXISTS, OR HE WOULD NOT ASK A QUESTION OR MAKE A STATEMENT.

Bible Reading of the Day: Read Psalm 119:30–32.
Verse of the Day: *"I have chosen the way of truth; I have set my heart on your laws" (Psalm 119:30, NIV).*

"Papa," Benjamin said, "let's play the 'True and Untrue' game!"

"Oh, I'm too tired," teased his father. Benjamin had come to the office with his father that morning and was tired of coloring all by himself.

"Oh, please, Papa," the boy begged. "Please?"

"What's the 'True and Untrue' game?" asked Dale, one of Papa's coworkers.

"It's a little game we've played with Benjamin for some time now, to help him understand what the terms 'true' and 'untrue' mean."

Papa hoisted little Benjamin onto his lap to begin the game. He cleared his throat, then said, "Dale's hair is purple."

"Untrue!" Benjamin shouted, pointing at Dale's hair, which was red.

"Peanut butter comes from chickens!"

"Untrue!"

"Dogs go 'woof!'"

"True!"

"This is my spleen," Dad said, touching his chin.

"Untrue!"

"You're a pretty smart kid," Dad said, laughing.

"True!" Benjamin announced proudly.

"I can't hear you!"

"Untrue!" Benjamin said, though he spoke louder than before.

"I love you!"

"True!"

"God loves you!"

"True!"

The game ended then as Dad poked Benjamin in his most ticklish spot and lifted him off his lap and onto the floor. Dale, who had watched the game, smiling the whole time, watched Benjamin return happily to his coloring.

"Where'd you come up with that game?" he asked Benjamin's father.

Papa shrugged. "Oh, I don't know. We've just always played it."

Dale grunted. "Well, I know plenty of adults who could benefit from a few rounds of 'True and Untrue.'"

Papa smiled and nodded. "I do, too, Dale," he said. "I do, too."

 TO DO: Play your own version of the "True and Untrue" game. What facts or concepts are always "true" or "untrue"?

 TO PRAY: "Lord, the 'Verse of the Day' is our prayer: 'We have chosen the way of truth; we have set our hearts on your laws.'"

17 Erin's Sweet Heart

GREED, OR STINGINESS, IS NOT JUST UNATTRACTIVE—IT'S WRONG.

Bible Reading of the Day: Read Ecclesiastes 5:10-14.
Verse of the Day: *"It is more blessed to give than to receive"*
(Acts 20:35, NIV).

Andrew excitedly watched his grandparents' car roll up the driveway. Grandma and Grandpa's visits were always fun. As soon as the car came to a stop, he ran to the driveway, opened Grandma's car door, and crawled onto her lap to give her a big hug.

When they were all inside the house, Grandma pulled two candy bars out of her purse. She gave one to Andrew and the other to his sister, Erin. "You can eat the candy now if you want," she said.

Andrew shook his head. "I'm gonna save mine for later," he announced. Erin nodded her agreement.

Later that night, the family sat around the kitchen table talking. Erin disappeared for a moment, then appeared with her candy bar. She carefully broke the candy into six equal parts. Then she placed a piece of candy beside each person at the table.

"That's so nice of you to share your candy with us," Grandma said. She picked up the piece Erin had set beside her and handed it back to Erin. "But I'm a diabetic, sweetheart, so I can't have any candy."

"I'll take it!" Andrew said, and, in an instant, he took the candy from his grandma's hand and popped it into his mouth. His parents' looks of disapproval didn't seem to bother him as he chewed a mouthful of candy.

Later that evening, Andrew went to his room, where he had stashed his candy bar under his pillow. He reached under the pillow, but the candy bar was gone! He searched around the bed, and then all around the room but couldn't find his precious candy. Finally, he ran out of the room and was just about to call for his mother when he saw Ashes, the family dog. Tiny scraps of candy wrapper lay all around the satisfied dog, who was licking her mouth. She had just eaten Andrew's candy bar, which he had been saving to eat all by himself!

Andrew reported the dog's misbehavior to his parents, but they simply shook their heads and instructed him to clean up the mess Ashes had made.

The next day, Mom and Grandma came home from shopping with a small brown bag, which Grandma handed to Erin. Erin looked in the bag, and her eyes opened wide in amazement.

"A whole bag of candy!" Erin said. "For me?"

Grandma nodded. "You may do anything you want with it."

Erin hugged her grandmother and ran off to share the bag with her brother.

 TO DISCUSS: Why do you think Grandma gave Erin a bag of candy? Why do you think Erin wanted to share?

 TO PRAY: "Lord, help us to be generous. Show us ways to share what we have with others."

18 Share and Share Alike

MAKING EXCUSES MEANS YOU WANT TO DO WHAT YOU WANT INSTEAD OF DOING WHAT GOD TOLD YOU TO DO.

Bible Reading of the Day: Read 1 Timothy 6:17–19.
Verse of the Day: *"Give generously to those in need, always being ready to share with others whatever God has given [you]"* (1 Timothy 6:18).

Miguel loved going to the carnival. He loved all the carnival sounds, smells, and tastes.

He jingled the coins in his pocket. A boy approached, carrying a long plastic tube that he whirled to make a high-pitched noise. Miguel turned to his friend, Victor, who walked along the fairway beside him.

"I am going to get one of those," he told Victor.

"I want one, too" Victor said.

"How much money do you have?"

Victor stopped walking and counted his coins. He was just a few cents short of the amount needed. He looked disappointed.

Miguel started walking faster, trying to ignore Victor's sad expression. *It's my money,* he told himself. *I can spend it any way I want. Besides, it's not my fault that I have enough but Victor doesn't.*

The two boys caught up to the man with the tubes and waited while he made change for another customer. Miguel noticed that the tubes were available in two sizes: the giant size that the other boy had, and a smaller size, which cost less. He knew he and Victor had enough money together to buy two small tubes, but he wanted one of the giant ones for himself. *I will share my toy with him,* he told himself. *I will let him play with it sometimes.*

But suddenly Miguel remembered what his father once told him. "Whenever you find yourself trying to convince yourself why it's OK to do something, you need to stop and listen to what you're saying. You're probably just making excuses to do what you want instead of doing what God has already told you to do."

Miguel sighed. He didn't want to share with Victor. But he knew that it would be better to share his money with his friend, so they could each buy a tube, than it would be to buy what he wanted.

"Can I help you?" the man with the tubes said to Miguel.

"Yes, sir," Miguel said. He smiled at Victor. "We'll take two . . . of the small ones."

Victor's mouth dropped open and he dug into his pocket for his money. Miguel suddenly knew that the expression on Victor's face was worth more than all the plastic tubes in the world.

 TO DO: Make it a family project to practice generosity by giving *something* away every day this week. For example, you can give away clothes, toys, loose coins, a smile, and a kind word.

 TO PRAY: "Lord, when we're tempted to be selfish, remind us of how you generously gave yourself for us."

19 A Tiny Request

GOD COMMANDS US TO BE GENEROUS.

Bible Reading of the Day: Read Deuteronomy 15:10-11.
Verse of the Day: *"Give to the one who asks you, and do not turn away from the one who wants to borrow from you" (Matthew 5:42, NIV).*

"Jim-mee!" Kara's childish voice broke the syllables of her stepbrother Jimmy's name into two drawn-out sounds. "Jim-mee! Me too! P'ease?" She held out her tiny palm.

Jimmy sat on a chair by the window, watching the city traffic outside their home. He held an unopened bag of chewy candies, and Kara had spied the familiar wrapper.

"Jim-mee! Me too! P'ease?" she repeated.

"No, Kara," Jimmy answered. "I'm saving these for later."

Kara thrust her lip forward in a pout, and she turned and walked away. Jimmy watched her leave, then whispered to himself as he put the bag of candy into his shirt pocket, "I'll wait until I can eat them all myself."

"Hello, Son," Jimmy's dad said at that moment, slapping his son on the back.

"I . . . I didn't know you were home, Dad," Jimmy said.

Dad nodded. "Got home a few minutes ago," he said. "Came in the back so I could leave my muddy shoes on the porch." Dad was a construction worker.

Jimmy wore a worried look but said nothing about his encounter with Kara, hoping his dad hadn't overheard anything. When Dad pulled up a chair and sat down facing Jimmy, he knew his hopes were empty.

Dad said, "You love Kara, and want her to learn the right things, don't you?"

"Yeah."

"I do, too," Dad said. "And one of the things I want her to learn is to be generous toward other people. You want to know why I want her to learn that?"

Jimmy nodded.

"Because God commands us to be generous, Jimmy. Jesus said, 'Give to the one who asks you,' and I want your little sister to be the kind of person who obeys God. Don't you?"

Jimmy nodded again.

"So," Dad said, standing up and putting his chair back in place, "anything you can do to help Kara learn to obey God and be generous—well, I'd just really appreciate that, any chance you get."

"Sure, Dad," Jimmy said.

Dad slapped Jimmy firmly on the back again and walked away, whistling as he left. Jimmy sat for a few moments, thinking. Finally, he jumped up and called for his little sister. "Kara!" he called. "I've got something for you!"

 TO DISCUSS: Do you think Jimmy was wrong to want to keep the candy for himself? Why or why not? Have there been times when you were tempted not to share with someone? What did you do?

 TO PRAY: "Lord, help us to give glory to you by our generosity."

20 Flower Power

GOD COMMANDS GENEROSITY BECAUSE HE VALUES GENEROSITY.

Bible Reading of the Day: Read Luke 21:1-4.

Verse of the Day: *"God loves the person who gives cheerfully. And God will generously provide all you need. Then you will always have everything you need and plenty left over to share with others"* (2 Corinthians 9:7-8).

Laura was visiting the nursing home where her grandmother lived. One of the patients suddenly complimented Laura on the fresh flower pinned to her dress.

"It's beautiful," the woman said.

"Well, then . . ." (Laura paused to pull the pin out of her dress) "I want you to have it!" She started to pin the flower on the woman's dress. The woman started to protest, but Laura insisted and finally won the friendly argument. As Laura turned toward her grandmother's room, the old woman sat, smiling, and stroking the flower as if it were made of gold.

"That's the third time I've seen you do that," said one of the nurses, who had come up behind Laura as she left the old woman. "What's going on?"

Laura shrugged and looked embarrassed. "Oh, it's no big deal. I wore a corsage that my dad gave me when I came to visit Grandma on Easter, and Grandma's friends couldn't stop talking about how beautiful it was. So I gave it to one of them. I wear a flower every time I come, now, 'cause it's so much fun to see somebody's face when I give it away, you know."

"But you have to pay for those flowers, right?" the nurse said.

"Well, yeah, but it's only a few dollars at the most, and I don't come every day." The nurse shook her head in amazement. "You're a saint," she said.

Laura rolled her eyes. "My grandma's the saint, not me. She taught me that giving things to other people can be a lot of fun. She says that when we give to others, we please at least three people."

"Three people?" the nurse echoed.

Laura nodded and raised one finger in the air. "We please the person we give to," she said, then raised a second finger. "And we please ourselves too. I think I get more fun out of giving those silly flowers away than any of the people I give them to."

"You said three people," the nurse reminded her.

"Oh yeah," Laura said. She raised a third finger in the air. "The third person we please is God. He likes it when we're generous to each other, because he really likes generosity. Grandma says it's something he values, you know, like we value gold."

"Or flowers," the nurse said.

 TO DISCUSS: God commands us to be generous because he values generosity. Do *you* value generosity? If so, how do you show that you value generosity? How *can* you show that you value generosity?

 TO PRAY: "God, when we don't have any material possessions to give away, help us to be generous with our time, our talents, and our affection for others."

21 Our Generous God

GOD VALUES GENEROSITY BECAUSE HE IS A GIVING, GRACIOUS GOD.

Bible Reading of the Day: Read Psalm 65:1, 9-13.
Verse of the Day: *"Freely you have received, freely give"*
(Matthew 10:8, NIV).

Jenny held hands with her friend, Kris, and Kris's mom and bowed her head. She felt odd as she listened to Kris's dad pray, thanking God for the food on the table and for many other things as well.

When Kris's dad said "Amen" and everyone raised his or her head, Jenny smiled nervously. "We don't do that at my house," she said.

"We always pray, especially before meals," Kris said. "Sometimes Dad prays for hours!"

"Really?" Jenny asked seriously.

Kris and her parents laughed. "No," Kris said. "It just seems like it."

Jenny accepted a bowl of vegetables that Kris's mom passed to her. She cleared her throat. "Why do you do it?"

Kris and her parents looked at Jenny with surprised expressions for a moment before Dad answered.

"We do it to give thanks to God for the food and everything he's given us," he said.

"After all," Mom added, "God is so generous with his blessings."

"What do you mean?" Jenny asked. "I mean," she added sheepishly, "you paid for all this food, right?"

Dad nodded. "Yes, but God gave me the ability to work, and I believe he gave me the job I have." He lifted a glass of water to his mouth and took a sip. "As a matter of fact," he said thoughtfully, "his generosity is an important part of who he is. He's not just generous sometimes, like when he feels like it. He is a gracious God, who is always giving."

"And he gives us lots of things we could never earn," Mom said. "Like the sunrise, the rain, the birds who sing outside our kitchen window, our families, . . . our friends."

Kris nudged Jenny with her elbow. "You never thought of yourself as a gift from God, did you?"

Jenny smiled. "No," she answered. "I never did. I'll try to remember that."

 TO DO: Think about the gifts you have freely received. Make a list that you can add to whenever you think of something. Keep the list somewhere handy where everyone can add to it.

 TO PRAY: "God, you are a gracious and generous God. You give us so much, we could never finish thanking you."

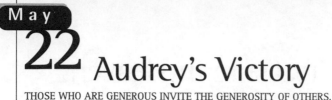

22 Audrey's Victory

THOSE WHO ARE GENEROUS INVITE THE GENEROSITY OF OTHERS.

Bible Reading of the Day: Read Psalm 112:1-5.
Verse of the Day: *"The generous prosper and are satisfied; those who refresh others will themselves be refreshed" (Proverbs 11:25).*

Lynn and Shawna rode with their friend Audrey to the baseball diamond. Audrey had volunteered to take her little brother to his baseball game, and her friends had volunteered to go along with her.

They watched the game for a few innings, then strolled down to the ice-cream stand a couple of blocks away. Each girl placed her order, and Audrey stepped to the window to pay.

"You're not paying for all that," Shawna protested.

"Sure I am," Audrey said. "You guys are keeping me company during Jason's game."

"But you paid for me the last time we went out together," Shawna said.

"No, I didn't," Audrey said. "Remember, you bought me that soft pretzel at the skating rink?"

"Yeah, but you bought me a soda at school yesterday, remember?"

"You two are ridiculous!" Lynn shouted. "I can't believe you're arguing about who gets to pay!"

"You're right, Lynn," Audrey said. She turned to Shawna. "See how ridiculous you're being?"

"Oh, no, you don't!" Shawna said. Her face got serious. "Come on, Audrey, I really want to pay. I feel like you're always paying for me."

"You guys are embarrassing!" Lynn shouted in frustration.

"I've got an idea," Shawna said. "Let's flip a coin to see who pays."

"OK," Audrey said. "To make it fair, let's have Lynn flip the coin." She pointed to a section of pavement a few feet away from the service window. "You call it while it's in the air, Shawna."

Shawna stepped next to Lynn, who flipped a nickel in the air. Shawna called "heads," and watched the coin hit the pavement and roll around until it settled a few moments later. It was "heads."

"Hah!" Shawna shouted in victory. "I pay!" She turned toward the window, where Audrey stood smiling. She held her friends' ice-cream cones in her hands.

"I already paid," she announced. "While you two were watching the coin."

Shawna shouted in good-natured frustration.

Lynn just shook her head. "I have the weirdest friends," she said.

 TO DISCUSS: Do you know kids who, like Audrey or Shawna, just love to be generous to their friends? Do you think they are usually rewarded or punished for their generosity?

 TO PRAY: "God, whenever we're tempted to act like generosity is a contest, or a game of 'Can you top this?', please keep us humble."

23 Treasure in Heaven

THOSE WHO ARE GENEROUS STORE UP TREASURES IN HEAVEN.

Bible Reading of the Day: Read Luke 12:27-34.

Verse of the Day: *"Your Father already knows your needs. He will give you all you need from day to day if you make the Kingdom of God your primary concern" (Luke 12:30-31).*

Mark and Marcy walked toward the store, hand in hand with their mother. Each held a shiny quarter Mom had given them as they got out of the car.

"While I'm doing my shopping," Mom told the children, "you may look around and decide what you want to buy with your money."

They arrived at the curb in front of the store. An elderly woman sat beside the door, holding a slotted can with which she accepted donations for a local charity.

Mark smiled as he started to walk past the woman. Then he turned back toward the woman and slipped his quarter into the can. She smiled warmly, and thanked him.

Marcy watched Mark with wide eyes but said nothing until she saw a row of vending machines as they entered the store. Tearing free of her mom's hand, she dashed to the machines and, after a few moments of excited inspection, dropped her quarter into one of the machines. Out came a handful of tiny multicolored candies, which Marcy ate happily as she walked the aisles of the store with her mother.

Marcy pushed the shopping cart as they left the store. The woman was still in her chair by the door, collecting donations as people passed by. She smiled at Mark.

"Thank you again, young man," the woman said. "God bless you."

Mark returned her smile and seemed to glow as he walked toward the car.

Marcy could see the satisfaction on her brother's face. "That's not fair," she said.

"What's not fair?" Mom asked.

"I should have given my money to the lady," she answered.

"Why didn't you?"

Marcy thought for a moment. "Because," she said. "Because I wanted candy. But my candy's all gone now."

"But Mark spent his money on something that lasts longer than candy," Mom said.

"He did?" Marcy asked.

"I did?" Mark asked.

Mom nodded. "Mark's *still* enjoying that quarter he gave away, isn't he?" she said to Marcy. "And even if he forgets all about it someday, God will remember."

Marcy appeared to be thinking hard. Suddenly her face brightened. "Mommy, can we come back here sometime?" Mom nodded and smiled. She knew what Marcy was planning.

TO DO: Give each member of the family a quarter (or a dollar) and instruct everyone to use that quarter to find a new way to be generous to someone tomorrow.

TO PRAY: "Lord, help us to store up treasure in heaven, rather than here on earth."

24 A Lesson in Priorities

THOSE WHO ARE GENEROUS ENJOY THE FRUIT OF PROPER PRIORITIES.

Bible Reading of the Day: Read Luke 12:13-15.
Verse of the Day: *"Real life is not measured by how much we own"*
(Luke 12:15).

"Wow!" Dad said to Nan. "That's some house your friend lives in!" He and Nan had just dropped off one of Nan's friends after a school event.

"Yeah, I guess so," Nan answered.

"You guess so? That house must have more rooms than Buckingham Palace. What do your friend's parents do?" Dad asked.

Nan shrugged. "Her dad's like some big important lawyer or something," she said.

"Wouldn't you like to live in a place like that?" Dad said, more to himself than to Nan. He took one more longing look at the impressive house as it faded out of sight.

"No!" Nan said, emphatically.

"What?" Dad asked. He hadn't even been sure Nan was listening.

"I said no, I wouldn't want to live in a place like that."

"Why not?" Dad asked, suddenly attentive.

"Because, Dad, there are lots of things more important than impressive jobs and fancy houses and lots of money."

Nan stopped speaking, but Dad said nothing. He suspected that Nan wasn't finished. He was right.

"Most days," Nan continued, referring to her friend, "Rachel doesn't even see her father. He's too busy making money. She says he's always talking about how she'll have it made when he dies; she'll never have to worry about a thing. But she just wishes her dad would quit trying to make so much money and spend time with her instead."

Nan was crying now. "You know what I think? I think Rachel's father is so wrapped up in making a lot of money that he can't see what's really important. I think if he would just stop trying to have the biggest house or the fastest car in the world, he might realize he's got a really cool daughter who just wants to know her daddy loves her."

Nan stopped talking, then, and they drove in silence for a while. It was Dad who finally broke the silence.

"You know what *I* think?" he said. "I think you've got to be the best friend—and the best daughter—in the whole world."

Nan wiped her tears with the back of her hand and leaned over to kiss her father. "I love you, Daddy," she said.

 TO DISCUSS: What do you think Jesus meant when he said, "Real life is not measured by how much we own" (Luke 12:15)? Be as specific as you can.

 TO PRAY: "Lord, we need help in keeping our priorities straight. Help us to remember that real life isn't measured by how much we own."

25 Father Knows Best

GOD IS SMARTER THAN WE ARE. THAT'S WHY WE'RE SMART WHEN WE DO WHAT HE COMMANDS.

Bible Reading of the Day: Read Isaiah 40:28-31.
Verse of the Day: *"Have you never heard or understood? Don't you know that the Lord is the everlasting God, the Creator of all the earth? He never grows faint or weary. No one can measure the depths of his understanding"* (Isaiah 40:28).

Marcy held her math textbook in her hand as she approached her dad. "Daddy, can you please help me with my math homework?" she asked.

Dad said, "Let's find Mom. She's better at math than I am."

Dad and Marcy showed Mom the math problems. "Oh, I see," she said, after a quick glance at the book. "This shouldn't be too hard for you, Marcy. Didn't your teacher explain this in class?"

Marcy shook her head sheepishly. "Beeler and I sort of missed that part," she explained, referring to her best friend, Nancy Beeler. "We got sent to the office for copying each other's homework."

"You what?!" Mom and Dad said in unison.

Marcy raised her hands defensively. "We couldn't finish it in time," she explained. "So I told her to do the first twenty problems and I did the last twenty problems. Then we just shared our answers with each other. I figured it wouldn't be so wrong, just this once, since we *meant* to do the homework."

Mom and Dad stared at Marcy for a few moments before Mom spoke. "Don't you think you went to the wrong person?"

Marcy looked confused for a moment. "What, you mean Daddy? That's why he said we should find you, 'cause you're better at math than he is."

"That's not what I mean. I'm talking about when you 'decided' it wouldn't be so wrong to cheat just this once," Mom said.

"Oh," Marcy said. She blushed. "I see what you mean. I tried to say it would be OK just this once, instead of . . . instead of remembering that only God gets to decide what's right or wrong."

"Whenever you do that, sweetie, you're bound to do the wrong thing," Mom said.

"Yeah," Marcy said. "If I were doing the right thing, I wouldn't have tried to make my own decision, huh?"

Mom smiled and nodded. Dad placed a hand on Marcy's shoulder. "God's smarter than any of us, Marcy. That's why we need to do what he says."

"Yeah, just like Mom's better than you at math, right, Dad?"

"Yeah," Dad answered. "Just like that."

TO DISCUSS: Who do you go to when you need help? Why do you go to that person? When do you seek God's help?

TO PRAY: "Lord, help us to remember to come to you when we need help in making a decision."

26 The Image of God

HUMAN LIFE IS GOOD AND PRECIOUS, BECAUSE EVERY HUMAN BEING WAS CREATED IN THE IMAGE OF GOD.

Bible Reading of the Day: Read Genesis 1:26-31.

Verse of the Day: *"God created man in his own image, in the image of God he created him; male and female he created them"* (Genesis 1:27, NIV).

"How did you save up sixty dollars?" Don asked his friend Patrick.

Patrick shrugged. "Mowing lawns and stuff," he said.

The two boys walked side by side down the aisles of the My-T-Mart until they reached the electronics section. "What video game are you going to buy?" Don asked. He was almost as excited as Patrick.

"I don't know." He pointed to a package. "I'm thinking of that one."

Don wrinkled his nose. "You've already got a basketball game." He pointed to another game. "Why don't you get *Slaughterhouse?*"

"Nah," Patrick answered. He turned and called to the store clerk, who unlocked the cabinet, allowing the boys to pull some of the games from the shelf to look at.

"Why not?" Don pressed. "It's the coolest game!"

"My parents won't let me," Patrick said. "They say it's too violent."

"That's why it's cool!" Don gushed. "Your parents are dumb."

Patrick wasn't happy that he wasn't allowed to buy *Slaughterhouse,* but he didn't like Don calling his parents dumb. "They're not dumb; they just don't want me playing a game like that."

"What's wrong with it?"

Patrick found himself in the unusual position of defending his parents for a decision he didn't like. He put the basketball cartridge back on the shelf and faced his friend. "How many people do you have to kill in *Slaughterhouse* to beat the game?"

Don wrinkled his nose again. "I don't know," he said. "A lot. What's the point?"

"My parents don't want me to think that killing people is a game," Patrick said.

"That's dumb," replied Don. "*Slaughterhouse* isn't gonna make you into some serial killer."

"That's not the point," Patrick answered. "Look, maybe it's not a big deal, but my parents are just trying to teach me to respect life, especially human life, because God made all of us in his image. And *Slaughterhouse* sure won't help me remember that, will it?"

Don started waving his hands back and forth in a gesture of surrender. "All right," he said, "I give up! Buy any game you want; I don't care."

Patrick smiled at his friend. *He's not so bad,* he thought. After all, Don had helped him realize—in a backward sort of way—how wise his parents could be.

 TO DISCUSS: What makes human life valuable to God? to others? to you? Do you think you can ever become less valuable? Why or why not? How can you show your respect for human life?

 TO PRAY: "Lord, teach us to have the same respect for human life that you have."

27 Marvelous Workmanship

HUMAN LIFE IS PRECIOUS TO GOD AT EVERY STAGE.

Bible Reading of the Day: Read Psalm 139:13-16.

Verse of the Day: *"Thank you for making me so wonderfully complex! Your workmanship is marvelous—and how well I know it"* (Psalm 139:14).

Eric's mother placed his hand on her large, round belly. She held it there. They stood silent and still. After a few moments, Mom and Eric jumped slightly at the same time.

"There!" Mom said. "Did you feel that?"

Eric stared at his mom's belly with wide eyes. When he spoke, it was in a whisper. "There's a baby in there," he said, lisping slightly.

Mom smiled broadly. She patted the couch cushion beside her, and Eric climbed onto the couch and snuggled up close to his mother.

"That baby is your little brother or sister," Mom explained. "Before long, you'll be able to hold the baby in your arms and help Mommy take care of him . . . or her."

"Is the baby sleeping now?" Eric asked.

Mom cocked her head to the side. "I don't know. He sleeps and wakes up just like you do. But I don't know if he's asleep or awake right now. God does, though."

Eric placed his hand softly on his mom's belly and rubbed it. "Does God know the baby's name?"

Mom stretched her arm around her first child. "Yes," she answered. "God's known your little brother or sister for the last eight months now, since even before his or her tiny heart started beating." She patted her belly. "God knew eight months ago whether you would have a brother or sister. He knew what color hair and eyes the baby would have, and whether he would be tall or short."

"Did God know me when I was in your belly?" Eric asked.

Mom sighed. She knew Eric could ask question after question. "Yes, he did. He knew you before you were born and took care of you and helped you to grow the whole time you were inside Mommy's belly."

"God loves me, doesn't he, Mommy?" Eric asked.

Mom's eyes filled with tears. "Yes," she answered. "He has always loved you. You were precious to him even before Mommy knew God had formed you in her belly."

Eric still rubbed his mom's belly. Her answer seemed to satisfy all his questions, and he and Mom sat side by side on the couch, silent, while the baby who had heard the murmur of their voices fell asleep inside her mother's womb.

TO DO: Take turns reading Psalm 139:13-16 to each other, substituting *God* and *he* for pronouns referring to God, and *you* or a name for pronouns referring to the person. For example: "God made all the delicate, inner parts of your body and knit you together in your mother's womb," or "God made all the delicate inner parts of Ramona's body." Discuss how you felt as you heard those words applied to you.

TO PRAY: "Lord, help us remember that our lives have been precious to you since the moment we were formed."

28 Police Story

GOD COMMANDS US TO PRESERVE LIFE.

Bible Reading of the Day: Read Genesis 9:1, 5-6.
Verse of the Day: *"To kill a person is to kill a living being made in God's image" (Genesis 9:6).*

Dad entered through the back door by the garage. Mom and Candi sat at the kitchen table eating breakfast together.

"You're home!" Mom said. She stood and helped Dad take off his police jacket, which bore large yellow letters on the back spelling *CHAPLAIN.* "Is everything OK?"

Dad volunteered as a chaplain to the city's police department and spent several nights a month riding in a cruiser with a police officer. Usually he got home in the middle of the night, but this night he was much later than usual. He slumped onto one of the kitchen chairs and rubbed his face with both hands. He looked very tired and sad. "There was a shooting last night," he said.

"Oh no," Mom said, sitting down beside Dad and rubbing his shoulder with one hand.

"What happened, Daddy?" Candi asked.

Dad shook his head slowly, then held out his hands to his daughter, who slid out of her chair and onto his lap. "Two boys got into an argument, Candi. One had a gun, and now the other one's dead."

"Did you know the boys, Daddy?"

"No, I didn't know them," he answered.

"Then why are *you* sad?" Candi asked.

Dad's lip started to quiver. He was crying.

Mom tried to answer Candi's question. "Daddy's sad because . . . because he doesn't like for anyone to die. None of us do." She thrust her hands under Candi's arms, lifted her off Dad's lap, and set her feet down on the kitchen floor. "Life is so precious, Candi; it's a gift from God. And someone who takes another person's life is destroying the most beautiful part of God's creation. That's why God commanded us not to kill, because every human being is made in the image of God."

Candi glanced shyly at her father, concern written on her face. "I wouldn't like it if somebody hurt something I made," she said solemnly.

Mom's eyes filled with tears. "That's right," she said, hugging her daughter. "And especially not if it was the most precious, priceless thing you'd ever created."

Mom whispered in her daughter's ear, and Candi tiptoed off to get ready for school. Then Mom knelt on the kitchen floor in front of her husband and wrapped her arms around him. And they held each other in the early morning quiet of the kitchen.

TO DISCUSS: Today's reading calls human life "the most beautiful part of God's creation." Do you think that's true? If so, why? Why does God command us to preserve life? (Hint: Genesis 9:6 gives a good clue.)

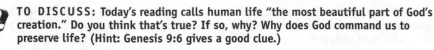

TO PRAY: "God, you've shown us that life is a precious gift. Help us to preserve and protect our own lives and those of others."

29 Source of Life

GOD VALUES LIFE BECAUSE HE IS THE SOURCE OF LIFE.

Bible Reading of the Day: Read Genesis 2:4-7.
Verse of the Day: *"The God who made the world . . . gives all men life and breath and everything else"* (Acts 17:24-25, NIV).

Ty helped his mom put the finishing touches on the scarecrow they had made for their vegetable garden. The scarecrow, formed by stuffing his dad's jeans and shirt with straw and hanging them on two poles tied into the shape of a *T,* stood guard in the middle of the garden to keep birds and other pests away from their carrots, lettuce, and other vegetables. They had used a deflated soccer ball stuffed inside a potato sack for the head. Ty himself had topped it off by tying an old felt hat to their creation.

Ty stood back to admire their work. "It looks pretty good, doesn't it, Mom?"

Mom brushed her hair out of her face and let out a weary sigh. "It sure does," she said.

"Now I know what God must have felt like when he made Adam and Eve," Ty said proudly.

Mom's head snapped in Ty's direction. "Oh, no, Ty," she said. "Don't say that."

Ty tossed a quizzical look at Mom. "Why not?" he said.

Mom wiped her forehead with a work-gloved hand. "Think about what you just said," she suggested. "I think you know the answer."

"Don't take things so seriously, Mom," he said.

"Well, do you really think you know how God felt when he made Adam and Eve?"

"No," Ty answered. "I guess not."

"Why not?" Mom asked.

"Well, 'cause that's just a scarecrow," he said. "It's not alive."

Mom nodded. "That's right. When God made the first man, he breathed the breath of life into him."

"I see what you mean," Ty said. "Plus, God made us in his own image, right?"

"Right. He gave more of himself to us humans than he did to anything else he created. That's why he values human life so much, Ty, because he is the source of the life that's in every one of us."

"God commands us to respect life because he values human life himself," said Ty. "And the reason he values human life so much is because he's the living God who gives life to us all."

"Wow," Mom said, clearly impressed with her son. She draped an arm across his shoulders and steered him back toward the house. "I think that deserves a tall glass of lemonade."

 TO DO: Make plans to show how much you value human life. You can do this in a big way, such as volunteering at a homeless shelter, or in a small way, such as sharing a kind word with someone.

 TO PRAY: "God, we owe you our very life. Help us to be grateful for life. Help us to value our life and the lives of others. Help us to respect life and to defend it."

30 Bushels of Love

RESPECTING LIFE ENRICHES LIFE.

Bible Reading of the Day: Read Matthew 10:29-31.
Verse of the Day: *"Don't be afraid; you are more valuable to him than a whole flock of sparrows" (Matthew 10:31).*

"I love you, a bushel and a peck," Sara sang softly as she brushed her grandmother's hair, "a bushel and a peck and a hug around the neck."

Sara stood behind Grandma's chair, gently drawing the brush through the gray tangles. "Do you remember singing that song to me, Grandma?" Sara asked. Grandma didn't answer. Grandma hadn't spoken to Sara in months. Sara didn't even know if her grandmother recognized her anymore.

"You used to sing that song to me all the time," Sara told Grandma. "And now I get to sing it to you."

"I love to brush your hair, Grandma," Sara said. "I remember you telling me when I was just a little girl, that God knew just how many hairs were on my head, and then you would pretend to count them. Do you remember that?"

Grandma sat stolidly, staring at the wall of her bedroom.

"One, two, three," Sara counted, her eyes filling with tears as she pretended to count the hairs on Grandma's head. "Four, five, six . . ."

Sara opened her eyes and suddenly realized that she had been dreaming. She sat in Grandma's bedroom, in the chair where Grandma had sat so many times while Sara had brushed her hair and sung to her and talked to her.

Grandma had come to live with Sara's family when she had no longer been able to take care of herself. Sara, her brother, and her parents knew that having Grandma live with them would turn their lives upside down. Everyone in the family took turns taking care of Grandma, staying home with her, paying attention to her.

Grandma had died three weeks earlier, and Sara missed her and still dreamed of her. But Sara's dreams were happy dreams, dreams that left her feeling warm and grateful and happy inside. The last couple of years of Grandma's life had been hard for her family, but they had been worth it for Sara, and she hoped she would remember those years for the rest of her life. Her eyes filled with tears.

"I love you, a bushel and a peck," she sang, "a bushel and a peck and a hug around the neck."

 TO DISCUSS: Remembering that other people's lives are unspeakably precious helps you remember that your own life is precious. What can you do today as a family to show how much you value human life?

TO PRAY: "Lord, we know that you love us more than a bushel and a peck. Help us to value our lives and those of others."

Crosses in a Row

ONE WAY TO RESPECT LIFE IS TO HONOR THOSE WHO HAVE SACRIFICED THEIR LIVES FOR OTHERS.

Bible Reading of the Day: Read John 15:9-13.
Verse of the Day: *"Greater love has no one than this, that he lay down his life for his friends" (John 15:13, NIV).*

Vijay gazed out of the car window at row after row of simple white crosses that dotted the green hillside. He watched wordlessly as his parents pulled the car to the side of the cemetery road. Father pushed a button, and the car trunk popped open. They got out and walked to the back of the car, where Vijay's parents removed a few garden tools and three small flowers.

Each member of the family took a garden trowel. Following his father's instructions, Vijay knelt at a simple grave and then, imitating his parents' movements, dug in the dirt at the foot of the grave marker. Vijay's parents planted their flowers in the dirt and then helped him to do the same.

The whole task took no more than fifteen minutes. As they stood, Vijay spoke. "Who is buried here, Father?" he asked.

Father answered with a man's name that the boy had never heard.

"Was he a member of our family?" Vijay asked.

"No," Father said.

"Why do we plant flowers on his grave?" Vijay asked.

"He was a soldier," Father answered. He made a sweeping motion with his arm to indicate the rows of white crosses. "All of these people were soldiers."

Vijay looked at the markers. There were too many to count.

"Before you were born," Father said, "your mother and I became citizens of this country. We were not born here. We have not had to fight for the freedoms we have. But these soldiers gave their lives for this country." He paused. "We come here every year," he said, pointing to the newly decorated grave, "to say thank you to this soldier for giving his life for our country."

"How did you choose him?"

Father cleared his throat. "We asked the people in charge of the cemetery."

Vijay nodded solemnly. His face brightened. "So we have adopted him?" he asked. Vijay knew that his parents had adopted him when he was just a baby.

Father smiled. "Yes," he said. "It is a small way to honor all those who gave their lives for their country."

Vijay took his parents' hands. They walked to the car and put their tools away in the trunk. As they drove away, Vijay again gazed out of the car window at row after row of simple white crosses.

TO DO: Decorate the grave of a family member, serviceman, or servicewoman today or this weekend.

TO PRAY: "Lord, help us to remember the people who have given their lives to serve others. We remember Jesus, especially—the Savior who gave his life for us all."

1 An Openhanded God

OVER AND OVER AGAIN, HE TELLS US THAT HE LOVES US AND HE JUST WANTS TO DO GOOD TO US.

Bible Reading of the Day: Read Isaiah 65:1-2, 12.
Verse of the Day: *"You open your hand and satisfy the desires of every living thing" (Psalm 145:16, NIV).*

"Come here, puppy," Inéz said. She wiggled a dog biscuit in front of the animal, which cowered in the bushes in the front yard. Inéz had discovered the puppy that afternoon, curled in a semi-collapsed box that one of the neighbors had placed at the curb for garbage pickup. She had coaxed it out of the box and into her yard with a bowl of leftovers she had claimed from the refrigerator. But the puppy had ducked into the bushes by Inéz's front steps and would not come out.

Mom watched as Inéz inched closer to the bushes. "Be careful," Mom warned.

"Why?" Inéz asked, without taking her eyes off the dog.

"I don't want him to bite you," Mom said.

"Oh, Mom," Inéz said. "It's just a puppy."

The words were barely out of Inéz's mouth when the puppy growled viciously and snapped the air near Inéz's hand. She jumped, dropping the biscuit in the dirt.

The puppy crept out from under the bush and quickly snapped up the biscuit. As he moved, Mom noticed that his coat was a mass of tangled and matted fur.

"I just want to help him," Inéz protested. "Why would he try to bite me?"

"He may be hurt," Mom answered. "Or maybe his master didn't take care of him properly."

Inéz grunted. "But I'm not going to hurt him," she said. "I just want to help him."

"I know that," Mom said. "But he doesn't know that. He's afraid of you."

"But that's silly! If he'd just let me help him . . ."

Mom nodded. She placed a hand on Inéz's back. "Now you know how God feels," she said.

"What?"

"Now you know how God feels," Mom repeated, "when people reject him and turn away from his commandments. Over and over again, he tells us that he loves us and he just wants to do good to us. But we don't listen, or we don't believe him, or we forget."

"So what do I do?" Inéz asked. She nodded toward the puppy. "About him, I mean."

Mom shrugged. "What do you think?"

"I could try doing what God does with us," she said. "I could just be patient and try to show him love. Think that'll work?"

"I think it's a good start," Mom said, and handed Inéz another dog biscuit.

TO DISCUSS: How has God shown his "openhandedness" to you? How can you be "openhanded" like God?

TO PRAY: "Thank you, Lord, for the kindness you've always shown to us. Help us to never take you for granted."

2 Ring of Promise

THE SEEDS OF MARITAL FAITHFULNESS ARE PLANTED IN YOUTH.

Bible Reading of the Day: Read Genesis 2:8, 18–23.

Verse of the Day: *"This is now bone of my bones and flesh of my flesh; she shall be called 'woman,' for she was taken out of man"* (Genesis 2:23, NIV).

Graham's thirteenth birthday had finally arrived. He and his parents went out together to a fancy restaurant, leaving his little sister at home with a baby-sitter.

Mom and Dad let Graham order any meal he wanted. When they were all done eating, Dad pulled out a small gift-wrapped box. Graham's eyes glittered as Dad passed the box to him.

"This is the most expensive birthday gift we've ever gotten you," Dad explained. "And the most meaningful."

Graham looked curiously at his parents. He held the box, unopened, in the palm of his hand.

"Open it," Mom said.

Graham tore off the wrapping paper to expose a felt box. He popped the box open to reveal a simple gold ring.

Graham flashed another curious look at his parents. This was certainly unexpected. He took the ring out of the box and tried it on. It fit perfectly.

"It's a promise ring," Mom explained. "Dad and I want you to keep this ring as a symbol of your faithfulness to your wife."

"Faithfulness to my *wife?*" Graham said, ignoring everything else that was said. "What wife? I'm not even married!"

"Not yet," Dad said. "But you may get married someday. And when you do, I hope you'll be able to give that ring to your wife on your wedding day and tell her that you've worn that ring ever since you were thirteen years old, to remind yourself every day to stay faithful to your wife—even before you knew who she was!"

"What do you mean by staying faithful to my wife?" Graham asked.

"Well," Dad said, "it means staying sexually pure and preparing yourself to be a good husband."

"After all, you may not know who your wife will be, but God knows," Mom said.

Graham flattened his hand on the table and looked at the ring with new appreciation. Then he looked up. "Thanks, Mom and Dad," he said. "This is the best birthday present ever."

 TO DO: Make "faithfulness keepsakes" for the whole family. Make bracelets out of yarn for everyone to wear. Or write a pledge of your faithfulness and provide a copy for everyone to have.

 TO PRAY: Pray for the children in the family and for each child's future husband or wife, asking God to keep them pure and prepare them to be good husbands, wives, mothers, and fathers.

3 The Positive Power of "No"

THE THINGS I SAY NO TO MAKE MY LIFE *BETTER,* NOT WORSE!

Bible Reading of the Day: Read John 10:7-10.
Verse of the Day: "And when we obey him, every path he guides us on is fragrant with his lovingkindness and his truth" (Psalm 25:10, TLB).

"Let's go see if we can sneak into the movie theater!" Tia suggested to her friends Anna and Heather. They stood on the sidewalk in front of the movie theater.

Anna shook her head. "Let's not," she said. "It wouldn't be right. It's just like stealing."

Tia threw up her hands in a gesture of frustration. "There you go again with that Christian 'I'm too good to do that' stuff!"

"It's not that," Anna protested, but Tia interrupted her.

"Every time I come up with an idea of what we could do, you always say no. It's like that's all being a Christian is—a bunch of rules saying, 'don't do this' and 'you can't do that.'"

"That's not true," Anna said.

Heather finally entered the conversation. "It does seem that way, Anna."

"But it's not like that at all," Anna said. She looked at the cars rushing past them as they talked. "That's like saying . . . well . . . like saying that getting your driver's license is all about not being able to do anything!"

"Huh?" Tia said.

"Yeah," Anna said, suddenly enthusiastic. "That's exactly what it's like. We can't wait to get our driver's license someday, right? That'll be so cool, right? We'll be able to go places, right?" Her friends nodded in unison. "But what about all the do's and don'ts you gotta learn before then, huh? You gotta learn how fast you can go and what all the signs and signals mean. Isn't that all a bunch of rules saying, 'don't do this' and 'you can't do that'?"

Heather shrugged. "Those are just things we learn to *get* a license."

"But you're willing to obey those rules," Anna said, "because you figure it's worth it, right? Because you'll be a lot freer once you have your license, right?"

"Well, yeah," Heather said.

"It's the same way with doing the right thing," Anna said. "All the things I say no to have made my life *better,* not worse! They're all worth it, because I have a lot more fun when I'm not scared or in trouble or whatever."

"All right, all right," Tia said. "We won't sneak into the movies." She smirked. "Let's rob a liquor store."

"Tia!" Heather and Anna cried in unison.

TO DISCUSS: How can saying no be a *positive* thing? How does saying no to wrong make your life better?

TO PRAY: "God, give us courage to say no when we're tempted to sin."

4 Don't Brag

DON'T PRAISE YOURSELF. LET OTHERS DO IT.

Bible Reading of the Day: Read Proverbs 27:1-2.
Verse of the Day: *"Don't praise yourself; let others do it!"*
(Proverbs 27:2).

"I'm better than you are! I'm better than you are!" Adrian taunted his little brother, Alex. He hurriedly tucked in his shirt. All that remained was for him to put on his socks and shoes. Then he would fulfill his promise of beating Alex in a race to see who could get dressed the fastest in the morning.

Alex's lower lip stuck out, but he didn't cry. He got his pants on, but his T-shirt got snagged while he was trying to pull it over his head. He wrestled with it, and finally got it over his ears, but Adrian was already pulling his last sock on.

"Just my shoes now. I'm gonna beat you! I'm gonna beat you!" Adrian sang.

Alex was sorry he'd ever agreed to race his brother.

Adrian crouched on the floor and swept an arm under his bed. He found one shoe but couldn't locate its mate. "Where's my other shoe?" he asked.

Alex pulled his socks on.

"Where's my other shoe?" Adrian asked, looking around frantically.

Alex had one shoe on.

Adrian heard the soft *scritch* sound of the Velcro fasteners on his brother's shoe. "I can't find my shoe!" he shouted. "It's not fair!"

Alex pulled on his second shoe, folded the fastener over tightly, and stood. "Done!" he said victoriously. "I win!"

"No fair!" Adrian said.

"You shouldn't have bragged so soon about winning," Alex said.

An idea suddenly occurred to Adrian. "You probably hid my other shoe, didn't you?" He stomped toward his little brother.

Alex opened the door of the bedroom they shared and held onto the doorknob. He turned back to face Adrian. "I never touched your shoe," he said. "It's still in the closet from when you threw it at me last night!"

Alex ducked through the doorway. Adrian turned and threw a glance at Alex's closet on the other side of the room. His shoe lay in plain sight atop a stack of Alex's toys.

 TO DISCUSS: Why do you think Adrian bragged about being better than his little brother? Do you ever brag? If so, why do you brag? If not, why not? Do you think bragging is good? Why or why not? Why is it better to let others praise you?

 TO PRAY: "Lord, we're sometimes tempted to toot our own horns. Help us to be humble."

5 Beth, Be Not Proud

SINFUL PRIDE IS BAD; HUMILITY IS GOOD.

Bible Reading of the Day: Read Proverbs 21:2-4.
Verse of the Day: *"Haughty eyes, a proud heart, and evil actions are all sin"* (Proverbs 21:4).

"Yyyyyes!" Beth shouted as she entered the family room. "I got the highest grade in my class on that social-studies report!"

"Congratulations," her big brother, Cal, said, barely glancing up from the TV.

"I knew I would," Beth said. She swaggered across the room like a drum majorette in a parade.

"Oh?" Cal asked. "How'd you know that?"

"We had to read our reports out loud in class, and I could tell mine was the best. Jenny Ramsdale's was stupid, and Howard's report was totally boring!"

"But yours was perfect, right?" Cal said, with barely disguised sarcasm.

"Uh-huh," she answered, not taking the hint. "I'm the smartest kid in my class, easy." She ran a hand through her hair as if she were posing for a picture.

"Guess you've never heard the story of the two roosters, have you?" Cal said.

"Two roosters? What story is that?"

Cal turned down the volume on the TV. "Oh, it's just a story about two roosters. Both claimed to be the best rooster in the barnyard. One day, they got into a fight. The rooster that lost ran away and hid in a secluded corner of the barnyard. The rooster that won climbed up on top of the chicken coop and started flapping his wings and crowing about how good he was. He crowed so loud that an eagle flying high overhead heard him. The eagle dove from the sky, carried the rooster off, and had a fine chicken dinner that night."

Beth stared at Cal. "What's that story supposed to mean?"

Cal shrugged. "I think you know," he said.

Beth pursed her lips and was silent for a moment. "I guess I was getting a little carried away," she said finally.

"A little?" Cal answered.

"OK, a lot," Beth admitted.

"It's OK to take pleasure in your achievements, Beth," Cal said. "But the Bible says that having a proud heart is a sin. It's better to stay humble."

"Kids," Mom said, sticking her head into the room. "It's almost time for dinner."

"What are we having?" Beth asked.

"Chicken," Mom answered.

Beth and Cal looked at each other and broke into laughter.

 TO DISCUSS: What do you think is the difference between taking pleasure in your achievements and being sinfully proud? How can you do your best and stay humble at the same time?

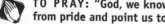 **TO PRAY:** "God, we know you monitor the pride levels of our hearts. Keep us away from pride and point us toward humility."

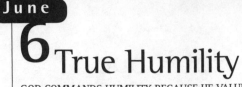

GOD COMMANDS HUMILITY BECAUSE HE VALUES HUMILITY.

Bible Reading of the Day: Read Romans 12:3-5.
Verse of the Day: *"Be honest in your estimate of yourselves, measuring your value by how much faith God has given you" (Romans 12:3).*

Rachel crossed her arms on her chest and slumped into her chair. She turned to her friend, Tracy. "I don't know why Mrs. Standish chose Julia to sing a solo," she said, referring to the girl who stood on the stage at the competition. "You can sing a lot better than she can."

"Shh," Tracy said. "She's doing great." The two girls sat in the auditorium of the largest school in the area, watching the final entries in the statewide vocal competition.

"Doesn't it make you mad that Julia's up there singing, when everybody knows you're the best soloist in the whole school?" Rachel asked. "I hope she loses."

"You should be rooting for her to win," Tracy protested, "instead of getting so upset. She's our last chance for our school to win a ribbon today."

"Don't you want her to lose?" Rachel countered.

"No!" Tracy said.

"But she took *your* solo!"

"It wasn't my solo. It wasn't anybody's solo."

Rachel waved a hand. "Aw, girl, you don't have to act all humble!"

"It's not an act," Tracy said, her eyes flashing. "It's just the truth. I don't want to think I'm better than I really am. That's all humility is. And that's the way God says we should be."

"So God says you should let Julia sing *your* solo?" Rachel asked, looking skeptical.

Tracy sighed. "Look, God may not want me to think I'm a terrible singer, but he doesn't want me to think I'm better than I really am, either. The Bible says for us not to think we're better than other people, because God doesn't like pride. He likes humility."

Julia finished singing, and Tracy joined the applause for her performance.

"So you really hope she wins?" Rachel said, her eyebrows arching like twin tents over her eyes.

"Yeah," Tracy said. "You know what else I hope?"

"What?" Rachel said.

"I hope you'll be quiet for a little while so I can hear the other singers," she said, jabbing her friend with an elbow.

TO DISCUSS: Why do you think God wants us to be humble? What do *you* think humility means? Do you think humility means not liking yourself? Do you think humility means thinking you're not as good as other people?

TO PRAY: "Jesus, thank you for helping us to look at ourselves honestly, rather than with pride or with a sense of inferiority. Both are displeasing to you."

Not Too Proud

GOD VALUES HUMILITY BECAUSE HE HUMBLED HIMSELF.

Bible Reading of the Day: Read Philippians 2:5-11.

Verse of the Day: *"Your attitude should be the same that Christ Jesus had" (Philippians 2:5).*

"Colleen!" Sidney's shout turned every head in the fast-food restaurant where Colleen ate with several of her friends. The mentally handicapped boy hurried across the restaurant with his arms outstretched.

"Sidney!" Colleen replied, smiling.

Sidney hugged her as if he hadn't seen her in years; in reality, he'd last seen Colleen four days earlier at the church both of their families attended. Colleen and Sidney talked for a few moments as Sidney's voice boomed over all the other conversations in the restaurant. Finally, Colleen turned and introduced Sidney to her school friends and explained that he was one of her friends from church.

"I gotta go," Sidney finally said, in his loud, faltering voice. He held a hand high in the air, which Colleen dutifully slapped in a high five. "See you, Colleen," he said, as he hurried off to rejoin his parents at the restaurant counter.

"How embarrassing!" said Kerri, one of Colleen's friends, when Sidney had left.

"Yeah," added another, "why didn't you just tell him to get lost?"

"I couldn't do that," Colleen answered in a horrified tone. "Sidney is my friend."

"You're serious?" Kerri said. "I thought you were just being nice. How can you have *him* for a friend?"

"What do you mean?" Colleen asked.

"Well," Kerri answered, "it's humiliating. He's retarded, isn't he?"

"Yeah. So?" Colleen said.

"I just don't think you should be *that* desperate for friends," Kerri decided.

"Kerri, you're a Christian," Colleen told her friend. She looked at one of the other girls. "You are, too, Angela. How can you be too proud to be Sidney's friend? Is Jesus too proud to be your friend? Didn't God stoop to *our* level when he became a man and died for our sins?" She shook her head. "If it takes humility to be Sidney's friend, then I don't have a problem with it. Maybe *you* should try it."

The girls around the table stared at Colleen. Then Kerri exchanged embarrassed looks with Angela, the other Christian at the table.

"She's right," Angela said quietly.

"I know," Kerri answered. She smiled sheepishly at Colleen. "I hate it when she's right."

 TO DO: Copy today's Bible reading onto a sheet of paper. Pass the paper around and allow each family member to circle or underline one word that refers to Christ humbling himself.

 TO PRAY: "Help us, Lord, when we're tempted to think that certain people are beneath our notice. Remind us that you humbled yourself in order to draw us to yourself."

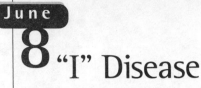

8 "I" Disease

HUMILITY INVITES RESPECT; PRIDE AND SELF-CENTEREDNESS INVITE SCORN.

Bible Reading of the Day: Read Isaiah 14:12-17.
Verse of the Day: *"Pride ends in humiliation, while humility brings honor" (Proverbs 29:23).*

Seth and his dad sat together at the school sports banquet. Seth's older brother, who had played on the high-school basketball team, was one of two students who were going to receive awards for their athletic achievements in high school.

The first student athlete to be given an award was the star of the school's football and baseball teams.

"Thanks for this award," the boy said. "I want to share a few memories of some of the plays that made me such a great athlete." He went on to talk about a touchdown pass he had caught and about the time he pitched for his baseball team in the regional championships. "I will always remember moments like that, when I had a chance to do something really great for my school. Thank you."

Seth and his dad joined the polite applause that followed the boy's speech. Seth's brother was announced next, and after his achievements were listed and his award was presented to him, he stepped up to the microphone and smiled.

"Thank you," he said. "It's really great to be honored like this, but I feel like the people who really deserve this award are my mom and dad, my teammates, and my coaches. They're the ones who worked hard and taught me things I could never have learned on my own. So I'd like to share this award with them. Thank you."

The audience rose in a standing ovation for Seth's big brother.

A few moments later, Dad and Seth walked to the car with Seth's big brother. "Your speech was a lot better than that other guy's," Seth said.

Dad placed a hand on Seth's shoulder. "I agree," he said. "But why do you think your brother's speech was better?"

"I don't know," Seth said. "It just was." He was silent for a few moments. "I didn't like that other guy's speech because all he did was talk about himself."

Dad nodded and said. "He did act like he had a bad case of 'I' disease."

"Eye disease?" Seth said, not understanding what his father meant.

"Yeah," Dad answered, his eyes twinkling. "All he talked about was, *'I* did this,' and *'I* did that.' That's probably why he didn't impress you. But your brother showed a humble spirit."

"Yeah!" Seth said, finally understanding. *"I* hope *I* never get 'I' disease!"

"I hope so, too," Dad said, laughing. "I hope so, too."

TO DISCUSS: What is "I" disease? How do you know when a person has "I" disease? What is the cure for "I" disease?

TO PRAY: "Jesus, you are the Great Physician, who cures us of 'I' disease. When you diagnose it in our lives, help us to be humble enough to submit ourselves to your treatment."

9 Pride's "Down" Side

HUMILITY WINS FRIENDS; PRIDE EARNS ENEMIES.

Bible Reading of the Day: Read 2 Chronicles 26:1, 16–21.
Verse of the Day: *"Pride leads to disgrace, but with humility comes wisdom" (Proverbs 11:2).*

"You're going to invite Brad?" Miles asked his friend, Tim. The two boys sat at the kitchen table. Tim was planning his birthday party. Miles had come over to Tim's house to help.

Tim shrugged. "My mom says I should invite all the boys in my class," he explained.

"But *Brad?*" Miles spoke the name as if it were a curse.

"What's wrong with Brad?" asked Mom, who had been putting dishes away in the cabinet behind the table.

Miles and Tim looked up suddenly, as if they were surprised that Tim's mom had heard their conversation. They exchanged wary glances. Then Tim spoke.

"Nobody likes Brad," he explained.

"Why not?" Mom asked.

"Well, he's always getting into fights and stuff," Tim said. "He . . . he acts like he's better than anyone else. He's always talking about how much money his dad makes—"

"And how he's smarter than anyone else in our class," Miles interjected.

"Yeah," Tim said, "like the time Miles won the spelling bee."

"What happened, Miles?" Mom asked.

"Well, I won the spelling bee for my grade, and then I won second place in the region," he explained. "After I got second place, Brad bragged to everybody that *he* would have won if *he'd* been in the regionals."

Tim looked at his mom. "He says stuff like that all the time. He's always getting people mad."

Mom nodded. "I see," she said.

"Do I have to invite him?" Tim asked.

"I'll let you decide," she answered.

"All right," Tim said. He paused, then began addressing an invitation with Brad's name on it.

Miles waited for Tim's mom to leave the room, then he leaned close to Tim. "Why are you sending him an invitation? Your mom said you could decide!"

"Yeah," Tim said, nodding. "She only says that when she knows I'll do the right thing."

 TO DISCUSS: Why do you think Brad had few friends? Why do you think Tim wanted to invite Brad to his party? Has pride ever hurt your friendships? Who do you think usually have more friendships: people who are proud or people who are humble? Why?

 TO PRAY: If pride has hurt one of your friendships or that of a family member, take a moment to ask for God's forgiveness and help to make amends.

10 First Chair

HUMILITY PROTECTS A PERSON FROM EMBARRASSMENT AND PROVIDES FOR HONOR.

Bible Reading of the Day: Read Luke 14:7-11.
Verse of the Day: *"For the proud will be humbled, but the humble will be honored" (Luke 14:11).*

Thad lifted his shiny trumpet out of its fur-lined case and headed toward the risers. He had been waiting a long time for this day, ever since the concert band tryouts.

Thad knew that his tryout had gone well, but he had stayed in the band room the rest of the afternoon and listened to the rest of the tryouts for the trumpet section. By the end of the day, he thought he knew who had won first chair in concert band. He didn't even have to check the seating chart on the wall.

He balanced his trumpet in his hand, rapidly fingering the valves, as he walked to the first chair in the trumpet section. He sat down and looked around the empty band room, soaking in the view from the position he'd wanted for two years: first chair, first trumpet.

Band members began to file in. Some ignored him. Others noticed him and nodded. Others seemed to give him a strange look.

They're probably jealous, he reasoned. He smiled to himself. *That's OK. Let 'em be jealous.*

Finally, when the band room was almost full, the band director, Mrs. Sawyer, entered the room and immediately caught Thad's eye, as if she'd come into the room looking for him. She walked over to the trumpet section.

"Thad," she said slowly, after clearing her throat, "did you happen to check the seating chart on your way into rehearsal today?"

Thad's eyes widened in a sincerely puzzled expression. "No," he answered.

Mrs. Sawyer cleared her throat again. "I see," she said. "You're . . . uh . . . sitting in the wrong seat. You're *second* chair. *First* chair belongs to Scott Medford."

Thad's mouth dropped open, and a deep red blush rose slowly from his neck to his hairline. He licked his lips and fumbled out an apology. It felt like every eye in the room was fastened on him as he scooted over, allowing Scott Medford to slip into the first chair.

Stupid, stupid, stupid, he scolded himself. *This is so embarrassing. Everybody must think I'm so stupid!*

Practice began, and Thad's embarrassment began to disappear. But in place of the embarrassment came a new realization. *It would have been way better if I'd been humble,* he thought. *Way better.*

TO DISCUSS: How was Thad's experience like the one Jesus described? Can you think of other places (besides banquets and concert bands) where people try to grab places of honor? How can humility in such places protect a person from embarrassment and provide for honor?

TO PRAY: "Lord, being humbled can be embarrassing. Help us not to seek places of honor but to honor you instead."

11 An Exercise in Humility

GOD OPPOSES THE PROUD BUT GIVES GRACE TO THE HUMBLE.

Bible Reading of the Day: Read James 4:4-10.
Verse of the Day: *"Humble yourselves before the Lord, and he will lift you up"* (James 4:10, NIV).

Jessica and Kayla's gymnastics instructor waved them over to the sidelines.

"I'd like to work with the two of you on a few problems I've noticed in your exercises," she said. She walked Jessica over to the bar in front of a large mirror. Placing one hand in the small of Jessica's back and the other on Jessica's ankle, she tried to show Jessica what she'd been doing wrong.

"I already know how to do it!" Jessica protested. She shrugged off her teacher's hands and insisted on performing the move herself.

The instructor shook her head. "No, dear, you're still making the same mistake," she began, but Jessica interrupted her again.

"I can do it!" she said loudly, and continued. The instructor watched her for a moment. But Jessica's exercise had not improved.

Finally, the instructor turned away from Jessica. She took a deep breath and nodded to Kayla, who stepped up to the bar. The instructor helped her position her feet and then, with one hand placed in the small of Kayla's back and the other on one of Kayla's ankles, began showing her the same movement she had tried to show Jessica.

Kayla listened carefully to the instructor and concentrated on doing exactly what she was told. Occasionally she would ask, "Like this?" or "Am I doing it right?" or "I did it again, didn't I?" The instructor would answer patiently and with a smile.

"Oh," Kayla finally cried in an excited voice. "I think I've got it now!" The instructor stepped away from the bar and watched as Kayla performed the move the instructor had shown her. "How was that?" Kayla asked when she had finished.

"Beautiful!" the instructor said. She clapped her hands together twice and smiled broadly. "That's excellent, Kayla. Just remember to keep your back straight."

"I will," Kayla said, beaming.

"I can do that," Jessica grumbled, watching Kayla's fluid movements.

"You could," the instructor said sternly, "if you just changed one thing."

"What?" Jessica asked.

"Your pride. I can't help you as long as you think you don't need help."

TO DISCUSS: What do you think was the difference between Jessica and Kayla? How do you think God "opposes" the proud? How do you think he shows grace to the humble?

TO PRAY: "Lord, you tell us that you oppose the proud and show grace to the humble. Reveal the areas of our life where we're proud. Point us in the direction of humility."

12 Like a Shield

GOD'S COMMANDMENTS ARE INTENDED TO SHIELD US FROM HARM.

Bible Reading of the Day: Read Psalm 33:13-22.
Verse of the Day: *"We depend on the Lord alone to save us. Only he can help us, protecting us like a shield" (Psalm 33:20).*

"Aw, Mom, do I have to?" Alan whined as his mom fastened his bicycle helmet under his chin.

"Yes," Mom said. "I'm afraid you have to."

"But why?" Alan protested.

"Now, Alan, you know better than to ask me that question," she answered. She straightened to her full height and placed her hands on her hips. "Why don't *you* tell *me*—why do I make you wear a helmet when you ride your bike?"

"Because it'll protect me if I fall," Alan answered in a singsong tone.

"So, do I make you wear a bike helmet because I hate you and want to make you miserable?"

"No," Alan answered in his singsong voice. "You do it because you love me and want to protect me."

"Very good, Class," Mom said with a laugh, in her best teacher's voice.

"But none of the other kids have to wear a helmet," he said. "I feel like a dork."

"Well, you're not a dork," Mom said. She smiled lovingly at him.

"Can I go now?" Alan asked, looking embarrassed by his mom's attention, even though no one else was around.

"You can go now," she said, gripping him by the shoulders and turning him to face the door. "Just remember one thing," she added.

"I know," Alan interrupted. "You love me."

"Well, yes, but I want you to remember one other thing."

Alan turned and faced his mom, impatience written on his face.

"Your helmet doesn't do you any good," she said, tapping her index finger on the top of his head, "unless you keep your head inside of it. OK?"

Alan rolled his eyes. "OK, Mom," he said. "I'll keep it on."

 TO DISCUSS: Why did Alan have to wear a helmet when he rode his bike? In what ways are God's commandments like Alan's bicycle helmet?

TO PRAY: Turn the "Verse of the Day" into a prayer: "Lord, we depend on you alone to save us. Only you can help us, protecting us like a shield."

13 The View from Above

WE SHOULD TRUST GOD'S VIEW OF RIGHT AND WRONG.

Bible Reading of the Day: Read Deuteronomy 10:12-21.
Verse of the Day: *"Fear the Lord your God and serve him"*
(Deuteronomy 10:20, NIV).

Cole and his parents stood on the curb watching the parade go by. Cole loved the bands that marched by in smart uniforms. The antique cars that drove by honking their horns were neat, too. He laughed at the clowns who tramped by, tossing pieces of gum and candy into the crowd. But he began to get impatient to see what was coming next.

"Daddy, what's coming next?" he would ask, along with "Mommy, are there more clowns?"

Finally, Cole's dad had an idea. He gripped Cole around the waist, whisked him into the air, and settled Cole on his shoulders.

Seated on Dad's shoulders, Cole felt as if he could see everything. He could see the clowns that had just passed. He could see the fire truck that was still a half block away. And he could see the 4-H float that was passing in front of him.

"I can see everything now," Cole said, "because I'm up high!"

After the parade was over, Mom and Dad sat on the curb on either side of Cole as they waited for the crowd to disperse.

"You liked being up on Daddy's shoulders, didn't you, Cole?" Mom asked.

Cole nodded enthusiastically. "I could see everything!" he said. He chattered about the cars, clowns, fire engines, and floats. "I was higher than anybody else!" he said.

"Oh, I don't know about that," Dad said, smiling. "I can think of someone who was still higher than you."

Cole frowned for a moment, then his expression brightened. "I know!" he said. "God was higher than I was!"

"That's right," Dad said, chuckling. "Just think how far you could see when you were on my shoulders. God can see even farther than that!"

"He can see all the way to . . . to . . . to everywhere!" Cole said.

"That's right," Mom agreed.

"God can see *forever!*" Cole realized.

Dad nodded. "You're right, Cole. That's very good. God can see forever, and he knows what will happen next, and even what will happen after that."

"That's why we should always listen to him and do what he says," Mom said, "because he can see a lot more than we can."

"Even more than I can see from Daddy's shoulders," Cole said solemnly.

"Even more than that," Dad said.

TO DISCUSS: Do you believe that God knows everything and is in control of your life? Do the choices you make reflect that belief?

TO PRAY: "O God, remind us that you can see higher and farther than we can see. Help us to trust you and to obey what you say."

14 R-E-S-P-E-C-T

RESPECT IS RIGHT.

Bible Reading of the Day: Read Leviticus 19:1-3.
Verse of the Day: *"Each of you must show respect for your mother and father" (Leviticus 19:3).*

Jason and Jarrod had just finished playing basketball with the youth group when Mom arrived to ask if they were ready to go home.

"Yeah, just a minute," Jarrod answered.

The boys kept talking with their friends while Mom waited. Finally, she interrupted the conversation. "OK, boys, it's time to leave."

"Just a second!" Jason answered impatiently.

The boys' mother propped her hands on her hips but said nothing. Just then, Pastor Ken, the boys' youth pastor, approached the group. He nodded to Jason and Jarrod.

"You guys got a minute?" he asked. "I'd like to talk to you."

Jason and Jarrod followed Pastor Ken across the room. Placing a hand on Jason's shoulder and his other hand on Jarrod's shoulder, he said, "Gentlemen, you see that woman over there?"

Jason and Jarrod looked back over their shoulders. The only woman in the room was their mom, who still stood by the door.

"That woman," Pastor Ken said, "is your mother."

"Yeah," Jason responded in a puzzled tone.

Jarrod sighed and faced his brother. "He means that we should treat Mom better than we just did. I guess we were pretty disrespectful, weren't we?" Jarrod asked Pastor Ken.

"A *little*," Pastor Ken answered, his voice dripping with sarcasm.

"But she always expects us to leave when *she's* ready," Jarrod protested.

"She looks pretty patient to me," Pastor Ken said. "Look, guys, God doesn't say 'Honor your father and mother . . . when it's easy.' If you're trying to say disrespecting your mom is OK because of this, or that, well then . . ."

"Well then what?" Jason asked.

Jarrod rolled his eyes at his brother. "Well then, we're trying to change what God has said is right, and that would be wrong."

"Right," Pastor Ken said.

Jarrod nodded to his brother. "We gotta get going," he said. He looked at Pastor Ken. "Our mom's waiting." He smiled.

Pastor Ken smiled back as he watched the twins walk out the door with their mom.

 TO DISCUSS: How do you know that respect for your parents is right? How can you show respect for your parents? Does a parent have to earn his or her child's respect? Why or why not? Is a person allowed to stop respecting his or her parents when he or she becomes an adult? Why or why not?

 TO PRAY: "Lord, help us to obey your command to honor our parents."

15 Where Respect Begins

RESPECT FOR OTHERS BEGINS WITH RESPECT FOR GOD.

Bible Reading of the Day: Read Malachi 1:6, 12-13.
Verse of the Day: *"Fear God and obey his commands, for this is the duty of every person" (Ecclesiastes 12:13).*

"Come on!" Bobby yelled as he darted in and out of the pews in the church sanctuary.

Trent heard his friend but didn't move from his spot on the last pew.

"Come on!" Bobby repeated. "What's the matter with you?"

"I . . . I'm not allowed to run in church," Trent said.

Bobby looked around at the empty sanctuary. "Nobody's here," he said.

"I know, but . . ."

Bobby tapped Trent on the arm and shouted, "You're it!" He dove between the pews and began scooting on the floor under the seats. Finally, he stopped. He poked his head out into the aisle. "Why don't you want to play?"

"I do," Trent said. "But we shouldn't be running and crawling around in the sanctuary."

Bobby got up from the floor and dusted off his knees. He looked at Trent and shrugged. "Why not?"

"Well," Trent said, "because this is God's house."

"I know that," Bobby said.

"Yeah, but my parents say we should show our respect for God by not running in church and not wearing hats in church and stuff like that."

"But—"

"My dad says that one reason people don't respect each other much anymore is because they don't respect God anymore," Trent said.

"You're just afraid your mommy's going to come in and catch you running in church," Bobby teased.

"No, I'm not!" Trent said at first. Then he changed his mind. "OK, I guess I am. Because if she saw me running around when I know I'm not supposed to, it would be like I don't respect *her,* either."

"Sort of like what your dad said, huh?" Bobby admitted.

"Yeah, I guess so."

"Let's go where we can play tag," Bobby suggested.

"OK," Trent said. "I'll tell my mom."

"I'll race you—" Bobby said as he started to run for the sanctuary doors. But he stopped suddenly and turned to face his friend. "Oh, yeah," he said. "I forgot—no running in God's house."

 TO DISCUSS: What are some ways you show respect for God? How does respect for others begin with respecting God?

TO PRAY: "Lord, we want to show our respect for you. Teach us to honor your name."

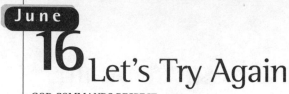
16 Let's Try Again

GOD COMMANDS RESPECT.

Bible Reading of the Day: Read 1 Peter 2:13-17.

Verse of the Day: *"Show proper respect to everyone"* (1 Peter 2:17, NIV).

Renee and her mom were having lunch at a restaurant with Kelly and her mom.

"I don't like this!" Renee said in a loud voice, pointing to her hamburger.

Mom gently laid her hand on Renee's forearm. "Let's try again, Renee," she said.

Renee frowned for a moment, then said, "Do I have to eat this?"

Her mother nodded. "I would like you to eat at least half of your hamburger and half of your french fries."

"No!" Renee shouted. "I don't want to."

"Let's try again," Mom said again.

Renee wrinkled her brow for a moment. "May I have some ice cream, please?" she said, emphasizing the last word.

Mom said. "If you eat *all* of your hamburger and fries, you may have ice cream."

Renee thought for a moment, then began eating her hamburger happily.

After dinner, the two girls went to the play area of the restaurant, leaving the mothers time to talk.

"Where'd you learn to do that?" Kelly's mom asked Renee's mom.

Renee's mom shrugged. "Oh, I don't know," she said. "We started playing 'Let's Try Again' a few weeks ago. Some of Renee's actions and attitudes started to really bother me, and I wanted her to understand that God commands us to respect each other. So I started explaining that to her. I wanted to teach her to be more respectful—you know, to say 'please' and 'thank you' and so on. So anytime she forgets her manners or says something rude, I give her a chance to correct herself by saying, 'Let's try again.' It seems to be working pretty well."

"It sure does," Kelly's mom said. "I should try that with Kelly."

"The game hasn't just helped Renee. It's helped *me,* too. Sometimes I have to say to myself, 'Let's try again,' whenever I find myself acting disrespectfully toward others—even toward Renee. The 'Let's Try Again' game is a good way to remember that God commands us to show proper respect to everyone—not just to our parents but to our nation's leaders, to our church leaders . . . basically to everyone."

"Mmm," said Kelly's mom as she finished chewing the bite of hamburger she had taken. "That's something *I* need to remember."

"Well, I'll be happy to play 'Let's Try Again' with you anytime."

Kelly's mom laughed. "You've got a deal!"

 TO DO: Play "Let's Try Again" with someone in your family sometime in the next twenty-four hours. If someone says something disrespectful or forgets to say "please" or "thank you," give that person a chance to try again to show proper respect for the other person.

TO PRAY: "Thank you, Lord, for the grace to try again when we mess up."

June 17
Respect for Elders

GOD COMMANDS RESPECT BECAUSE HE VALUES RESPECT.

Bible Reading of the Day: Read Leviticus 19:32; Proverbs 20:29.
Verse of the Day: *"Show your fear of God by standing up in the presence
of elderly people and showing respect for the aged. I am the Lord"
(Leviticus 19:32).*

Jess and Katherine had never been to such a big family reunion before. They had driven
several hours in the car to get there. When they arrived, they couldn't believe how many
people were gathered in the park's clubhouse—and everyone was related to them!

Jess and Katherine spent the afternoon playing lawn darts, volleyball, badminton,
and kickball with the other kids, while the adults sat around the picnic tables in the
park, talking and eating.

Jess grew tired toward the end of the afternoon and decided to take a break. He
sat beside his parents in what seemed to be the only empty seat in the whole building.
Several of his cousins were already seated, eating pie and cake.

A few moments later, Jess watched his grandmother hobble into the clubhouse.
She walked between the rows of picnic tables, looking from side to side.

"Here, Grandma!" Jess yelled. He leaped up from his seat beside his mom and
darted to Grandma's side. "You can sit in my seat." He took Grandma by the hand and
led her to the spot he had just vacated. For the next few minutes, Jess stood by the
table, listening to the conversation. Then he noticed his grandmother looking at the
food table. He leaned his mouth close to her ear.

"Can I get you something to eat, Grandma?" he asked.

Grandma smiled sweetly. "Thank you, dear," she said. "I would like a tiny piece
of that apple pie I smell."

Jess leaped into action. He scooped a large piece onto a plate—Grandma liked
"tiny" pieces that took up a lot of space on a plate—and carried it to her. A few
moments later, Jess returned to the field beside the clubhouse and joined a game of
"freeze tag" that was just getting started.

On the way home that evening, Dad spoke to Jess.

"Son, I was proud of you today."

"Why?" Jess asked.

"Because of the way you treated Grandma," Dad answered. "You gave her your
seat. You helped her to get some food. You treated her with respect. I'm proud of you
for that."

"Thanks, Dad," Jess said. He smiled. It felt good to hear his dad say that he was
proud of him.

TO DISCUSS: God commands us to show respect to our elders, especially to the
elderly. Since respect is a godly value, how can you show respect for people who are
older than you?

TO PRAY: "We value respect, Lord, because you value respect. Open our eyes to the
people around us who are deserving of our respect."

18 Boys, Girls, and Plumbers

GOD VALUES RESPECT BECAUSE EVERY HUMAN BEING WAS CREATED IN HIS IMAGE.

Bible Reading of the Day: Read Ephesians 5:33–6:5, 9.
Verse of the Day: *"I see very clearly that God doesn't show partiality. In every nation he accepts those who fear him and do what is right"* (Acts 10:34-35).

"Girls are stupid!" Jeremy shouted.

"Oh, yeah?" his cousin, Leah, answered. "Well, boys are gross and disgusting!"

"Oh, yeah?" Jeremy countered. "Girls are—"

"Hey!" said Jeremy's dad, interrupting the shouting match. "What's going on here?"

"She doesn't know how to play this game right," Jeremy complained.

"He's just a stupid, gross *boy!*" Leah answered, spitting out the last word as if it were the worst insult one human being could hurl at another.

"I see," said Dad. "It sounds like you two are having trouble playing together." He gripped the children's hands and walked them over to the couch. "I don't like it when you call each other names and act like girls are stupid and boys are disgusting."

Dad paused and squeezed Leah's hand in his. "Tell me, Leah, who made you? Who decided that you would be a girl?"

She thought for a moment. "God?" she answered.

Dad nodded, then turned to Jeremy. "And who made you?"

"God," Jeremy answered, sounding as if he thought the question was too easy.

"Right," Dad said. "And God made *you* in his image," he said, pointing to Leah. "And he made *you* in his image," he said, pointing to Jeremy. "Let me ask you something else," he added. "What about dark-skinned people? Did God make them?"

"Yes," Jeremy answered.

"And light-skinned people?"

"God made them, too!" Leah said.

"What about teachers? And plumbers?"

"God made them all, Dad!" Jeremy answered.

"That's right. He made them all, and he made them all *in his image.* That means every one of them deserves to be respected as a human being who's made in the image of God. That means you," he said—turning to his son—"should respect girls. And you,"— he said to Leah—"should respect boys. Do you think you can do that?"

"I guess," Leah said, shrugging.

"I can do it better than you can!" Jeremy taunted as he jumped up from the couch. Leah chased him out of the room.

Dad sighed. "One step at a time," he said with a chuckle.

 TO DO: Take turns listing all the varieties of people who are worthy of respect (including various races, nationalities, and occupations, as well as both sexes). Make the activity fun and lighthearted, but make it meaningful as well.

TO PRAY: "God, help us to remember that everyone is worthy of respect."

19 God's Masterpiece

SELF-RESPECT HELPS US TO RESPECT OTHERS.

Bible Reading of the Day: Read Ephesians 2:10-22.
Verse of the Day: *"Thank you for making me so wonderfully complex!
Your workmanship is marvelous—and how well I know it" (Psalm 139:14).*

Adam had been having a rough day. He had broken one of his favorite toys. He had struggled for a long time to put together a simple puzzle that he had completed easily several times before. He had even knocked his baby brother's milk over at the lunch table. Finally, angered by the kind of day he was having, he had answered his mother disrespectfully and loudly when she asked him to put some of his toys away.

After Mom sat him in a chair by himself for a while, she called him over and patted the couch cushion next to her. She had a piece of paper in her hand.

"Adam," Mom said, "I want to show you a list of names I heard a person call someone." She read the names off one by one: "'Stupid.' 'Dummy.' 'Clumsy.' 'Bad.'"

She balanced the paper on Adam's knees. "What do you think about those names?"

"They're not very nice," Adam said.

"What do you think a person should do if someone calls him names like that?"

Adam shrugged. "Tell him to stop, I guess."

"What if I told you the person who used all those names was you?" Mom said.

Adam's eyes widened. "I didn't—" he started. Then a look of realization crossed his face. He remembered using those names that day. He looked at his mom. "I didn't call anybody those names. I was talking to myself."

"Would it be OK for somebody else to call you those names?" Mom asked.

"No," Adam answered.

"Why not?"

"Because they're not nice. They're mean."

"That's right," Mom said. "They're not respectful. No one should call you these names. You shouldn't either. I want you to respect yourself. You know why?"

Adam shook his head.

"Because you're my son," she said, "but also because you're God's masterpiece! God made you in his image when he made you a part of our family. And he remade you in his Son's image when he made you a part of God's family!"

Adam studied his mom's smiling face without speaking.

"And when you respect yourself, Adam, it will be easier for you to respect others. But if you call yourself 'stupid,' it'll be easier for you to call others names, too."

"I'm sorry," he said. He hugged his mom. "I'll treat myself nicer from now on."

"Good," Mom said. "I'd like that."

 TO DISCUSS: How do you show that you respect yourself? Why do you think respecting yourself helps you to respect others?

 TO PRAY: "Lord, when it comes to respecting others, help us not to leave ourselves out. We can't respect others if we don't respect ourselves."

20 The New Principal

THE BENEFITS OF RESPECT AREN'T ALWAYS IMMEDIATE; BUT RESPECT IS BETTER IN THE LONG RUN.

Bible Reading of the Day: Read Romans 13:1-7.
Verse of the Day: *"Give everyone what you owe him: If you owe taxes, pay taxes; if revenue, then revenue; if respect, then respect; if honor, then honor" (Romans 13:7, NIV).*

Kay was horrified. Only two days of school had passed, and already she'd been sent to the principal's office.

The lunchroom lady, Mrs. Vanderhorn, had accused her of making a rude gesture behind her back. Kay was embarrassed by the woman's accusation, and she was terrified of going to the principal's office. Everyone at school said the new principal was tough.

She entered the principal's office, carrying in her hand the piece of paper detailing the lunch lady's report. After a few moments, one of the office staff ushered her into the principal's office. Kay shut the door behind her and turned to face the new principal.

"You?" Kay asked. The word was out of her mouth before she could stop it.

"Hello, Kay!" Mrs. White said, smiling broadly and looking as surprised as Kay.

Kay's mouth hung open. Mrs. White had been her counselor at a Christian camp the summer before last. She had heard that the new principal's name was Mrs. White, but she had never suspected that it would be the woman who had been her camp counselor.

They chatted for a few moments, then Mrs. White gingerly took the report from Kay's fingers. Kay flushed with embarrassment as Mrs. White read it.

"Did you do what this report says you did?" Mrs. White asked.

"No, ma'am," Kay answered. "I don't know why she thinks I did, but . . ."

The principal waved the paper back and forth slowly in the air. She seemed to be thinking. Finally, she spoke. "Kay," she said seriously, "the summer I was your counselor at camp, I probably got to know more than a hundred girls, and I don't remember *one* who was more polite and respectful than you were."

Kay smiled shyly at Mrs. White.

"That hasn't changed, has it?" Mrs. White asked.

"No, ma'am," Kay said. "I don't think so."

Mrs. White smiled warmly. "I don't think so either," she said. "I'll talk to Mrs. Vanderhorn."

"Oh, thank you, Mrs. White," Kay gushed. "Thank you so much."

"You're welcome. And now I think you'd better get to class."

Kay nodded and turned to leave. She stopped as she opened the door and turned with a smile. "Welcome to Stuart School," she said.

"Thank you," the new principal answered.

TO DISCUSS: Do you think it's always easy to show respect? Why or why not? Do you think showing respect always "pays off"? Why or why not? How can you show respect to those in authority (school, government, church, and so on)?

TO PRAY: "Heavenly Father, help us to respect those in authority over us, even when respect doesn't come easily."

21 Star Attraction

RESPECT KEEPS US FROM OFFENDING OTHERS AND MAKES US MORE ATTRACTIVE.

Bible Reading of the Day: Read Luke 23:32-33, 39-43.

Verse of the Day: *"Take delight in honoring each other" (Romans 12:10).*

Mandy stood in line watching the filming of a network television show at the amusement park.

"I can't believe it's really *him,"* she gushed to her friend, Carla. "We're actually going to meet Brad Jansen!"

Mandy and Carla each had posters of Brad Jansen, the teen star of the television show, *Ventura Highway,* tacked all over the walls of their bedrooms. They had seen every episode of his show and thought he was the coolest boy in the world. And now they had a chance to meet him and get his autograph!

As they waited, a young woman brought a tray of sandwiches onto the set and set them next to Brad's chair. When the filming stopped for a moment, Brad snatched one of the sandwiches and bit off a corner.

"No! No!" he said, spitting what he had bitten into his hand. He looked around for the woman who had brought the sandwiches and located her standing to one side of the set. He picked up the tray and thrust it into the young woman's stomach.

"I said 'no cheese,' didn't I?!" he shouted. The woman stared wordlessly at him, her face flushing with embarrassment. "Can't you get a simple sandwich order right? Are you a total moron?"

He yelled at her for a few more moments before ordering her to get some more sandwiches. "And get it right this time," he added.

"Did you see that?" Carla whispered to Mandy, still staring at the retreating back of the handsome actor.

"Yeah," Mandy said. She swallowed hard.

The two girls stood side by side in silence as the actors of *Ventura Highway* started filming the next scene. Finally, Mandy broke the silence.

"Are you thinking what I'm thinking?" she asked.

"Yeah," Carla said, her voice flat.

Mandy blew out a long sigh and shook her head. The two friends put their pens and paper back in their pockets and left the line.

"Well," Carla said as they walked away, "that was a waste of time."

"Not really," Mandy said. "Now I can clear up some space for new posters!"

"Me too!" Carla agreed, laughing.

 TO DISCUSS: Why do you think Brad Jansen became suddenly unattractive to Mandy and Carla? In the story of Jesus' crucifixion (today's Bible reading), who do you admire more—the repentant (and respectful) thief, or the thief who scoffed at Jesus? Why? In what ways do you think showing proper respect can make a person more attractive and admirable to other people?

TO PRAY: "Lord, help us to honor each other with our respect."

22 Praise and Punishment

RESPECT PROTECTS US FROM CONDEMNATION AND PROVIDES FOR PRAISE.

Bible Reading of the Day: Read Romans 13:2-4.
Verse of the Day: *"The authorities do not frighten people who are doing right, but they frighten those who do wrong. So do what they say, and you will get along well" (Romans 13:3).*

Four-year-old Chad raced into his mother's arms after Sunday school.

"Mommy!" he cried. "Look what I got!" He showed her a bright yellow sticker on his shirt, bearing the words, "Good job!" in bold black letters.

"Where did you get that?" Mom asked.

"Teacher gave it to me," Chad said. "She said I was the most *r'pectful* student in her class this week!"

"Respectful? Wonderful!" Mom said, clapping her hands. "What did you do to earn that sticker?"

He quickly remembered. "I put my crayons away as soon as the teacher said, and I never talked when she was talking . . . like I do sometimes."

Mom tousled Chad's hair. "That's wonderful, Chad. I'm so proud of you."

Just then, Chad's eight-year-old sister Penny walked up. "My teacher wants to talk to you," Penny said. She had a grouchy expression on her face.

"Why?" Mom asked. Chad listened with interest.

"I don't know," Penny answered. "I . . . I might have said some bad things."

"Like what, sweetheart?" Mom asked.

Penny shrugged. "I . . . I *might* have called the teacher a mean old lady."

"Penny, you didn't!"

Penny nodded sadly. "I'm sorry, Mom! I didn't think she could hear me."

"That doesn't matter, Penny. What you said was very disrespectful."

"I know," Penny muttered.

Mom glanced from her son to her daughter. "I want you two to remember what you feel like now. Chad, you feel happy and proud, don't you?"

The boy nodded.

"You feel that way because you were respectful in Sunday-school class. And Penny, you feel sad and a little ashamed right now, don't you?" She watched Penny nod. "So," Mom continued, "which do you like better—the way you feel when you've been respectful to other people, or the way you feel when you've been disrespectful?"

"Respectful!" both children answered.

"Good," Mom said. She took her children's hands in hers. "Now, Penny, let's go apologize to your teacher."

 TO DO: Write a note of appreciation to someone in authority over you (a boss, a teacher, a pastor). Tell that person how much his or her authority has meant to you over the years.

TO PRAY: "God, thank you for reminding us that respecting others protects us from bad feelings and provides praise too."

23 Staying Close

RESPECT FOR OTHERS ENRICHES OUR RELATIONSHIPS.

Bible Reading of the Day: Read 2 Samuel 9:6-10.
Verse of the Day: *"A real friend sticks closer than a brother"*
(Proverbs 18:24).

Tess and Cora were rollerblading together at the city park when they saw Stephanie, one of their classmates. The two girls waved at the same time, and Stephanie waved back from across the wide lawn.

"Didn't you and Stephanie used to be friends?" Cora asked, as she and Tess paused by the drinking fountain to take a break and tighten the laces on their inline skates.

"We still are," Tess answered.

"Yeah, but I mean, didn't you use to be really close friends?"

"Yeah, I guess so." Cora was right; Tess and Stephanie used to be extremely close. They spent almost all their spare time together. They could even complete each other's sentences. But Stephanie had a few habits that bothered Tess. She would make fun of Tess in front of their other friends. She often interrupted when Tess was speaking, and when Tess would object or get upset, Stephanie would respond with a comment like, "Grow up" or "Get a life!" Stephanie would even pull Tess's hair and punch her in the arm when Tess did or said something she didn't like.

For a long time, Tess had put up with her friend's behavior, but as she matured, she realized that Stephanie's conduct was disrespectful. But when she told her friend how she felt, Stephanie became angry and treated Tess even more rudely than before.

Since that time, Tess had tried to remain Stephanie's friend, but refused to let Stephanie be disrespectful and boss her around.

"So what happened?" Cora asked, interrupting Tess's thoughts.

"What?" Tess said, before she belatedly understood Cora's question. "Oh," she answered, "we just kinda drifted apart."

"Why?" Cora asked, pressing for an answer.

"Is it OK with you if I don't answer that question?"

Cora shrugged. "Sure," she said.

"I thought so." Tess smiled at her friend. "That's why I really appreciate your friendship. You, uh . . . you respect me, and I respect you."

"Well, sure," Cora said. "Isn't that what friends are supposed to do?"

"Yeah," answered Tess. "It sure is."

TO DISCUSS: In today's Bible reading, who respected whom? In the story above, how did Tess show respect for Stephanie, even though she disagreed with her? How did Cora show respect for Tess? How do you think showing respect to others strengthens and enriches your relationships?

TO PRAY: "Lord, even when we disagree with friends, help us to respect them."

24 Make Up Your Mind

CHOOSING TO DO RIGHT IS EASIER WHEN YOU'VE ALREADY MADE UP YOUR MIND.

Bible Reading of the Day: Read Daniel 1:3–8.
Verse of the Day: *"I am determined to keep your principles, even forever, to the very end" (Psalm 119:112).*

David followed his buddies around the corner and into the alley beside the laundromat.

"What are you guys doing?" he said.

"You'll see," Neil answered.

"Yeah," said Paul. He cast a furtive glance to his left, then to his right. "OK, show him," he told Neil.

Neil smiled and dug into his pocket. After a careful look behind him, he pulled a pack of cigarettes from his pocket.

David's mouth dropped open. "You guys are gonna *smoke?*"

"No," Paul answered. *"We* are gonna smoke."

"Yeah," Neil said. "It's like a club, OK?"

David shook his head. "Not me," he said.

"Come on," Neil said. "You're not wimping out on us, are you?"

"No," David said, shrugging. "I'm just not doing it."

"Whatever," Neil said. He tapped a cigarette out of the box and stuck it between his lips. He offered one to Paul, who aped his friend's actions.

"See you guys later," David said. He started to walk away.

"Wait a minute," Neil said, dropping the cigarette from his mouth as he called out to David. "You're really leaving?"

David took two steps back toward his friends. "Hey," he said, "I made my mind up a long time ago that I wasn't gonna do that stuff."

"So you're just leaving?" Paul said.

"If you're gonna smoke," David answered.

Neil and Paul looked at each other. Neither had lit his cigarette.

"So where are you going?" Neil asked.

"I don't know," David answered. "Anywhere but here." He turned and started to leave.

Neil and Paul exchanged glances again. After a moment of hesitation, Neil crumpled the pack of cigarettes and threw it into the dumpster. "OK," he said. He turned to Paul. "Let's go."

"Where to?" Paul asked.

"Anywhere but here," Neil answered, as he trotted to catch up to David.

 TO DISCUSS: Do you think it was easy for David (in the story above) or Daniel (in the Bible reading) to stand up for their beliefs? Why or why not? What would have made it easier for Daniel and David to do the right thing?

 TO PRAY: "God, when we're afraid to speak out, please give us the courage to stand up for our beliefs."

25 Everybody Does It!

FRIENDS WHO TRY TO TALK YOU INTO WRONG CHOICES ARE LIKELY TO HURT YOU, NOT HELP YOU.

Bible Reading of the Day: Read 1 Peter 4:1-5, 19.
Verse of the Day: *"In everything set them an example by doing what is good"* (Titus 2:7, NIV).

John walked with his friends, Andy and Todd, to the pond.

"Don't walk so fast," John complained. "I can't keep up." He had to work harder than his friends because his left foot was in a cast. The cast was removable—John could take it off when he took a shower, for example—but the doctor had given him stern instructions not to swim or play sports until the toe he had broken last week was fully healed. Otherwise, the doctor had informed him, the toe would not heal properly and would probably require surgery.

As they got closer to the pond, Andy and Todd's strides grew longer, and John fell behind. When he reached the pond, he noticed that his friends had left their towels, shoes, and shirts on the bank and were already in the water.

"Come on in, John," Todd called. "The water's great!"

"Yeah," said Andy. "Come on!" He pitched forward under the water.

"I can't," John answered. "You guys know what the doctor said."

"Oh, a little water's not going to hurt anything," Andy said, splashing water in John's direction.

The day was hot, and John knew that the water would feel so good. But he shook his head. "I don't want to have to have an operation," he said.

"You won't," Todd said. "It's just a toe."

"Yeah, don't be such a wimp," Andy said.

John looked at the gleaming water. The little pond had never looked so clean and inviting. *And swimming wasn't too different from taking a bath, was it?* he reasoned within himself.

John shook his head again. "I'd get in trouble if I went swimming," he said. "My parents would kill me."

Andy looked from one side of the pond to the other. "I don't see your parents," he said sarcastically. "Do you?"

John hesitated just a moment before he sat down on the bank and started carefully removing his cast. As he did, he seemed to be arguing with his conscience. "I know I shouldn't do this," he whispered. "I'm gonna be sorry."

 TO DISCUSS: Do you think John's friends showed concern or lack of concern for him? Why? Do your friends ever entice you to join them in wrong or harmful behaviors? Do they act "very surprised" that you won't? Do they ever "say evil things about you" when you refuse to participate in their actions as the Bible reading mentions? What does today's Bible reading say is a proper response when such things happen?

 TO PRAY: "Help us, Lord, to have the proper response when friends 'say evil things' about us. Help us also to follow your way, even if no one else does."

26 High Voltage

SEXUAL INTIMACY IS A POWERFUL FORCE, ONE THAT SHOULD BE KEPT BETWEEN A HUSBAND AND WIFE.

Bible Reading of the Day: Read Hebrews 13:4.

Verse of the Day: *"Give honor to marriage, and remain faithful to one another in marriage" (Hebrews 13:4).*

Samantha was helping Dad fix the lamp in her bedroom.

"Now," Dad instructed her, "you always have to be very careful when you're working with electricity, Sam." He unscrewed the light assembly from the base of the lamp, then slipped off the cardboard piece that covered the wires and placed his screwdriver in one of the screws that held the wires in place. *"Yeeoww!"*

Samantha immediately saw sparks. "Daddy, are you all right?" she asked.

Dad shook his hand up and down in the air. "Yeah, Sam, I'm fine." Dad looked behind Sam's bedside table, then faced his daughter with a sheepish expression. "I forgot to tell you the most important thing to remember when you're working with electrical things." He reached behind the table and pulled the lamp's plug out of the wall outlet. "Always make sure they're unplugged first!"

"Are you sure you're not hurt, Daddy?" Sam asked.

"Yes, I'm fine. But I could have been hurt. That's why you always need to be careful with electricity."

"I don't think I like electricity," Sam said, only half joking.

"Sure you do," Dad said. "It's what powers your lights and your fan and your CD player. But the same force that does all those things can hurt you too."

Dad concentrated for a few moments on replacing the switch in Samantha's lamp.

"There," he said. "All done." He plugged the lamp in and switched it on. "Works fine." He motioned for Sam to sit down. "Electricity is a powerful force, Sam, and in that respect, it's a lot like something else I want to talk to you about."

Sam looked at him curiously.

"Someday soon," Dad continued, "you're going to begin dating, and you're going to start thinking about getting married, and so on. When you do, I want you to remember that shock I just got. I want you to understand that sexual intimacy is a lot like electricity. It's a powerful force, Sam, and it can be a wonderful thing if you respect it and use it the way God intended. But it can hurt you too. As long as sex is kept between a husband and wife, it's a beautiful and awesome thing. But if it's not between a husband and wife, it's even more dangerous and harmful than electricity."

"OK, Dad," Sam said, with a twinkle in her eye. "I'll remember that. I don't want to get burned . . . like you did!"

TO DISCUSS: What are society's beliefs about sexual intimacy outside of marriage? How do these beliefs conflict with God's desires?

TO PRAY: A parent could pray the following: "God, help us to honor marriage and to treat it with the respect and care that it deserves. We acknowledge that sexual intimacy belongs *in* marriage, *not* outside of it. In Jesus' name. Amen."

27 God and Good

GOD ALONE KNOWS WHAT IS GOOD.

Bible Reading of the Day: Read Genesis 1:1-12.
Verse of the Day: *"No one is good—except God alone" (Mark 10:18, NIV).*

"Dathan, would you like some of Mommy's eggs?" Mom asked her two-year-old.

"Don't like eggs," Dathan said. He sat at the breakfast table with his mother, father, and sister, Carlene.

"Would you like some of Mommy's sausage?" Mom asked.

"Don't like saufage," Dathan answered.

"It's really good, Dathan," Dad said. He spooned a bite of eggs into his mouth and chewed, smiling and wiggling his eyebrows.

"No! Don't like saufage!" Dathan insisted.

"All right, then," Mom suggested, "why don't you have a bite of Daddy's toast?"

"Don't like toast," Dathan said.

"You don't like anything this morning, do you?" Mom said.

"You just don't know what's good," Dad teased.

"Of course not," said Carlene matter-of-factly. "Nobody does, except God."

Mom and Dad stopped chewing and turned to look at Carlene. Her comment surprised them.

"It's true," Carlene said confidently. "Only God knows what's good. Right, Dad?"

"Yes," Dad answered slowly. "You're right, Carlene. We may agree or disagree with what God says is good, but ultimately he's the only one who knows what is good and what is bad."

"We just need to listen to him and follow what he says is good," Mom added.

"Does that mean Dathan has to like eggs and sausage?" Carlene asked.

Dad chuckled. "Well, Dathan's allowed to decide whether he thinks eggs and sausage *taste good*. That's called 'taste' or 'opinion.' But when it comes to moral decisions—right and wrong—none of us are allowed to decide what's good or bad. Only God can decide that."

TO DISCUSS: What's the difference between taste (or opinion) and right or wrong? Are you allowed to decide what foods taste good? Are you allowed to decide what's right or wrong? What's the difference?

TO PRAY: "God, remind us that only you can decide what's good or bad, right or wrong. Help us to agree with you and follow what you say is good."

28 It Was Good

TO BE GOOD IS TO BE LIKE GOD.

Bible Reading of the Day: Read Genesis 1:14-25.
Verse of the Day: *"They raised their voices in praise to the Lord and sang: 'He is good; his love endures forever'"* (2 Chronicles 5:13, NIV).

Tasha ran into the cabin so fast that she nearly tripped and fell. "Look what I caught!" she said.

She ran to Rebecca, her counselor at Camp Wonderlake, and gingerly opened her cupped hands.

"A butterfly!" Rebecca said. "It's beautiful, Tasha. Where did you catch it?"

"By the creek." She opened her hands a little wider so she and Rebecca could study the vivid colors and intricate designs of the butterfly's wings.

"Isn't God's creation incredible?" Rebecca whispered. "Just look at how perfect it looks."

"Yeah," Tasha cooed. "It sure is."

Rebecca grabbed her Bible off the table beside her cot and turned to the first chapter of Genesis. "Can I read you something from the Bible?" she asked.

"Sure," said Tasha, still gazing at the butterfly.

Rebecca began reading the Creation account from the Bible, pausing every time she read the words, "And God saw that it was good." When she finished, she closed the Bible and said to Tasha, "When God created this world—all the mountains and oceans, and trees, and animals—he said it was good."

"It is," Tasha said.

"Yeah," answered Rebecca. "But what does that mean?"

Tasha threw a look of confusion at Rebecca.

"See, Tasha, when God created the heavens and the earth, the only standard for good that existed was God himself. So when he called his creation 'good,' he was saying it reflected his own goodness, because there was nothing else to compare it to."

"So," Tasha began, looking back and forth between Rebecca and the butterfly, "when we say something is good, we're saying . . . we're saying . . . it's like God?"

"Yes!" Rebecca cried. "That's right. To be good is to reflect God's nature. That's what 'good' means."

Tasha nodded slowly. She smiled at Rebecca. "That's good," she said. "That's good."

TO DISCUSS: Six times in the first twenty-six verses of Genesis 1, God calls his creation "good." Why do you think he said this word six times?

TO PRAY: "God, we acknowledge that you are the only standard of good that exists. Help us not to rely on our own opinions when we need to make moral choices."

29 God's Image

TO REFLECT THE IMAGE OF GOD IS TO ACHIEVE THE HIGHEST GOOD.

Bible Reading of the Day: Read Genesis 1:26-31.
Verse of the Day: *"As the Spirit of the Lord works within us, we become more and more like him and reflect his glory even more"* (2 Corinthians 3:18).

"Do that again," Grandmother said.

"Do what again?" her grandson, Kwok, asked.

"The way you laughed just then," Grandmother answered. "You look just like your father when you do that."

"I do?" Kwok responded. He jumped up and raced to the bathroom to gaze at his reflection in the mirror. He studied his reflection from every angle and tried repeating the laugh that had caught his grandmother's attention.

He returned a few moments later. "It doesn't work," he said.

Grandmother smiled. "Maybe it only works when you're not trying to make it work."

"Besides," Kwok said, "I thought I always looked like my father."

"You do," Grandmother admitted, "but when you do certain things, the resemblance is even stronger."

"Is that how it is with God's image?" Kwok asked.

"What do you mean?" Grandmother asked.

"Well, you said that I always look like my father, but when I do certain things, I look even more like him."

"Yes," Grandmother said.

Kwok frowned as if trying to think so hard it hurt. "The Bible says we're made in God's image," he continued. "But don't we look more like him when we do certain things?"

Grandmother's mouth opened slightly. She looked surprised. "Yes," she said, "in a way, I think you're right. Human beings *are* created in the image of God. But we don't always act like it, do we?"

"But when we do good," Kwok suggested, smiling, "the resemblance is stronger, like you said."

"There," Grandmother said, "you did it again!"

"What?"

"You looked just like your father."

"Which one—God or Dad?"

"Both," Grandmother said, her eyes twinkling.

 TO DISCUSS: Why do you think God called his creation of man "very good," rather than just "good"? What can you do this week to reflect God's image in your actions?

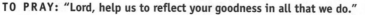 **TO PRAY:** "Lord, help us to reflect your goodness in all that we do."

30 Min's Mistake

THERE IS OFTEN A DIFFERENCE BETWEEN A WRONG CHOICE AND A POOR CHOICE.

Bible Reading of the Day: Read Proverbs 10:19-21, 31-32.
Verse of the Day: *"The godly speak words that are helpful, but the wicked speak only what is corrupt" (Proverbs 10:32).*

Mom noticed that Min was in a bad mood when she came home from school, but she said nothing until after dinner, when Min was alone in her room.

"Is something wrong?" Mom asked as she entered Min's room.

Min started crying. "Oh, Mom! Why do I have to have such a big mouth?"

"What do you mean?" Mom sat next to Min on the bed.

"Jackie told me she really liked my sweater. I felt embarrassed because Jackie always wears really nice clothes, and I couldn't think of anything to say. So I just blurted out, 'Oh, this old thing? I've got lots of sweaters that are even nicer than this!' . . . Well, I didn't realize until I'd said it that Hannah was standing there too!"

Mom nodded, but it was obvious to Min that her mom didn't understand the importance of what she had just said.

"Mom," she said, her voice quivering, "this sweater was a gift from Hannah!"

Mom's eyes widened slightly and her mouth formed a silent "O."

"I apologized as much as I could to Hannah, but I could tell her feelings were hurt. . . . I didn't mean it!"

Mom wrapped her arms around Min and gently stroked her long black hair. "I know you didn't," she told Min. "We all make mistakes. But it's a mistake you can learn from."

Min sniffed and said nothing, but Mom could tell she was listening.

"You may not have made a *wrong* choice, like you would have if you had intended to hurt Hannah," Mom said, "but you did make a *poor* choice. You see, Min, usually when we don't know what to say, it's better to say nothing . . . or, in your case today, to keep your words to a minimum."

"I should have just said, 'thank you,' and nothing else, right?" Min offered. "If I had, I wouldn't feel so bad right now."

"You're right," Mom agreed. "But remember, there is sometimes a difference between a wrong choice and a poor choice. Wrong choices are always poor choices, but poor choices are not always sinful. You can't help but regret how you made Hannah feel, but don't feel guilty. What you said was a mistake, not a sin."

Min wiped the tears from her cheeks. "Thanks, Mom," she said. "I'm going to call Hannah and apologize for what I said. And from now on, I'm going to try to remember to keep my mouth shut when I don't know what to say!"

 TO DISCUSS: What could Min have done to prevent hurting Hannah's feelings? Why is it important to think before speaking?

 TO PRAY: "Lord, help us to avoid hurting others. But when we do make a mistake and hurt someone, help us to make things right."

1 Wrong Measurements

PEOPLE WHO MEASURE THEMSELVES BY THEMSELVES AND COMPARE THEMSELVES
WITH THEMSELVES ARE NOT WISE.

Bible Reading of the Day: Read 2 Corinthians 10:12-18.
Verse of the Day: *"For it is not the one who commends himself who
is approved, but the one whom the Lord commends" (2 Corinthians
10:18, NIV).*

Tyree liked helping his father. Dad was really good at building things and fixing things.
Tyree always felt proud and happy when he and Dad worked together.

He also was glad that his dad was starting to give him more responsibility. They
were installing sturdy shelving in the storeroom of a food pantry near their home, and
Dad had let Tyree run the circular saw they used to cut the shelves.

"Tyree," Dad mumbled through a mouthful of nails, "could you please bring me
three shelves?"

"Sure, Dad," Tyree answered. He leaped to the short lengths of lumber he'd cut
and stacked and grabbed three pieces off the top. As he picked them up, he was
horrified to notice that they were all different lengths!

He took them to his dad. "I, uh, didn't get 'em all the right size," he said.

Dad took the three shelves from his son and laid them on the floor of the storeroom.
"You're right," he said, scratching his head. "How'd you measure them?"

"I just laid a board on top of the board I was cutting and drew a line."

Dad nodded. "Did you use the same board every time?"

Tyree shook his head. "No," he answered. "But they should all be the same length."

Dad smiled. "There's your mistake," he said good-naturedly.

Tyree's mouth opened in a silent *O* shape. He slapped his forehead as though he
should have known all along what he was doing wrong. Every time he cut a board,
he would use that board to measure the next. If the board he'd just cut was just a tiny
bit smaller or larger than the last one he cut, he would be using a whole different
measurement every time he cut a shelf.

"I'm sorry, Dad," he said.

"Oh, that's all right, Son," Dad answered. "That's a mistake we've all made. Just
make sure you always use the right measurement *every time* you cut."

Dad's words sounded familiar. Then Tyree remembered. "Just like choosing right
from wrong," he told his dad. "We need to make sure we always measure our decisions
against the only standard that counts—God. Right, Dad?"

"That's right," Dad answered. "Always measure against the original."

"I'll remember that from now on," Tyree said. "I promise."

 TO DISCUSS: What standard do you most often rely on to decide what's right or
wrong: What your parents say? What your friends say or do? What the law says? What
you think? Or do you compare your choices with God and his character?

 TO PRAY: "Lord, thank you for your reminder that you are the only true standard
of right and wrong."

2 More than a Matter of Taste

THERE ARE SOME THINGS THAT AREN'T NECESSARILY RIGHT OR WRONG.

Bible Reading of the Day: Read Romans 14:1-4.
Verse of the Day: *"I always try to maintain a clear conscience before God and everyone else"* (Acts 24:16).

"Everything is black and white to you, isn't it?" Blair asked, as he sat beside Tina on the dock. Their fishing poles dangled in the water beneath the dock.

"What do you mean?" Tina asked.

"Well, you're always talking about right and wrong."

"Well, OK," said Tina, "but there are lots of things that aren't right or wrong."

"Like what?"

"OK, like some people like strawberry ice cream. Some think vanilla ice cream tastes better. Neither one is wrong; it's just that they have different tastes."

"Uh-huh," Blair said.

"Or, suppose your parents won't let you stay out past midnight, and mine say I have to be home by eleven o'clock. Your parents aren't wrong, and mine aren't either. They're trying to choose what's best for their kids."

"So how do you tell the difference?" Blair asked.

"The difference?"

"Yeah, between things that are right or wrong and things that are just, you know, different tastes, or stuff like that."

Tina thought for a moment. "Well," she said, "if the Bible says it's wrong, then it's wrong. If the Bible says it's right, then it's right."

"What if the Bible doesn't say anything about it?" Blair's eyes lit up. "Like, the Bible never says, 'Thou shalt not pull Tina's hair.'" He grabbed a handful of Tina's hair and yanked.

"Ouch!" Tina said, gripping Blair's wrist and holding it while he continued to hold her hair. "You're right," she said, speaking very fast, "but we also know something is right if it's like God, and something is wrong if it's *not* like God. And God is love, the Bible says, and 'love does no harm to its neighbor,' and you're hurting me, so let go!"

Blair let go of Tina's hair. "You think you're so smart, don't you?"

Tina rubbed her head. "Smart enough to know one thing," she said.

"What's that?" Blair asked.

"You're all wet!" she said, as she pushed him into the water.

 TO DISCUSS: Can you name something that's a matter of taste rather than a matter of right and wrong? Can you name something that's a choice between a wise and an unwise action that's not necessarily a matter of right and wrong? Can you name something that's a choice between good, better, or best, that's not necessarily a matter of right and wrong? How can we tell the difference between those things and matters of right and wrong?

TO PRAY: "Lord, help us not to confuse taste with truth. Help us to recognize truth when we see it and to follow it."

3 Fort Providence

GOD'S LOVING COMMANDS PROTECT US LIKE THE WALLS OF A FORT.

Bible Reading of the Day: Read Psalm 31:19-21.

Verse of the Day: *"Blessed is the Lord, for he has shown me that his never-failing love protects me like the walls of a fort!" (Psalm 31:21, TLB).*

Kevin lay on his stomach in the sand. He kicked his feet and stared contentedly at the sand castle he and his dad had just completed. They had formed large towers at each corner with the help of Kevin's sand pail. The towers were joined by four solid walls. The castle keep sported a soda-straw flagpole with a candy-wrapper flag.

"It's neat," Kevin said.

"Yeah," Dad said. He seemed almost as pleased as his son.

"How long will it take the ocean to wash it away?" Kevin asked.

Dad turned his head to check the approaching tide. "It won't reach our castle until after we leave to go home."

"Good." Kevin reached out his hand to straighten the flagpole. Suddenly his eyes brightened, and he smiled at his dad. "Wouldn't it be neat if we had castle walls around our house?"

Dad opened his mouth to answer, but Kevin kept talking.

"We could have a bridge that we would let down only if we knew it was safe, and nobody could get in unless they knew the secret password!"

Dad nodded, smiling. He leaned on his elbow in the sand. "You know, Kev," he said, "we sorta do have castle walls around our house."

Kevin sucked his bottom lip under his teeth, an expression he often wore when he was thinking.

Dad continued. "Our home is protected by God's commandments," he said.

Kevin blinked uncertainly.

Dad rolled over onto his back and pulled Kevin onto his chest. "See, Kev, God loves us. And he gave his commands to us for our own good, just like Mommy and Daddy tell you to eat all your vegetables or not to play in the street because we love you and want to take good care of you. God's commands are like a wall of protection around us, just like the walls of a fort or a castle. That's one of the reasons God gave his commandments—to protect us from a lot of bad things."

"I still wish we lived in a castle," Kevin said.

Dad nodded. "Yeah, then I could throw you in the dungeon when you don't eat your vegetables!"

"I'd throw *you* in the dungeon!" Kevin countered as he and his father rolled over in the sand, laughing and trading threats of imprisonment.

 TO DISCUSS: Do the walls of a castle or fort protect those who decide to stay outside the walls? Whom do they protect? How can you stay inside the walls of God's protection?

 TO PRAY: "God, thank you for the protection of your commands."

4 Endowed by Their Creator

A GOVERNMENT MAY HONOR YOUR BASIC RIGHTS AS A HUMAN BEING, BUT IT DOES NOT *GRANT* THEM–GOD DOES THAT.

Bible Reading of the Day: Read Psalm 82.
Verse of the Day: *"What joy for the nation whose God is the Lord"* *(Psalm 33:12).*

"Daddy, can you help me with my homework?" Juan José asked as he entered the family room, where his father sat at the computer.

"Yes, Juan José," Dad said. He swiveled in his computer chair. "What are you working on?"

"We have to memorize the Declaration of Independence," Juan José answered. He handed his textbook to his dad.

"Let me hear what you've memorized so far," Dad said.

"OK." Juan José inhaled. He began and, with an occasional hint or help from Dad, recited the first sentence. He continued, "'We hold these truths to be self-evident, that all men are created equal, that they are endowed by their Creator with certain unalienable rights . . .'"

"*¡Excelente!*" Dad exclaimed, using the Spanish for "excellent." "Let me interrupt you there. That's a really important part of the Declaration of Independence. I want to be sure you understand what you're saying."

"I don't have a clue what I'm saying," Juan José explained.

"Well, it means that every man and woman has certain rights, which aren't given to us by the government; they're given to us by God, the God who created us."

"Uh-huh," Juan José said.

"You see, Son, the very basis of this idea of personal 'rights'–the right to life or liberty, for example–is the fact that there is a God, and he is the one who by his nature defines what is right and what is wrong. A government may honor your basic rights as a human being, but it does not grant them; God does that. Do you understand what I'm trying to say?"

"I don't think so," Juan José answered.

"Let me put it this way: Your right to live or your right to be free is given to you by the righteous God, the one from whom all moral judgments–including human rights–are derived. That's not just me talking; that's the basis on which the United States of America was founded."

"Wow!" Juan José said. "I guess I didn't realize the Declaration of Independence said all that."

"You're not the only one," Dad answered with a smile. "A lot of judges don't realize it either!"

 TO DO: Find a copy of the Declaration of Independence and tack it to your bulletin board or refrigerator this week to remind you that all men and women have been "endowed by their Creator with certain unalienable rights."

TO PRAY: "Thank you, Lord, for the rights and freedom you have given us."

5 Built-in Radar

MEMORIZING GOD'S WORD CREATES INNER RADAR FOR FINDING THE RIGHT WAY.

Bible Reading of the Day: Read Psalm 119:97-105.
Verse of the Day: *"Your word is a lamp to my feet and a light for my path" (Psalm 119:105, NIV).*

"Oh!" Tyler said excitedly to his mom, who sat next to him. "We're in the clouds!"

Mom looked past her son and out the window of the airplane. Wispy strands of whiteness floated by the window. "We sure are!" she said.

"Mommy," Tyler said, his eyes wide with trepidation, "are we going to crash?"

"No, sweetheart. Why would we crash?"

"Because the man who's flying the plane can't see where we're going."

"Oh, don't worry, Tyler," Mom said, "the pilot has a thing called 'radar' that tells him where he should go even when he can't see."

"Oh," Tyler said. He smiled at his mom and then turned his face back toward the window to watch the clouds go by.

Mom watched him for a moment, then turned back to what she had been doing. She held a stack of index cards in her hands. On the front of each card was a Bible verse, and on the back was the verse reference. She would read or glance at a card, then try to recite the verse without looking at the hand-printed words on the card.

"Mommy," Tyler said, interrupting her memorization efforts again, "what are you doing?" When she told him, he asked, "Why?"

She thought for a moment, trying to decide how to explain the importance of Scripture memorization to her young son. Finally, a thought came to her.

"You know how the pilot of this plane has radar so he can find his way even through clouds and darkness?" she asked.

Tyler nodded.

"Well, by memorizing Bible verses," she said, showing him the cards, "I put parts of God's Word in here," she said, pointing to her temples with her index fingers. "That gives me a sort of built-in radar, so that even when things get foggy or dark in my mind or in my life, I can find the right way . . . by using God's Word."

"Oh," Tyler said, seemingly satisfied. "Mommy?"

"Yes, sweetheart?"

"Can your radar find my shoes?"

Mom looked down at Tyler's feet. Both shoes were gone. She laughed. "I think I can do that myself," she said, releasing her seat belt so she could search for Tyler's shoes under the seats.

 TO DISCUSS: How can memorizing God's Word help you make right choices? How many Bible verses do you know by heart? Take turns reciting Bible verses until someone is stumped. (Younger children can receive help or can recite the same verse more than once.)

 TO PRAY: "Lord God, I need the 'radar' that your Word and your Spirit provide to find my way each day."

6 Family Commandments

TREATING OTHERS AS YOU WOULD LIKE TO BE TREATED IS THE BEGINNING OF JUSTICE.

Bible Reading of the Day: Read Luke 6:27-31.
Verse of the Day: *"Do for others as you would like them to do for you"* *(Luke 6:31).*

Dad and Mom sat everyone down around the dining room table for a family meeting.

"I think you're all old enough," Dad said to his four children, "to help Mom and me decide on some family laws that would be fair for everybody."

Suddenly, the room was filled with suggestions as Brittney, Kyle, Melissa, and Michelle began talking all at once. Someone suggested that one rule should be "Don't talk when someone else is talking." Brittney suggested "Don't be bossy." After about thirty minutes, the family had twenty-one "commandments," from "No hitting" to "Ask permission to use things." Mom posted the family commandments on the refrigerator.

Almost two weeks later, Brittney spoke up at the dinner table. "We have too many commandments," she said. "I can't remember them all."

Kyle added, "God gave only ten commandments. Why do we have twenty- one?"

Mom and Dad smiled and agreed. By the time dinner was over, the family had revised their "commandments" to five: "Be nice" (no hitting, kicking, yelling, etc.); "Be clean" (keep yourself, your room, the house, and yard clean); "Be polite" (don't interrupt, say please and thank you, etc.); "Be helpful" (do your chores, etc.); and "Be obedient" (do what Mom and Dad say). They posted the new commandments on the refrigerator.

That week, Mom and Dad heard Michelle tell Brittney, "Be polite," which reminded Brittney not to interrupt her older sister. They also heard Kyle reminding Michelle to "Be clean" and pick up the magazines she had spread out on the living room floor. And once, Melissa leaped up from her seat on the couch, disappeared for a few moments, then returned, explaining that she had forgotten to "Be helpful" by doing her chores, one of which was taking the trash out.

Soon, however, Melissa made another suggestion at the dinner table. "Remember how we used to have twenty-one family commandments, and we narrowed them down to only five?" The others at the table nodded. "Well," she said, "I think we can have only *one* family commandment that will include all of the others."

Everyone stopped eating to listen to Melissa's suggestion. She beamed proudly at her brother, sisters, and parents.

"Well, what is it?" Kyle asked.

"Do for others as you would like them to do for you."

The others were silent for a few moments. Finally, Mom broke the silence. "You're right," she said. "If we obey that commandment, we'll obey the others, won't we?"

 TO DO: Post your own "family commandments" on your refrigerator.

TO PRAY: "Lord, help us to do for others as we would like them to do for us."

7 Missing Markers

FAIRNESS ASKS, "HOW WOULD *YOU* FEEL?" UNFAIRNESS ANSWERS, "THIS IS DIFFERENT."

Bible Reading of the Day: Read Psalm 106:1-3.
Verse of the Day: *"Happy are those who deal justly with others and always do what is right" (Psalm 106:3).*

Nakeesha counted her colored markers for the third time, hoping that she had counted wrong the first two times. But she had counted correctly. Two markers were missing.

"Somebody took my markers!" she told her friend Karissa. Recess had just started, and the other desks in the classroom were empty.

"How do you know?" Karissa asked.

"Look! They're gone. The red and the—the dark purple."

"Are you sure you didn't lose them?" Karissa suggested.

"No!" Nakeesha answered, her eyes flashing. "Somebody stole them!" She looked around the classroom with narrowed, suspicious eyes. "Maybe it was Tanya. No, I bet it was Christopher."

"Why?" Karissa asked.

"Because he's a thief. He's always stealing things from people."

"That's not fair," Karissa said. "You don't know that."

"Leave me alone!" Nakeesha snapped. Her eyebrows shadowed her eyes. "I should take something from everyone in this whole class," she muttered. "That would teach them not to mess with my markers!"

"You can't do that," Karissa whispered in a pleading tone.

"Yes, I can!" Nakeesha said.

"You're going to take something from *everybody* because *one person* took something from you?"

"Yeah!" Nakeesha answered. She stepped up to the desk in front of her hers.

"Nakeesha!" Karissa said, stamping her foot. "How would you feel if someone took your things because somebody else took theirs?"

"This is different," Nakeesha said.

"Why?"

"Because my markers are special. I only use them for special things, like . . ." She stopped suddenly, as if she had just remembered something. She turned away from her friend and dashed toward the closet, where her art frock was hanging. She dug frantically in the large pockets and pulled out two markers—a red one and a dark purple one. Her eyes grew wide, and she looked sheepishly at her friend, who stood with her hands propped on her hips.

"Funny, huh?" Nakeesha said.

"Yeah," Karissa answered, shaking her head. "Real funny."

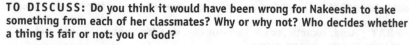

TO DISCUSS: Do you think it would have been wrong for Nakeesha to take something from each of her classmates? Why or why not? Who decides whether a thing is fair or not: you or God?

TO PRAY: "Lord, we want to be fair because you are fair."

8 First in Line

GOD COMMANDS US TO TREAT OTHERS FAIRLY.

Bible Reading of the Day: Read Leviticus 19:13-16.
Verse of the Day: *"Follow justice and justice alone"* (Deuteronomy 16:20, NIV).

"I'm first!" Troy insisted.

"No, you're not, I am!" countered Shawna.

"I am!" Troy said, shoving Shawna out of his way.

Shawna grunted and shoved back but was immediately restrained by Brenda, their Bible school teacher.

"He took my place in line!" Shawna protested.

"Did not!" Troy said.

"Did too!" Shawna said.

"Stop it, both of you," Brenda said. "You're supposed to be waiting in single file. We can't go to the playground until everybody's in line."

"But I got in line first!" Shawna said.

"No, you didn't!" Troy said. "I did."

Brenda placed one hand on Troy's shoulder and the other on Shawna's shoulder. "One of you is not being fair, because taking turns and waiting for your turn in line is a part of being fair with other people. If you get in line ahead of another person, you're not being fair, and that's wrong."

Troy looked at Shawna, but Shawna stared at the tiles on the floor beneath her feet.

"Now, I don't know which one of you really was first, but do you think it's fair for the whole class to wait to go out on the playground while you two argue about who was first?"

"No," Troy answered.

"No," Shawna said.

"So," Brenda continued, "if you two can't work this out quickly, I'm going to have to make you continue this discussion at the back of the line so the rest of the class doesn't have to wait for you."

Troy looked at Shawna again, but she wouldn't meet his gaze.

"All right," Brenda said. "Let's go to the end of the line."

"No, wait," Shawna answered. "Troy was first. He should go first."

Brenda nodded with satisfaction. "Thank you, Shawna. That's only fair, isn't it?" She looked at the line, where the rest of the class waited in single file. "Troy, you may lead the way to the playground now. Everybody walk, don't run!"

 TO DISCUSS: Is taking turns (and waiting in line) a way to be fair to other people? If not, why not? If so, why? Can you think of more ways to be fair to other people?

TO PRAY: "Lord, sometimes we want our own way. We want to be first. Help us to put your desires above our own."

9 Fairness and Friendship

GOD COMMANDS JUSTICE BECAUSE HE VALUES JUSTICE.

Bible Reading of the Day: Read Genesis 18:18-19.
Verse of the Day: *"Follow justice and justice alone"* (Deuteronomy
16:20, NIV).

"Hey, Dad, can I invite Jon and Alex over to spend the night tomorrow night?" Andre asked his father, who was on their small back porch grilling dinner.

Dad thought for a moment, then answered with a shrug. "Sure," he said. "What about Ben?"

Andre wrinkled his nose. "I don't think I should invite him."

"Why not?" Dad asked.

"Well," Andre said, speaking slowly. "He doesn't get along with everybody as well as Jon and Alex and I do."

"Oh?" Dad said.

"He's always trying to be first at everything," Andre explained, "and sometimes he cheats at games—stuff like that."

Dad nodded slowly. He flipped a sizzling hamburger over. "I guess I understand that," he said.

Father and son stood together in silence for a few moments as a light breeze blew the smoke from the grill away from them. Finally, Dad broke the silence. "You really value your friendships with Alex and Jon, don't you?"

"Well, yeah," Andre said. "They're cool."

"Why?" Dad asked.

"Well . . . because . . . because they like most of the things I do."

"Like fairness?" Dad asked.

Andre looked sideways at his dad, as if surprised by the question. "Yeah," he said. "I guess so."

Dad nodded. "Good. Fairness is a good thing to value in a friend." He flipped another burger. "That's one of the things God valued in his friend Abraham."

Flames started to leap through the coals. Dad grabbed a plastic water bottle on the table next to him and squirted water into the flames until they disappeared.

"I think," Dad continued, "that was one of the reasons God chose Abraham to become the father of the nation of Israel. He recognized in Abraham a friend who valued many of the same things he did." Dad waved his long-handled spatula around in the air to emphasize his words. "God values justice, Andre. That's why he commands *us* to be fair and just with each other." He paused for a moment. "I think it's good that you value fairness—and that you value friends who share that value."

TO DISCUSS: Do you like to be treated fairly or unfairly? Do you know anyone who likes to be treated unfairly? Do your friends value fairness? How do you know? Why do you think God commands us to treat others fairly? Do you treat others fairly?

TO PRAY: "Help us, heavenly Father, to treat others fairly."

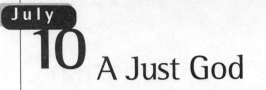

July
10 A Just God

GOD VALUES FAIRNESS BECAUSE HE IS A JUST GOD.

Bible Reading of the Day: Read Revelation 15:1-4.
Verse of the Day: *"Follow justice and justice alone"* (Deuteronomy 16:20, NIV).

Nicole slid hard into second base, stirring up a cloud of dirt and dust.

"Yer *out!*" the umpire bellowed.

Nicole jumped up and stared incredulously at the umpire. "Out?" she yelled. "How can you call me out? I was safe!"

The umpire shook his head. "I'm afraid not, Nicole," he said gently but firmly.

Nicole shook her head and slumped off the field. The play had ended the game, and she had to join her teammates as they lined up to congratulate the other team.

Johnny stood behind her in line and whispered sympathetically in her ear. "I can't believe *your own dad* called you out," he said. "Are you mad?"

Nicole shook her head. "No," she said. "He's always fair. I shouldn't have tried to stretch it into a double."

Dad and Nicole walked off the baseball field together. "Tough play, huh?" he said. "You're not upset with me, are you?"

Nicole shook her head but didn't answer.

"I had to call you out," Dad explained. "I couldn't treat you differently from the other players."

"I know," she said. "You had to be fair."

"That's right," Dad said. "Do you know why?"

"Because it wouldn't be fair," Nicole said.

Dad smiled. "Yeah, but why is fairness right?"

"Well," Nicole said, stalling, "because God says we should be fair."

Dad nodded. "Uh-huh," he said. "Why does God say we should be fair?"

"Because . . . because he . . . he likes fairness."

"Right," Dad said. "He *values* fairness. But why does he value fairness?"

"Oh, I don't know!" Nicole said in a frustrated tone as she tossed her baseball glove into the cab of Dad's truck. "Because *he's* fair!"

"Absolutely right!" Dad said, chuckling. "That was a pretty good guess."

"Yeah, I guess it was, wasn't it?" Nicole said. She climbed into the cab of the truck and sat down; her father climbed in behind the wheel. "Oh, uh, Dad?"

He looked at her. "Yes?" he said.

"You were right," she answered. "I *was* out."

TO DO: Make up new rules for a favorite game. Make the rules unfair. Play the game the new way for a while, then play it the old way. Which way is more fun?

TO PRAY: "Great and marvelous are your actions, Lord God Almighty. Just and true are your ways. You are just and fair in everything you do. Help us to reflect your character in our actions by being like you, by being fair with others." (Prayer based on Revelation 15:4.)

11

Follow Jusice

ACTING JUSTLY PLEASES GOD AND PROMOTES FRIENDSHIP.

Bible Reading of the Day: Read Jeremiah 7:5-7.
Verse of the Day: *"Follow justice and justice alone"* (Deuteronomy 16:20, NIV).

Paula and Lilly were jumping rope together on the sidewalk in front of Paula's house when a girl whose family had just moved in down the block approached. Without speaking, the girl watched them play for a while. Paula, who had noticed her when she first approached, at last said, "Hi! Would you like to skip rope with us?"

The new girl nodded. When Paula asked her name, she answered shyly, "Faith."

Lilly suggested that Faith should hold one end of each rope and Paula should hold the other ends so they could play Double Dutch. The two girls got into position and Lilly jumped between the rotating ropes.

"OK," Lilly said after she had taken her turn, "you go next, Paula."

Paula handed the ropes to Lilly and tried a few times, but she always seemed to get tangled up in the ropes right away.

"OK, OK," said Lilly, "let me try again." She held out the ropes to Paula.

"Wait a minute," Paula said. "It should be Faith's turn."

"That's OK," Faith said.

"See?" Lilly said and extended the ropes in Paula's direction again.

"No," Paula said. Then she turned to Faith. "Go ahead," she said softly. She took the ends of the ropes out of Faith's hands. Smiling shyly, Faith waited until Lilly and Paula were turning the ropes, and she jumped between them and moved her feet up and down and back and forth with more skill than either of her new friends. Before long, Paula and Lilly were laughing with excitement and cheering Faith's skill.

Later that evening, Dad came into Paula's room as she was listening to music. "I saw what you did this afternoon," he said. He explained that he had been watching from the window when Paula had insisted that Faith get a turn. "I'm sure it pleased God that you made sure the new girl was treated fairly. The Bible says that God loves righteousness and justice, and you acted justly today."

Paula smiled. "I think Faith and I are going to be friends."

Dad stood to leave. "Good. That's another reward for being fair. So you pleased God and made a new friend by treating someone else fairly. Not bad."

"I can think of another reward for being fair," Paula suggested.

"What's that?" Dad asked.

"I made you happy too, didn't I?"

Dad smiled and wrapped his daughter in a big hug. "You sure did," he said.

TO DISCUSS: Have you treated others fairly today (or this week)? If so, how? Do you think your action pleased God? Did it please anyone else? Did your actions start or strengthen a friendship? Can you think of any other reward your action produced?

TO PRAY: "Holy Spirit, please show us how to be fair to others."

12 The "What If?" Game

IF EVERYONE PURSUED JUSTICE, THE WORLD WOULD BE A BETTER PLACE.

Bible Reading of the Day: Read Psalm 11:4-7.
Verse of the Day: *"For the Lord is righteous, and he loves justice. Those who do what is right will see his face" (Psalm 11:7).*

"How long until we get to Grandma's house?" Reed asked in an impatient tone.

Mom turned around in her seat to face Reed and his sister, Rachel, in the backseat. "Honey, we left home only a half hour ago! Grandma's house is almost three hours away."

"I'm bored," Reed said.

"Mommy, Reed's looking at me!" Rachel whined. "Tell him to stop looking at me!"

"I have an idea," Mom said. "Let's play the 'What If?' game."

"OK," Reed said. "I want to go first!"

Rachel protested. "Mommy, he always gets to go first."

"OK, Rachel, you go first," Mom said, and, before Reed could protest, she began the game. "What if . . . everybody in the world played fair?"

"Ooh, I know!" Reed said, raising his hand in the air as if he were in school.

"I know," Rachel said. "If everybody in the world played fair" —she smiled at her brother— "Reed wouldn't always get to go first."

"Who went first today, huh?" Reed asked.

"Mommy, he's teasing me," Rachel said.

Mom turned to Reed. "Your turn,"she said.

"If everybody in the world played fair," Reed answered quickly, "we wouldn't need so many, like, umpires and referees and people like that. People would just admit if they were safe or out or whatever, because they'd play fair."

"Very good," Mom said. She turned to Rachel. "Your turn again."

Rachel's forehead wrinkled as she thought. "People wouldn't get into arguments on the playground."

"That's excellent, Rachel," Mom said. "You're right; if everyone played fair, they would get along much better with each other, wouldn't they?"

"My turn!" Reed said. "If everybody in the world played fair, Dad wouldn't yell at the television set so much when he's watching sports."

"Hey!" Dad protested. "No fair bringing me into this game!"

Mom and Dad exchanged smiles, and Mom said, "I've got a new question. What if . . . everybody in our *family* played fair?"

"I know!" Reed and Rachel said at the same time.

Reed looked at Mom, then at his sister. "You go ahead," he told Rachel.

"We would get along much better with each other, wouldn't we, Mommy?"

"Yes," Mom answered. "We would!"

TO DO: Play your own version of the "What If?" game.

TO PRAY: "Jesus, help us to 'play fair' with others."

Food Fight

TREATING OTHERS FAIRLY INVITES THE PROTECTION AND PROVISION THAT COMES FROM OBEYING GOD.

Bible Reading of the Day: Read Psalm 37:27-31.
Verse of the Day: *"For the Lord is righteous, and he loves justice. Those who do what is right will see his face" (Psalm 11:7).*

"Food fight!" Ray scooped up a handful of mashed potatoes and heaved it across the table at B. J., who responded by flinging his milk carton at Ray.

"Cut it out, guys!" Aaron cried. "You're going to get us all in trouble."

But it was too late. A full-fledged food fight had erupted, and everyone at the table except Aaron was soon involved. Peas, pudding, chicken nuggets, and pizza slices flew across the table, into hair, onto clothes, and on innocent bystanders.

As quickly as it had begun, it ended. Mr. Sawyer appeared—seemingly out of nowhere—and clamped a hand on Ray's shoulder and B. J.'s shoulder. The lunchroom monitor's booming voice halted the food fight and froze everyone at the table.

"You're all in big trouble," Mr. Sawyer said. "You're going to clean this mess up, and then you're all coming with me to the principal's office." Ray, B. J., Aaron, and their other friends at the table silently cleaned up the mess they had made. When they were finished, Mr. Sawyer marched them all to the office.

"Mr. Sawyer," Ray said as they approached the principal's office. "Aaron shouldn't get in trouble with the rest of us."

Mr. Sawyer looked at Ray. "Why not?"

"He had nothing to do with the food fight," he said.

"That's OK, Ray," Aaron said gloomily.

"He tried to stop it," Ray insisted, ignoring Aaron.

Mr. Sawyer looked from Ray to Aaron, then scanned the faces of the other boys. "Is this true?" he asked. The boys all nodded.

"OK, Aaron," Mr. Sawyer said. "Looks like you're off the hook. You can go."

Aaron turned to go, and the other boys followed Mr. Sawyer into the principal's office. Ray and several of the others returned to class later. As Ray took his seat at the desk next to Aaron's desk, Aaron leaned over and whispered, "Thanks."

Ray looked embarrassed. He shrugged. "It's OK," he said.

"Why'd you do it?" Aaron asked.

Ray hesitated. Finally, he said, "Remember in baseball when Coach kept getting us confused, and he kept trying to give you credit for something I did? You'd always say, 'No, Coach, that was Ray.' You were fair with me. I wanted to be fair with you."

Aaron smiled. Without even realizing he was doing it, he breathed a quick prayer. *Thank you, God, for keeping me out of trouble.*

TO DISCUSS: How did God keep Aaron out of trouble? How did obeying God's command to treat others fairly protect and provide for Aaron? How can you enjoy God's protection and provision?

TO PRAY: "Lord, we need the provision and protection that your Word provides. Help us to stay out of trouble by obeying your commands."

14 Keep Knocking

FAITHFULNESS IN PRAYER IS ESSENTIAL TO SUCCESS IN MAKING RIGHT CHOICES.

Bible Reading of the Day: Read Luke 11:5-10.
Verse of the Day: *"Ask and it will be given to you; seek and you will find; knock and the door will be opened to you" (Matthew 7:7, NIV).*

"Hey, Dad, watch this!" Mindy called to her father, who was just getting home from work. She dribbled toward the basketball hoop in their driveway and, in one smooth motion, leaped and dunked the basketball through the hoop.

"Excellent!" Dad said. "You're getting really good, Mindy."

"I should be," Mindy said, propping the basketball between her hip and forearm as she walked beside her dad. "I practice every day. Sometimes I even get pointers from Brad, the kid down the street who plays for the high school."

"Keep it up," Dad said. "You'll break Brad's records someday."

Mindy beamed at her dad, then returned to the driveway to shoot more baskets as Dad went in the house. Mindy's mom greeted him with a smile and a kiss. Then she told him some news that wiped the smile off his face. Mindy had gotten in trouble—again—for lying to her mother. Dad changed his clothes and returned to the driveway to talk to Mindy.

"Your mother told me you lied to her again," he said.

Mindy nodded gloomily. "I'm trying to be good, Dad, I really am," she said. She placed the basketball on the pavement and sat on the ball. "I'm trying really hard. It's just not working."

Dad crouched beside her. "That's because the key to making right choices isn't *trying*, honey."

"Well," Mindy said, throwing her hands in the air, "I've tried praying about it!"

"You have?"

"Yeah. I asked God to help me, and nothing's changed."

"Have you kept asking?" Dad asked. Mindy's question was written on her face, so he continued. He nodded toward the basketball hoop. "How good would you be at basketball if you took one or two shots a month?"

Mindy rolled her eyes. "Terrible," she said.

"Well," Dad said, "maybe that's why you're struggling so much with lying to your mom. Sure, you've prayed about it—once or twice. But if you really want to make right choices, you need to show as much faithfulness in prayer as you do in basketball."

"You're right," Mindy said. "I'll start praying every day . . . starting today!"

"Good!" Dad said. "Now, how about a game of 'Around the World'?"

"OK," Mindy said. "But first I have to go apologize to Mom."

TO DISCUSS: Do you think you could do better at making right choices if you prayed every day? Why or why not? Have you asked God to help you make right choices? What do you need to do in order to make right choices?

TO PRAY: "Lord, we want to make a habit of coming to you for help in making right choices. We depend on you for direction."

15 Squares and Rectangles

FAILURES AREN'T ALWAYS SINS.

Bible Reading of the Day: Read 2 Corinthians 12:6-10.
Verse of the Day: *"For when I am weak, then I am strong"*
(2 Corinthians 12:10).

Mom held Micah's schoolbook in her hands. "All right," she said in her best teacher's voice, "what is a square?" She was quizzing him to help him prepare for an important test at school.

"A parallelogram with four equal sides and four equal angles," Micah answered.

"Very good," Mom said. "What's a parallelogram?"

"Uh," Micah said, "it's . . . a figure where the sides are even with the other sides."

"Right," Mom said. "Each side is parallel to the opposite side. What's a rectangle?"

Micah thought for a moment. "A parallelogram with four equal angles."

"Good!" Mom said. "Is a square always a rectangle?"

Micah nodded. "Yup," he said.

"Is a rectangle always a square?"

"No," he said confidently.

Mom slapped the covers of the book shut and said, "I think you're ready."

"I hope so," Micah said. "I don't want the other kids making fun of me again like they did when I flunked the last quiz. They make me feel so . . . so guilty."

Mom looked at her son with sympathetic eyes. "I understand that. It's hard when people make fun of you. And I'm glad you're determined to do your best. But you don't have to feel guilty, no matter what the other kids do. Failures aren't always sins, you know."

"They're not?"

"No," Mom said. She opened the textbook again to the illustrations of squares and rectangles. She laid the book on the table in front of Micah. "Failures and sins are like rectangles and squares. Sins are like squares; they're always failures. When you sin, you also fail."

"Just like a square is always a rectangle."

"Right," Mom said. "But failures aren't always sins. Sometimes they are, but sometimes they're not. We all fail, because we're all human. You may fail a quiz, or you may fail to give me a phone message, or you may fail to win a race. But those aren't necessarily sins."

"Just like rectangles aren't always squares," Micah suggested.

Mom rubbed the top of Micah's head. "Right."

 TO DISCUSS: How are failures and sins related? How are they different? Do you ever fail at something? How can you tell if your failure is a sin?

TO PRAY: "Lord, as humans, we can't help but fail sometimes. Help us to learn the difference between sinful failures and innocent failures. And if we sin, remind us to seek forgiveness from you."

16 Temptation Frustration

BEING TEMPTED TO DO WRONG ISN'T A SIN; GIVING IN TO TEMPTATION IS, HOWEVER.

Bible Reading of the Day: Read Mark 1:9-13.

Verse of the Day: *"For we do not have a high priest who is unable to sympathize with our weaknesses, but we have one who has been tempted in every way, just as we are—yet was without sin" (Hebrews 4:15, NIV).*

Mom entered Joy's bedroom to kiss her daughter good-night. She sat on the edge of Joy's bed and talked for a few moments about the day's events.

As Mom rose to leave, Joy gripped her wrist and gently tugged, indicating she didn't want her to leave yet.

"What is it, dear?" Mom asked.

Joy hesitated for a moment the way people do when they're not sure what to say—or whether to say anything at all. Finally, she spoke.

"You know how I wanted to buy that new *Green Daze* CD, and you said I couldn't?"

Mom nodded.

"Well, I snuck into your room and got into your purse tonight. I was going to take the money out of your purse and buy it anyway."

"You took money out of my purse!?"

"No," Joy answered quickly. "I was going to," she explained. "I got into your purse and found the money and everything . . . but I put the money back and closed your purse." Joy's eyes filled with tears. "I'm so sorry, Mom!" she cried.

Mom wrapped her arms around her daughter and hugged her for a few moments.

"I feel so awful!" Joy mumbled through her tears.

"Oh, Joy," Mom said, "don't be sorry. You made the right choice. You were tempted to do wrong, but you made the right choice. Everybody faces temptation."

"But I feel so bad," Joy answered.

"I know, dear, but being tempted isn't a sin; giving in to temptation is. You might have waited a little longer than you should have to make the right choice, but you did make the right choice when you were tempted."

"So you're not mad at me?"

Mom smiled. "No, dear. If I got mad at you every time you were tempted, I'd be mad all the time, wouldn't I?"

"Yeah," Joy said, smiling. "I guess so."

"Even Jesus was tempted," Mom said, "but he did not sin."

"I'm glad I made the right choice, Mom," Joy said.

"I am too," Mom answered.

 TO DISCUSS: What is the difference between *temptation* and *sin?* Do you think you'll ever stop being tempted to do wrong? Do you think you can resist temptation and choose to do right? If not, why not? If so, how?

TO PRAY: "Lord, as Jesus taught his disciples to pray, lead us not into temptation, but deliver us from evil."

17 Weak Spots

TEMPTATION TO DO WRONG IS OFTEN STRONGEST WHEN YOU ARE WEAK.

Bible Reading of the Day: Read Luke 4:1-4.
Verse of the Day: *"My grace is sufficient for you, for my power is made perfect in weakness" (2 Corinthians 12:9, NIV).*

Billy lugged his duffel bag out of the car and followed his father up the steps. As soon as he entered the door, Mom ran to him and gave him a hug and a kiss. Sharon, his little sister, arrived a moment later.

"How was camp?" Mom asked.

Billy's tired eyes brightened instantly. "It was so cool, Mom," he answered. "I can't wait to go back next year."

"Well," Mom said, "you'll have to tell us all about it."

"Yeah," Billy said, nodding. "Right now I'm really tired, though. Can I just go up to my room for a while?" Billy had been looking forward to a long nap in his own bed all the way home from Camp Kickapoo.

Mom gripped Billy's duffel bag and took it out of his hand. "I'll take this down to the laundry room," she said. "You go on upstairs. I'll call you when dinner's ready."

Billy trudged wearily up the steps. Sharon followed closely on his heels. When he reached his bedroom and opened the door, he was immediately surprised by a large paper banner that hung on the wall over his bed. A magic-marker message—"Welcome Home Billy"—was scrawled in large childish letters on the banner.

Billy turned around to see Sharon smiling with pride in her handiwork. He smiled back, then turned to look at the poster again.

It was then he noticed that Sharon's banner was held to the wall by several thumbtacks—several of which pierced his favorite football poster.

She put holes in my best poster! he thought. *She's ruined it—RUINED IT!* In spite of his weariness, anger rose in him as he whipped around to face his sister.

"How could you?" he asked, his voice rising to a shout. Instantly, while words still formed in his mouth, he saw the smile disappear from Sharon's face.

Billy stopped. Sharon wore a look of innocent confusion as the muscles in Billy's jaw tightened and the expression of anger on his face was replaced with another, softer, expression.

He inhaled deeply and exhaled slowly. "How could you do something so nice for me?" he asked, and was instantly rewarded by the reappearance of a smile on Sharon's face.

"It was fun," she said. She hugged her brother. "I missed you," she said.

He hugged her back. "I missed you too," he answered.

 TO DISCUSS: Are you more tempted to do wrong when you're tired, lonely, or weak in some other way? If so, what can you do to get ready for temptation at those "weak" times?

 TO PRAY: "Lord, prepare us for those moments when we're tempted to sin. Help us be victorious over temptation."

18 Shortcuts

TEMPTATION TO DO WRONG OFTEN COMES IN THE FORM OF A "SHORTCUT."

Bible Reading of the Day: Read Luke 4:5-8.

Verse of the Day: *"The highway to hell is broad, and its gate is wide for the many who choose the easy way. But the gateway to life is small, and the road is narrow, and only a few ever find it"* (Matthew 7:13-14).

As soon as Holly and Dad buckled their seat belts, Dad steered the car out of the church parking lot. He stopped at the alley behind the church and leaned forward over the steering wheel to look both ways. Then he turned the car into the alley.

"Daddy!" Holly cried. "You're going the wrong way!"

"No, I'm not," Dad said.

"Uh-huh," Holly insisted. "The sign said 'one way' and pointed the other way."

"Well," Dad said, "I'm only going to this street right here."

"But isn't that breaking the rules?" Holly asked.

"Well, technically it is," Dad said. "But if I turned right back there, I'd have to go all the way around the block to get to this same spot."

He stole a glance at Holly's face. She looked unconvinced.

Dad continued. "It would take a lot longer to go the other way, Holly, and I'm in a hurry."

Dad pointed to the sign over the road. "See, I have to get here to get onto the expressway."

"You can break the rules, can't you, Daddy?" Holly said, in an understanding voice.

"Well, no, Holly," he said. "Daddy has to follow the rules too. But if I didn't take that little shortcut, I might be late picking up your sister from school."

"So, it's OK to break the rules sometimes," Holly said, deep in thought.

"No," Dad answered, "I don't want you to think that."

"But some rules are dumb, aren't they, Daddy?"

"It's not that, Holly," Dad said. "It's just that . . . well," he said, suddenly very uncomfortable. He knew it would be useless to try to change the subject. He sighed.

"Holly," he said slowly, watching the expressway traffic as he talked, "Daddy did something wrong back there. I was in a hurry, and it seemed quicker—easier—to do the wrong thing . . . but I broke the rules, and I shouldn't have. I'm sorry." He glanced away from the traffic to gauge his daughter's reaction to his confession, but Holly's head leaned against the car door. She had fallen asleep.

Dad smiled and shook his head. "Out of the mouths of babes," he said.

TO DISCUSS: Sometimes temptation to do wrong may seem like taking a "shortcut," like the shortcut to power the devil offered Jesus in the wilderness. Name a time when you were tempted to do wrong because it seemed quicker or simpler than doing right. How can you fight the temptation to take shortcuts?

TO PRAY: "Holy Spirit, whenever we're tempted to take the easy way out, help us not to give in to temptation."

19 Strength Training

RESISTING TEMPTATION MAKES YOU STRONGER.

Bible Reading of the Day: Read Luke 4:9–14.
Verse of the Day: *"Resist the devil, and he will flee from you"*
(James 4:7, NIV).

Yan trudged across the gymnasium floor and dropped her gym bag at her mother's feet.

"I am so weak," she said. "I don't think I can walk another step."

Mom smiled. "I'll carry your bag," she said. "Did Coach work you too hard?"

"She's trying to kill us!" Yan said. "She made us spend forty-five minutes in the weight room today."

Mom chuckled and said. "She's just trying to make you stronger."

"Stronger?" Yan squealed. "Stronger? I can barely lift my own arms right now. How am I supposed to jump and run?"

"Well, you're tired right now. But every weight you lift makes it easier to lift the next one."

"Yeah, right." Yan said. They arrived at the car, and Mom opened the door for Yan and set her gym bag on the floor.

"Really," Mom insisted as she got in on the driver's side. "The reason your coach makes you work out with weights is to make you stronger so you can jump higher and run faster."

"I got offered drugs again," Yan said, in a flat voice.

"What did you do?" Mom asked, her voice suddenly heavy with concern. Drugs seemed to flow through Yan's school like water through a faucet.

Yan shrugged. "I said no, what else?"

"Was it hard?"

"No. It was hard the first few times because I thought everybody would think I was weird or something. But now it's easy to say, 'No way!'"

Yan suddenly turned to her mom, smiling. "Maybe saying no to bad things is like lifting weights."

"What do you mean?" Mom asked.

"Well, you said Coach just wants to make us stronger, right? Every weight we lift makes the next one easier." She turned in her seat to face Mom squarely. "Maybe every time I say no to temptation, I get a little bit stronger. You know, like I used to be embarrassed when I said no to stuff, and now I just say *no!*"

Mom smiled at Yan. Her eyes filled with tears. "You just keep getting stronger, then," she said. "You just keep saying no."

TO DISCUSS: Can you think of a temptation that used to be hard for you to resist? Do you think resisting temptation has made you stronger? What temptation is hard for you to resist right now? How can you get stronger in fighting that temptation?

TO PRAY: "Lord, we need your strength each day to resist temptation. Here's what we'd like to say no to." Have each family member silently pray about a temptation he or she is facing. After the prayer time, you might discuss ways to resist temptations.

Power Source

THE POWER TO RESIST TEMPTATION COMES FROM GOD.

Bible Reading of the Day: Read Judges 16:4-20.

Verse of the Day: *"No temptation has seized you except what is common to man. And God is faithful; he will not let you be tempted beyond what you can bear. But when you are tempted, he will also provide a way out so that you can stand up under it"* (1 Corinthians 10:13, NIV).

"This is going to be sooo cool!" Shawn said. He and his older brother Dustin were unpacking their new home computer and setting it up together. "I feel like I'm the last kid in my whole school to get a computer," he said.

As they worked, unpacking the various components and connecting all the cords and cables, Shawn told Dustin that he'd been kicked out of the public swimming pool for a whole week.

"What for?" Dustin asked.

"I pushed Janet Kline into the deep end," he said. His brother looked up from his work as if he knew there had to be more to the story. "She had all her clothes on," Shawn continued. He paused another moment before saying, "This was during the break, when only adults and little kids are allowed to swim."

"Why would you do that?" Dustin said, his voice betraying his amusement.

"I don't know," Shawn whined. "The guys kept saying I should do it, and . . . well, it was just so tempting, you know?"

Dustin nodded, smiling. "You should've just said no."

"I don't know why, but I just can't seem to resist temptation. How do you do it?"

"How do *I* do it?" Dustin echoed Shawn's question. He fished around behind the computer, connecting cables. "Well," he said, "I don't."

"You don't?" Shawn said. "What's that supposed to mean?"

Dustin rotated the computer monitor and sat down. "I don't have the power to resist temptation," he said, "and neither do you. Trying to resist temptation all by yourself would be almost like trying to run this computer without electricity."

"Well, then, what am I supposed to do?" Shawn asked.

"The power to resist temptation comes from God," Dustin said. "You need to depend on him every day—every moment—to give you the power you need. Like the Lord's Prayer says, 'Lead us not into temptation, but deliver us from evil.'"

Shawn nodded. "Oh," he said. He flipped the power switch on the computer, but nothing happened. "What's wrong?" he asked his brother.

"Same thing that's causing your problem," he said. He held up the electrical plug to the computer. "It's not plugged in to the power it needs."

 TO DISCUSS: What was the true source of Samson's power—his hair or the Lord? What is the source of your power? How can you plug in to God's power to resist the temptations you face?

 TO PRAY: "Lord God, only you can help us to resist temptation. We don't want to be fooled into relying on our own strength. Guide us, Lord, in your truth."

21 Who's the Boss?

GOD'S A GOOD BOSS TO HAVE.

Bible Reading of the Day: Read Exodus 20:1-7.
Verse of the Day: *"I am the Lord your God" (Exodus 20:2).*

"You have a boss?" Megan's eyes widened in amazement.

Megan's mother had taken her to work with her for the first time and had introduced Megan to the men and women in the office where Mom worked as an accountant.

When Mom introduced Megan to Rachel Hardaway and explained that Rachel was her "boss," Megan stared at her mother with a shocked expression. "I didn't know mommies had bosses!"

Mom laughed. "A lot of people do, Megan. Almost everyone has a boss."

Megan pointed to Rachel Hardaway. "Does *she* have a boss?"

Mom nodded. "Yes. And *her* boss has a boss."

Megan thought hard. "Well," she said slowly, "who's the boss of all those bosses?"

"That's a very good question," Mom answered. "What do you think?"

"The president?" Megan offered.

"Even the president of the company has a boss," Mom said. "Lots of bosses, in fact."

Suddenly, Megan's eyes brightened. "I know!" she announced. "God's the boss!"

"That's right, Megan," Mom said, hugging Megan and lifting her into her arms. "And do you know *why* God is the boss of all of us?"

Megan's face grew serious, and she thought hard. Finally, she shook her head.

"Because," Mom explained, "God made every one of us. And he made everything around us."

"Does everybody do what he tells them to do?" Megan asked.

"No," Mom said. "Some people don't even admit that God is the boss. They think they can be their own boss. And they try to decide for themselves what things are good and what things are bad."

"There must be a lot of people who decide bad things."

Mom nodded sadly. "What about you, Megan? Are you going to try to be your own boss?"

Megan's expression became determined. "No. I think God's a good boss to have."

Mom hugged her daughter even tighter. "He's the best, Megan. The very best!"

TO DISCUSS: What about you? Are there times when you're tempted to be your own boss? If so, what are those times? Why do you think Megan said "God's a good boss to have"? Do you agree or disagree? Why?

TO PRAY: "When we want to go our own way, lead us back to your way, Lord."

22 When It's Not Easy

IF YOU DO WHAT'S RIGHT ONLY WHEN IT'S EASY, YOU WON'T DO THE RIGHT THING
VERY OFTEN.

Bible Reading of the Day: Read Genesis 6:5-22.
  Verse of the Day: *"So Noah did everything exactly as God had
  commanded him" (Genesis 6:22).*

Erin hung her head. She'd never felt so ashamed in her life. Her mother had caught her
and several of her friends smoking cigarettes in the vacant lot down the street from
their apartment building.

"Erin Marie," her mom said, "I can't believe you would do such a thing."

"It wasn't my idea," Erin offered.

"It doesn't matter *whose* idea it was," Mom said. "What matters is that you did
something you knew was wrong. You disobeyed me."

"I know," Erin said. She still hadn't looked at her mother.

"Where'd you get the cigarettes?" Mom asked.

"Suzette had them. I don't know where she got them." She lifted her eyes to meet
her mom's gaze. "I wasn't going to at first, really I wasn't," she explained. "But
everybody would have laughed at me!"

Mom's expression had been hard, but after she took a deep breath, her face
softened before she spoke. "It can be hard to do the right thing sometimes," Mom said.
"If it were always easy, everyone would do it. But if you only do what's right when
it's easy, you won't do the right thing very often."

"I should have never listened to Suzette," Erin said.

"That's true," Mom said. "Who *should* you have listened to?"

Erin cocked her head to the side. An unspoken question showed in her expression
for a moment. Then it disappeared. "I should have listened to God. I should have done
what he wanted me to." She paused. "Right?"

"Right," Mom said. "Your friends might have laughed at you. Your choice still
would've been hard—"

"But I wouldn't feel so rotten," Erin said.

"And you wouldn't be grounded, either," Mom added.

"I'm grounded?" Erin asked.

Mom rolled her eyes at her daughter. "Don't tell me you didn't see that coming,"
she said.

"Yeah." Erin sighed. "I guess I did."

 **TO DISCUSS: Do you think it was easy for Noah to do everything God commanded
him to do? Do you think Noah was glad he obeyed God? Why or why not? Why is it so
hard sometimes to make the right choice? Why do you think we should do the right
thing even when it's hard?**

 **TO PRAY: "Heavenly Father, making the right choice isn't always easy. But with your
help, we *can* make the right choices."**

23 Guarded by God's Rules

RULES CAN BE LIKE A WALL OF PROTECTION.

Bible Reading of the Day: Read Galatians 3:23-24.
Verse of the Day: *"The commandments of the Lord are right. . . . They are a warning to those who hear them; there is great reward for those who obey them"* (Psalm 19:8, 11).

Becky held her grandma's hand as they walked together toward the swimming pool. They had to walk around the tall brick wall that surrounded the pool area and enter through the shower rooms at the front of the facility.

"It sure doth take a long time to get to the thwimming pool," Becky said, a slight lisp sounding in her speech because of a missing front tooth.

"Yes, it does," Grandma answered. "It wouldn't be so far if we didn't have to walk all the way around that wall."

"Why don't they juth take the wall down?" Becky asked as they entered the shower rooms.

Grandma kicked off her sandals. "The wall is there to protect people," she said. "If it weren't for that wall, a little child could wander away from his house and into the pool area. He could fall in and get hurt."

"Or drown!" Becky said, her eyes wide with alarm.

"Yes." Grandma nodded seriously. They sat together on the bench inside the shower room. "Or an older child might be tempted to go swimming when there's no lifeguard on duty. That could be very dangerous too. It's the same way with the rules your parents make you obey, like 'don't play with knives.'"

"Or 'don't play in the threet.'"

"Right!" Grandma said.

"Or 'don't play with matcheth.'"

Grandma's eyes twinkled. "I can see you know the rules," she said. "Those rules are like a wall your parents built around you to keep you safe."

"Or 'don't run in the houth.'"

"Or 'don't hide peath in your ear.'"

"Oh, that's a good one!" Grandma said, laughing. "You should eat all your peas."

Becky nodded solemnly. "We have a lot of rulth at our houth."

"That's wonderful," Grandma said. "Do you know *why* that's wonderful?"

"Why?" Becky asked, curiosity sparkling in her eyes.

"Because it shows that your parents love you very much. They make those rules to keep you safe and to help you grow up to be big and strong and happy."

 TO DISCUSS: How do your parents' rules protect you? How can God's rules, or commandments, act like a wall of protection around you? When was the last time you thanked your parents for their protection? When was the last time you thanked God for his protection?

TO PRAY: "Thank you, God, for your protecting rules."

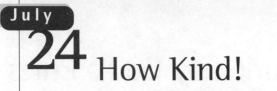

24 How Kind!

KINDNESS—EVEN A SMALL ACT OF KINDNESS—IS GOOD.

Bible Reading of the Day: Read 1 Thessalonians 5:15-24.
Verse of the Day: *"Always try to be kind to each other and to everyone else"* (1 Thessalonians 5:15, NIV).

Dean's dad steered the car into the parking space at the Mega Mall, turned the engine off, and opened his door. By the time Dad did all that, Dean was already out of the car.

"Wait a minute, Dean," Dad said. "Get back in the car for a second."

Dean did what his dad said but asked, "Why?" as he climbed back in the car.

"Shut your door, please," Dad said. He started the car again and Dean shut his door. "I did a pretty bad job of parking," Dad explained. "I realized when I opened my door that I was taking up two parking spaces."

"So?" Dean responded.

Dad backed up and parked the car again, this time centering it carefully between the yellow lines that marked each parking space. "Well, Son," he said, "I parked in the closest space I could find, and there was another space right next to it. If I took *two* spaces, that means that someone else would have to walk farther—maybe much farther—to get to the mall."

"Well, yeah," Dean said. "People do that all the time."

"I know, but once I noticed what I'd done, don't you think it would have been unkind to make someone walk farther just because I did a poor job of parking?"

Dean shrugged. "But you'd never know who had to walk farther."

They got out of the car again and started walking to the mall.

"The fact that I don't know a person doesn't give me the right to be unkind," Dad continued.

"I guess you're right," Dean said. "But it seems like such a small thing."

"It is," Dad said. "But the difference between kindness and unkindness is often in the small things."

"I get what you're saying," Dean said. "It's like this—" He jogged a few steps ahead of his father and opened the door to the mall. He made a grand sweeping gesture with his left hand while holding the door open with his right.

"Why, thank you, Dean," Dad said. "How kind of you!"

Dean nodded grandly as he followed his dad into the mall. "I thought so too," he said.

 TO DO: Be alert for an opportunity to show a small act of kindness to someone in the next twenty-four hours. Be prepared to report your act to your family tomorrow.

 TO PRAY: "Lord, we want to be kind and loving. Show us the opportunities we have for doing so this week."

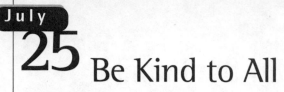

25 Be Kind to All

DO YOU DECIDE WHAT'S RIGHT, OR DOES GOD?

Bible Reading of the Day: Read Luke 6:32-35.

Verse of the Day: *"Always try to be kind to each other and to everyone else"* (1 Thessalonians 5:15, NIV).

Sarah glared down the sidewalk at the person approaching. She stood with other members of her church youth group on the city sidewalk, passing out coupons for free ice-cream cones as a combined service and witnessing project. Sometimes a person would stop and ask why they were giving away free ice-cream cones, and they would use that opportunity to explain God's love and the plan of salvation to the person. Everything had been going great, and Sarah was enjoying herself—until she saw the girl who now walked toward her.

"It's Hillary Whitson," she hissed to her friend Teri.

Teri turned and squinted against the bright sunlight. "Yeah," she said. "Sure is."

"Is that all you can say?"

"What am I supposed to say?" Teri asked.

"This is Hillary Whitson we're talking about—the girl who thinks she's better than everyone else in our grade. She's gonna walk right by us!"

"So give her a coupon," Teri suggested.

"I'm not going to give her a coupon!" Sarah's voice dripped with indignation. "She's always treating us like we're dirt."

"That doesn't mean we should treat her that way," Teri said.

"Well, it doesn't mean I have to be nice to her," Sarah countered.

Teri cocked her head as if she had just thought of something. "Actually, I think you do," she said.

"What do you mean?" Sarah asked, her eyes narrowing with suspicion.

"Jesus said, what good is it if you're only nice to people who are nice to you? He said we should love our enemies, remember?"

"Well, I'm not going to do it," Sarah decided. "I don't have to be nice to Hillary Whitson!"

"You don't?" Teri said. She gave her last coupon to a passerby. "Who decides what's right, then—you or God?"

Sarah looked back and forth from Teri's face to Hillary's approaching form. "Ooh," she said at last, "you make me so mad sometimes." She took a step toward Hillary and extended a coupon for a free ice-cream cone.

 TO DISCUSS: Do you think we should be kind only to people who are kind to us? Why or why not? Do you think kindness is right only when it's easy? Why or why not? Is it right to be kind even when it's hard? even when we don't feel like it? even when someone doesn't deserve it? Have you shown kindness to someone in the last twenty-four hours? If so, tell each other about that experience.

TO PRAY: "Lord, help us to be kind to everyone, even those whom we find hardest to love."

26 All in the Family

GOD COMMANDS US TO BE KIND TO OTHERS.

Bible Reading of the Day: Read Colossians 3:12-15.
Verse of the Day: *"For this very reason, make every effort to add to your faith . . . brotherly kindness; and to brotherly kindness, love"* (2 Peter 1:5-7, NIV).

"Hey, dork!" Josh said as he walked into the garage and saw his little brother, Tad, leaning over his bicycle. He reached out a hand as he walked past Tad and slapped his little brother's head.

Tad dropped the wrench he was using to tighten his bicycle chain and rubbed his head. "That hurt!" he said.

"Duh!" Josh responded. "It was *supposed* to hurt." He kept walking through the garage, entered the house, and walked to the refrigerator.

A few moments later, Mom walked into the kitchen through the garage door. She saw Josh standing in front of the refrigerator, peeling the wrapper off a Popsicle. She sat down at the kitchen table and studied Josh for a few moments.

"What's wrong?" Josh asked, when he noticed his mom watching him.

"I was just wondering where you learned to treat your brother that way," Mom said. "I was weeding the garden. I saw what you did and heard what you said."

A guilty look surfaced on Josh's face.

"How can you be so unkind to your brother?" Mom asked.

"He's my brother, Mom," Josh said, a defensive tone in his voice.

"So, you're telling me it's OK to be unkind to people in your own family?"

"No," Josh said.

"Good," Mom said. "Because I know that's not true. God commands us to be kind to each other, but he doesn't say 'except for little brothers.'"

"I'm sorry," Josh said. He hung his head, and his hair covered his eyes.

Mom took his chin gently in her hand and lifted his face until his eyes met hers. Her voice softened. "Josh, a Christian family isn't a place where we can ignore God's commands; it's a place where we can practice them. If we can get good at following God in our own family, we'll be better at following him out in the world."

Josh nodded. "I'm sorry," he repeated. "I'll try to be kinder to Tad."

Mom smiled. She nodded toward the garage door. "There's a little boy out in the garage who's trying to fix his bike," she said.

A small smile creased Josh's face. "I bet he could use some help, huh?"

"I bet he could," Mom said.

TO DISCUSS: God commands us to be kind to "each other" and to "everyone else." Who do you think is included in those two phrases? Can you think of anyone those phrases ("each other" and "everyone else") *don't* include? What are some of the ways we can be kind to the people in our family?

 TO PRAY: "Jesus, we want you to show your love and kindness through us."

27 The Tyke and His Trike

GOD COMMANDS KINDNESS BECAUSE GOD VALUES KINDNESS.

Bible Reading of the Day: Read Jeremiah 9:23-24.
Verse of the Day: *"We have proved ourselves by our purity, our understanding, our patience, our kindness, our sincere love, and the power of the Holy Spirit" (2 Corinthians 6:6).*

Mom sat with her sister at the picnic table in the backyard, watching Evan and his cousin playing in the driveway. Evan's new red-and-white tricycle gleamed in the sunlight as he rode it around the driveway. His cousin Vincent sat on the low brick wall that lined the driveway, swinging his legs and kicking the wall with his heels.

Finally, Evan stopped riding the tricycle he had gotten for his birthday, trotted across the driveway to the fence, and reached over the fence to pet the family dog for a few moments. As he petted the dog, however, he saw Vincent slowly climb down from his seat on the wall, stroll over to the tricycle, and sit down on it.

"No!" Evan shouted. He forgot all about the dog and ran to his tricycle. "I'm not done riding it," he said, and waited for Vincent to get off the tricycle seat.

Mom waited a few moments, then walked over to Evan, who was furiously pedaling the tricycle in circles around the drain in the center of the driveway.

"That's a really nice tricycle, isn't it?" Mom said.

Evan nodded and stopped pedaling. "I can make it go really fast," he said.

"You really love it, don't you?" Mom asked.

Evan nodded again. "It's the best birthday gift I ever got!"

Mom crouched beside the tricycle and took one of Evan's hands into her own. "You know how you *value* this tricycle, how you think it's really neat?"

Evan nodded.

"Well," Mom continued, "God values things in much the same way. But you know what he thinks is even neater and better than tricycles?"

Evan didn't move. He looked at Mom with curiosity.

Mom smiled. "God really loves kindness, Evan," she said. "He thinks being kind to other people is really, really neat—just like you think this tricycle is neat."

As Mom stood, she mussed Evan's hair. Then she walked back toward the picnic table where her sister, Vincent's mom, still sat. Before she reached the table, however, she saw a smile cross her sister's face. She turned to look back at Evan. She watched as Evan rode his tricycle to the low brick wall where Vincent sat.

"Do you wanna take turns riding my neat tricycle?" Evan asked.

Vincent smiled and jumped off the wall.

 TO DO: Post a sheet of paper on the refrigerator. Have everyone in the family list one chore or task that he or she needs help doing. The whole family can model kindness by doing one of the tasks for someone else this week.

 TO PRAY: "God, we know that you command us to be kind because you value kindness. Help us to be kind to each other and to everyone else—even those we find it hard to be kind to—because we know that pleases you."

28 The Kindness of God

GOD VALUES KINDNESS BECAUSE HE IS KIND.

> **Bible Reading of the Day: Read Psalm 145:17-21.**
> Verse of the Day: *"Since God chose you to be the holy people whom he loves, you must clothe yourselves with tenderhearted mercy, kindness, humility, gentleness, and patience" (Colossians 3:12).*

Janna studied her reflection in the dressing room mirror, then stepped through the curtains to show her friends.

Tammy shook her head, smiling. "That dress makes you look like your mom!" she said, stifling a giggle.

Janna looked confused. "What do you mean?" she said. She stepped in front of another mirror. "I think my mom's pretty!"

"Yeah," said Gretchen, "but who wants to look like her mom?"

"It could be worse," Tammy said. "The last one she tried on made her look like her dad!" Both girls laughed.

Janna shook her head and turned sideways to look at her reflection from a different angle. "I like it," she said. "I'm going to buy it."

That evening, Janna told her father about the incident in the clothing store.

"You're right," Dad said. "Your mom is a very pretty woman."

"I know," Janna said. "They were just trying to be funny."

"You do look like your mother, you know," Dad said. "You're both beautiful."

Janna smiled shyly. "I look a little like you, too," she said. "Everybody says I have your nose."

Dad ran a hand over his bald head. "At least you don't have my hairline!" he said, chuckling. Then his face got serious. "I'm glad you got your mother's good looks, but you know who I want you to look like even more?"

"Who?" Janna asked.

"Your Father—your heavenly Father. I think you resemble him more and more each day, and that makes me really happy. I think you even resembled him when you were in that store, when you refused to say unkind things about your mom and dad." He winked lovingly at Janna. "You see, Janna, God is kind. Kindness is a part of his nature. The Bible says his lovingkindness lasts forever. It's just a part of who he is. And when *you're* kind—whether you're kind to your parents or your friends or somebody you don't even know—you look and act like him . . . no matter what your friends say about your clothes!"

Janna smiled. She laid her head on her dad's chest. "Thanks, Dad," she said.

 TO DO: Using Psalm 136 as a pattern, take turns listing the many things that show God's kindness. (For example, one person may say, "He gave me loving parents," after which the whole family responds, "His kindness lasts forever." Someone else may say, "He sent Jesus to die for my sins," and then all respond, "His kindness lasts forever.")

 TO PRAY: "Lord, thank you for the kindness you showed by sending Jesus to die for us. Help us to be kind this week in many practical ways."

29 Pennant Race

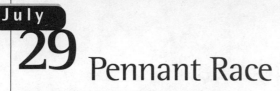

KINDNESS BRINGS OUT KINDNESS IN OTHERS.

Bible Reading of the Day: Read 2 Samuel 10:1-2.
Verse of the Day: *"Always try to be kind to each other and to everyone else"* (1 Thessalonians 5:15, NIV).

"Wow!" cried Nathan. "What a game!"

He and his dad leaped out of their seats in the baseball stadium after their favorite team had come from behind—twice—to win the game in thirteen innings.

"It *was* great, wasn't it?" Dad said.

"Thanks for buying the tickets and taking me, Dad," Nathan said.

"You're welcome, Son, but I didn't buy the tickets."

"You didn't?" Nathan said.

Dad shook his head. "The tickets were given to me by Mr. Grant."

"He just *gave* them to you?"

Dad shrugged. "Yeah, I helped him cut down a few trees a few weeks ago, so he said when he got a pair of tickets for this game, I was the first person he thought of."

"He just *gave* them to you?"

Dad nodded, smiling. "Out of the goodness of his heart," he said.

"Wow," Nathan said. "That's really cool."

"Well, we'll have to be sure to let him know how much fun we had and how much we appreciate his kindness."

Just then, as they walked through the stadium gate and onto the large concrete plaza, Nathan spied a man selling sports pennants. "Can I get one, Dad?" he asked.

Dad nodded, and Nathan dug into his pocket for money. He raced over to the man, bought a pennant bearing the home team logo, and then dashed back to his dad's side as they walked together toward the car.

"What are you going to do with that pennant, Son?" Dad asked. "Are you going to hang it on the wall in your bedroom?"

Nathan twirled the pennant in his hand. "No," he answered proudly. "I'm going to give it to Mr. Grant."

Dad's eyes opened wide, and he smiled broadly. "I think that's a wonderful idea," he said. "A wonderful idea."

 TO DISCUSS: Although Nahash's kindness to David was rewarded by David's efforts to be kind to Nahash's son, David's kindness to Hanun was not rewarded by Hanun. (The rest of the story of David and the Ammonites is found in 2 Samuel 10:3-19.) Sometimes that happens. Kindness is not always rewarded in this life, but which do you think usually has more positive benefits: kindness or unkindness? Why?

 TO PRAY: "Lord, help us see the ways that our kindness to others often brings kindness back to us. "

30 Kind Heart

A KIND PERSON BENEFITS HIMSELF AND OTHERS.

Bible Reading of the Day: Read Proverbs 11:16–17.

Verse of the Day: *"Always try to be kind to each other and to everyone else"* (1 Thessalonians 5:15, NIV).

"My candy!" Whitney said. She gripped the clear bag of hard candy tightly.

"No," Mom said as she knelt beside Whitney. "I asked you to hold the candy until we got to the nursing home. Now that we're here, Mommy needs the candy."

"I don't want to," Whitney said, her voice a whimper.

"But Whitney, honey, that candy is diabetic candy. It's made especially for people who can't eat other kinds of candy."

Whitney didn't answer, nor did she release her hold on the candy.

"Why don't I put you in charge of passing out the candy?" Mom suggested.

Whitney nodded solemnly but still hugged the candy to her chest. Mom rose then, gripped Whitney's shoulder, and walked through the open doors of the nursing home. Immediately inside the door, Mom and Whitney met a white-haired woman in a wheelchair. "Would you like a few pieces of candy?" Mom asked her, explaining that "Whitney would be glad to share with you . . . wouldn't you, Whitney?"

Whitney still looked unconvinced about giving away the candy, but she reached into the plastic bag and pulled out two brightly wrapped pieces. She slowly handed them to the lady.

"Oh, thank you so much," the woman said. She accepted the candy without taking her eyes off Whitney's face. "You're such a nice little girl."

Whitney smiled as she followed her mom to the nurses' station at the back of the lobby. As her mom talked to the nurse on duty, Whitney wandered over to a thin, wrinkled man who sat in the lobby watching a game show on television. Whitney dug into her bag of candy and offered a couple of pieces to the man.

The man reached out with a quivering hand and took the candy from Whitney's hand. "Thank you," he said, his speech slurred but his eyes smiling and radiant.

Whitney ran to her mom's side. "More, Mommy," she said. "I want to do more."

Mom smiled and for the next forty-five minutes led Whitney in and out of several rooms in the nursing home. Whitney gave candy to everyone she saw. Finally, Whitney had only a few pieces of candy left.

"We're all done," Mom explained to Whitney. "Thank you for your help."

"It was fun," Whitney answered, her eyes sparkling. "Can we do it again?"

Mom nodded. "Soon," she said. "We'll do it again soon."

TO DISCUSS: What changed Whitney's mind about sharing the candy? Which do you think was more enjoyable for her: having a bag of candy, or having the benefits of showing kindness to others? Have you ever been blessed because you showed kindness to someone else? If so, tell about it.

TO PRAY: "Lord God, your daily kindness to us encourages us to be kind. Thank you, Lord, for the opportunities you provide for us to be kind."

Old Elmer

KINDNESS PROVIDES A GOOD REPUTATION AND BRINGS HONOR TO GOD.

Bible Reading of the Day: Read Proverbs 14:21-22, 31.

Verse of the Day: *"He who oppresses the poor shows contempt for their Maker, but whoever is kind to the needy honors God"* *(Proverbs 14:31, NIV).*

"Grandma! Grandma!" Ty ran into the storeroom of the small restaurant his grandmother had owned and run ever since he could remember.

"Ty," Grandma said, "who's watching the cash register?" Ty was supposed to be running the cash register. He sometimes helped his grandma after school.

"I asked Holly to cover for me real quick," he explained. "Grandma, that man—the one with the long beard—he left without paying."

"Uh-huh," Grandma said, sounding disinterested.

"Should I catch him? Should I call the police? Wh-what should I do?" he stammered in a frantic tone.

"What?" Grandma asked, then before Ty could repeat himself, she said, "Oh, never mind him."

"But you can't just let him walk out without paying!"

"He never pays," Grandma said.

"What!" Ty cried. "You mean he's done this before?"

Grandma turned away from her work counting cans and took Ty's face in both of her hands. "That's Old Elmer," she said. "He's an old man with no family and no money. He comes in two or three times a week for a bowl of soup and some crackers. Been coming here since before your grandpa died."

"You just let him eat without paying?" Ty asked.

"Well, sure," Grandma said. "Wouldn't you?"

"But Grandma, you can't afford to just give food away," Ty protested. "You've got a business to run."

"And I've always done just fine, haven't I?" she answered. "Old Elmer isn't going to eat me out of my restaurant. Besides, I can't help it. When I see him eating his soup at that corner table—the same table every time he comes in—I feel like the smile of God just fills this place. It sure fills my heart to know I'm helping Elmer out."

Ty's eyes fastened on his grandmother. He had always loved and respected her, but never more than at this moment. He understood now more than ever why so many people seemed to think his grandma was special.

Because she was.

TO DISCUSS: What did Grandma's act of being kind to Old Elmer do for Elmer? What did her own kindness do for *her?* How does being kind to the needy honor God? How does being kind provide a good reputation? What other blessings and benefits come from being kind to others?

TO PRAY: "Jesus, we want to honor your name by being kind to everyone we meet. "

1 Trust in the Lord

WE OBEY GOD'S COMMANDS NOT BY TRYING, BUT BY TRUSTING.

Bible Reading of the Day: Read Proverbs 3:5-8.

Verse of the Day: *"Trust in the Lord with all your heart; do not depend on your own understanding. Seek his will in all you do, and he will direct your paths" (Proverbs 3:5-6).*

"Relax!" Suzanne said. She stood waist deep in a large swimming pool with her friend Linda. Suzanne held her hands out, palms up, in a pleading gesture. "You'll never learn to swim by fighting the water. You have to give in and let the water hold you up."

"I know," Linda admitted. "But I just—I guess I'm just afraid of sinking."

"Do you want to do the floating exercises again?" Suzanne asked. She was the captain of the school swim team and gave swimming lessons every summer.

"No," Linda said. "I know I won't sink." She inhaled deeply. "Let's try it again."

Suzanne placed her hands under Linda's stomach as Linda stretched out on the surface of the water. Linda began moving her arms and legs as Suzanne had instructed her. After a few moments, Suzanne took her hands away, and Linda kicked her way to the side of the pool.

"I did it!" Linda shouted. "I did it, didn't I?"

Suzanne laughed. "Yeah," she said. "You did."

When Linda's lesson was over, she walked with Suzanne to the locker room. "You're going to be swimming better than me in no time," Suzanne said.

"Yeah, right!" Linda said, laughing.

"I wouldn't be surprised. You do everything else better than I do."

"Like what?"

"Well . . . you're the perfect Christian. You never say or do anything wrong."

"That's not true," Linda said.

"Yes, it is," Suzanne insisted. "I'm serious," she said. "How do you always manage to do the right thing?"

Linda scratched her head. She could see that Suzanne was serious. "I don't know," she said. "It's . . . it's a lot like swimming. You're always saying I need to stop trying so hard and let the water hold me up, right?"

"Yeah," Suzanne said. "So?"

"So that's not too different from obeying God and doing what he says. It's not so much that I *try* to do good and be good and all that stuff; I just stay as close as I can to God, and trust *him* to do the work. It's not trying so much as it's trusting, because I don't have the power to do good, but he does. So I just trust him day by day to help me do the right thing."

 TO DISCUSS: How is making right choices like learning to swim? How can you show by your actions that you trust God with all your heart?

TO PRAY: "Lord, help us trust you to help us do the right thing through your Spirit, who lives within us. "

2 I Don't Understand

OBEYING GOD'S COMMANDS—EVEN WHEN WE DON'T UNDERSTAND THEM—
IS SMART.

Bible Reading of the Day: Read Joshua 6:1-16, 20.

Verse of the Day: *"Trust in the Lord with all your heart; do not depend on your own understanding. Seek his will in all you do, and he will direct your paths" (Proverbs 3:5-6).*

Molly and James leaned forward with excitement. They were on their way to their cousins' new house in the country.

"I can't wait to see the animals they have," Molly said. Their cousins had told them about their stable, where they kept many different kinds of animals.

"I wish they had horses," James said.

"Yeah, that's like the only kind of animal they didn't get," Molly answered. "Daddy, what's a rhea?"

Dad looked up from the map he held in his lap as he waited for a traffic light to change. "Huh?" he said, then suddenly realizing he had heard her question, he answered, "I don't know, honey. It's a bird. Some kind of bird."

The traffic light changed to green, and Dad drove through the intersection, then pulled to the curb in the small town they were in. "That's odd," he said, turning to his wife. "Pat said to turn right at the light."

"What's odd about that?" Mom asked.

"On the map that looks like the long way around. I should just be able to follow this county road here," he said, pointing to a line on the map. "It looks a lot easier and quicker going this way."

"But Pat should know his way around, don't you think?"

Dad didn't answer. He steered the car back into the street and began driving again, consulting the map instead of his brother's directions. After they had driven for about fifteen minutes, Dad came to a stop at an intersection. In front of them the road was blocked. Mom and Dad sat in silence, gazing at the roadblock.

"Are we there yet?" James asked.

"No," Mom said. "We're not there yet."

"Are we lost?" Molly asked.

"No," Dad answered. "We just found out why Uncle Pat gave us the directions he did." He turned the steering wheel and headed the car back in the direction from which they'd come. He folded the map as he drove and put it away. "I should have followed his directions in the first place," he said.

 TO DISCUSS: Have you ever gotten lost or confused because you didn't follow directions? Do you think Joshua and the Israelites fully understood the directions God gave them for conquering Jericho? Did Joshua follow God's directions anyway? Do you always understand God's commandments? Do you think it's better to obey God's commandments even when you don't understand them? Why or why not?

 TO PRAY: "Help us, Lord, so that we don't let pride stand in the way of following your directions."

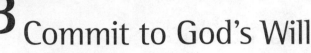
3 Commit to God's Will

ARE YOU COMMITTED TO DOING THE RIGHT THING?

Bible Reading of the Day: Read 2 Timothy 1:8-12.
Verse of the Day: *"Trust in the Lord with all your heart; do not depend on your own understanding. Seek his will in all you do, and he will direct your paths" (Proverbs 3:5-6).*

Crysti and her friend Mary had been playing together all afternoon in Crysti's sandbox in the shade of her house.

"I'm thirsty," Mary announced.

"I could go ask my mom for a drink of water," Crysti suggested.

"I don't want water. I want something that tastes good."

"She might let us have some lemonade."

"Yeah," Mary said, her eyes brightening. "Or some soda pop!"

Crysti stood and brushed the sand off her pants. "I'll go ask."

"Wait! Ask her for some cookies, too."

Crysti scratched her head. "She probably won't let us. It's too close to dinnertime."

"Tell her we need the cookies for a game we're playing."

Crysti shook her head. "That would be lying. I can't lie to my mom."

"Why not?"

"Because," Crysti explained, "I don't like to lie to my mom because it's wrong, and because it would hurt her feelings, and because I don't ever want to do that."

"So you *never* tell a lie?" Mary asked, unbelieving.

"Well," Crysti said, hesitating, "I try not to. And I especially try not to tell lies to my mom."

"How are we supposed to get cookies, then?"

Crysti shrugged. "I don't know." She thought for a moment, and she suddenly heard her mother call her from the window above her head.

"Crysti," Mom said, "would you and Mary please come to the kitchen?"

Crysti and Mary ran into the house together and met Crysti's mom in the kitchen. Two cups of lemonade and two large chocolate cookies sat on napkins on the kitchen counter.

"You can each have one cookie," Mom said, her eyes twinkling, "even though it's close to dinnertime." She kissed her daughter on the cheek. "I'm so glad my little girl is committed to telling the truth." She smiled and left the kitchen. The two girls watched her leave.

"Whatever *that* means," Crysti said.

 TO DISCUSS: A commitment is like a promise. Are you committed to seeking God's will and doing the right thing? What kind of specific commitments (promises) have you made? (For example, to tell the truth, to stay away from drugs, and so on.)

TO PRAY: "Lord, we're committed to following your path."

4 He Will Direct Your Paths

OBEYING GOD'S COMMANDS PUTS YOUR LIFE ON THE RIGHT PATH.

Bible Reading of the Day: Read Isaiah 26:3-7.

Verse of the Day: *"Trust in the Lord with all your heart; do not depend on your own understanding. Seek his will in all you do, and he will direct your paths" (Proverbs 3:5-6).*

The trail seemed to end at the creek. Lauren, Jason, and their dad had set out from their car three hours earlier on a backpacking trip, but the trail had been washed out in places, and darkness had fallen before they located their campsite beside a wide creek at the foot of the canyon. Dad searched the dark banks of the raging creek for the campsite but was unable to find it.

"OK," he said, facing the two children, "so we can't find our campsite. But we do know the way back to our car."

Dad, Lauren, and Jason shouldered their packs and began the laborious three-hour trip back up the mountain. The trail was now shrouded in darkness.

"Jason," Dad said as they started back up the canyon, "grab your sister's backpack and hold on to it. Lauren, you can hold on to my backpack." He pointed his flashlight at the trail. "And Lauren, watch where I step, and just walk where I do." He turned and began walking slowly up the trail. Because they followed each other so closely, Dad would frequently shine his light on a slippery rock or an exposed root.

"Be careful here," he would say, pointing his flashlight at the danger.

Lauren would then turn her flashlight on the spot and turn herself to make sure her brother could see it. "Dad says be careful here," she would say.

Three hours later, the backpacking trio arrived in the parking lot again. They were weary, wet, and dirty, but they were unharmed. Lauren and Jason dropped their backpacks to the pavement beside their car and hugged their father.

"That was scary," Jason said.

"Yeah," Lauren added, "but we made it, didn't we, Daddy?"

"That's right, Lauren," Dad said. "We made it, safe and sound. You want to know the main reason we made it back safely?"

They nodded.

"Because you followed me every step of the way and did everything I told you," Dad continued. "If you had tried running off on your own, or had stopped following me, we'd still be wandering around in the dark—or worse."

The children hugged their father again. "I'm glad we followed your feet, Daddy," Jason said.

"Me too," Dad answered. "Me too."

 TO DISCUSS: Have you ever tried "running off on your own" instead of following God's commands? If so, what happened? Is life always easy when God directs your paths? Why or why not?

 TO PRAY: "Heavenly Father, we want you to choose the path that we will follow."

5 Cindy's Trip

EVEN YOUR FRIENDS CAN TRIP YOU UP.

Bible Reading of the Day: Read Proverbs 13:14-20.
Verse of the Day: *"He who walks with the wise grows wise, but a companion of fools suffers harm"* (Proverbs 13:20, NIV).

"I don't see why you won't let me hang around with Shannon," Cindy protested. She folded her arms and stared at her empty dinner plate. "Why do you hate her so much?"

"We don't hate her at all," Dad replied calmly. "But Shannon doesn't always make the wisest decisions."

"And we don't want her to influence your decisions," Mom added.

"She won't," Cindy insisted. "I don't always do everything she says."

"That's good," Dad said, "but we still think the wisest thing is for you not to be around her as much."

Cindy said nothing for the next few moments. Finally, she asked to be excused from the table. Her parents agreed.

Cindy picked up her dinner plate and silverware from the dining-room table to take them to the kitchen sink. She turned and took several strides toward the kitchen.

Buster, the family dog, roused from his station beside Cindy's chair when she got up and followed her into the kitchen. At the kitchen door, however, Buster tried to dash ahead and got tangled up in Cindy's legs. Buster let out a pained yelp. Cindy lost her balance, let out a shocked cry, and tumbled to the floor.

Mom and Dad jumped up from the table and ran to the kitchen door. Cindy lay on the floor next to her scattered silverware and upturned plate. Buster had already sought sanctuary under the kitchen table.

"Cindy!" Mom cried. "Are you all right?"

Cindy rubbed her elbow. She nodded. "I think I just scraped my elbow."

Dad looked at her arm. He nodded. "Nothing serious. Does it hurt?" he asked.

"No, I'm OK," Cindy said. "Really. Buster just got between my legs and tripped me up." She called to Buster, who ran to her arms and licked her face. "He didn't mean to hurt me."

Cindy suddenly looked from her dad's face to her mom's.

"I guess that's kinda like me and Shannon, isn't it?" Cindy said. Mom and Dad listened attentively. "She doesn't mean to hurt me, but—but I guess even your friends can trip you up sometimes, huh?"

Mom nodded. "That's why you have to be careful where you walk."

"And who you walk with," Dad said. He patted Buster on the head and then helped Cindy get back up on her feet.

 TO DISCUSS: Do you have any friends that sometimes "trip you up" by their bad influence? Are you ever a bad influence on your friends? How can you be more careful in the future to avoid tripping up your friends or to avoid letting them trip you up?

 TO PRAY: "Lord, we don't want to be bad influences on our friends; nor do we want to be 'tripped up' by a friend's bad advice. Help us to make wise choices."

6 Opportunity Knocks

A SPIRIT OF REVENGE WILL JUSTIFY WHAT A SPIRIT OF LOVE WILL RECOGNIZE AS WRONG.

Bible Reading of the Day: Read Leviticus 19:16-18.
Verse of the Day: *"Don't say, 'I will get even for this wrong.' Wait for the Lord to handle the matter" (Proverbs 20:22).*

Monica turned to her mother and screamed.

"Stop the car!"

Mrs. Jackson slammed her foot on the brakes, watching in the rearview mirror as a rusty brown pickup truck stopped just in time to avoid a collision. She turned to her daughter, who sat beside her in the front seat.

"What's wrong?" Mrs. Jackson expected Monica to say they had almost run over an animal, but Monica pressed her face against the window and pointed at the line outside the movie theater.

"That's Jimmy," she whispered, "in line with Susan Brock."

Mrs. Jackson's eyes widened. "You mean I almost had an accident because you saw some old boyfriend going to the movies with someone else?"

Monica rolled her eyes without turning to face her mother. She just didn't understand. Jimmy wasn't just "some old boyfriend." It had been months now since her former friend, Gina Price, had broken them up and stolen Jimmy away. Jimmy and Gina had been going together ever since. And now he was in line at the movies with pretty Susan Brock.

"Monica Jackson!" Her mother was still stewing over their near accident. "Don't ever do that to me again. Do you hear me?"

"Yeah, Mom," Monica muttered, still watching Jimmy and Susan. "I'm sorry."

Jimmy, who was ahead of Susan in line, had turned away from her and was now talking with Nate and Alex, two of his closest buddies. As her mom began to pull the car back into traffic, Monica saw that Jimmy was there with his friends, and Susan was accompanied by her parents. They weren't there together at all.

Too bad, she thought as she turned around and settled back into the seat. *Then Gina would know how it feels to have someone steal your boyfriend.*

An idea began to form in her head. After all, she *did* see Jimmy at the movies with Susan. She wouldn't be lying if she told her former friend what she saw. And if Gina *assumed* that Jimmy was going out on her . . . Monica smiled. It was a golden opportunity. *Besides, she needs to know how much she hurt me. Then maybe she'd think twice before doing it again.*

 TO DISCUSS: Monica is not planning to lie to her "former friend." She's simply planning to tell Gina what she saw—that Jimmy and Susan were standing in line together at the movies. Are Monica's plans wrong or right? Explain.

 TO PRAY: "Lord, help us recognize unloving attitudes when they arise in our heart and mind. And please help us choose to act in love toward others."

7 Dear Diary

DON'T TRY TO JUSTIFY OR EXCUSE UNLOVING BEHAVIOR.

Bible Reading of the Day: Read Romans 12:9, 17–21.
Verse of the Day: *"Don't let evil get the best of you, but conquer evil by doing good"* (Romans 12:21).

Monica said good night to her mother and closed her bedroom door. She reached into the drawer of her nightstand, pulled out her diary, and began to write:

Saw Jimmy in line at the movies today. He was talking to Susan Brock. He was with friends, and she was with her parents.

I can't wait to see Gina tomorrow. I'll smile like we're still friends and tell her that I saw Jimmy and Susan in line together at the movies. I'll tell her how pretty Susan looked and how close they were standing. That ought to give Gina something to think about. With any luck, she'll throw one of her temper tantrums around Jimmy. He'll finally see what she's really like. Maybe they'll even get mad and break up.

The best part of it is, I'll only be telling the truth. I won't be doing a thing wrong. Just teaching my former best friend a lesson.

She finished writing, set her diary on her bedside table, turned out the light, and rolled over to go to sleep. But sleep would not come. Something was bothering her. After tossing and turning for a long time, she turned on the light beside her bed and stared at the poster-covered walls for a few moments.

I know God said we should love each other, she thought, feeling as if she were talking not only to herself, but to Someone else as well, *but this is different.*

She frowned. *I mean, Jimmy was* my *boyfriend first. Gina had no right to do what she did.* She stood for a moment, then plopped back down onto the edge of her bed. *It was wrong for* her *to do what* she *did, not for* me *to do what* I'm *going to do.*

She turned out the light and lay back on her bed, waiting for sleep to come.

TO DISCUSS: Do you agree that Monica wouldn't be doing anything wrong to carry out her plan? Why or why not? What command is Monica forgetting? What do you think Monica should do? What would you do?

TO PRAY: "Lord, we need your strength to avoid letting evil get the best of us. May we conquer evil by doing good."

8 The Confrontation

GOD COMMANDS US TO LOVE EACH OTHER.

Bible Reading of the Day: Read 1 Corinthians 13:1-5, 13.
Verse of the Day: *"And now these three remain: faith, hope and love. But the greatest of these is love"* (1 Corinthians 13:13, NIV).

Monica rolled out of bed and rubbed the sleep out of her eyes. It had seemed to take forever for her to fall asleep last night. She had spent half the night thinking about her plan to tell Gina—the "former friend" who had stolen her boyfriend, Jimmy—that she had seen Jimmy and Susan Brock at the movies. She didn't plan to mention that Jimmy had been at the theater with a couple of his friends and Susan had been standing in line behind Jimmy with her parents.

She had spent hours wrestling with the rightness and wrongness of her decision but had fallen asleep determined to get even with Gina.

I've made my decision, she told herself as she got dressed. She rushed through breakfast and arrived at school in time to see Gina standing at her locker near the chemistry lab. She glanced up and down the hall for any sign of Jimmy. The coast was clear.

"Hi, Gina," she said sweetly.

Gina's eyes widened at Monica's greeting. "I've got something I need to tell you." Monica took a deep breath. "I've been really mad at you for going out with Jimmy. I blamed you for breaking me and Jimmy up, and I've thought about ways to get even with you. But I finally had to admit that it would be wrong because—well, because I'm a Christian and God tells me to love you." Monica blushed. "Plus, I just realized this morning that you were one of the best friends I've ever had, and I'd—I'd really like to try to be friends again. What do you think about that?"

The first bell rang. "I'll see you later, OK?" Monica said, inwardly congratulating herself for the effect her words had obviously had on Gina. Gina's eyes had clouded with tears as if she couldn't believe what she had heard. Monica nearly skipped down the hall with self-satisfaction.

Throughout the day she thought about the encounter. She knew that she had done the right thing, and maybe even saved a good friendship. In her heart she knew that even though she had planned to teach Gina a lesson, she'd really taught herself. And from now on, she would remember what God's love was really like.

 TO DISCUSS: What do you think Monica would have gained by "teaching Gina a lesson"? Do you think she gained less or more by acting lovingly toward her instead? First Corinthians 13:5 says that love "keeps no record of when it has been wronged." What does that mean? Do you ever keep track of someone's "wrongs" against you? Do you need to change anything in your attitudes or actions in order to obey God's command to love others (even those who have hurt you)?

TO PRAY: "Heavenly Father, when people make us angry, we want to get even sometimes. Show us how to reflect your love instead of getting even."

9 "Give a Love"

GOD COMMANDS LOVE BECAUSE GOD VALUES LOVE.

Bible Reading of the Day: Read 1 John 4:7-11.

Verse of the Day: *"Dear friends, let us love one another, for love comes from God"* (1 John 4:7, NIV).

Heather and Robyn sat with their parents in their large family room.

"Heather," Mom said, "would you show little Ian where the toy chest is?" Mom nodded toward three-year-old Ian, who was visiting with his parents.

"Sure," Heather said, jumping up.

"I'll go too," Robyn said. She reached out a hand to Ian. He smiled and gripped her hand, and he and Robyn followed Heather out of the room.

Mom and Dad chatted for a long time with Ian's parents and lost track of time after a while. Finally, Ian's father looked at his watch.

"Oh, my," he said. "Look at the time. It's well past Ian's bedtime."

They stood together, and Mom and Dad led the way out of the room and down the hall to the playroom. Heather and Robyn sat in the center of the room, surrounded by toys, while Ian carried toy after toy back and forth from the toy box, which was now nearly empty.

"How's it going?" Ian's mother asked the girls.

"Oh, fine," Heather answered.

"Yeah," Robyn agreed. "We've been having fun, haven't we, Ian?"

The boy nodded happily and bobbed up and down in the middle of the room as if he were one of the toys from the toy box.

"Just one question, though," Heather said, raising a finger like a teacher.

"What's that?" Ian's dad said.

"Ian keeps saying something, and we can't figure out what it means."

"Oh?" the boy's dad said. "What?"

"It sounds like he's saying 'give a love,' or something like that."

Ian's mom and dad exchanged smiles. "Oh, that," his dad said. "That's exactly what he's saying."

"What does it mean?" Robyn asked.

"It means he wants a hug," his mother answered. "That's all. 'Give a love' means 'I want a hug.'"

"Oh!" Heather and Robyn said together. They laughed and held out their arms. Ian fell between them, and they both hugged him.

 TO DISCUSS: Even though Ian was a little child, he had already learned to value love and the signs (or tokens) of love, like hugs and kisses. That's why he kept saying "give a love." Can you tell that God values love by the things he says? If so, how? If not, why not? Do you think God would command us to love each other if he didn't think love was good and important? What's your favorite way to "give a love"?

 TO PRAY: "Show us, Lord, the many ways that we, as a family, can show your love to others, particularly to those less fortunate than we are."

10 Love Comes from God

GOD VALUES LOVE BECAUSE GOD IS LOVE.

Bible Reading of the Day: Read 1 John 4:16-19.
Verse of the Day: *"God is love"* (1 John 4:16).

"Mom, Curtis pushed me!" Tina cried as she burst into the house.

"Did not!" Curtis protested, following closely on her heels.

"Did too!" Tina said, barely holding back the tears in her eyes. "I hate you!"

"All right now," Mom said. "That's enough. Both of you come sit at the table." The children sat in chairs on opposite sides of the kitchen table.

"Tina," Mom said, "you don't hate your brother. At least I hope you don't."

"Well . . . ," Tina said, hesitating, "I don't love him."

"You should," Mom said, "because love is right. You know that. God commands us to love each other because he values love. And he values love because *he* is love."

"I know," Tina said. She glared across the table at Curtis. "I try to love him, Mom, I really do. But then he goes and does something really mean."

"And you, Curtis," Mom said, turning to her son. "You ought to love your sister."

Curtis said, "I can't, Mom. She's my *sister.*" He spoke the word with a snarl.

"Well, you're right," Mom said, "in a way. Neither one of you can love the other . . . not on your own, at least."

"What do you mean?" Tina asked.

"Well, love doesn't come from us," Mom said. "So we can't manufacture it. It comes from God." She reached out and turned over one of Tina's hands. "Just like those stains on your hands come from the berry patch."

Tina flashed a guilty look at her mom. "We were in the raspberries again."

"I know," Mom said. "I can tell. When you've been in the raspberries, you come home wearing the evidence. The berry juice just rubs off, doesn't it?"

Curtis and Tina nodded.

"It's the same with loving someone else when it doesn't come easily. Wishing won't help. And trying won't help. Love comes from God, because he is love. So if you want to love someone, you've got to start letting God's love 'rub off' on you. If you live in God—and I know you both do—you've got to give his love a chance to grow in you, through daily prayer and Bible reading, for example. The more time you spend with him, the more your attitudes toward each other will change."

"I guess we need to go wash our hands now, don't we?" Curtis asked.

Mom nodded. "You need to do something else, too."

Curtis looked from his mom to his sister. "I'm sorry," he said to Tina.

"Me too," Tina answered. She stood. "Let's go," she said to Curtis.

 TO DISCUSS: How can you love someone when it doesn't come naturally or easily? Will wishing or trying help? Why or why not?

 TO PRAY: "Loving God, we admit that we can't love anyone on our own. Thank you for helping us to love others."

11 Secret Service

LOVE BRINGS SATISFACTION, NOT DEPLETION.

Bible Reading of the Day: Read Hebrews 13:1-3.

Verse of the Day: *"Continue to love each other with true Christian love"* *(Hebrews 13:1).*

"Wanna do something fun?" Mom asked.

Little Judy nodded her head vigorously. Her older brother and sister were both old enough to go to school, and she was left alone every day with Mom.

"You and I," Mom whispered, though no one else was home, "are going to be . . . *the Secret Service!"*

Judy's eyes widened. She whispered back to her mom, "What's that?"

"You'll see," Mom said. "Come with me."

Mom led the way into the kitchen. She explained to Judy that the two of them were going to spend the day doing secret acts of love for other people. And they did.

First, they baked a batch of chocolate-chip cookies, tied them with bright red ribbon in wrapping paper, and placed bundles of cookies on everyone's pillows—including their own, "To keep the secret," Mom said.

Judy giggled gleefully as they next tiptoed onto the screened porch of their neighbor's house and left a bundle of cookies by the door for Mrs. Hastings, the woman who lived alone next door.

Finally, they left a bundle of cookies in their mailbox and sat together on the living room sofa, waiting and watching for the mail carrier to come. When the truck pulled up to their mailbox to drop off their mail, Mom and Judy closed the curtains and looked at each other, smiling and laughing at their "secret service."

"This is so much fun, Mommy," Judy said.

"Yes, it is," Mom said. "Do you know *why* it's so much fun?"

"Because . . . ," Judy said, thinking. "Because it's fun!"

Mom smiled again. "That's right," she said, "because showing love to others is fun. You see, giving love away isn't like giving cookies away. You have fewer cookies than when you started, don't you?"

Judy nodded.

"But," Mom continued, "when you give love away, you don't *lose* anything. You don't have less love than when you started; you have *more!"*

"Can we be the Secret Service tomorrow, too?" Judy asked.

Mom nodded. "As long as you've got enough love left!"

"I have lots and lots," Judy said. "More than before, just like you said."

TO DO: Start your own "secret service." You might clean a room, color a picture, walk a dog, or send new socks or slippers to grandparents with no return address on the package— whatever you think of. Make it your goal to perform your "secret service" sometime in the next seven days.

TO PRAY: "Lord, you poured out your love by sending your Son, Jesus, to die for us. We want to be generous in our love for others this week."

12 Puppy Love

LOVE INVITES LOVE; HATRED REPELS LOVE.

Bible Reading of the Day: Read Galatians 5:13-15.
Verse of the Day: *"Continue to love each other with true Christian love"* *(Hebrews 13:1).*

"Dad! Dad, look at this one! He's so cute!" After weeks of pleading, Margie had finally convinced her dad that she was ready to take care of a puppy. He had taken her to the animal shelter to see if they could find a dog to adopt.

Margie pointed to a sandy brown-and-white pup in a cage. "Isn't he precious?" she cooed.

"Yes, he is," Dad answered, "except that one's a 'she,' not a 'he.'"

Margie poked her fingers through the cage and petted the puppy's long, curling hair.

"What about that one?" Dad asked. He pointed to another puppy in the cage. "I think he's even prettier than that one."

Margie shook her head. "I don't like him as much," she said.

Dad's eyes gleamed with wisdom. "Why not?"

"Because," she said, hesitating. "Because I've been watching him. Look at him," she said, pointing as the animal snarled at the puppy next to him. "He keeps growling at the other two and pushing them out of the way. He seems kinda . . . kinda mean, you know?"

Dad nodded. "Yes," he said, "I think you're right." They stayed for a few moments and looked at other dogs, but when they left the animal shelter, Margie cradled the sandy pup in her arms.

"I think you made a good choice," Dad said. He patted the dog's head. As they got into the car and started the long drive home, Dad turned the conversation into a new area. "You know, Margie, I think those puppies at the shelter have something to teach us today. You chose this puppy because she seemed more loving and good-natured than that black-and-white one, didn't you?"

Margie nodded. "He was kinda mean," she said.

"But he really wanted your attention," Dad suggested.

"Yeah, but he was mean to the other dogs," Margie said.

"So this puppy got what that other puppy wanted because she seemed more loving?"

"Yeah," Margie said. "I guess that's the way love works, isn't it, Dad? I mean, when people are mean and stuff, it's usually because they want something. But mean and hateful people end up not getting what they want. But loving people—and puppies— they usually end up a lot better off, don't you think?"

Dad smiled. "I think," he said, nodding, "that's exactly what I think."

 TO DISCUSS: What do you think about what Margie said? Do you agree? Disagree? Why? How do you show your belief that loving actions and attitudes are better than mean and hateful actions and attitudes?

 TO PRAY: "Gracious God, you command us to love others. Lord, by your grace, we can show genuine compassion and love."

13 Proceeds of Love

LOVE PROTECTS US FROM STRIFE AND PROVIDES FOR PEACEFUL RELATIONSHIPS.

Bible Reading of the Day: Read Proverbs 10:11-12.
Verse of the Day: *"Hatred stirs up quarrels, but love covers all offenses"* *(Proverbs 10:12).*

Trudy plopped onto the school bus seat beside her friend Abby. She leaned across Abby and peered out the window.

"There goes Jaclyn Kayliss," Trudy said. She glared at a girl walking past the line of school buses. "She got kicked off her bus again."

"What for?" Abby asked.

"What for?" Trudy echoed. "Abby, this is Jaclyn Kayliss we're talking about." Trudy rolled her eyes when she saw Abby's blank look. "She got in a big fight on the bus this morning, her and Bobby Marshall duking it out like a couple of boxers."

"Really?" Abby said. She shook her head as she watched Jaclyn disappear around the corner of the school building.

"What's wrong?" Trudy asked, responding to Abby's sad expression.

"Oh, I don't know," Abby said. "I guess I just feel bad for Jaclyn."

"You feel bad for Jaclyn?" Trudy said. "Jaclyn Kayliss?" she repeated.

Abby shrugged as the school bus doors closed. "Yeah, why?"

"Come on, Abby, she gets into more fights than anybody in the whole school."

Abby inclined her head to one side in an expression of bemusement. "She's always been nice to me," she said.

"Of course she's nice to you. It's like you love everybody in the world."

"I'm so sorry," Abby said sarcastically. "I should try not to get along with other people so much—is that what you're saying?"

"No," Trudy answered. "You know what I mean. *Of course* Jaclyn Kayliss is going to like *you*—you're probably the only person in the school that doesn't hate *her.*"

Abby looked at her friend thoughtfully. "Well, that ought to tell you something right there," she said. "If you love others, you're not just doing *them* good, you're doing *yourself* good too. . . . Hatred just causes problems and arguments. Love *prevents* a lot of problems and stuff."

"I guess I never thought of it that way," Trudy said.

"Maybe that's why God tells us to love each other, Trudy," Abby said. "Because he knows loving others is a lot better for us."

"I guess he should know, right?" Trudy suggested.

Abby nodded and smiled. "Yeah," she said.

 TO DO: Make a family "covenant" to speak words of love to each other in order to promote peaceful relationships.

 TO PRAY: "God, thank you for the wisdom of your commands. Remind us that your commands are given to us for our own good. Help us to see the many ways love protects us and provides for us, and help us to obey your command to 'love one another' more and more."

14 Pleasant Surprise

TREATING EVERYONE WITH LOVE CAN PRODUCE PLEASANT SURPRISES.

Bible Reading of the Day: Read James 2:1-9, 12-13.
Verse of the Day: *"If you really keep the royal law found in Scripture, 'Love your neighbor as yourself,' you are doing right"* (James 2:8, NIV).

"I can't believe I have to stand next to Lyle at our concert!" Amber said. She sat at the table and helped her parents wrap presents for her brother's birthday party.

"What's so bad about that?" Mom asked.

Amber let out a hopeless sigh. "He's *only* the biggest nerd in our whole school!" She looked at her parents' faces and saw no understanding there. "If I stand next to Lyle, people might think I *like* him!"

"Would that be so terrible?" Dad asked.

"He's a *nerd,* Father," Amber said. "I don't want people thinking I like him."

Dad turned to Mom and smiled. "I'm glad you didn't feel that way," he said.

"Me too," Mom said. She leaned over the table and exchanged a kiss with Dad.

"Stop it," Amber said. She often admonished her parents for kissing in front of her. She reached for the tape dispenser. "What's that all about, anyway?" she asked.

Dad smiled. "If your mom hadn't been nice to nerds, you wouldn't be here today."

"What do you mean?" Amber asked.

"Your mother was one of the most popular girls in school," Dad explained. "And I was sort of a nerd."

"Sort of?" Mom scoffed.

"OK," Dad said, laughing. "I *was* a nerd. I wasn't popular at all, especially with the girls. Your mom was one of the few people in school who were actually nice to me."

"Once I got to know him as a friend," Mom said, "I realized that he was one of the smartest and funniest people I'd ever met." She leaned over the table and, in a low voice, told Amber, "And once I taught him how to dress, he wasn't bad looking, either!"

Amber laughed. "That's too much!" she shouted. "Dad was a nerd."

"The point is," Mom said, "if I had chosen to act hatefully toward your dad, I would have missed out on the greatest man in the world."

"When you treat *everyone* with love," Dad explained, "instead of just the popular kids or the most lovable people, you often receive some pleasant surprises."

"So you're saying I shouldn't be so upset about standing next to Lyle," Amber said. Her parents didn't answer, and she fell silent for a moment. "He can be a really nice person," she admitted. "But I'm *not* marrying him, OK?"

Mom and Dad laughed. "OK," Dad said. "That's fine with us."

 TO DISCUSS: Has treating someone with love ever produced a pleasant surprise for you? If so, describe it. Do you think we should love only the most popular people or people who are most like us? Or everyone? Is there anyone you need to treat with more love than you have been doing?

TO PRAY: "Lord, help us to love people no matter what they're like, instead of loving only those we feel are worthy of love. "

15 Facts and Feeling

RIGHT AND WRONG ARE NOT DETERMINED BY FEELINGS.

Bible Reading of the Day: Read 1 Corinthians 13:4-13.
Verse of the Day: *"Lord, let your constant love surround us, for our hopes are in you alone" (Psalm 33:22, TLB).*

Mom lifted her gaze from the newspaper to her daughter, who sat at the kitchen counter eating a bowl of Fruit Flakes cereal. "Tara," she said, "doesn't your friend Janet live on Morgan Street?"

"She's not my friend anymore," Tara mumbled.

Mom repeated her question. "Doesn't her family live on Morgan Street?"

Tara shrugged. "Yeah," she answered. "Why?"

"There was a fire on Morgan Street last night," Mom explained, laying the paper down on the counter. "Two families were burned out of their homes."

"Did anybody die?" Tara asked.

"No, everybody got out in time. But one of the families was named Turner."

"That's Janet's family," Tara said. "It's got to be."

Mom shook her head sadly. "We should find out what we can do to help. I'm sure we have extra blankets and clothing and things they could use. The paper says the house was a total loss."

"Do we have to?" Tara asked.

Mom looked at her daughter with confusion in her expression. "What do you mean?"

Tara sighed. "It's just that Janet's been really cruel to me and my friends this year at school, and . . . well, I just don't feel like helping her, that's all."

Mom nodded solemnly. "I'm sorry to hear she's been cruel to you," she said, her voice soft. "I guess I can understand your feelings. But feelings don't determine what's right or wrong, Tara. God does."

"You mean, even though she's been cruel to me and my friends all year, I still have to . . . like . . . be all loving to her?"

"Only if you want to do the right thing," Mom answered.

"Whether I feel like it or not," Tara said flatly.

"Whether you feel like it or not," Mom answered. "Because, like I said, feelings don't determine what's right or wrong—"

"Yeah, I know," Tara interrupted. "God does." She took a final bite of Fruit Flakes and stood. "I guess I've got some T-shirts and sweaters I could bag up for Janet."

Mom took her daughter's cereal bowl and placed it in the sink. "I knew you'd do the right thing," she said.

 TO DISCUSS: Do you think it was easy for Tara to decide to help Janet's family? Why or why not? What determines right and wrong? Do your feelings sometimes make it harder to choose right? Should you choose right anyway, even when it's hard?

TO PRAY: "Our feelings sometimes lead us to take the easy way out when it comes to showing love to people we don't like. Give us your strength, Lord, to do right."

16 Contend for the Faith

ALWAYS BE READY TO STAND UP FOR YOUR FAITH.

Bible Reading of the Day: Read Jude 1-3.
Verse of the Day: *"Always be prepared to give an answer to everyone who asks you to give the reason for the hope that you have" (1 Peter 3:15, NIV).*

Bo stomped into the garage, where his dad was working on the family car.

"What's wrong with you?" Dad asked.

"It's Coach," Bo said, referring to the coach of his swim team. "He knows I'm a Christian, and he keeps calling me things like 'Holy Bo' and 'God Squad.'"

Dad wiped his hands with a grease rag and leaned against the car. He nodded thoughtfully as Bo kept talking.

"And it's like he purposely tries to get me mad and make me do something wrong, you know? Like he *wants* me to mess up."

Dad nodded again. "It's like he's trying to test your faith."

"Yeah," Bo said, as if surprised that his dad understood.

"Reminds me of your first summer playing in the Little League," Dad said.

"It does?" Bo asked. "How?"

Dad smiled. "You stepped up to the plate, and your coach started lobbing balls at you. You swung and missed three times. Finally the umpire called, 'Strike three! You're out!' You turned around then and, without moving away from the plate, started crying and yelled to me, 'Daddy! He won't let me hit it!'"

Bo smiled for the first time since entering the garage. "I did that?"

"You sure did," Dad said, returning Bo's smile. "Of course, I had to walk you off the field and explain to you that the pitcher wasn't *supposed* to let you hit it. 'His job is to pitch the ball,' I said, 'and your job is to hit it. That's baseball.'"

Bo rubbed his chin and leaned back against the car beside his father.

"Sometimes," Dad continued, "we make the same mistake with our faith. We forget that the devil is going to attack our faith—and sometimes he's going to do it through people, even through people who are otherwise decent folks."

"So," Bo said, "the devil's 'job' is to attack my faith."

Dad nodded. "You can count on that. He will do that every day of your life in one way or another."

"*My* job," Bo said slowly, "is to stand up for my faith and to let Coach see what being a Christian is all about."

Dad slapped his son on the back. "That's right! You may not hit a home run every time, but you just stand in there and take your swings, and you'll do all right."

 TO DISCUSS: Do people ever tease you for being a Christian or for trying to make right choices? How do you respond when people try to test your faith? Are there good ways and bad ways to stand up for your faith? Can you give examples?

 TO PRAY: "God, it's not always easy to stand up for our faith. Give us your courage when our faith is put to the test."

17 Like Pure Gold

MORAL PURITY IS GOOD.

Bible Reading of the Day: Read Exodus 37:1-24.
Verse of the Day: *"Make every effort to live a pure and blameless life"*
(2 Peter 3:14).

"Now, remember," Todd told his nephew, Kenny, "you have to keep this a secret." Todd opened the door to the jewelry store and stood aside to let Kenny enter ahead of him.

"I will," Kenny promised. "I'm really good at keeping secrets."

Todd and Kenny approached the counter and explained to the salesman that Todd was shopping for an engagement ring. The man congratulated him as he pulled out a tray of gold rings and began showing them to Todd.

Kenny climbed onto a cushioned chair and leaned on the glass display case. "Those are pretty," he said.

Todd picked a ring out of the velvet-covered tray. He turned the price tag over and grimaced. "Iit'll have to cost a lot less than this one, that's for sure."

Kenny pointed to a tag dangling from one of the rings. "What's '14K' mean?"

Todd looked around for the salesman, but he had gone to help another customer. "I think it means, like, how much gold is in the ring."

"Aren't they all gold?" Kenny asked. The rings all looked gold to him.

"Well, it's like, if it's fourteen karats—that's what '14K' stands for—then it's got more real gold in it than if it says '12K' or something like that."

"That's right," the salesman said as he returned to the counter. "Twenty-four karats is pure gold."

"Pure gold," Kenny repeated in a reverent tone.

"And pure gold is the best," Todd explained to his nephew as he picked up another ring. "That means there's nothing but gold in it. No, uh, plastic or aluminum or other metals or stuff like that."

"I like pure gold," Kenny said.

Todd chuckled. "You're not the only one. But I can't afford this." He returned the ring to the tray. He looked over a few other rings, thanked the salesman, and led the way out of the store.

"Cassie likes pure gold too, doesn't she, Todd?" Kenny said.

Todd nodded. "I'm sure she does. Everybody likes pure gold. When something's pure, it's worth more. It's better."

"Like pure gold?" Kenny asked.

"Yeah," Todd answered, "like pure gold."

 TO DISCUSS: Can you name some pure things that you like (pure gold, pure milk chocolate, pure water)? God wants us to be pure. He doesn't want our lives to be all messed up with impurities like sin. Of course, we can't do that on our own, but God can make us pure.

TO PRAY: "Lord, teach us to rely on your help in keeping our lives pure."

18 Jenna's Perspective

WHO DECIDES WHAT IS RIGHT OR WRONG? GOD—AND ONLY GOD.

Bible Reading of the Day: Read Genesis 39:1-10.
Verse of the Day: *"Make every effort to live a pure and blameless life"*
(2 Peter 3:14).

"I can't believe you're letting me watch this show, Dad!" Jenna said.

"I can't believe it, either," Mom said.

Dad smiled. He sat on the couch with his arm wrapped around his wife. Jenna curled up on the floor in front of the couch as the theme song to the hit television show *Hollywood Boulevard* came on.

"Why are we watching this show?" Jenna asked. She knew this was the episode in which Marla, one of the main characters, was supposed to fall in love with Brant.

"Let's just watch it for now," Dad suggested.

The show was half over when, at the commercial break, Dad turned down the sound and shifted his position on the couch. "What do you think Marla's going to do, Jenna?" he asked his daughter.

Jenna coughed nervously. She suspected her dad was ready to turn the television off. "I think she's going to, uh, go to bed with Brant."

"But they're not married, are they?" Dad asked.

Jenna shook her head.

"You think Marla feels that what she's doing is OK?"

Jenna nodded. *"She* thinks so, because she said she waited until Brant's divorce was final, so that no one could come between her and the man she loves."

"What do *you* think?" Dad asked.

"It would be wrong," Jenna said.

"Why?" Dad asked.

"Because she and Brant aren't married."

"So?" Dad asked. "Who are you to say Marla shouldn't do what she thinks is right?"

Jenna looked shocked. "I—I, uh, I'm not the one who says that," she answered. "God says so. He says we should be pure, and what Marla's thinking of doing isn't pure. Just because Marla says it's right doesn't make it right; it's what God says that matters."

Dad leaned back on the couch again and reached for the remote control. "You're right," he said. "You're absolutely right. In fact, you may have some friends at school tomorrow who need to hear a godly perspective on tonight's episode of *Hollywood Boulevard.*" He smiled and turned the sound up on the television.

 TO DISCUSS: In today's Bible reading, Potiphar's wife tried to tempt Joseph to surrender his purity. How did Joseph react? Did Joseph try to decide right and wrong by himself, or did he act according to what God said was right?

 TO PRAY: "Father, we love you. We worship you, and we adore you. We want to glorify your name by seeking your help to live pure and blameless lives."

19 Hammer Time

GOD COMMANDS PURITY IN THOUGHT, WORD, AND DEED.

Bible Reading of the Day: Read Ephesians 4:29; 5:1-4.
Verse of the Day: *"Do not let any unwholesome talk come out of your mouths, but only what is helpful for building others up according to their needs, that it may benefit those who listen" (Ephesians 4:29, NIV).*

Simon held the board still while Dad held the nail he was trying to hammer into the board, which was going to become part of the roof for the doghouse they were making. Dad lifted the hammer into the air and brought it down—partly on the nail and partly on his hand. Dad let out a yelp and dropped the hammer.

"Are you OK?" Simon asked, concern written on his face.

Dad shook his hand vigorously in the air. "Yes," he said. He inhaled sharply, the air whistling through his teeth. "It sure does hurt, though," he said.

A few moments later, Dad lifted the hammer again and went back to work. He handed the hammer to Simon and let him pound in the last nail. As they lifted the roof and prepared to attach it to the doghouse, Simon asked his dad a question.

"Dad," he said, "haven't you ever said a bad word? Ever?"

Dad stopped working and studied his son's face. He knew what had prompted Simon's question—his reaction to pain without cursing when he hit his hand with the hammer. He shook his head. "Not since I was a little boy," he said.

"Why?" Simon asked.

"Well," Dad answered, "because God tells us that he wants us to be pure—in thought, word, and deed. His Word says, 'Don't let any unwholesome talk come out of your mouths.'"

"What's that mean?"

"Well, 'unwholesome talk' means bad words, mean things you might say about somebody else, gossip—things like that."

"Mr. Henderson sometimes says bad words," Simon said, referring to the father of one of his friends.

Dad nodded. "I know," he said. "Do you?"

Simon thought for a moment. "I did once," he said. "But I didn't like it."

"I'm glad to hear you didn't like it," Dad said with a smile. "It's a lot better to say good things instead of bad things, isn't it?"

"Yeah," Simon agreed, smiling. "Even when you hit your hand with a hammer, huh, Dad?"

Dad returned Simon's smile. "Even then, Son," he said. He lifted the hammer and hit the nail squarely on the head.

TO DO: Place a hammer on the table or kitchen counter today to remind everyone in the family that God commands purity in thought, word, and deed.

TO PRAY: "Lord, may we be pure in our thoughts, words, and deeds."

20 Motorcycle Madness

GOD COMMANDS PURITY, BECAUSE HE VALUES PURITY.

Bible Reading of the Day: Read Philippians 1:9-11.
Verse of the Day: *"Have I lied to anyone or deceived anyone? Let God judge me on the scales of justice, for he knows my integrity" (Job 31:5-6).*

Grant burst in the back door after a hot, sweaty session of backyard football with a few of his friends.

"Thirsty?" Mom asked.

"Yeah," he answered. "I'm dying of thirst."

"How about a glass of ice water?" Mom said. She held a glass in her hand.

Grant reached out and grabbed the glass. "Thanks, Mom," he said. He lifted the glass to his mouth but stopped before taking a drink. "What's this?" he asked. He held the glass up in front of his face. "There's dirt in this water!"

"Oh, don't worry about that," Mom said. "It's cold and wet, isn't it?"

"Yeah, but I don't want to drink . . ." Suddenly a knowing expression crossed Grant's face. "What's this all about, Mom?"

Mom reached for a magazine on the kitchen counter and set it down on the table in front of Grant. "I was running the sweeper in your bedroom this afternoon, and I found this under your desk," she said.

Grant blushed. It was a copy of *Motorcycle Madness,* a magazine a friend had given him that featured pictures of motorcycles and women in skimpy clothes.

"I just figured," Mom said, "that you wouldn't mind putting impurities into your body, since it doesn't seem to bother you to put impurities into your mind and heart."

"Oh," Grant muttered, making the connection between the dirty water his mom had given him to drink and the pictures he'd been looking at.

"Grant," Mom said, "the pictures aren't very pure, are they?"

Grant shook his head. "No," he answered, "they're not."

"I want you to stay pure, Grant," Mom continued. "I value purity . . . because *God* values purity. That's why he commands us to be pure, to live pure and blameless lives—because he knows that purity is a good thing, a valuable thing."

"Yeah," Grant said. "I'm sorry, Mom." He turned the glass of dirty drinking water around in his hand. "I guess I value purity too."

"Good," Mom said. "Now, would you like a glass of clean water?" She picked up the magazine, carried it to the wastebasket, and threw it away.

Grant nodded. "Yes, please," he said. He looked at the magazine, resting atop the trash bin of coffee grounds, eggshells, and other garbage. "Thanks, Mom," he said.

 TO DISCUSS: Why does God command us to live pure lives? How does your life show that you value purity in your own thoughts, words, and deeds?

TO PRAY: "Lord, help us to have the mind of Christ when it comes to our thought life. We want to make a covenant with you to guard what we watch, listen to, and read."

21 God Is Pure

GOD VALUES PURITY, BECAUSE GOD IS PURE.

Bible Reading of the Day: Read Isaiah 6:1-7.
Verse of the Day: *"Holy, holy, holy is the Lord Almighty; the whole earth is full of his glory" (Isaiah 6:3, NIV).*

Missy and April were playing croquet together in the backyard at Missy's house. Missy's father stood at the grill on the back porch, barbecuing their dinner.

April knocked her ball into Missy's ball, sending it far from the closest wicket. Missy watched her ball roll farther and farther away, and then, in frustration, said a word she had heard April say many times in anger.

Missy didn't say the word very loudly, but she suddenly felt afraid when she heard her father call from the porch.

"Missy, April," he called, "would you both come here for a minute?"

The girls joined Missy's dad by the grill. He pointed to a hot dog he had dropped onto the wood slats of the porch. "Either of you want that hot dog?" he asked.

"Eeww, gross!" April said. Missy wrinkled her nose and shook her head.

"Why not?" Dad said.

"It's dirty," Missy answered.

"Oh," Dad said. "You're right. It's not very clean. Like your language just now. You see, girls," Dad said, "purity isn't just good for the things you put into your mouth; it's good for the things that come out of your mouth. Purity is right, and impurity is wrong. Do you know *why* purity is right?"

Both girls shook their heads.

"Because God commands us to be pure," Dad answered. "God commands us to be pure because God values purity. Do you know *why* God values purity?"

Again they shook their heads.

"Because God is pure," he said. He took a red-hot coal out of the grill and held it in a pair of tongs as he told them the story of Isaiah in the temple. "When Isaiah saw the holiness and purity of God, he was terrified because of his own impurity and sinfulness, until an angel touched his lips with a hot coal and told him his sin and guilt were gone. That's how pure God is," Dad explained, "so pure that nothing impure can survive in his presence. That's why purity is right—"

"And impurity is wrong," Missy said, finishing her dad's sentence. "I'm sorry, Dad."

"Well, here," Dad said, holding the smoking coal toward his daughter with a teasing look in his eyes. "Let me touch your lips with this coal! That'll make everything better!"

"No!" Missy screamed, as she and April ran away laughing.

TO DISCUSS: Why was Isaiah ashamed? How does the knowledge of impurity in our lives cause us to feel?

TO PRAY: "God, you are pure and holy, and you command us to be pure. Please purify our thoughts, Lord. Purify our words. And purify our lives so that we may please you in all that we do."

22 Smoke Alarm

DOING RIGHT IS EASIER ONCE YOU'VE COMMITTED TO GOD'S WAY.

Bible Reading of the Day: Read Psalm 119:9-16.
Verse of the Day: *"How can a young person stay pure? By obeying your word and following its rules" (Psalm 119:9).*

Uncle Jim's hacking cough echoed through the small house as Pete skulked in the front door and tried to sneak into the bathroom.

"Pete!" Uncle Jim called. He appeared suddenly in front of Pete.

"Hi, Uncle Jim," Pete said.

"Where ya been, boy?" Uncle Jim asked. Pete had agreed to stop by Uncle Jim's house after school to help him hang some shutters.

"I, uh, hung out with a couple of friends after school," Pete said.

"Oh," Uncle Jim said. "Is that why your breath smells like cigarette smoke?"

Pete dropped his hand. "Yeah," he muttered, not meeting his uncle's gaze. "I guess so. The guys were just messing around, you know?" he said. "I was ashamed to say no."

"You should have been ashamed to say yes," Uncle Jim barked, which triggered a prolonged coughing spell.

"Uncle Jim, you know what it's like," Pete said in a pleading tone. "You started smoking when you were a kid, didn't you?"

"Yes!" the man answered loudly. "And it took me thirty-five years to stop. And now all that garbage I took into my lungs is killing me, slowly but surely. I don't want you making the same mistake."

"I know," Pete said. "It's just that—well, the guys—"

"I know all about the guys," Jim said. "They think it's 'cool' to smoke. They test you and tempt you and try to get you to take the same impurities into your body as they do." He coughed. "I know it's hard, Son, but it'll be a whole lot easier if you decide ahead of time that you're going to keep yourself pure, in soul *and* body."

"But how do I do that, Uncle Jim?"

Uncle Jim sighed. "Doing the right thing is easier," he said, "if you've already made your mind up before temptation hits. You need to decide *now* what your answer's going to be when your 'friends' offer you a cigarette. Commit *now* to obeying God's Word and following his commands, and trust him every day for the strength to avoid temptation or, if you can't avoid it, to resist it when it comes."

"I've never really done that, I guess," Pete said.

"Now's as good a time as any to commit to God's way," Uncle Jim answered.

Pete looked at his uncle with a serious expression. "OK," he said.

Uncle Jim gripped Pete's shoulder firmly in his hand, and they both closed their eyes while Pete started to pray, committing himself to following God's way.

TO DISCUSS: Do you ever face temptation to think, say, or do impure things? Have you committed to following God's way when temptation hits? How can you do that?

TO PRAY: Take turns praying, promising God that you will follow what he says is right and that you'll stay pure by obeying his Word and following its rules.

Clean Hands and Hearts

PURITY PROTECTS US FROM GUILT AND PROVIDES FOR SPIRITUAL VITALITY.

Bible Reading of the Day: Read Psalm 24:3-6.

Verse of the Day: *"How can a young person stay pure? By obeying your word and following its rules" (Psalm 119:9).*

Mom leaned out the back door and called to her daughter, who was playing in the neighbor's yard. "Sheila! It's time to eat!"

A few moments later, Sheila came in and saw the dinner table already set with plates, napkins, silverware, and bowls of steaming food. She started to sit down in her usual seat next to Dad, who sat at the head of the table.

"Sheila, honey," Mom said, "please go wash your hands first."

"Do I have to?" she asked.

"Yes, you have to," Dad answered. "Please hurry," he added.

Sheila returned to the table a few moments later after washing her hands, and the family ate dinner. Afterward, Dad reached for the Bible and opened to Psalm 24 for devotions. "'Who may climb the mountain of the Lord?'" he read. "'Who may stand in his holy place? Only those whose hands and hearts are pure, who do not worship idols and never tell lies. They will receive the Lord's blessing and have right standing with God their savior. They alone may enter God's presence and worship the God of Israel.'"

"I know why you read that," Sheila said when he had finished.

"Why?" Dad answered coyly.

"Because I didn't want to wash my hands before dinner."

He smiled. "That's right," he said. He winked at his daughter.

"You see, honey," Mom offered, "we want you to wash your hands before you eat because, if you don't, the dirt and impurities and germs can make you sick."

"They can?" Sheila asked.

Dad closed the Bible and returned it to its place on the sideboard. "That's why we require you to have clean hands when you come to the table. And it's sort of the same reason God wants you to have a pure heart."

"Will I get sick if I don't have a pure heart?" Sheila asked innocently.

"In a way," Mom said. "If you have any impurity in your life, it can make you feel guilty and even shameful, and those things can make you feel far from God."

"I don't want to be far from God," Sheila said.

"We don't want that, either," Mom said. "And God doesn't want that."

"Clean hearts are important, aren't they?" Sheila said.

Dad nodded, and Mom added, "And clean hands are too!"

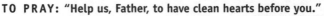

TO DISCUSS: What good things does today's Bible reading say will happen to "those whose hands and hearts are pure"? How does God's command to be pure protect us from guilt and shame? Each time you wash your hands this week, remember the importance of clean hands—and clean hearts.

TO PRAY: "Help us, Father, to have clean hearts before you."

PURITY PROTECTS US FROM CORRUPTION AND PROVIDES FOR GOOD WORKS.

Bible Reading of the Day: Read Titus 1:15–16.

Verse of the Day: *"To the pure, all things are pure, but to those who are corrupted and do not believe, nothing is pure" (Titus 1:15, NIV).*

"Thanks for coming over, Rudy," Darbi said as she opened the door for her friend. "I don't know what's wrong with it. Sometimes it works fine, but sometimes it acts really weird." She led the way through the house to the family den. "There it is," she said, as she opened the door to the den and pointed to the home computer on the desk.

Rudy rubbed his hands together and sat down on the desk chair facing the computer. "OK," he said. "Let's see what we've got here."

He started opening and closing applications on the computer, alternately typing on the keyboard and working the mouse that controlled the cursor on the computer screen. After about fifteen minutes, he turned the computer off. Then he stood, moved the monitor, and began taking the cover off the computer unit itself.

"Can you tell what's wrong with it?" Darbi asked, hovering over Rudy like a concerned mother hen.

"Well," he said, as he pulled the cover off to expose the chips, circuits, and other components that formed the "guts" of the computer. "This could be part of your problem right here."

Darbi stared at the dusty interior of the computer, looking for something that looked broken or disconnected. "What?" she asked. "I don't see anything."

"Do you have a vacuum cleaner?" Rudy asked. "With a small, thin attachment?"

Darbi disappeared and, a few moments later, came back in with a canister vacuum cleaner, a thin, flat nozzle attached to the hose.

Rudy took the hose from her. "Home computers tend to attract a lot of dust and other stuff," he explained, "because of carpets and plants and other things."

"You mean my computer just needs to be vacuumed?" Darbi asked.

Rudy shrugged. "Dust and other junk can get into your computer and mess it up. There are a lot of sensitive pieces to a computer. Dust and dirt can really corrupt your computer and make it not work right."

"Wow," Darbi said. "I never thought of cleaning my computer's insides."

Rudy spent the next half hour cleaning his friend's computer. When they put it back together and tried it, everything seemed to be working much better. "Now, that may have been all it needed," he said. "But if it still doesn't work right, you may want to take it to be professionally cleaned."

"OK," Darbi said. "I never knew clean 'insides' could be so important."

TO DISCUSS: What effects did the impurities inside Darbi's computer have on how it worked? Do you think impurities on *your* "insides" have effects too? Like what? How can staying pure in thought, word, and deed make your life "work better"?

TO PRAY: "Lord, we need you to check us out spiritually from the inside out. Remove anything impure that's inside of us."

25 A Pure World

THE BLESSINGS OF PURITY ARE NUMEROUS.

Bible Reading of the Day: Read Psalm 51:10–12.
Verse of the Day: *"Create in me a pure heart, O God, and renew a steadfast spirit within me"* (Psalm 51:10, NIV).

Mom, Carrie, and Anthony were standing in line at the bank.

"This line is too long," Anthony complained. He studied the other lines in the bank to see if any were shorter, but they all looked about the same length.

"I have an idea!" Carrie announced. "Let's play the 'What If?' game!"

"OK," Mom said. "What if . . . everyone in the world was pure in all of his or her thoughts, words, and deeds?"

Carrie and Anthony grew suddenly quiet, forgetting the long line and concentrating on imagining a world where everyone was pure.

"I know!" Carrie said. "We could go to any movie we wanted . . . because they'd all be rated 'G'!"

Mom chuckled. "Very good, Carrie," she said.

"I know," Anthony announced. "People wouldn't paint all those bad words on the walls near our school."

"Yeah," Carrie agreed. "And I could watch any TV show I wanted, instead of having to ask you first!"

Mom nodded. "I think you're both right," she said. "Anything else?"

Anthony placed his finger on his chin in a thoughtful gesture. "They wouldn't have to put those stickers on CDs!"

"That's right," Mom agreed. "We wouldn't need 'parental advisory' stickers, would we?"

"Bobby Nelson wouldn't always be getting in trouble for telling dirty jokes at school," Carrie offered, frowning in obvious disapproval of Bobby's behavior.

"Excuse me, ma'am," a man in a police officer's uniform said to Mom as he stepped up to her in line.

"Oh, I'm sorry," Mom said. "Are we being too loud?"

"No," the man said quickly, "not at all. I was just listening to your little game—I couldn't help but overhear—and I wanted to join in." He turned to Carrie and Anthony. "If everyone in the world was pure in thought, word, and deed, it would make my job a whole lot easier. I might even be able to retire early!"

Carrie and Anthony smiled. Mom said, "Thank you, Officer."

He nodded, smiling. "Thank *you*, ma'am."

 TO DO: Play your own "What If?" game on the subject of purity. See what you can add to Carrie and Anthony's ideas.

TO PRAY: "Lord, it's hard for us to imagine this world being pure. Help us to remember that a pure world starts with us doing our part to stay pure. Please help us to be pure in thought, word, and deed."

26 The Cart and the Horse

OBEYING GOD'S COMMANDS WILL NOT SAVE US, BUT SAVING FAITH WILL
PRODUCE OBEDIENCE.

Bible Reading of the Day: Read Galatians 3:10-11; 5:16.
Verse of the Day: *"The righteous will live by their faith"* (Habakkuk 2:4).

Krystal came crying into her classroom at her Christian school. All the other children were still on the playground.

"What's the matter, Krystal?" her teacher, Miss Stacy, asked. Miss Stacy placed a gentle hand on each of Krystal's shoulders and pulled her close.

Krystal struggled to control her sobbing, and finally managed to explain. "I—I was playing hopscotch with Bethany, and—and I fell down and then I said a bad word."

"Did you hurt yourself?" Miss Stacy asked.

"N-no," Krystal answered. "But now I won't go to heaven!"

"What?" Miss Stacy asked, her voice still soft. "What makes you think that?"

"My mommy and daddy are teaching me how to make right choices. But now I've done a bad thing, and I won't get to go to heaven."

Miss Stacy hugged Krystal and stroked her hair gently. She smiled slightly. She knew Krystal's parents, and she knew they had not intended to give their daughter that impression. "Oh, Krystal, that's not true," she said.

"It's . . . it's not?" Krystal said. Her crying subsided slightly, and she looked up at Miss Stacy with big, round eyes.

"No," the teacher said, erasing her smile. "Not at all. You're getting the cart before the horse."

"I am?" Krystal asked.

Miss Stacy nodded. "Didn't you ask Jesus to live in your heart?" she asked.

Krystal sniffled and nodded solemnly.

"And don't you love Jesus?"

"Oh, yes," Krystal answered. She wiped a tear from her cheek with the back of her hand.

"Krystal, *that's* what makes you a Christian. That's why you get to go to heaven."

Krystal didn't speak, but her tears had stopped flowing.

"Saying a bad word isn't going to change any of that. But loving God and being a Christian should make you want to do good things, not bad things."

"Oh, I do," Krystal said, her face suddenly bright. "I want to be good . . . for Jesus!"

Miss Stacy laughed and hugged Krystal again. "I know you do, Krystal. We all do."

 TO DISCUSS: How would you answer the questions Miss Stacy asked Krystal ("Did you ask Jesus to live in your heart?" and "Do you love Jesus?")? Do you think making right choices saves us or gets us to heaven? Do you think a saving faith in Jesus Christ helps us make right choices? Explain.

 TO PRAY: After the above discussion, take turns praying for family members and friends who need to know the truth of Jesus' love.

27 The Prayer Plan

PRAYER IS A KEY TO MAKING RIGHT CHOICES.

Bible Reading of the Day: Read 2 Thessalonians 1:3-4, 11-12.
Verse of the Day: *"We pray that God, by his power, will fulfill all your good intentions and faithful deeds" (2 Thessalonians 1:11).*

"What's that?" Mika asked his friend Daniel. He pointed to a letter-sized piece of paper posted on the refrigerator door in the kitchen of Daniel's house.

"What, that?" Daniel said. "That's our prayer plan." The paper consisted of two columns. On the left side of the sheet was a column of numbers, one to thirty-one; on the right side of the page, opposite each number, was a short word or phrase.

"What's a prayer plan?" Mika asked.

Daniel shrugged. "It's just something we do as a family." He scratched his head; he wasn't sure if Mika would understand, so he wanted to explain it as well as he could. "My parents want me and my sister to grow up to love God and make right choices. So they try to teach us, you know, what things are right and what things are wrong."

Mika nodded.

"But if we're really going to learn how to do right all the time, it's going to take more than that. So every day me and my sister and my parents, we pray for each other, that God will make us good." He pointed to number one on the prayer plan. "So, like, on the first of the month, we pray for each other that we'll all be sure of our salvation."

He moved his finger to number two on the list. "On the second day of every month, we pray for each other to be loving; on the third—" he moved his finger down to the next item on the prayer plan—"we pray for each other to show respect."

"Oh, I get it," Mika said. He looked at the last item on the sheet of paper. "And on the thirty-first of the month, you pray for each other to have a love for God's Word."

Daniel nodded. "So that's our prayer plan."

"It's like a game!" Mika said.

Daniel had never thought of their prayer plan as a game before. "I guess it is," he admitted. "Sort of. It *is* fun. But it's serious, too."

"I like your prayer plan," Mika said.

"I do too," Daniel agreed.

TO DO: Take a few minutes to brainstorm your own "prayer plan" to help you pray for each other as a family. You may wish to include the godly virtues discussed in this book, such as justice, mercy, purity, humility, generosity, and so on, as well as the fruits of the Spirit included in Galatians 5:22-23, and any other values or convictions you desire for each other.*

TO PRAY: "Lord, help us to be faithful in our prayer lives."

*See the back of this book for a Suggested Prayer Plan for Your Family.

28 The Fear of the Lord

OUR FEAR OF GOD SHOULD MAKE US AFRAID TO DISOBEY HIM; OUR LOVE OF GOD
SHOULD MAKE US WANT TO OBEY HIM.

Bible Reading of the Day: Read Deuteronomy 31:9-13.
Verse of the Day: *"I will make an everlasting covenant with them
that I will not turn away from them, to do them good; and I will put
the fear of Me in their hearts so that they will not turn away from Me"*
(Jeremiah 32:40, NASB).

"Your dad is *huge!*" Darcelle said as she and Shanaya walked down the steps of
Shanaya's house on their way to the store.

Shanaya smiled. She was used to her friends being surprised the first time they
met her dad. "Yeah," she answered. "He used to be a football player."

"You mean, for like, real football?" Darcelle asked.

Shanaya nodded. "He's retired now, but he played for a couple different teams."

"Wow!" Darcelle thought for a moment. "Aren't you afraid of him?"

"Afraid of him?" Shanaya echoed. "Why would I be afraid of him?"

Darcelle stooped down and picked up a tiny twig off the sidewalk. "Because he
could snap you" —she broke the twig between her fingers— "like this!"

Shanaya laughed and shook her head. "No," she said. "I'm not afraid that he'll
hurt me. I mean, he may be big and strong, but he's really loving too. I love it when
we cuddle together, and when he lets me sit on his lap."

"Girl, as big as *you* are?" Darcelle said. "You sit on his lap?"

"Uh-huh," Shanaya answered. They reached the corner opposite the store and
waited for the traffic lights to change.

"You're telling me that your dad never gets mad at you or anything like that?"
Darcelle said.

Shanaya thought for a moment. "Yeah, he gets mad sometimes. But you know
what I hate even more than when I make him mad? When I know I've disappointed
him . . . or hurt him. *That's* what I'm afraid of, I guess: I'm afraid of hurting him. I'm
afraid of disobeying him . . . and disappointing him."

"I'd be afraid too," Darcelle said, "if my dad was the size of an apartment
building!"

The light changed, and the girls crossed the street. "I keep telling you, it's not like
that," Shanaya insisted. "I know my dad loves me, and I love him. So I'm afraid to
disobey him, yeah, but it's like . . . it's like my respect for him makes me afraid to
disobey him, and my love for him makes me *want* to obey him."

 TO DISCUSS: Is Shanaya's relationship with her dad like your feelings about your
parents? If so, how? If not, how are your feelings different? Do you think Shanaya's
"fear" of her dad is anything like the "fear of the Lord"? If so, how? If not, how is it
different? Does your respect for God make you afraid to disobey him? Does your love
for him make you want to obey him?

TO PRAY: "Lord, we want to fear you in a healthy way. We also want to love you,
Abba Father."

29 Don't Be Misled

USUALLY WHEN WE MAKE A WRONG CHOICE, IT'S NOT BECAUSE WE DIDN'T KNOW
WHAT WAS RIGHT; IT'S BECAUSE WE DESIRED WHAT WAS WRONG.

Bible Reading of the Day: Read James 1:12-16.
Verse of the Day: *"Do not do as the wicked do or follow the path
of evildoers" (Proverbs 4:14).*

Heidi's wide eyes gazed up at her mother with a combination of fear and sadness. She
stood on the top step of her house, facing the front door, which her mother had just
opened. Two police officers stood behind her.

"What's this all about?" Mom asked.

"Ma'am," a female officer said, "this young lady tried to shoplift several items
from McCracken's Department Store."

Mom looked from the officer to her daughter. "Is this true, Heidi?" she asked.

Heidi nodded solemnly. "Yes," she whispered.

"If it's all right with you, ma'am," the officer said, "we'll turn her over to your
custody, since this is her first offense."

"Yes," she said. "Thank you, Officers."

Mom and Heidi walked the few steps to the staircase, and Mom sat on the second
step. "What did you take?" she asked her daughter.

"Well," Heidi said, "I just saw this really cool jumper, and I knew we'd never have
enough money to buy it." She stopped. "I'm sorry."

"Didn't you know what you were doing was wrong?"

Heidi's gaze dropped. "Yes," she answered.

"If you knew it was wrong," Mom asked, "why did you do it?"

Heidi opened and closed her mouth several times. Finally, she shook her head and
said, "I just wanted it, Mom. I'm sorry. I feel so awful."

When Mom looked up, there were tears in her eyes. "Heidi," she said, "I know it's
hard to choose right sometimes—especially when doing wrong seems so attractive and
so easy. But the path of evildoers leads to disappointment and destruction, Heidi."

"I know, Mom," Heidi said. "I never want to feel this horrible again."

Mom nodded. "Good. Because the devil wants you to think that the evil desires
that lead to wrong choices are going to get you what you want; but don't you believe
it! The Bible says that evil desires lead to evil actions, and evil actions lead to death."

"I believe it," Heidi said. "I've learned my lesson."

"I hope so," Mom said. She draped an arm around Heidi's shoulders and hugged
her. "I surely hope so."

 TO DISCUSS: When you make a wrong choice, is it usually because you didn't know
it was wrong, or because you just didn't want to do what was right? Have wrong
choices ever gotten you what you wanted? (Be honest!) Are the things you get from
wrong choices satisfying? Why or why not? How can you better resist temptation?

 TO PRAY: "Lord, doing what's wrong seems to come so easily. Yet we feel so awful
when we sin. Forgive us, Lord, for the times when we do slip up. Help us to choose
the right path again."

30 Ryan's Repentance

WHEN WE MAKE WRONG CHOICES, WE SHOULD BE QUICK TO REPENT AND SEEK GOD'S FORGIVENESS.

Bible Reading of the Day: Read 1 John 1:8–2:3.
Verse of the Day: *"If we confess our sins, he is faithful and just and will forgive us our sins and purify us from all unrighteousness"* (1 John 1:9, NIV).

Ryan and Matt didn't know they were being watched.

The two brothers were playing in the side yard together. Their uncle watched them from the house, through the large window that overlooked the side yard.

Suddenly, Ryan's left hand gripped the plastic baseball bat at the same time that Matt's fingers closed around the other end.

"I want it," Ryan said.

"I had it first," Matt protested.

"No, you didn't," his brother disagreed.

Instead of carrying the argument any further, however, Ryan closed his right hand into a fist and swung, connecting with the side of Matt's face in a solid punch. Both boys immediately released the bat, which fell to the ground. Matt's eyes widened in pain, and his hands quickly covered the reddening skin on the side of his face.

Ryan swallowed and, even before his brother's first cry pierced the air, dashed toward the house. Running into the living room where his father sat talking to Uncle Dan, Ryan flung himself into his father's lap.

"I'm sorry, Daddy," Ryan sobbed. "I'm really, really sorry."

Ryan quickly spilled a surprisingly accurate account of his actions, and just as he was finishing, a tearful Matt staggered into the room, still clutching his face.

Neither boy knew that their dad already knew the details of what had happened from Uncle Dan's eyewitness account. But Dad took Matt and Ryan into his arms. He looked at the rising welt on the side of Matt's face.

"Ryan," he said, "have you told Matt that you're sorry?"

Ryan looked at his brother with big eyes. "I'm really, really sorry," he said.

Matt didn't speak but sniffed and nodded slightly, as if accepting his brother's apology.

Dad turned to Ryan. "You made a bad decision, Ryan," he said, "but you did the right thing coming to me and telling me the truth about what you did. I forgive you, and I think your brother forgives you." He hugged his sons. "Now, Ryan, I want you to go upstairs and help Matt clean up as much as you can, OK?" Ryan nodded and started to turn, but his father stopped him. "And Ryan," he said. "Don't do that again, OK?"

"OK, Daddy," Ryan said.

TO DISCUSS: What wrong choice did Ryan make? What was good about what he did afterward? How should we be like Ryan when we do something wrong?

TO PRAY: "Help us, Lord, to be quick to confess any sin and turn from it."

31 Anchored to God's Word

THE BIBLE HELPS US KNOW AND CHOOSE RIGHT.

Bible Reading of the Day: Read Psalm 119:57-64.
Verse of the Day: *"I have hidden your word in my heart, that I might not sin against you" (Psalm 119:11).*

Grandpa and Nolan scanned the harbor, which was filled with boats and ships of all sizes. The wind gusted through their hair, and the waves slapped and splashed at the posts of the dock on which they stood.

"What's that boat called, Grandpa?" Nolan asked.

"That's a cargo ship," Grandpa said. "And the one right behind it is an oil tanker."

"Look at that one go!" Nolan shouted. A speedboat, bumped and buffeted by the waves, sliced through the water. They watched the activity at the harbor in silence for a few more moments. Then Nolan noticed a single boat, sitting alone atop the water, well out from the docks. "What kind of boat is that, Grandpa?" he asked, pointing.

Grandpa peered out in the harbor. "That's a yacht. It's a big pleasure boat."

"What's it doing out there?"

"Well," Grandpa said, "She may just be waiting for the water to calm down."

Nolan stared at the yacht. "Won't the wind blow it around?" he asked.

Grandpa shook his head. "No," he said, "because her anchor holds her in place." He pointed to a huge anchor hanging from one of the carrier ships docked nearby. "See that anchor at the front of that ship?" he said to Nolan. "Well, that yacht out there has an anchor too. She's dropped anchor and is just going to sit there, moving up and down with the water but not going anywhere."

"Oh," Nolan said, without taking his eyes off the yacht. "That's pretty neat."

"Yes, it is," Grandpa said. He turned and watched Nolan's face for a few moments. "Come to think of it, Nolan," he said, "you have an anchor too."

"I do?" Nolan tuned his eyes on his grandfather.

"Yup," Grandpa said. He inhaled the salty sea air. "Sometimes, you're going to be like that boat out there. Storms are going to come into your life. Problems are going to toss you back and forth. Other people are going to tempt you to sin. At times, it's going to seem hard to know what's right and what's wrong." Grandpa fastened his eyes on Nolan. "But if you put your anchor down into God's Word—if you've read and learned what God says about right and wrong—that will help you wait out the storms, and help you know—and choose—what's right."

"That's why you read the Bible so much, isn't it, Grandpa?" Nolan asked.

Grandpa nodded.

"I want to read the Bible too," Nolan said. "Just like you."

 TO DISCUSS: How can we be "anchored" in God's Word? How does that help us know and choose right?

 TO PRAY: Pray today's Bible reading responsively, each person praying a verse or a sentence, putting the thoughts of the psalmist into your own words if you wish.

1 Don't Be a Lazybones

LAZINESS MAY BE EASIER, BUT WILLINGNESS TO WORK AND DILIGENCE IN WORK ARE BETTER.

Bible Reading of the Day: Read Proverbs 6:6–11.
Verse of the Day: *"Laziness brings on deep sleep, and the shiftless man goes hungry" (Proverbs 19:15, NIV).*

Will and Richard stared at the pile of firewood in the driveway. Their dad had assigned them both the job of carrying the wood to the back door and stacking it in two rows.

"There must be a million logs there," Richard muttered.

Will inhaled deeply and exhaled loudly. "Well," he said, slipping a pair of work gloves over his hands, "we'd better get to work."

"You go ahead and get started," Richard said. "I'll be right back."

Will began tossing the logs into the wheelbarrow he had taken from the shed. When the wheelbarrow was full, he wheeled it to the back door and started stacking the logs. When he returned to the woodpile for a second load, Richard was sitting on the logs, wearing the headphones to his portable CD player.

"Where have you been?" Will asked.

Richard shrugged. "I just got my CD player, that's all."

"Well, why are you just sitting there?"

"You had the wheelbarrow," Richard said. "I had to wait for you to get back."

Will rolled his eyes and started tossing more logs into the wheelbarrow. Richard slipped his work gloves on and leaned over to help, but his motion caused the CD to skip. By the time he had positioned the CD player, Will had filled the wheelbarrow.

Will threw his brother a disgusted look as he pushed his second load of logs to the back of the house. Richard helped his brother stack the logs, although he handled about half as many logs as Will did. For the next couple of hours, Will worked steadily while Richard stopped working frequently. Finally, the boys loaded the last logs into the wheelbarrow and added them to the stack Will had started earlier that day.

Suddenly Dad came around the corner of the house.

"You're all done?" Dad asked as he approached.

Will looked up at his father, weariness showing on his face. "Yes, sir," he answered.

Dad studied the two boys, comparing Will's sweaty clothes and dirty face with Richard's tidy appearance. "Thank you," he said. He met Will's eyes. "I appreciate all your hard work."

Dad went into the house, and Richard turned to Will. "That sounded like he was only talking to you."

Will grabbed the wheelbarrow's handles and turned it toward the shed to put it away. He smiled. "Maybe he was."

 TO DISCUSS: How would you have felt if you had been working with Richard? Why? Would you have acted differently? If so, how? What was wrong with Richard's behavior? What was good about Will's behavior?

 TO PRAY: "Lord, help us to be faithful in our work."

2 Lim's First Customer

GOD COMMANDS US TO WORK AND NOT BE LAZY.

> **Bible Reading of the Day:** Read 1 Thessalonians 4:11-12.
> **Verse of the Day:** *"A lazy person is as bad as someone who destroys things" (Proverbs 18:9).*

"Let's go ride the Destroyer!" Nat said.

Lim looked at his watch. "I can't," he said. "I have to go help my mom."

Lim was spending the weekend at the fairgrounds with his family, who were earning money by selling food at a booth close to the grandstand. His parents had given him certain hours every day when he had to work. He swept the floor, wiped counters, and helped fill the orders his mother and father took from customers. The rest of the time, he could ride the rides and walk around the fairgrounds with Nat, a new friend he had just met. Nat's parents were showing their horses at the fair.

"Why do your parents make you work every day?" Nat asked. "My parents don't make me work."

Lim wrinkled his nose. "I don't know," he said. "They just do." He promised to meet Nat when he finished working, then jogged to the tent that sheltered his family's booth. He strapped on an apron and was ready to work a few minutes early.

He worked with his mom for a long time, waiting on customers. Finally, when there was no one standing at the counter, Lim turned to his mom.

"Mom," he said, "why do you and Dad make me work? Nat doesn't have to help his parents."

Mom wiped her hands on her apron. "I don't know why Nat's parents don't ask him to work," she said, "but your dad and I want you to for several reasons."

"Like what?" Lim's tone was curious, not defiant.

"Well," Mom answered, "one reason is that we need your help. You are part of our family, and we could not stay in business without your help."

Lim nodded. He knew that his parents worked very hard, and he sometimes wished they had more people to help them.

"Also," Mom continued, "your father and I want to teach you to work. We don't want you to grow up lazy. That would not please us, and it would not please God."

Lim thought about his mother's words. He didn't want to grow up lazy; he wanted to know how to work hard, just like his parents.

Just then, a customer approached the counter. Lim turned to his mother. "Can I wait on this customer myself?" he asked.

His mother nodded. Lim wiped his hands on his apron and stepped up to the counter.

TO DISCUSS: Why is it important for a person to work, rather than be lazy? Name some work that you've done this week. Why do you think it pleases your parents when you work hard? Why do you think it pleases God when you work hard?

TO PRAY: "Lord, guard us against a desire to be lazy."

3 Carrier of the Year

GOD COMMANDS US TO WORK BECAUSE HE VALUES WORK.

Bible Reading of the Day: Read 2 Thessalonians 3:6-12.
Verse of the Day: *"Whatever you do, work at it with all your heart, as working for the Lord, not for men" (Colossians 3:23, NIV).*

Mandy raced to meet her brother at the door. Chris was a lot older than she was; he was in high school and was old enough to drive a car.

"Look, Chris!" she said, waving a page of the neighborhood newspaper in his face. "Look what I got!"

Chris closed the door behind him and took the paper from Mandy's shaking hand. He glanced at the headline, then looked back at his sister.

"Right here," she said, realizing that her brother had not seen her picture at the bottom of the front page. She poked her finger at the paper.

He finally located her photograph under the headline "Carrier of the Year."

"Wow," he said. "That's terrific, Sis." He read the short paragraph beneath her picture, describing why Mandy had been selected as their Carrier of the Year.

"It says here you're one of the hardest-working kids ever to deliver *The Sentinel*," Chris said, smiling. "'A valuable part of *The Sentinel* team,' it says. That's terrific, Sis," he repeated.

"I get a twenty-dollar gift certificate to Mama Mia's," she said, referring to a popular restaurant in their town.

Dad walked up and draped an arm on Mandy's shoulders. "I think she deserves it," Dad said. "She's worked hard."

"I sure have," Mandy said, beaming with happiness. "Sometimes my hands get really sore from folding and wrapping all those papers. And my legs used to get sore from riding my bike to deliver them!"

"But I'm really glad you do it," Dad said. "And I think God is too."

"He is?" Mandy said. "Why?"

"Well," Dad said, "because God values hard work as much as we do . . . more, I guess. That's why he commands us to 'work with our hands' and not to be lazy." Dad smiled. "So, Mandy," he said, "are you taking anybody with you to Mama Mia's?"

"I want to take you and Mom *and* Chris," she said.

"I think that would cost more than twenty dollars," Dad warned.

"That's OK," Mandy said. "I've got some money saved up to pay for the rest."

"I'll tell you what," Dad said. "Why don't I pay for the rest? We'll call it our 'hard worker of the year' award."

"All right!" Mandy said.

 TO DISCUSS: If your family had a "hard worker of the year" award, who do you think would receive the honor? Why? Why does God command us to work?

TO PRAY: "Lord, teach us to value work as you do. "

4 Always Working

GOD VALUES WORK BECAUSE HE IS ALWAYS WORKING.

Bible Reading of the Day: Read John 5:1-17.
Verse of the Day: *"This should be your ambition: to live a quiet life, minding your own business and working with your hands, just as we commanded you before"* (1 Thessalonians 4:11).

"Tamika!" Mom said as she looked into her daughter's room. "It's bedtime."

"But, Mom," Tamika objected, "I'm not done cleaning my room."

Mom frowned at Tamika. "I asked you to clean your room a long time ago, Tamika."

"I know," Tamika said. "I started to, but then I found this!" She held up a talking stuffed toy she thought had been lost. "He was under my bed."

Mom smiled and shook her head. "Well, I'm glad you found your toy, Tamika. But it's bedtime now. I'll be back in a few minutes to pray with you."

Mom left and returned after Tamika had changed into her pajamas and brushed her teeth. Tamika knelt beside her bed, and Mom knelt next to her daughter.

"Are you ready to pray?" Mom asked.

Tamika's eyebrows wrinkled together. "Mommy," she said thoughtfully, "does God stay up past my bedtime?"

Mom smiled. "Yes, God stays up past your bedtime. The Bible says he never sleeps or takes naps. He's always ready to listen to your prayers."

"He's open twenty-four hours a day!" Tamika said. "Like that store on the corner."

Mom chuckled. "I guess so," she said.

"Doesn't he get tired?"

"No," Mom said. "Because he's God. He's always awake, always listening for your prayers, always working, always waiting to help you." Mom looked around at Tamika's room, which was still messy. "And he never stops working," she said, her eyes twinkling, "just because he found an old toy!"

Tamika's mouth dropped open as she realized her mom was talking about her. Then she smiled again. "I'll clean my room real good tomorrow, OK, Mommy?"

"OK," Mom said. She kissed Tamika on the cheek. Then they both folded their hands and bowed their heads while Tamika started praying.

 TO DISCUSS: Does God ever stop working? Is he ever "off duty"? Why does God command us to work? Why does God value work? Unlike God, we sometimes get tired. God wants us to take breaks to rest from work, but he also wants us to take breaks from our rest in order to work! Do you think hard work is right? Why or why not?

TO PRAY: "Heavenly Father, we need your balanced attitude about work and rest. Help us to achieve the right balance."

5 Better than Boredom

WORK IS BETTER, BY FAR, THAN IDLENESS.

Bible Reading of the Day: Read Proverbs 24:30-34.
Verse of the Day: *"Lazy hands make a man poor, but diligent hands bring wealth" (Proverbs 10:4, NIV).*

Lori spotted Chelsea in the hallway on the first day of school.

"Chelsea!" she called. She hadn't seen her friend since the beginning of summer vacation. She caught up with Chelsea and they walked together to the cafeteria, trying to catch up with each other.

"What was your summer like?" Lori asked.

"Ugh!" Chelsea answered, making a face as if she had just taken a bite out of a lemon. "It was horrible!"

"Why?" Lori asked.

"It was boring," Chelsea answered, "totally boring. What was your summer like?"

"Great!" Lori answered, in her usual breezy way.

"Well, what was so great about it?" They arrived at the cafeteria and found an empty table.

Lori shrugged as she pulled a sandwich out of her lunch bag. "I don't know," she said. "I had sort of a job working for my uncle at his animal hospital, sweeping floors and emptying wastebaskets, stuff like that."

"Yuk!" Chelsea said. "That doesn't sound like fun."

"Well, at least it wasn't boring!" Lori said.

Chelsea opened her milk carton and took a sip. She wiped her mouth with her sleeve. "You *liked* sweeping floors and emptying trash?"

"Not exactly," she said. "But my uncle paid me."

"How much did he pay you?"

"Well," Lori said shyly, "it wasn't a lot, but I saved some of it. Plus, it was a lot better than just sitting at home watching game shows!"

Chelsea rolled her eyes. "I can believe that," she said. "I got so bored, I couldn't stand it! There wasn't anything to do!"

Lori smiled. "I'm going to work there again next summer. Do you want me to ask my uncle if you can help too?"

Chelsea's eyes brightened. "Would you? That would be so great!" she said.

TO DISCUSS: A popular poem in an old American schoolbook once ended, "Oh! We may get weary, and think work is dreary; 'tis harder by far, to have nothing to do." Do you think that's true? If so, why? Who do you think had a better summer vacation, Lori or Chelsea? Why?

TO PRAY: "Sometimes we're tempted to be lazy. Help us, Holy Spirit, to value hard work."

6 Splitting Wood

HARD WORK CAN BE ITS OWN REWARD.

Bible Reading of the Day: Read Proverbs 14:20-23.
Verse of the Day: *"All hard work brings a profit, but mere talk leads only to poverty" (Proverbs 14:23, NIV).*

Luke watched as his dad split wood. He swung a large, two-sided ax in a circular motion, in a rhythm that nearly hypnotized his son.

"Whoosh! Whack! Crack!" went the sound of his dad's work, and Luke and Dad exchanged smiles from time to time. Both seemed happy; Luke enjoyed watching, and Dad enjoyed working. He used a big, flat-topped segment of log as a base. On this he set the pieces to be split. With a rocking windup, he slung the ax over his head and into the wood with splitting force. Many of the logs split completely with one blow. In others, however, the ax lodged deep into the grain; without removing the ax, Dad lifted it aloft again and slammed the wood once more onto the log base, splitting it neatly into two pieces.

With the largest sections of wood, he created a crack into which he placed a metal wedge, called a mall. Dropping his ax, he would then use a sledgehammer and, in the same fluid motion, would drive the wedge deep into the wood.

"Daddy," Luke said, when at last his dad took a break in his work. "Do you like chopping wood?"

Dad wiped the sweat off his forehead with his sleeve. He inhaled deeply, leaned his sledgehammer against the stump, and sat down on the log beside his son. "Yes, I do," he said. "I like chopping wood."

"Is it hard?" Luke asked.

Dad nodded. "Yes, it's hard work, all right."

"Then why do you like it?"

"I suppose I like it," Dad answered, "partly *because* it's hard work. You may be too young to understand this now, Luke, but hard work can be very satisfying. It feels good to work. It's even fun sometimes."

"It is?" Luke asked, amazement in his voice.

"Oh, yeah," Dad said. "When I get into a rhythm swinging that ax or sledgehammer, the motion and effort of the work can be as much fun as rowing a boat."

"Daddy?" Luke said, twisting his face into a hopeful expression. "Can I chop wood with you . . . when I get bigger?"

Dad nodded. "When you get bigger, Son," he said, "I hope you'll still want to."

 TO DISCUSS: Have you ever enjoyed working for the work itself? If so, tell about it. What was fun or satisfying about it? Of all the kinds of jobs you do (cleaning your room, taking out trash, and so on), which do you enjoy most? How can you make the others more fun? Do you take more satisfaction out of a job done well or one done poorly? Why?

TO PRAY: "Heavenly Father, please grant us the satisfaction of knowing that our tasks are done well."

7 The Broken Lamp

WHEN YOU DO SOMETHING WRONG OR UNWISE, DON'T MAKE EXCUSES. INSTEAD, ADMIT YOUR WRONG AND ASK FORGIVENESS.

Bible Reading of the Day: Read Psalm 32:1-6.

Verse of the Day: *"Then I acknowledged my sin to you and did not cover up my iniquity. I said, 'I will confess my transgressions to the Lord'—and you forgave the guilt of my sin"* (Psalm 32:5, NIV).

Jenny and her friend Christy were playing a rowdy game with Jenny's cat in the living room. Jenny knew they should calm down and find something else to do, but they were having too much fun.

Suddenly, Christy rolled the cat's ball between Jenny's legs. Jenny jumped to her feet and, in the act of rising, upturned one of the end tables beside the couch. In seconds, the end table lay on its side, and the glass lamp that had been on the table lay in pieces on the floor.

Jenny's dad, who had heard the crash, came into the room while Jenny and Christy were still staring at each other in shock—and horror.

"What happened?" Dad said as he entered the room. He saw the glass lamp on the floor. "Are you all right?" He looked from Jenny to Christy. They both nodded.

"It wasn't my fault, Dad!" Jenny yelled. "Honest!"

Dad knelt beside the table. "Don't step in this glass," he ordered.

"It was an accident, Dad," Jenny said defensively. "It wasn't my fault."

Dad nodded as he picked up the bigger pieces of broken glass. Finally, he lifted his gaze and looked at Jenny. His expression was soft. "I know it was an accident," he said, "but that's not what I want to hear from you, Jenny."

"You want me to tell you I did it on purpose?" Jenny asked, looking confused.

"No, that's not what I mean," he answered. "I haven't yet heard the most important words to say when something like this happens."

"I said I didn't mean to do it," Jenny answered defensively.

"But that's not the same as saying, 'I'm sorry,'" Dad said. He saw Jenny's expression change from confusion to embarrassment. "When you do something wrong or even when you cause an accident, the most important thing to say is not 'It wasn't my fault' or 'I didn't mean it.' The most important thing to do is to admit what you did and take responsibility—and ask forgiveness."

"I'm . . . I'm sorry, Dad," Jenny said. She looked at the broken lamp, one of her mom's favorites. "I really am."

"That's more like it," Dad said. Then he smiled. "Why don't we clean it up together?"

 TO DISCUSS: Do you have trouble admitting it when you do something wrong? Do you try to make excuses, or do you usually take responsibility? What's the most important thing to do or say when you do something wrong, even if it was an accident? Why do you think that's important?

 TO PRAY: "Lord, when we sin, even unconsciously, help us to take responsibility and admit that we were wrong. "

8 Know Right, Do Right

TRUTH IS OF NO USE UNLESS IT IS OBEYED.

Bible Reading of the Day: Read Romans 2:5-10.
Verse of the Day: *"If we claim to have fellowship with him yet walk in the darkness, we lie and do not live by the truth"* (1 John 1:6, NIV).

Mom and Dad heard the garage door opening and raced to the door together. When they opened the door between the kitchen and the garage, their daughter Robin was putting her bike away where it belonged.

"Where have you been?" Mom asked. "We've been worried sick about you!"

"The streetlights came on a long time ago," Dad said.

Robin knew that she was supposed to be home before the streetlights came on. She smiled sheepishly. "I got lost on the way home from Jayda's house," she explained.

Her mom and dad exchanged confused glances as they turned and walked back into the house. Robin followed.

"You know your way home from Jayda's house," Mom said.

"I know it," Robin said, "but I was already late, and I thought I could save time by going a different way." She slumped into a chair beside the kitchen table. "But it didn't work. Am I in trouble?"

"Well, Robin," Dad said, "you know the rules. It doesn't do much good to know the right way if you don't follow it, does it?" he said.

Robin searched his face. He seemed to be talking about more than just coming home late.

"Mom and I are glad you're safe," he said. "But we want you to remember that doing the right thing involves more than just knowing the right way. You have to choose to *follow* the right way too."

"Mom, Dad," Robin said, "what are you talking about?"

Mom sighed and peered into her daughter's eyes. "We found this in your bedroom today," she explained. She laid an empty package on the table.

Robin looked at the package. It looked similar to a pouch of tobacco. Robin's face registered shock, then she started laughing. "I'm sorry, Mom and Dad. I just can't believe you would think that's real. It's an empty bubble gum pouch."

Mom looked relieved. "I'm so glad," she said.

"I know better than that," Robin said. "Besides, I think tobacco's gross."

Dad smiled and sighed. "I'm glad to hear that," he said. "But do me a favor. Don't buy that kind of bubble gum anymore, OK?" he said.

 TO DISCUSS: Did *knowing* the right way home do Robin any good? Why not? Does knowing what's right guarantee that we'll make right choices? What else should we do?

TO PRAY: "Lord, help us to know the right thing and do the right thing."

9 Whose Rules Rule?

DOING THINGS OUR OWN WAY—INSTEAD OF GOD'S WAY—CAN GET US INTO
A LOT OF TROUBLE.

Bible Reading of the Day: Read Genesis 4:1-7.
Verse of the Day: *"If you do what is right, will you not be accepted?
But if you do not do what is right, sin is crouching at your door;
it desires to have you, but you must master it" (Genesis 4:7, NIV).*

Paul heard a loud noise in the backyard. He ran toward the noise and saw his little brother, Greg, kneeling beside the lawn mower.

"What happened?" Paul said, as he stood beside Greg.

Greg wore a frown. "I ran over a big branch." He lifted one end of the stick. The other end was lodged in the blade of the lawn mower.

Paul pushed the lawn mower on its side and looked underneath. A tangled mess of wood and metal could be seen. He whistled. "How did you miss seeing this?"

Greg shrugged. "I don't know," he said.

Paul cocked his head to one side. "You *did* look for rocks and sticks before you started mowing, didn't you?"

Greg looked as though he didn't want to answer. "I like doing things my own way."

Paul knew that his brother hadn't walked through the yard picking up rocks and sticks the way their father had taught them. "Well, your 'own way' has sure messed up the lawn mower. I don't know if I can fix this."

The brothers carried the lawn mower into their dad's workshop and started trying to fix it. They were still working when Dad got home. Dad was upset about the lawn mower, but he didn't get mad when Paul and Greg explained what had happened, and why. Instead, he put his arm around his younger son.

"Greg," he said, "I understand that you like doing things your own way. All of us do. It's natural. It goes way back to the days of Cain and Abel, when Cain tried to worship God his own way, while Abel did things God's way. I do pretty much the same thing. Most of the time, when I make a wrong choice, it's not because I didn't know which way was right; it's usually because I wanted to do things my own way—instead of doing things God's way."

Greg studied the mangled blade of the lawn mower. "Doing things our own way sure can get us into a lot of trouble," he said.

Dad smiled ruefully. "Yeah," he said. "I've found that out a time or two myself."

TO DO: Break a twig into small pieces. Have everyone in the family carry a piece of the twig in his or her pocket or purse today to remember that doing things our own way—instead of God's way—can get us into a lot of trouble.

TO PRAY: *"Abba* Father, help us to live our lives your way, rather than by our own rules."

10 Laurel's Chore

FAITHFULNESS IS GOOD; UNFAITHFULNESS IS BAD.

Bible Reading of the Day: Read Luke 16:10-12.
Verse of the Day: *"Now it is required that those who have been given a trust must prove faithful"* *(1 Corinthians 4:2, NIV).*

"Do I have to?" Laurel whined.

Mom looked surprised. "Laurel, you know we all have chores in this house. That's part of being a family."

Laurel's head sagged. "I'm just tired of taking out the trash," she said. "Why can't somebody else take out the trash?"

Mom wore a serious but gentle expression. "We all have chores to do, Laurel. I do laundry and do most of the cooking. Your dad washes dishes and does the yard work. Your brother sweeps the floors and feeds the dog."

"I know," Laurel said, her voice a whine. Then her face brightened. "What if I paid Tommy some of my allowance to take the trash out for me?"

Mom chuckled. "No, I don't think so," she said.

"Why not? As long as it gets done, what difference does it make who does it?"

"It makes a big difference," Mom answered.

"Why?" Laurel said, a trace of defiance entering her voice.

"Dad and I don't just give you chores because there's work to be done," Mom said.

"Well, then, why *do* you make me do chores?" Laurel asked.

Mom hesitated only a moment before answering. "One reason," she said, "is to help you learn to be faithful."

Laurel said nothing, but looked at her mom with an expression of uncertainty.

Mom continued. "We want to be able to depend on you, Laurel," she said. "We want to know that, when you get older, you'll be faithful to God, and to your family, and to others. But becoming a faithful person, a dependable person, doesn't happen overnight."

"So, you're saying I'm supposed to learn something from taking out garbage?" Laurel asked.

Mom smiled broadly and said. "We want you to learn how to be faithful, how to fulfill a responsibility, how to be the kind of person who can always be counted on."

"I haven't been doing that with my chores, have I?" Laurel asked.

Mom shook her head. "Not yet," she answered, smiling softly.

Laurel took a deep breath. "All right," she said. "From now on, you can count on me. I'll be the best trash-taker-outer there's ever been." She saluted like a soldier.

Mom returned her salute. "Outstanding!" she said.

TO DISCUSS: What are your chores? Do you do them faithfully or do you need to work harder at being faithful and dependable? How can doing your chores like you're supposed to help you develop faithfulness?

TO PRAY: "Help us, Lord, to be faithful over all that we have to do this week."

11 More Important Matters

GOD COMMANDS US TO BE FAITHFUL.

Bible Reading of the Day: Read Matthew 23:23, 37.

Verse of the Day: *"Now it is required that those who have been given a trust must prove faithful" (1 Corinthians 4:2, NIV).*

Jesse sat on the couch and pointed the remote control at the television, flipping from channel to channel. His older brother John came into the room.

"Hey, Jesse," John said, "are you ready for me to take you to Zach's house?"

"Naw," Jesse answered. He continued his channel surfing.

"Well, come on," John said. "We're going to be late."

Jesse didn't take his eyes off the television screen. "I'm not going," he said.

John just stared at his baby brother in silence for a few moments. Finally, John said, "I thought you told Zach you were going to the fair with him and his parents."

"I did," Jesse said, "but I don't feel like it now."

"So you're going to let your friend down, just like that?"

"It's no big deal," Jesse said. "Besides, I don't like the fair. It's dumb."

"That's not the point, Jesse. You told Zach you'd go with him."

"I'll call him and tell him I . . . I'm sick or something."

"Lying to your friend isn't the answer."

"Well, then, what *is* the answer, Mr. I'm-in-College-Now-and-I-Know-Everything?"

John sat on the couch beside his brother. When he answered his brother's question, his voice was soft and patient. "Jesse, you told your friend that you would go with him. It may not seem like a big deal to you, but I bet it is to Zach. He's counting on you to do what you said, and if you let him down, I think you'll be making a poor choice."

Jesse rolled his eyes. "Why don't you leave me alone? This is just between me and Zach."

John hesitated a moment, then answered, "It *is* between you and Zach, but it's also between you and God."

"How?" Jesse said.

It was John's turn to shrug. "God commands us to be faithful. In fact, once when Jesus was talking to the Pharisees, he called God's command to be faithful one of the most important parts of the law, along with justice and mercy." He paused. Jesse was no longer watching the television screen.

Jesse glanced at the clock on the wall. "I guess I still have time to make it to Zach's house," he said. He met his brother's eyes for the first time in their conversation. "Will you still take me?"

"I've got my jacket on," John answered. "I might as well!"

 TO DISCUSS: What does it mean to be faithful to your friends? Who are your most faithful friends? How do your friends know they can count on you?

 TO PRAY: "Lord, we want to be faithful in our relationships and in our tasks. Make us faithful people, Lord."

12 A Faithful Priest

GOD COMMANDS FAITHFULNESS BECAUSE HE VALUES FAITHFULNESS.

Bible Reading of the Day: Read 1 Samuel 2:27-30, 35.
Verse of the Day: *"Now it is required that those who have been given a trust must prove faithful"* (1 Corinthians 4:2, NIV).

Mom and Dad sat in the school auditorium and waited anxiously for Seth to stand up. Seth was scheduled to be one of three students to speak in the special program sponsored by a local program against drugs.

They watched Seth fidget on his chair on the platform while the first speaker, a fourth-grade student, stood and read the short speech she had prepared. She spoke on how she didn't want to take drugs because she wanted to be a gymnast when she grew up, and she didn't want to hurt her body with drugs.

Then a fifth grader, stood. He said he didn't want to take drugs, either, because "drugs are bad for you, and they make you do all kinds of dumb things."

Finally, after waiting and fidgeting for what seemed like hours, Seth walked to the edge of the tiny grade-school stage and unfolded the single sheet of paper he had held in his hands since the program had started.

"I don't want to take drugs because my parents have taught me the difference between right and wrong, and I know drugs are wrong. If I took drugs, I would disappoint my mom and dad, who would find it hard to trust me ever again. Taking drugs would also be wrong because God says I should take care of my body, because my body is his temple since he lives in my heart. I want to be faithful to God, so I don't ever want to take drugs."

When the program was over, Mom and Dad strode side by side to the platform and hugged their son.

"I'm so proud of you," Mom said.

"I am too," Dad added. "You did a great job, Son. You know what I liked best about what you said?"

Seth smiled. "You liked it that I didn't want to disappoint you, right?"

Dad smiled. "I liked that," he admitted, "but I also liked the fact that you said you would refuse drugs because you want to be faithful to God. And I'm sure God liked your speech too—because he values faithfulness."

"Thanks, Dad," Seth said. "Thanks, Mom."

Mom and Dad smiled. "Thanks for being such a faithful son," Mom said, as they walked together toward the refreshment table.

TO DISCUSS: Today's Bible reading reveals that God values faithfulness, because he wanted Eli to be a faithful priest. Was Eli a faithful priest? Do you think Eli's sons were faithful priests? What did God decide to do, since Eli and his sons were unfaithful? Can you think of someone who was a faithful priest? (Hint: Read Hebrews 2:17–3:1.) Has anyone ever described you as faithful?

TO PRAY: "Lord, help us to value faithfulness, because we know you value faithfulness."

13 Faithful Forever

GOD VALUES FAITHFULNESS BECAUSE HE IS FAITHFUL.

Bible Reading of the Day: Read Psalm 146:1-6.

Verse of the Day: *"The Lord himself goes before you and will be with you; he will never leave you nor forsake you. Do not be afraid; do not be discouraged" (Deuteronomy 31:8, NIV).*

"I don't understand her," Margaret said as she hung up the phone.

"Who?" Mom asked. She stood at the kitchen counter cutting up vegetables.

"Oh," Margaret said, "Stacy, a girl from school who used to be my friend."

"I remember Stacy," Mom said. "She's the girl who has the trampoline in her backyard. What do you mean she 'used to be' your friend?"

"I've tried to be her friend," Margaret answered, "but it's like Stacy changes friends more than I change my socks! She used to be 'best friends' with Heather Albright but now they don't get along at all. Then she started hanging around with Janet, but she can't stand Janet anymore. Now she says she can't be *my* friend."

"Why not?"

Margaret rolled her eyes. "Because I'm friends with Janet!"

"I see," Mom said.

Margaret looked at her mom. "Well, I sure don't! I don't understand. How can a person be your friend one day and then *not* your friend the next day?"

"I'm glad you don't understand," Mom said.

"You are?" Margaret's face was a mask of confusion. "Why?"

Mom set her knife down and leaned on the counter with both hands. "The reason you don't understand Stacy's behavior is because you are a faithful friend, Margaret. Because you're faithful, you value faithfulness in others. That's why you don't understand the behavior of people who aren't faithful like you are."

Margaret nodded thoughtfully, and Mom continued.

"And when you're faithful, Margaret, you're like God. He is the most faithful friend you'll ever find. Even if all your earthly friends desert you, God will still love you and be your friend, no matter what."

"That's the kind of friend I want to be," Margaret said.

Mother and daughter fell silent for a few moments until Margaret asked, "So why is Stacy the way she is?"

"I don't know," Mom said. "But I do know one thing."

"What's that?"

"I'm sure glad *you* are the way you are!"

 TO DISCUSS: Do you have any friends like Margaret? Who is the most faithful friend you have? Do you have any friends more faithful than God? Do you think God will ever stop being your friend? Why does God command faithfulness? Why does God value faithfulness? Why is it right for you to be faithful?

 TO PRAY: "Lord, thank you for your faithfulness. Teach us how to be faithful friends like you."

14 A Faithful Man

FAITHFULNESS BRINGS BLESSINGS FROM GOD AND OTHERS.

Bible Reading of the Day: Read Proverbs 28:14-20.
Verse of the Day: *"A faithful man will be richly blessed, but one eager to get rich will not go unpunished" (Proverbs 28:20, NIV).*

Norman was thrilled—his grandfather was taking him out to breakfast that morning! Norman knew that his grandfather went to a restaurant for breakfast every week, but Norman had never gotten to go along. He was out of bed and dressed and waiting at the window almost a half hour before his grandpa arrived to pick him up.

When they got to the restaurant, Norman was amazed as Grandpa led him to a corner table where several people already sat. They were all as old as Grandpa! Grandpa introduced Norman to everyone, and Grandpa's friends laughed and talked to Norman and to each other like old friends often do.

As they were leaving the restaurant and walking to the car, Norman asked, "Grandpa, do you eat breakfast with those same people every week?"

Grandpa nodded. "We've been eating together for more than thirty years now."

"Wow!" Norman said. "Are they all as old as you?"

Grandpa chuckled as he and Norman climbed into the cab of his old truck. "Yup," he said. His eyes crinkled at the edges as he added, "Some are even older!"

"Did you meet them at the restaurant?" Norman asked.

"No," Grandpa said. "I've known those characters for years. Charley was in my wedding," he said. Norman remembered Charley was the large man in overalls. "Dan and I went to school together. Ed and I worked together at the mill, oh, some thirty years ago."

"They've been your friends that long?" Norman asked.

"Longer, some of 'em," Grandpa said. He paused and stared out the windshield of the truck. He didn't start the engine. He didn't look at Norman as he spoke. "Be faithful to your friends, Grandson," he said. A faraway look entered his eyes. "Charley gave me my first Bible. My parents weren't Christians, and we hardly ever went to church. Charley stopped by every Sunday, and we've been going to church together for over sixty years now.

"Ed saved my life once at the mill. And Dan—well, Dan's about the funniest man I know. His sense of humor has brought me through some awful tough times." Grandpa sighed and reached for the key. He put it in the ignition and started the truck.

"I like your friends, Grandpa," Norman said.

"I do, too, Grandson," Grandpa said.

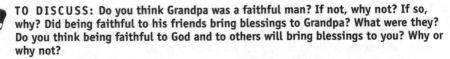

TO DISCUSS: Do you think Grandpa was a faithful man? If not, why not? If so, why? Did being faithful to his friends bring blessings to Grandpa? What were they? Do you think being faithful to God and to others will bring blessings to you? Why or why not?

TO PRAY: "We want the blessings that faithfulness brings. With your help, Lord, we'll be people who are known by our faithfulness."

15 Earning Trust

FAITHFULNESS INVITES TRUST.

Bible Reading of the Day: Read Nehemiah 13:11-14.
Verse of the Day: *"Now it is required that those who have been given a trust must prove faithful"* (1 Corinthians 4:2, NIV).

"Kendra," Mom said, as she stumbled in the front door with her arms full of grocery bags, "what are you doing home? I thought you were supposed to baby-sit the Johnson kids this afternoon."

Kendra's mouth dropped open, and her eyes widened. She turned her head to glance at the clock on the wall. "I was!" she said. "But I got on the phone with Felicia, and I . . . I guess I kind of forgot."

"Oh, Kendra!" Mom said, setting the bags down on the kitchen counter. "Mrs. Johnson's probably wondering what happened to you. Hasn't she called?"

Kendra smiled sheepishly. "I don't know," she said. "I've been on the phone."

"Well," Mom said, sighing and glancing at the clock, "you'd better call her."

Kendra picked up the phone and dialed Mrs. Johnson's number. Moments later she hung up and turned to her mom. "She said she already missed her doctor's appointment, so she doesn't need me anymore."

Mom balanced a package of frozen vegetables in her hand. She sighed again. "Did you apologize?"

"Yeah," Kendra said, nodding. "She said she forgives me. But I still feel terrible."

Mom wrapped her arms around Kendra. "I know," she said.

"Do you think Mrs. Johnson will call me the next time she needs a baby-sitter?" Kendra asked. She and Mom both wore worried expressions. Kendra recalled that her parents had only recently allowed her to baby-sit. The Johnson children were a perfect way to start because they were well behaved and lived only a few houses away.

"I don't know," Mom said honestly. "You may have to earn her trust again."

"Maybe I should call her back," Kendra said.

"What would you say?" Mom asked.

"I would . . . I would tell her I really, really want to earn her trust again, and if she'd give me another chance, I'd work really hard to be more, you know, faithful."

"I think that's a good idea, Kendra. Mrs. Johnson would probably appreciate that."

"And maybe I should offer to baby-sit for free the next time," Kendra added.

Mom smiled. "That's an even better idea," she said. "I'm sure Mrs. Johnson would appreciate *that!*"

TO DISCUSS: According to today's Bible reading, why did Nehemiah choose Shelemiah, Zadok, Pedaiah, and Hanan to take charge of the temple storerooms? Why do you think people tend to trust people who have been faithful in the past? Have you earned the trust of others because of your faithfulness? Why or why not?

TO PRAY: "All of us want to be trusted, Lord. Please grant us the opportunities to prove our trustworthiness. If we fail at our responsibilities, give us the humility to earn back the trust that we lost."

16 Like Daniel

THE LORD PRESERVES THE FAITHFUL.

Bible Reading of the Day: Read Psalm 31:21-24.

Verse of the Day: *"The Lord preserves the faithful, but the proud he pays back in full" (Psalm 31:23, NIV).*

"How do you remember to pray every day?" Kara asked her friend Bonnly.

Bonnly blinked at Kara as though he had not understood the question. Bonnly and his family had left Cambodia, his native country, only a few years earlier, but he already spoke English very well. "How do I remember to pray every day?" he repeated.

"Yeah," Kara said. "Like, most days I forget. You know, I either have homework, or there's a really good TV show on, or one of my friends comes over, and I forget to pray. I don't mean to, though. But you told me you pray every day."

Bonnly still wore a confused look. "Yes. I do not forget to pray," he explained, "because praying is very important to my family."

"Well," Kara said, looking a little embarrassed, "praying is important to me, too."

"I will explain like this," Bonnly said. "When I was tiny child, my family had to leave our house in Cambodia because the soldiers did not like my parents. They did not like us to pray and told us that if we didn't stop, they would take our house away."

Kara listened, her eyes wide with fascination. She knew her friend had come from far away, but she didn't know that his family had been driven from their home.

"But my father said we would never stop praying. He tried to tell the soldiers to become Christians, but they would not listen."

"Wow," Kara said. "Just like Daniel! Did they throw you in a den of lions?"

Bonnly smiled shyly. "No," he said. "But we had to leave our house to escape the soldiers."

"Were they going to kill you?" Kara said, her face suddenly serious.

Bonnly shrugged. "I don't know. I don't remember. But I remember the refugee camp where we lived before we came to this country."

"So," Kara said, her voice filled with awe, "you lost your house and everything because you wouldn't stop praying?"

"No," Bonnly said, smiling. "Father says we escaped to this country because we wouldn't stop praying. He says God answered our prayers much—" he stopped as if he couldn't think of the next word— "much greater than we thought."

Bonnly smiled again. "We pray every day still," he said.

Kara returned her friend's smile. She didn't say it, but she couldn't help thinking, *I want to be more faithful in prayer too—like Bonnly and his family.*

TO DISCUSS: How did God reward Bonnly and his family's faithfulness? Are you faithful in prayer? Do you sometimes forget to pray? Do you, like Kara, want to be more faithful about praying to God every day? If so, how can you do that?

TO PRAY: "Lord, thank you for preserving the faithful."

17 Fan the Flames

DAILY PRAYER AND BIBLE READING ARE FUEL FOR THE FLAMES OF OBEDIENCE TO GOD.

Bible Reading of the Day: Read 2 Timothy 1:3-6.
Verse of the Day: *"Keep alert and pray. Otherwise temptation will overpower you" (Mark 14:38).*

Dylan and his dad were camping in the woods. They had started early that morning and had walked about five miles into the woods before taking off their backpacks and making camp. They set up their tent together, then Dad started a fire.

"A fire is very important on the trail," Dad told Dylan. "It turns a cold, dark campsite into a temporary home."

"Plus, it cooks our dinner!" Dylan said.

"That's right," Dad agreed. Before long, Dad and Dylan sat beside a crackling fire. Dad put a pot of water on the fire, and soon they were spooning hot noodles into their mouths, and Dad was sipping hot coffee.

"What happens if the fire goes out, Dad?" Dylan asked.

Dad shrugged. "We'd just have to start over," he answered. "But it's much easier to keep the fire going than it is to try to revive it."

Dylan nodded and swallowed a mouthful of noodles. "But as long as we pay attention to it, and keep putting sticks on it, we'll be all right, won't we, Dad?"

Dad smiled and nodded. Then his face got serious as he thought of something. "You know, Dylan," he said, "it's sort of the same way with us."

Dylan squinted at his dad. "What do you mean?"

"Well, you want to obey God and please him, right?"

"Uh-huh," Dylan answered.

"But you know you can't do that all by yourself, right?"

Dylan nodded. "I need God's help."

"That's right," Dad said. "You see, Dylan, your heart is like that fire. If you pay attention to it, and keep feeding it like you would a fire, it'll produce obedience to God just like that fire produces flames."

Dylan grabbed a dry stick from the ground beside the fire and placed it in the flames. "Only I don't put sticks in my heart!" he said.

Dad chuckled. "No."

"But I can pray every day, can't I, Dad?"

"Right," Dad said. "And reading your Bible will help you obey God, too."

Dylan nodded. He understood. He picked up another stick and added it to the fire. "I want to keep our fire going."

"So do I," Dad answered.

 TO DISCUSS: Can you please God and obey him all by yourself? Why or why not? Whose help do you need? Do you think praying and reading your Bible every day will help you make right choices? Why or why not?

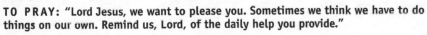 **TO PRAY:** "Lord Jesus, we want to please you. Sometimes we think we have to do things on our own. Remind us, Lord, of the daily help you provide."

18 The Meanest Kid

GOD DECIDES WHAT IS RIGHT OR WRONG.

Bible Reading of the Day: Read 1 Peter 3:8-12.
Verse of the Day: *"Be compassionate" (1 Peter 3:8, NIV).*

Tyeka couldn't believe her eyes. Kevin, the boy who lived next door, was sitting on his front steps, crying. She watched him for a few moments, trying to decide what to do.

Normally, Tyeka would have run to comfort someone who was crying. But Kevin was different. Kevin was probably the meanest person she knew. He was cruel to his own family's pets and constantly teased Tyeka's dog, Mittens. He even tore her dolls apart. For those reasons and more, Tyeka tried not to feel sorry for Kevin.

As she watched, his cries seemed to get louder, as if he knew she was watching. *Why should I feel sorry for him?* she asked herself. But even while she was thinking the words, she knew she would be wrong to try to pay him back by being mean, even though he was mean to her.

Finally, she threw up her hands and walked over to Kevin. "Are you OK?" she asked.

"Go away!" Kevin shouted.

Tyeka turned away, her feelings hurt. But after a moment she turned back and sat on the step next to Kevin.

"What's wrong?" she asked.

Kevin sniffed loudly and wiped his tears with his sleeve. "You wouldn't understand."

"Maybe I would," she said.

"I locked myself out of my house," he said. "And my parents won't be home all day."

"You're home alone?" Tyeka asked. When he nodded, she really did feel sorry for him. She wondered if this were the first time he'd spent the whole day by himself. "You don't have to stay here," she said. "My mom's home. You could . . . you could come over to my house until your parents get home."

Kevin looked at Tyeka with surprise. "I could?" he said, as if he didn't believe her. She nodded. He wiped his face on his sleeve. "Is—is that OK with your mom?"

Tyeka stood. "We could ask her."

Kevin smiled. "OK," he said.

Kevin followed Tyeka into the house. Tyeka saw a shocked look appear on her mom's face when they entered the room, but it quickly disappeared. After Tyeka explained what had happened, she saw a proud look on Mom's face. That look helped her realize that she had done the right thing by being nice—even to the meanest boy she knew.

 TO DISCUSS: Do you think Tyeka did the right thing? Why or why not? Do you think it was easy for her to show compassion to Kevin? Why or why not? Do you think Tyeka acted as though *she* decided what was right or as if *God* decided? Who says it's right to be compassionate?

 TO PRAY: "We need your compassion, Lord, to fill us and overflow toward those who need it most.

19 Good At Something

GOD COMMANDS US TO BE COMPASSIONATE.

Bible Reading of the Day: Read Ephesians 4:32–5:2.

Verse of the Day: *"Be kind and compassionate to one another, forgiving each other, just as in Christ God forgave you" (Ephesians 4:32, NIV).*

Grant sat beside his baby sister, Nina, in the middle seat of the minivan and played with her as she sat in her car seat. About halfway home from his older sister and brother's school concert, he started crying softly.

"What's wrong, Grant?" Dad said, when he noticed his son's tears in the rearview mirror.

Grant shook his head, not wanting to talk. But Mom turned around in her seat and urged him to tell her why he was crying.

"I'm not good at anything," he said between sniffles. "Ellen plays the piano, and Todd plays the saxophone," he said, pronouncing it "sassophone." "But I'm not good at anything."

"Oh, Grant," Mom said. "That's not true at all. Just because you haven't started music lessons yet doesn't mean you're not good at anything."

"Yes, it does," Grant said. His lower lip projected out from his face in a pout.

"No, it doesn't," Mom answered. "In fact, I think you're the best in the family at something."

Grant's sniffles quieted, and his lower lip returned to normal. "I am?" he asked.

Mom nodded. "You're the best in the family at being compassionate."

"What's that mean?" Grant asked, his face expressing doubt.

"Who can make little Nina stop crying better than anyone else?" Mom asked.

"I can," he answered softly.

"And who cuddles in Mommy's lap when a TV show or letter makes her cry?"

"I do!" Grant answered, his mood lightening.

"And," Ellen added from the seat behind Grant and the baby, "who is always feeling sorry for stray animals and birds with broken wings?"

"Me!" Grant answered.

"That's right," Mom said. She pointed her finger at Grant's chest. "You are a very compassionate young man. That's something you're very good at."

"And that's an important thing to be good at," Dad added, "because God wants us all to be compassionate."

"And I am!" Grant said. His tears and sniffles had disappeared, and he was smiling happily.

 TO DISCUSS: Today's Bible reading includes one of God's many commands to be compassionate. What does it mean to be compassionate? Have you done anything compassionate today? If so, what? Did you do anything compassionate yesterday? If so, what? Do you think you can do anything compassionate tomorrow? If so, how?

TO PRAY: "Lord, help us to be good at showing compassion to others."

20 Traffic Jam

GOD COMMANDS COMPASSION BECAUSE HE VALUES COMPASSION.

Bible Reading of the Day: Read Luke 10:30-37.
Verse of the Day: *"Show mercy and compassion to one another"* (Zechariah 7:9, NIV).

"This is a bad traffic jam, isn't it, Dad?" Dale said.

Dad sighed and tapped his thumb on the steering wheel. "Yes, it is, Dale," he answered. "And it's going to make us late getting home."

"Dad, look!" Dale pointed ahead, across two lanes of traffic. Dad looked where he was pointing. A woman stood behind her car, which apparently had broken down in the high-speed lane of the three-lane highway. She paced back and forth behind her car, her hand on her forehead, a worried look on her face.

"That's why we're not going anywhere!" Dale said, irritation surfacing in his voice. Other drivers honked or shouted at the woman as they passed by. Suddenly, Dad switched on his hazard lights and steered the car onto the shoulder.

"What are you doing?" Dale asked.

"Stay in the car," Dad said. "I'll be right back."

Dad jumped out of the car and dodged through the creeping traffic to the woman's car. Dale watched, fascinated, as his dad pointed to the woman's car, then to the side of the road where Dale sat. The woman got behind the steering wheel of her car, and Dad pushed her car, inching it across the two lanes of traffic until it was parked in front of their car. Dale noticed that the woman was crying, but smiling. Dale saw her mouth form the words "thank you" as Dad jogged back to their car and got in.

"I'll call the highway patrol at the next pay phone I can find," he told his son as he started the car and steered it back into the traffic, which was flowing a little faster now.

Dale helped his dad find a pay phone at the first exit off the highway. As soon as Dad made the call, Dale had a question ready.

"Dad, why did you stop to help that lady when we were already going to be late?"

Dad smiled at his son's question. He thought for a moment before answering. "You know what the story of the Good Samaritan teaches, don't you?"

Dale nodded. "That it's good to help people."

"Yes," Dad said, *"and* it shows us that God values compassion. We could have been like the priest in the story, or the other man, who passed by without helping. But it's much better to show compassion when you have the chance."

Dale thought about what his dad had done. "I'm glad we stopped," he said, smiling. "That was fun!"

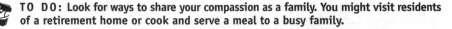 **TO DO:** Look for ways to share your compassion as a family. You might visit residents of a retirement home or cook and serve a meal to a busy family.

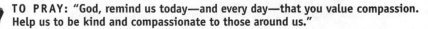 **TO PRAY:** "God, remind us today—and every day—that you value compassion. Help us to be kind and compassionate to those around us."

21 Betsy's Doll

GOD VALUES COMPASSION BECAUSE HE IS COMPASSIONATE.

Bible Reading of the Day: Read Psalm 103:8-13.
Verse of the Day: *"The Lord is compassionate and gracious, slow to anger, abounding in love" (Psalm 103:8, NIV).*

"Marilyn, will you hold my doll for me?" Betsy asked her big sister.

"Shh!" Marilyn answered. "I'm busy."

"But she wants you to hold her," Betsy pleaded. Marilyn turned an angry look on her sister. "I'm watching my favorite TV show, so leave me alone!"

Betsy tramped away, crying softly, but Marilyn ignored her. Mom came into the room a few moments later, holding Betsy's doll. She sat on the couch behind Marilyn.

"What are you watching?" Mom asked.

"Frontier Doctor," Marilyn answered. "Did you know that the actor who plays Luke on this show is a Christian? I read about him in a magazine."

"That's interesting," Mom said.

Marilyn turned back to face the television. "I think that's so cool."

"Why?"

"Well, because, you know—he's a Christian, we're Christians, you know."

"Oh," Mom said. "You, um . . . you like it when you find out that others share your faith."

"Yeah," Marilyn said. "That's it."

Mom waited a few moments, until a commercial break interrupted the program Marilyn was watching. Then she said, "You know what you were telling me about the actor on that show?" She waited until she saw Marilyn nod. "God feels the same way, I think."

"What do you mean?"

"You have something in common with that actor, because you're both Christians, right?" Mom said. Marilyn nodded again. "Well, God likes it when you show that you have things in common with him. For example, the Bible says he's a compassionate God, who is slow to anger and abounding in love. So, naturally, he likes it when you are compassionate too. You could say that he *values* compassion."

Marilyn suddenly noticed her sister's doll in Mom's arms. She blushed. "I guess I wasn't very nice to Betsy, was I?"

Mom smiled patiently. "You could have been more compassionate."

Marilyn got out of her chair and stood. "Can I borrow that doll?" she asked. She took the doll from her mom's arms, then stepped to the television and turned it off. She shrugged. "I probably watch too much TV anyway."

 TO DISCUSS: Why does God command us to be compassionate? Why does God value compassion? Is God compassionate? If so, how do you know? Do you want to be more compassionate, like God? How can you start?

 TO PRAY: "Lord, we want to be compassionate because you value compassion, and because you are compassionate."

22 Blessing and Compassion

COMPASSION INVITES BLESSING FROM GOD.

Bible Reading of the Day: Read Exodus 1:8-17, 20-21.

Verse of the Day: *"Therefore, as God's chosen people, holy and dearly loved, clothe yourselves with compassion, kindness, humility, gentleness and patience" (Colossians 3:12, NIV).*

Andrea tiptoed into her mother's bedroom. Mom sat on the edge of her bed, crying. Her hands covered her face and muffled her sobs. Her back was turned to the door, so she didn't see Andrea as she walked softly to the bed.

"Mom?" Andrea whispered. "Are you crying?"

Mom straightened with a jolt. She snatched a tissue out of a box on the bedside table and wiped her eyes and nose. "Andrea!" she said. "When did you come in?"

Andrea didn't answer. "What's wrong?" she asked. "What are you upset about?"

Mom wiped her eyes. "Oh, I'm not upset," she said.

"Yes, you are," Andrea insisted, "or you wouldn't be crying."

Mom shook her head. "I'm not upset or sad." She patted the bed next to her, motioning for Andrea to sit down beside her. She inhaled deeply before speaking. "I spent the afternoon at the center for handicapped children." Andrea knew that her mom volunteered several days a month to work with people with handicaps.

"There was a young girl there who's very badly handicapped." Mom paused for a moment, then smiled and continued. "She's had a very hard life. Well, everyone at the center knew that she hadn't spoken a word in . . . in a long time. Years, maybe."

Andrea placed her hand on Mom's shoulder.

"Anyway," Mom went on, "today, I fed that young girl lunch; she's not able to feed herself. Some of the soup dribbled down her chin, and when I . . ." —Mom lifted the tissue to her mouth and paused for a moment— "when I wiped it off, she said thank you!"

Mom started to cry again, and Andrea's eyes filled with tears too. Andrea wrapped her arms around her mom and hugged her close.

"That's really cool, Mom," Andrea said.

"Yeah, it is," Mom said. "Isn't it? It's just so—so wonderful when something like that happens." She straightened her back and peered into her daughter's eyes. "Andrea, when you're obedient to God in serving other people, he gives *you* far more blessing than you can *ever* give someone else."

TO DISCUSS: How did God reward the Hebrew midwives for their compassion toward the Israelite babies in Egypt? How did God reward Mom for her compassion? Do you think what Mom said is true ("When you're obedient to God in serving other people, he gives *you* far more blessing than you can *ever* give someone else.")? Has anything like that ever happened to you?

TO PRAY: "Holy and gracious God, may we be clothed in your compassion from head to foot. May we also wear a garment of praise."

23 Fun and Compassion

COMPASSION CAN BE FUN!

Bible Reading of the Day: Read Acts 3:1-11.
Verse of the Day: *"When darkness overtakes the godly, light will come bursting in. They are generous, compassionate, and righteous" (Psalm 112:4).*

Bethany was the first to see the man. She and her brother Ben had just walked out of the department store with their father. Sitting on the sidewalk was a whiskered old man in stained clothing. An upturned hat sat beside him on the pavement, and a handwritten cardboard sign pleaded with passersby to "Help the Homeless."

Ben stiffened and Bethany swerved behind Dad. To their surprise, however, Dad stopped. He crouched down and extended his hand toward the man.

The man looked suspicious at first, then slowly reached out and shook the hand Dad had offered him. Dad introduced himself and his children by name, then said, "We're just about to catch a quick lunch at the cafe down the street. We'd be happy to have you join us."

The man looked from Dad to Bethany, then to Ben and back to Dad again.

"Sure," he answered with a shrug. "Why not?"

Dad smiled, and helped the man to his feet. The four of them walked to the cafe. As they ate, Dad drew the man into a conversation about his life. The man confessed to struggling with an alcohol problem and warned Ben and Bethany never to start drinking. "No good ever came of it for me," he said.

When they finished eating, Dad paid for their meal. They paused in front of the little cafe to say good-bye to the man. He shook Dad's hand, thanked him for the meal, and smiled at Bethany and Ben as he turned to walk back to his corner.

"That was really cool, Dad," Ben said excitedly. "He was a nice man."

"I think he liked you and Bethany too," Dad said.

"It was so cool hearing about all the places he lived," Bethany said. She shook her head in amazement. "He used to live in—what was that one place he said he lived in?"

"Argentina," Ben answered.

"Hey, Dad," Ben said. "Can we take him out to lunch next time we come downtown?"

Dad nodded. "We can try," he said, then added, "Why?"

Ben cocked his head. "I don't know," he replied. "I just liked it."

"Yeah," Bethany agreed. "It was fun."

Dad smiled. "I'm glad you think so," he said.

TO DISCUSS: Do you think it was fun for Peter and John to heal the beggar at the temple? Why? Do you think it was fun for Bethany, Ben, and Dad to take the homeless man to lunch? Why? Have you ever had fun showing compassion? If so, tell about it.

TO PRAY: "May your joy, Lord, create a tidal wave of compassion within us."

24 Beauty and Compassion

COMPASSION CAN BE BEAUTIFUL!

Bible Reading of the Day: Read Romans 15:1-3.

Verse of the Day: *"Each one of us needs to look after the good of the people around us, asking ourselves, 'How can I help?'"* (Romans 15:2, *The Message*).

Ronita's Sunday school class was interrupted by the arrival of a new student, who was escorted in by the Sunday school superintendent.

Like everyone else in the class, Ronita noticed that the new boy had only one arm; his left arm was missing. Nobody said anything as the boy sat in the seat to Ronita's right. Ronita smiled at the newcomer, as the teacher continued the Bible story she was telling.

After a few minutes, the class seemed to return to normal. The teacher had seemed nervous at first, but when everyone acted normally instead of staring at the boy or talking about him, she seemed to relax.

Finally, the teacher looked at the clock on the side wall. "Oh my," she said, "it's time to dismiss." She closed her book and smiled at her students. "Thank you for listening so well," she said. She clapped her hands together. "Now, let's do our closing exercise together, shall we?"

Ronita's mouth suddenly dropped open as she watched the teacher begin the ceremony they used every week at the end of class.

"Let's make our churches," the teacher said, clasping her hands together and extending her index fingers straight up to form a steeple. "Here's the church and here's the steeple," she started, and then stopped abruptly, realizing what she had done. She had forgotten all about the new boy who had only one arm! Her face flushed red as she realized that her actions had made things very awkward and difficult for the newcomer.

Suddenly, however, Ronita had an idea. She reached her left hand across her body and placed it in front of the new boy. "Here," she said cheerfully. "We can make our church together!"

The boy blinked at Ronita for a moment, then smiled. He lifted his only hand, his right hand, and intertwined his fingers with the fingers of Ronita's left hand. Together they extended their index fingers into the shape of a steeple and joined the teacher's voice to complete the rhyme: "Here's the church and here's the steeple. Open the doors and see all the people."

The teacher smiled at Ronita and the new boy. The Sunday school lesson had never been more beautiful or more meaningful.

TO DO: Join hands with the person next to you to form a church and steeple and recite the rhyme, "Here's the church, and here's the steeple. Open the doors and see all the people."

TO PRAY: "Lord, as people of compassion, help us to see beyond a person's looks and connect with his or her heart instead."

25 God and Ice Cream

GOD'S COMMANDS SHOW US WHAT HE LIKES, WHAT HE DOESN'T LIKE, WHAT HE THINKS IS GOOD, AND WHAT HE THINKS IS BAD.

Bible Reading of the Day: Read Psalm 119:65-68.
Verse of the Day: *"You are good and do only good; teach me your principles" (Psalm 119:68).*

Lee stood at the ice-cream counter with his dad and Pastor Martin. His dad and the pastor were good friends, and Lee liked it when they invited him to do things with them.

"What flavor ice cream would you like, Lee?" the pastor asked. "It's my treat."

Pastor Martin and Dad argued in a friendly way for a few moments, but Pastor won the argument and repeated his question to Lee.

"Chocolate, please," he said, smiling in anticipation.

A few moments later they each had an ice-cream cone. They walked outside, crossed the street, and sat on a bench in the small park across the street from the ice-cream parlor.

After a few moments of conversation between him and Dad, Pastor Martin turned to Lee. "You know, Lee," he said, "I think I can guess your favorite ice-cream flavor."

Lee smiled and raised his shirt sleeve to wipe the chocolate from around his mouth.

"It's chocolate, isn't it?" Pastor Martin said.

Lee nodded. "You knew because I'm eating chocolate ice cream now," he said matter-of-factly.

Pastor Martin nodded. "That's part of it, yes," he admitted. "But I've noticed something every time I've seen you order ice cream. You always order chocolate! Did you know that's the same way I can tell what God likes?"

Lee's forehead wrinkled, and he flashed a puzzled look at the pastor. "You know what flavor God likes?"

Pastor and Dad laughed together. "No," Pastor said. "But I can tell the things he does like by paying attention to the 'orders' he gives."

Lee said nothing, but his expression revealed that he didn't understand what the pastor meant.

"When you order chocolate ice cream," Pastor said, "it shows me that you like chocolate ice cream. Well, when God tells his people to love each other . . ."

"It shows that he likes love!" Lee said, finishing the pastor's sentence.

"That's right!" Pastor answered. "And when God tells us to forgive each other . . ."

"It shows that God likes forgiveness!"

"Exactly. Now do you see what I mean?"

Lee nodded. He licked his cone. "I think God likes chocolate ice cream too," he said.

Pastor Martin laughed. "He probably does, Lee. He probably does."

 TO DISCUSS: What's your favorite flavor of ice cream? Can you figure out other things God likes (in addition to love and forgiveness) by remembering the commands he has given?

TO PRAY: "Almighty God, as we learn more about you, we learn more of your likes and dislikes. Thank you for these private glimpses of you."

26 Cucumbers and Berries

WE WILL REAP WHAT WE SOW.

Bible Reading of the Day: Read Galatians 6:7-10.

Verse of the Day: *"Don't get tired of doing what is good" (Galatians 6:9).*

Lisa strode into the barn and flopped onto a bale of hay. Her mother was filling a bucket with water from the faucet in the corner.

"Hi, Lisa," Mom said cheerily. "What have you been up to?"

Lisa watched her mom work for a moment before answering. She wore a sulky look. "Sharon doesn't want to come to my birthday party this year."

"She doesn't?" Mom said.

Lisa shook her head. "She says she's supposed to go somewhere else. But I think she just doesn't want to come."

"Is this the same Sharon who gave you that sweater she knitted herself last year?" Mom asked. She set the bucket on the floor and filled a second bucket.

Lisa's expression grew even darker. "Yes," she said. She had hoped her mom had forgotten that, but Mom never seemed to forget anything. Lisa had unwrapped Sharon's sweater and started laughing and making fun of the sweater. She had even called it "stupid." All the other girls at the party had laughed too, except for Sharon.

Mom picked up the two buckets. "Can you give me a hand?" she asked Lisa.

Lisa and her mom walked toward the old farmhouse they lived in.

"Would you grab a handful of strawberries off that vine for me?" Mom asked.

Lisa stepped into the garden and leaned over before she realized what her mom had asked her. "Mom," she said, straightening her back, "these are the cucumbers."

"Oh, I know I planted cucumbers there, but I thought maybe you could pull a couple of strawberries off anyway."

"What are you talking about, Mom?" Lisa asked. "I can't get strawberries off a cucumber vine." A sudden change in Mom's expression triggered a realization in Lisa's mind. "Oh," Lisa said. "I see what you're doing."

"What?" Mom asked innocently.

"This has something to do with me and Sharon, doesn't it?" Her mom smiled. "You're saying I'm getting what I deserve, aren't you?"

Mom shook her head. "No," she said. "I'm suggesting you're getting the crop you planted. The Bible says we will reap what we sow. You can't expect to harvest kindness and friendship unless you plant seeds of kindness and friendship."

"You're right, Mom," Lisa said. She started to step out of the garden.

"Wait a minute," Mom said. "See if there are any ripe cucumbers on that vine. Talking about food has made me hungry!"

 TO DO: The next time you eat cucumbers or strawberries, remember that "you will always reap what you sow" and ask God to help you live in a way that pleases the Spirit of God.

TO PRAY: "Lord, help us to live in a way that pleases you."

27 Glory Stories

GIVING GLORY TO GOD REMINDS US THAT HE IS A GOOD GOD, WHO IS GOOD TO US.

Bible Reading of the Day: Read Mark 7:31-37.
Verse of the Day: *"Glory and honor to God forever and ever. He is the eternal King, the unseen one who never dies; he alone is God"* (1 Timothy 1:17).

Frank and his friend Jarrod sat together at the table as Frank's mom set bowls of steaming soup in front of them.

"I don't like this kind of soup!" Alicia, Frank's little sister, whined.

"I'm sorry, Alicia," Mom said, "but this is what we're having for lunch."

Alicia stopped whining, but she wore a grouchy look on her face. Later, as the four of them were finishing their lunch, Alicia started whining again.

"I don't want to take a nap today," she said. "I'm too big to take naps."

Frank and Jarrod exchanged smiles. "It sounds like you really need a nap, Alicia," Frank said.

"Do not!" Alicia answered sullenly.

"That's a really grouchy look on your face, Alicia," Mom said. She winked at Frank. "Maybe it's time for a 'glory story.'"

"What's a glory story?" Jarrod asked.

"It's just something we do in our family," Frank explained. "When one of us starts feeling grumpy or sad or something like that, we share a glory story."

"What *is* a glory story?" Jarrod repeated.

"It's a story that gives glory to God," Mom offered. "It's like a testimony we tell to each other when one of us starts getting negative. Giving glory to God reminds us that he is a good God, who is good to us."

"I'll tell a glory story," Frank volunteered. He looked at his sister. "I remember once when you were lost at the beach, I was really, really scared, because I didn't want to lose my baby sister. So I prayed really hard while I looked, and then Mom found you at the lifeguard station."

Alicia's eyes widened. "I was scared too!"

"But God helped us find you," Mom said. "I'll tell a glory story," she added. "You had to have an operation when you were just a tiny baby, and we all prayed that the operation would be a success." She reached her hand over to Alicia and rubbed her daughter's cheek. "I'm so thankful to God that it was."

"See?" Frank said, turning to his friend. *"That's* a glory story."

Jarrod nodded and looked at Alicia. She was no longer whining. She—and everyone else at the table—was smiling broadly.

 TO DO: Tell your own "glory stories" to each other, to remind each other that God is a good God, who is good to you.

 TO PRAY: "Gracious Lord, you are so good to us. We praise your name today. You deserve all glory and honor."

28 Playground Battleground

DOING THE RIGHT THING IS SOMETIMES UNPOPULAR.

> **Bible Reading of the Day: Read Daniel 3:1-12.**
> **Verse of the Day:** *"Surely God is my salvation; I will trust and not be afraid. The Lord, the Lord, is my strength and my song; he has become my salvation" (Isaiah 12:2, NIV).*

Janine saw it all.

She was walking from the swings to the monkey bars on the school playground. Suddenly, a boy named Marcus placed a hand squarely in the middle of John's back.

"Get out of my way!" Marcus yelled. He pushed John, whose arms waved in the air for a moment like twin windmills before he fell off the monkey bars. John hit the ground with a thud.

Janine ran over to where John lay. John was curled in a heap, crying. Janine looked at Marcus, who still sat atop the monkey bars, defiance written on his face.

A teacher arrived then and checked John for broken bones. "What happened?" she asked.

"He pushed me!" John cried, pointing at Marcus.

"Did not!" Marcus answered. He fastened a pair of innocent-looking eyes on the teacher. "I never touched him!"

Janine looked in disbelief from Marcus back to John.

"Did anyone see what happened?" the teacher asked.

Janine looked at the other kids standing around. Everyone had seen what had happened, but no one wanted to say anything. She looked at Marcus, who glared threateningly at the crowd. She knew that he could beat her up; he was the biggest bully in their grade.

"I saw," Janine finally said, after looking around the circle of silent faces. She sighed, as if she were getting herself in trouble; in a way, maybe she was. "Marcus and John were both climbing on the monkey bars," she said quietly, still knowing that Marcus would hear her. "Marcus said, 'Get out of my way,' and pushed John." She looked only at the teacher as she talked, and when she finished, she turned her head to look at John.

John's face was streaked with dirt and tears, but he smiled. Janine smiled back. The teacher told Marcus to report to the principal's office while she took John to the school nurse. Then she turned to Janine.

"Thank you for telling the truth," she said. "I know it wasn't easy."

TO DISCUSS: Today's Bible reading is about three young men who did the right thing even though it got them in trouble with the king. How is that like Janine's story? How is it different? Have you ever done the right thing even though it made you unpopular? If so, tell about it. Did Janine do the right thing? Why or why not? What would you have done if you had been in Janine's situation? Should we do the right thing only when it's popular? Why or why not?

TO PRAY: "Lord God, help us to do the right thing even in difficult situations."

29 But If Not . . .

DOING RIGHT IS STILL RIGHT EVEN WHEN IT SEEMS HARD OR UNREWARDING.

Bible Reading of the Day: Read Daniel 3:13-18.
Verse of the Day: *"The God whom we serve is able to save us"*
(Daniel 3:17).

"Look!" Manny said. He looked at his friend Davis with wide eyes. His hands held a wallet he had found in the alley behind the mobile home park where they both lived.

"Where'd you find that?" Davis asked in a hoarse whisper.

"Right here!" Manny answered. "Laying right here on the ground."

"How much is in it?" Davis asked.

Manny thumbed through the money. "At least a hundred dollars."

"There's more than that," Davis countered. He stuck a finger into the open billfold. "There's got to be—" he counted through the ten- and twenty-dollar bills—"over *two* hundred dollars!"

The boys exchanged broad grins. "What do you want to do with it?" Davis asked.

Manny flipped through the credit cards and found a driver's license. He showed it to his friend. "We should give it back," he said. It doesn't belong to us."

"It does now!" Davis argued. "Think of all the things we could buy with that money."

"But it belongs to *him,*" Manny said, pointing to the photo on the driver's license.

"Manny," Davis said in a pleading voice, "this is more money than we've ever seen in our entire lives! Think of what we could do with it."

Manny nodded. "I know," he said. "But I think we have to give it back."

Davis closed his eyes and let his head lean backward. "I don't believe this."

Manny folded the wallet and stuffed it in his jacket pocket.

"You know," Davis said, "the guy who lost it probably won't even miss it."

"Sure he will," Manny said. "It's got his driver's license and credit cards in it."

"We could just give him back the wallet and tell him we found it empty. He'll be so glad to get the wallet back, he won't miss the money that much."

Manny shook his head and started walking toward his trailer.

"He probably won't even give us a reward, you know," Davis said bitterly as he walked beside his friend.

"Maybe not," Manny said. "But it still wouldn't be right to keep it, would it?"

"I guess not," Davis said sadly.

 TO DISCUSS: People who do right aren't always rewarded for doing right, at least not in this life. Today's Bible reading tells about three young men who decided to do the right thing even if it cost them their lives. How is that like Manny's story? How is it different? What do *you* think Manny and Davis should do with the money? Why? Do you think we should do right even when it's hard or there's no reward? Why or why not?

TO PRAY: "Lord, you command us to do right even when the right way is hard. Be with us, Lord, during those times."

30 Through the Fire

GOD DOES NOT PROMISE THAT WE WILL ESCAPE PAIN OR HARDSHIP IF WE CHOOSE
RIGHT, BUT HE DOES PROMISE TO BE WITH US.

Bible Reading of the Day: Read Daniel 3:19-27.

Verse of the Day: *"When you go through deep waters and great trouble,
I will be with you. When you go through rivers of difficulty, you will not
drown! When you walk through the fire of oppression, you will not be
burned up; the flames will not consume you"* (Isaiah 43:2).

Susan stomped into the house and up the stairs. She walked through every room of the
house and finally stopped outside Ludmilla's door. Ludmilla was an exchange student
who had been living with Susan's family for several months. When Ludmilla came to
live with them for the school year, Susan and her family had been overjoyed to discover
that she was a Christian.

Susan rapped on Ludmilla's door.

"Come in!" Ludmilla called.

Susan opened the door and stuck her head into the room. Ludmilla sat cross-
legged on her bed with a book opened on her lap. "Where's Mom?" Susan asked.

Ludmilla smiled. "I think she took Carrie to her ballet lesson," she said, referring
to Susan's sister.

Susan groaned and stepped into the older girl's room.

"What's wrong?" Ludmilla asked.

"I had to stay after school today," she said as she flopped down on Ludmilla's bed.
"My teacher had to leave the room, and when she came back, she caught the class
shouting and shooting spitballs and told us we all had to stay after school."

"Oh," Ludmilla said. "I see."

"But I didn't do any of that stuff. I wanted to, but I stayed in my seat while
everyone was going crazy around me." She pouted. "I didn't do anything wrong, and
I got punished with the rest of them."

"You did the right thing," Ludmilla said, "and you were punished anyway."

Susan nodded. "Yeah!" she said. "It's not fair. I thought being good was supposed
to keep me out of trouble."

Ludmilla smiled. "Many times it does. But God does not promise that doing good
will always make things easy. But he does promise to always be with us, even when
life is hard."

"Even when we have to stay after school?" Susan asked.

"Yes," Ludmilla said. "Even when we have to stay after school."

 TO DISCUSS: In today's Bible reading, Shadrach, Meshach, and Abednego were
thrown into a hot furnace even though they had done nothing wrong. Was God with
them? How did God help them? Does God promise you won't ever have problems if you
make right choices? What does he promise?

 TO PRAY: "Lord, you promise to always be with us. You also promise that we can
have joy in your presence. We need this joy when we're going through hard times.
Thank you, Lord."

1 Too Hot to Handle

DOUBTING GOD'S GOODNESS IS OFTEN THE FIRST STEP TOWARD DOING WRONG.

Bible Reading of the Day: Read Genesis 3:1-6.
Verse of the Day: *"No good thing will the Lord withhold from those who do what is right" (Psalm 84:11).*

Everyone in the family laughed at Danise, the baby. She sat in her mother's lap, stretching and straining for the hot pepper that was in her father's hand.

"No, Danise," Mom told her. "You don't want what Daddy's got."

The others laughed at the child's insistence. Danise saw her father eating the yellow peppers and thought she wanted some too.

"Why don't you give her one, Dad?" Dionna suggested. "Let her have a taste."

Dad shook his head and screwed the lid of the jar full of peppers shut. "No," he said, chuckling. "I know she wants it, but it would be cruel to let her have it."

"You could give her just a taste," Dionna said.

"Girl," Mom said, shaking her head, "do you want your baby sister to cry all afternoon? If your daddy even touched Danise's tongue with that pepper, she'd be hurting the rest of the day!"

"But she wants it!" Dionna protested.

"She *thinks* she wants it," Dad said. "But she doesn't *know* any better."

Dad walked across the kitchen, put the jar of peppers in a cabinet, and shut the door. A few moments later, Danise had forgotten the peppers.

Dad sat down next to his older daughter. "Sometimes we all act a lot like Danise," he said.

"What do you mean?" Dionna asked.

"We all strain and complain after something God has told us to stay away from, and we sometimes think he's just being stingy or spiteful by not letting us have what we want—or what we think we want."

"When all the time," Mom added, "God's loving us and not wanting to see us hurt. Yet we go on doubting him and questioning him like he was trying to hurt us."

"But if we remember God loves us," Dionna said, "like you love Danise, we'll be a lot better off, won't we, Daddy?"

Mom and Dad both smiled at Dionna.

"We sure will," Dad answered. He turned to the baby in Mom's arms and touched her on the nose. "Just like Danise will be better off if she stays out of the hot peppers!"

 TO DISCUSS: Do you ever strain and complain after something God has told you to stay away from? Do you sometimes think he's just being stingy or spiteful by not letting you have your own way? Have you ever wanted something that you later realized was bad for you? Do you think it would be easier to obey God if we believe today's "verse of the day"? Why or why not?

TO PRAY: "Lord, when we're tempted to doubt your goodness, guide us back to the truth. "

2 Standard Equipment

DOING RIGHT IS NOT OPTIONAL, IT'S *CRUCIAL*.

Bible Reading of the Day: Read Hebrews 12:14-17.
Verse of the Day: *"Try to live in peace with everyone, and seek to live a clean and holy life, for those who are not holy will not see the Lord"* *(Hebrews 12:14).*

Dad and Shelly went to the car dealership to pick up a brand new car. Dad planned to leave their old car as a trade-in.

"This is the first new car I've ever owned," Dad said as they climbed into the new car.

Shelly inhaled. "It smells so good!" she said. Then she looked at the car's sound system. "I still don't understand why we couldn't get a CD player."

"I told you, Shelly, a CD player costs extra. The radio and tape deck are standard equipment, but the CD player is optional. It would have cost more."

"Darbi's car has a CD player," Shelly announced, referring to one of her friends.

"I know," Dad said as he drove out of the car lot. "But we can't have everything we want, can we?"

"Not in our family!" Shelly countered, a trace of sarcasm surfacing in her voice.

"That reminds me, Shelly," Dad said. "Mom tells me that some of Darbi's language has been rubbing off on you."

Shelly clucked her tongue and rolled her eyes. "I've just cussed a couple times, Dad," she said. "It's not like I'm making a habit of it."

"I hope not, Shelly. You know how your mom and I feel about those kinds of words."

"I don't see what the big deal is," Shelly said. "I'm still a Christian. A few bad words aren't going to keep me out of heaven."

"That's true," Dad answered. "But I don't want you to make the mistake of thinking that right choices . . . are . . . optional. See, Shelly, doing right isn't like a CD player in a car; it's more like a steering wheel or an engine. It's not optional—it's standard equipment. We can't just decide, 'Well, I'm going to heaven, so it doesn't matter how I act,' or, 'I can do this because I know God will forgive me.'"

"I'm not doing that," Shelly protested.

"Maybe not, but I don't think you're taking your sin very seriously," Dad said. "I'm glad you're a Christian, Shelly, you know I am. But being a Christian doesn't make living a clean and holy life unnecessary . . . it makes it possible!"

Shelly shook her head. "I'm sorry, Dad," she said. "I'll do better from now on."

Dad smiled. "I'm sure you will," he said.

 TO DISCUSS: Is it OK for Christians to sin? Why or why not? Is it OK for us to sin as long as we plan to ask for God's forgiveness later? Why or why not? How can we live clean and holy lives?

 TO PRAY: "Lord, help us to remember that you command us to obey you. Help us to live clean and holy lives."

3 The Finish Line

TO PERSEVERE IS TO DO RIGHT EVEN WHEN IT IS HARD OR WHEN YOU ARE TIRED.

Bible Reading of the Day: Read Galatians 6:4-5, 9-10.
Verse of the Day: *"Don't get tired of doing what is good. Don't get discouraged and give up, for we will reap a harvest of blessing at the appropriate time" (Galatians 6:9).*

Killian slumped down onto the kitchen floor. "I don't want to clean up!" she said.

Mom smiled. She and Killian had been baking cookies and brownies all afternoon for a church sale. She could tell that her daughter was tired and was tempted to let her stop working. But instead she sat down next to Killian on the floor.

"We've worked really hard, haven't we?" Mom said.

Killian frowned. "And I don't want to clean up," she repeated.

"But cleaning up is part of the job," Mom answered. "Don't you think we should stick with the job until it's finished?"

"I don't want to," Killian said, smacking the floor with her hand. Her action created a cloud of flour from the fine film that coated the floor.

Mom laughed and patted the floor with her hand, sending up another cloud. Killian responded by hitting the floor with both hands. Soon they were laughing and rolling together on the flour-covered floor, dusted from head to toe with flour. Mom said. "Killian, do you know why I want you to help clean the kitchen?"

"Because you don't want to do it alone!" Killian answered, her eyes sparkling.

Mom smiled. "That's part of it," she admitted. "It is a lot more fun to do something with you than to do it by myself. But I also want you to help me because I want you to learn how to persevere."

"How to p-p-what?" Killian said, unable to pronounce the big word.

"I want you to learn how to persevere. To persevere means to do what you should even when it's hard, or even when you're tired. It means to finish a job you've started."

"You don't always p-per-persevere," Killian said.

"What do you mean?" Mom said.

"You didn't finish sewing my new jumper," she said.

Mom looked surprised. Killian was right. She had promised to make a new jumper for her daughter and hadn't touched it in weeks. She smiled. "All right," she said. "I'll make you a deal. If you help me finish the job of cleaning the kitchen, I'll let you help me finish your jumper too!"

"OK," Killian answered, suddenly cheerful. "I was going to help you anyway," she whispered confidentially.

Mom laughed and rolled Killian over and over in the flour on the floor.

TO DISCUSS: Is it good to finish jobs you've started? Why or why not? What does it mean to "persevere"? Do you sometimes get discouraged and feel like giving up? How can you do what you should even when it's hard or when you're tired?

TO PRAY: "Lord, we need your help to persevere when hard tasks come our way."

4 Peter, John, and Denny

PERSEVERANCE OBEYS GOD RATHER THAN MEN.

Bible Reading of the Day: Read Acts 4:1-3, 16-20.
Verse of the Day: *"We must obey God rather than men!" (Acts 5:29, NIV).*

"Are you trying to make the rest of us look bad?" asked Michael, the biggest kid in the class, looking menacingly at Denny.

"What do you mean?" Denny asked innocently. He glanced at Travis and Clay, two of Michael's friends.

Michael poked his finger in Denny's chest. "You get an A on every test we take," he said. "And the rest of us get C's and D's. If it wasn't for you, Miss Preston might make the tests easier. But you have to go and make the rest of us look dumb. You better not make us look bad on the next test, you hear?"

Michael and his friends left, and Denny sat cross-legged on the playground. What was he going to do? His parents had always taught him to do his best in school, but he didn't want to get beat up by Michael and his friends. And he knew that if he told Miss Preston or his parents, Michael would probably beat him up anyway.

I could just try to get a B, he thought. *That wouldn't be so wrong. Maybe Michael won't beat me up.* But even as he tried to think of a solution, he knew he couldn't give in to the bully. His parents had taught him to always do his best, and he knew it would be wrong to give in to Michael's threats.

Denny stood and searched the playground for Michael. He finally spotted him, standing with Travis and Clay by the drinking fountain. He took a deep breath and walked over.

"Michael," he said, "you can get mad if you want to, but I'm not going to get bad grades just for you." His mouth was as dry as a desert. He licked his lips. "It . . . it wouldn't be right."

Michael smiled sweetly. "You're right, Denny," he said. "It wouldn't be right. What made you think I wanted you to get bad grades?"

Denny blinked at Michael. What was going on? He looked from Michael to Travis and Clay. They were looking over his shoulders. He turned. "Miss Preston," Denny said. "I . . . I didn't know you were there."

"Is there any problem here, Denny?" she said.

Denny turned and looked at Michael, then at Travis and Clay. "No, ma'am," he said.

Miss Preston turned her gaze on Michael. He smiled. "No problem at all, Miss Preston."

"Good," the teacher answered. "I'll be watching to make sure you keep it that way."

TO DISCUSS: Peter and John persevered and did the right thing in the face of persecution. How was Denny's situation like theirs? How was it different? Were Peter and John right to persevere? Why or why not? What can we learn from Peter and John's—and Denny's—example?

TO PRAY: "Lord, when others try to force us away from your will, help us to keep our eyes on you and to persevere. "

5 On Wings like Eagles

THE STRENGTH TO PERSEVERE COMES FROM GOD.

Bible Reading of the Day: Read Isaiah 40:27-31.
Verse of the Day: *"Even youths will become exhausted, and young men will give up. But those who wait on the Lord will find new strength"* (Isaiah 40:30-31).

Blake sat beside his mother and listened carefully as the visiting missionary stood before the church and told about his experiences in Japan, where he had served for seven years. He told of some of the differences between the customs of Japan and the customs of the United States. The missionary also explained that he had only recently won his first convert to the Christian faith! The missionary then clapped his hands together, bowed slightly, and said he would answer questions from the congregation.

A man two rows in front of Blake raised his hand. "Was it hard to work for almost seven years without seeing any results from your work?"

The missionary nodded. "Oh, yes," he said. "I knew before I arrived in Japan that my job would be difficult. The Japanese are always very polite, but most are very resistant to the gospel. Still, it was hard to keep going at times."

Blake tapped his mom's arm. "Can I ask a question?" he whispered.

"Go ahead," Mom whispered back.

Several others asked questions before the missionary called on Blake.

Blake stood to ask his question. "How did you keep trying even when nobody was listening to you?"

The missionary looked at Blake with appreciation. "That's a very good question, young man," the missionary said. "It can be hard to keep trying, even if you know what you're doing is right." He cleared his throat. "I think the only way I kept going through those first six-and-a-half years was in God's strength. I stayed very close to God, and I honestly believe his Spirit gave me the strength to persevere. Otherwise, I probably would have given up about six years ago!"

The missionary started to answer another question, but he stopped and faced Blake again. "Now that I think about it," he continued, "that's true for all of us. It's hard to keep on doing good in the face of hardship or persecution. It's natural to get tired and feel like giving up. But the Bible tells us, if we wait on the Lord, he will give us strength and help us keep going without getting tired. That's not just true for missionaries in Japan," the man said. "It's true for you, too."

Blake smiled at the missionary as he returned to his seat beside Mom. The missionary smiled back.

TO DISCUSS: Where does the strength to persevere come from? According to today's Bible reading, who finds new strength? What do you think it means to "wait on the Lord"? Do you need to persevere in something you're doing right now? How can you keep going, even if you're tired and feel like giving up?

TO PRAY: "Lord, we're not like the Energizer Bunny, who keeps going and going. We get tired sometimes. Give us your strength, Lord, when we're weary."

6 Carl's Win

GOD COMMANDS PERSEVERANCE.

Bible Reading of the Day: Read Hebrews 12:1-3.
Verse of the Day: *"Never get tired of doing good"* (2 Thessalonians 3:13).

Carl tossed his running shoes onto the front seat and got into the car. "I can't believe you're making me do this," he told his father.

"I'm not making you do it, Son," Dad replied. "You agreed to this when you joined the track team."

"Yeah, but I don't want to be on the track team anymore. I'm sick of it! I haven't even won a single race. But you won't let me quit!"

Dad drove in silence for a few moments, while Carl moped. Finally, Dad cleared his throat. "Carl," he said, "how many models do you have on that shelf in your room?"

Carl was puzzled by the shift in the conversation, but he closed his eyes to picture his room in his mind. He counted the model cars, ships, and planes he and his dad had made together, a collection he was proud of. "I don't know," he answered at last. "Around nineteen or twenty."

"How many of those models would you have finished if I had let you give up when you wanted to?" Dad asked.

Carl knew what his dad was going to say now. "I don't know," he said, the sullen tone entering his voice again.

"Well," Dad said. "I think I do. I don't think you'd have a single model on that shelf if I hadn't insisted that you finish each one."

They drove a while in silence. Then Dad said, "Carl, I want you to learn to persevere . . . not just in building models, but in running track, in doing schoolwork—and especially in following Jesus." Dad inhaled deeply and exhaled slowly. "You see, Son, God commands us to persevere. He wants us to obey him when it's hard as well as when it's easy. Sticking with the track team is good practice for learning how to persevere in your faith . . . understand?"

Carl wasn't smiling, but his tone had softened. "I guess," he said, as Dad pulled to a stop at the track field. He got out and leaned back in the car to grab his running shoes. "I don't have to like it, do I?"

Dad smiled wryly. "No," he said with a sigh. "You don't have to like it."

Dad met Carl back at the car after the track meet ended. Carl was sweaty and dirty, but he was smiling. "I won the 100-yard event, Dad!" he said. "I actually won!"

"I know," Dad said, smiling. "I saw. But be careful, Son."

"What?" Carl asked, the smiled disappearing from his face. "Why?"

Dad's smile appeared again. "You're starting to sound like you like it!" he said.

TO DO: Choose a family project—like putting together a model or a jigsaw puzzle—that requires patience and perseverance, and complete it together. As you work on it together, talk about perseverance and why it's important.

TO PRAY: "Heavenly Father, help us to never get tired of doing good."

7 Carl's Award

GOD COMMANDS PERSEVERANCE BECAUSE GOD VALUES PERSEVERANCE.

Bible Reading of the Day: Read Revelation 2:1-3.
Verse of the Day: *"Never get tired of doing good"* (2 Thessalonians 3:13).

Carl sat beside his mother and father at the annual sports banquet. He watched several of his teammates on the track team win awards.

"I won't win anything," he whispered to his mom.

"Why not?" she asked.

"I only won one race all year!" he answered, as if his mom's question were silly. But even as he whispered to his mom, he heard his name called.

Carl stood and walked nervously to the front of the banquet hall. The room was filled with kids who played sports at Carl's school, and their parents—and even some grandparents. Carl wore a puzzled look as he took his place next to Coach Watkins.

"There are many young men and women on our sports teams who could be given this award," the coach said, "but I can't think of anyone who deserves it more than this young man. This was Carl's first year on the track team. He ran every track meet, and though he ran well, someone always seemed to finish a few steps ahead of him. But Carl never gave up, and he won his first event in the next-to-the-last meet of the year. So our 'Perseverance Award' goes to Carl Hughes!"

The crowd erupted in applause. Carl said a quick "thank you" and returned to his table with the trophy Coach Watkins had given him.

On the way home that evening, Carl repeatedly looked at his trophy as if he couldn't believe it was actually his.

"We're proud of you, Carl," Dad said.

"More important," Mom suggested, "I think God's proud of you too."

Carl's expression reflected his puzzlement.

"Think about it," Mom said. "People only give awards for things they value. The fact that your coach gave you an award for perseverance shows that he thinks somebody sticking with something through difficulty is a good thing."

"I almost didn't," Carl said, exchanging a glance with his father.

"But you did," Mom said. "And that's what matters. But I think God's proud of you too, Carl, because I know God values perseverance too. He was always telling people and churches in the Bible that he liked their perseverance."

"I never thought about that before," Carl said softly. He looked at his father's eyes in the rearview mirror. Dad was watching the road. "Hey, Dad?" he said. Dad looked at his son in the mirror. "Thanks for not letting me give up."

TO DISCUSS: In today's Bible reading, why did the Lord praise the church at Ephesus? How does that show what he values? Do you think perseverance is a good thing? Do you try to work hard and not give up? Can you give an example of when you persevered?

TO PRAY: "Lord, thank you for the times when you wouldn't allow us to give up."

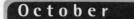

8 Kari's Question

GOD VALUES PERSEVERANCE BECAUSE GOD PERSEVERES WITH US.

Bible Reading of the Day: Read Deuteronomy 31:1-6.
Verse of the Day: *"[Love] always protects, always trusts, always hopes, always perseveres" (1 Corinthians 13:7, NIV).*

Mom tucked Kari into bed and sat down beside her on the edge of the bed.

"Mom," Kari asked, "do you ever get tired of being a mommy?"

Mom raised her eyebrows at her daughter's interesting question—particularly since she asked at the end of a day that had been hard and tiring for Mom. "Well," Mom answered honestly, "sometimes I get tired of cooking dinner and doing laundry and making beds."

"I thought you liked doing those things," Kari said innocently.

Mom chuckled. "No, sweetheart," she said. "Sometimes those tasks are harder than at other times; but doing laundry and making beds are never my first choices of what I'd like to do."

"Then why do you do those things?"

"Because they need to be done," Mom answered. "But even when I'm tired of doing all that, I'm still not tired of being your mommy."

"You're not?" Kari asked.

Mom shook her head as she played with a strand of Kari's hair. "Kari," she said softly, "do you think God ever gets tired of being God?"

Kari's mouth dropped open as if she were surprised by the question. Her forehead wrinkled in thought, and she twitched her nose as she always did when she was thinking. "I think he gets tired of us doing bad things and saying bad words," she said in her tiny voice. She paused for a moment before continuing. "But I don't think he gets tired of being God."

Mom smiled and nodded. "I don't think so, either," she said, "and even if he does, he won't give up because he loves us. The Bible says that love always perseveres."

"What does that mean?" Kari asked.

Mom touched noses with her daughter. "It means God will never leave us or fail us. He'll never get tired of being God and give up."

"I'm glad," Kari said, "because if he did get tired, who would take his place?"

"I don't know," Mom said, laughing. "I don't know."

 TO DISCUSS: The verse Mom referred to in the story above is the "Verse of the Day." What are some other ways of saying that God perseveres? (He'll never give up, never leave us, never forsake us, never fail us.) How does it make you feel to know that God perseveres for you and with you?

TO PRAY: "Thank you, God, for never giving up on us."

9 Janice's Maturity

PERSEVERANCE PRODUCES MATURITY.

Bible Reading of the Day: Read James 1:2-4, 12.
Verse of the Day: *"Consider it pure joy, my brothers, whenever you face trials of many kinds, because you know that the testing of your faith develops perseverance" (James 1:2-3 NIV).*

"Don't pay any attention to them," Chrissy told the girl in the wheelchair. She glared at the group of kids in the corner of the cafeteria who had been making fun of the new girl. "Just because this is a Christian school doesn't mean the kids are all Christians."

The girl smiled. "Oh, I know!" she said. "By the way, my name's Janice."

"I'm Chrissy." Chrissy walked down the hallway beside her new friend. "It must be hard being in that wheelchair all the time," she said.

Janice shrugged. "Sometimes. I've gotten used to it."

"How long have you been, you know, in the wheelchair?"

"Since I was little. I've got a bone disease," Janice answered.

"That's too bad," Chrissy said. They continued down the hallway, slowly. *She's so nice,* Chrissy thought. *And normal.* She thought of the kids who had made fun of Janice in the cafeteria. "Do kids make fun of you a lot?"

Janice shook her head. "Not too much. Mostly they avoid me, like they're afraid to look at me or talk to me. But that doesn't bother me too much. . . . I mean, I'd probably be just like them if I weren't in a wheelchair."

They had arrived at Janice's classroom. Janice nodded toward the room. "I'm going to get ready for my next class," she said. "Thanks for walking with me."

Chrissy smiled and turned toward her own room. "Sure," she said. "See you later." As she walked down the hall, she saw Mr. Sanders, one of her teachers.

"I see you've met Janice," Mr. Sanders said.

Chrissy smiled. "Yeah," she said. "She's pretty cool."

"She is, isn't she?" Mr. Sanders said.

"Yeah," Chrissy answerd. "She seems so . . . I don't know, grown up for her age."

Mr. Sanders nodded. "She's had to do a lot of growing up because of her handicap. She's been through a lot of tough times, things that would shatter a lot of people's faith. But she's stood up under it really well, and I think it's made her more mature than a lot of kids her age."

"Yeah," Chrissy said, a hint of admiration in her voice. "I hope some of her rubs off on me."

 TO DISCUSS: Why do you think Chrissy admired Janice? Do you think Janice's perseverance had anything to do with her maturity? If so, how? The Bible says perseverance will make you "mature and complete, not lacking anything" (James 1:4, NIV). What do you think that means? Has your faith ever been tested? If so, tell about it. What should we do when our faith is tested?

TO PRAY: "Lord, help us to persevere toward maturity in Christ."

10 Jamal's Character

PERSEVERANCE PRODUCES CHARACTER.

Bible Reading of the Day: Read Romans 5:1-5.
Verse of the Day: *"We also rejoice in our sufferings, because we know that suffering produces perseverance; perseverance, character; and character, hope" (Romans 5:3-4, NIV).*

"I've got an idea!" Lucas announced. He stood beside his bike with his friends Bobby and Jamal, who sat on their bikes. "Let's sneak into Old Man Potter's place and swipe some apples!"

"Old Man Potter's got a gun," Bobby countered.

"Are you scared?" Lucas asked.

"No, but . . ."

"I'm not going," Jamal said, matter-of-factly.

"Why not?" Lucas said. "Are you scared too?"

Jamal shook his head. "No," he answered. "I just don't steal stuff, that's all. You should know that, Lucas."

"Well, I'm going," Lucas announced. He turned to Bobby. "Are you with me?"

Bobby looked from Lucas to Jamal, hesitating.

Jamal turned the handlebars of his bike away from Lucas. "Come on, Bobby," he said. He started riding away as Lucas started shouting, calling him "Chicken."

Jamal had only pedaled for a few moments when he heard Bobby.

"Wait up!" Bobby said. Jamal braked his bike and turned to wait.

Bobby was panting, out of breath, when he pulled his bike alongside Jamal's. Jamal nodded to his friend without saying anything. As he started to go, Bobby stopped him.

"Wait," Bobby said, still panting. "How'd you stand up to Lucas so easy?"

"Oh, that," Jamal said. He shrugged as if it was no big deal. "I've said no to Lucas so many times, I don't even have to try anymore."

"But isn't it hard?" Bobby asked. "He makes you feel so . . . so dumb if you don't do what he says."

Again Jamal shrugged. "I guess it was hard the first few times. But I just kept saying no. I said it, no matter how much he made fun of me or got mad at me." He smiled. "He'd probably have a heart attack if I said yes to any of his ideas now!"

"I bet he would!" Bobby agreed, as he and Jamal turned their bikes and started pedaling toward home.

 TO DISCUSS: How did Jamal get good at saying no to Lucas? How did Jamal's perseverance lead to the development of character (the strength to do right things)? What might have happened if Jamal hadn't kept saying no to wrong choices?

 TO PRAY: "Lord, no one likes to suffer. But you tell us in your Word that suffering produces perseverance, which produces character. May each of us reflect Christ in our character."

11 Sammy's Success

PERSEVERANCE PRODUCES SUCCESS.

Bible Reading of the Day: Read Hebrews 11:24-27.

Verse of the Day: *"Moses kept right on going because he kept his eyes on the one who is invisible" (Hebrews 11:27).*

Sammy gritted his teeth and fought to hold back the tears as he sat on the bottom row of bleacher seats in the school gymnasium. He had failed—for the fifth time—to climb the rope in his physical education class. He was the only kid in his class who couldn't climb the rope.

As the teacher dismissed the rest of the class, they all jogged by Sammy. Some made unkind comments, like Wade, who said, "Hey, Sammy, what's it like to be a sissy?"

Sammy's friend Brad said, "Don't worry, Sammy. It's no big deal."

But it was a big deal to Sammy. He waited for his classmates to disappear into the shower room before walking over to the teacher.

"Mr. Jacobs?" he said. The teacher turned to face him. "Can I . . . can you . . . is there any way I can get extra practice climbing the rope?"

Mr. Jacobs paused to consider Sammy's request. "You don't have to do that, Sammy," he said finally. "We won't be doing any more rope climbing since we're not doing fitness tests anymore."

"I know that. I just want to pass the rope test."

The teacher looked like he was about to say no. At last he said, "I'll tell you what, Sammy. I'll leave the ropes up for one more week. How's that sound?"

"Thanks, Mr. Jacobs," Sammy said. He turned toward the shower room with a tiny smile on his face.

Every day that week Sammy went to the gym after school. He hung on the ropes until his hands were red and sweat broke out on his forehead. After three days, he could still only pull himself a few feet off the floor. His shoulders and arms were so tired, he felt like giving up. When he tried to climb on the fourth day, his arms were so tired he could barely hold the rope. He positioned his feet to hold his weight so he could rest for a moment. Then he took a deep breath and pushed his body up the rope with his legs.

Suddenly, Sammy's eyes opened wide. He looked down at the position of his feet on the rope. He realized that he had been trying to *pull* himself up the rope with his arms instead of *pushing* his body's weight with his legs! He climbed all the way to the knot at the top of the rope, then descended. He had done it! He had climbed the rope.

He pumped his right arm in the air. "Yes!" he cried. "Yyyyes!"

TO DISCUSS: Do you know how many times Moses had to visit Pharaoh before the Egyptian king let the Israelites go? (Ten; see Exodus 7–12.) Do you think Moses might have felt like giving up? What did both Moses and Sammy do that helped them succeed? Do you think the reward was worth the effort to Moses? To Sammy? According to Hebrews 11:27, how can you keep "right on going" when it's hard?

TO PRAY: "Lord God, help us learn that we need to persevere if we want to succeed."

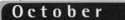

12 Good Fear

WHY DOES THE BIBLE TELL US TO FEAR GOD?

Bible Reading of the Day: Read 1 Samuel 12:1, 14-18.
Verse of the Day: *"But be sure to fear the Lord and serve him faithfully with all your heart; consider what great things he has done for you"* *(1 Samuel 12:24, NIV).*

"Dad, I don't understand something," Trevor said as he helped his dad unload suitcases from the car. They had just arrived at Trevor's cousins' house for a weekend visit. "Why does the Bible tell us to fear God? I mean, God loves us, right?"

Dad nodded as he and Trevor passed Trevor's little brother, Kyle. Kyle stood nose-to-nose with B. J., his cousins' St. Bernard. "Don't worry, Kyle," Dad said, as Kyle faced the hairy beast with wide eyes, "he's gentle. He won't hurt you. Go ahead, pet him."

Kyle tentatively stroked the big dog's fur. By the time Dad and Trevor had reached the porch with the suitcases, Kyle had wrapped his arms around B. J.'s neck.

Dad turned as he and Trevor set down the suitcases inside the house. "I haven't forgotten your question, Trev," he said. "We're supposed to fear God *like the Bible says.* Some people don't fear God at all. They think he's like a senile old grandfather who will let them get away with whatever they want. Other people forget that God loves them. They fear him as if he were a mean old dictator."

Suddenly, Trevor and Dad heard a cry outside. They ran for the door and saw Kyle pressed against the car door, crying. Uncle Dave held B. J.'s collar.

"What happened?" Dad asked.

"Everything's OK," Uncle Dave explained. "Kyle was petting B. J. when he started running toward the car." Dave shrugged. "B. J. is a loving dog, but he doesn't like it when people run away from him. So B. J. trotted after Kyle and growled at him. Of course, that scared Kyle—didn't it, little buddy?" Kyle nodded.

Dad knelt on the pavement beside Kyle. "B. J. didn't want to hurt you, Son; he wants to be your friend. He'll probably even lick your face if you let him."

Kyle smiled shyly. "He already did," he said.

Dad winked. "Just be careful not to run away from him, OK?"

Moments later, Kyle was playing with B. J. again. Dad and Trevor returned to their task of unpacking the car.

"Now," Dad said, "you were saying you don't understand what it means to fear God."

"I think I do now, Dad." Trevor watched B. J. lavishing love on little Kyle. "I think I do."

 TO DISCUSS: What do you think helped Trevor understand what it means to fear God? How do you think the fear of God is like Kyle's "fear" of B. J.? Do you think God wants us to fear him so we won't "run away" from him? Do you think we can love God and fear him too? If not, why not? If so, how?

TO PRAY: "Awesome God, we respect you and want to serve you faithfully."

13 Uncle Jack and God

WE KNOW WE CAN TRUST GOD'S COMMANDS BECAUSE WE KNOW WE CAN TRUST GOD.

Bible Reading of the Day: Read Psalm 78:1-7.

Verse of the Day: *"Trust in the Lord and do good" (Psalm 37:3, NIV).*

"I have to go to bed early tonight," Melissa told her mother, "'cause Uncle Jack's taking me fishing tomorrow."

Mom tucked the bedcovers around her daughter. "Oh?" she said. "Is that so?"

Melissa nodded solemnly. "He said we have to leave the house when it's still dark outside!" she said, obviously excited by the prospect of leaving on a fishing trip before sunrise.

Mom sat down on the side of the bed. "What makes you think Uncle Jack's going to take you fishing tomorrow?" she asked, with a teasing tone in her voice.

"Because he said so!"

"But why do you believe what Uncle Jack says?" Mom asked, a serious look on her face.

"Well, because," Melissa answered, as if ending all discussion.

"Because why?" Mom pressed.

Melissa sighed dramatically. "Because Uncle Jack wouldn't say we were going fishing and then not take me fishing!"

Mom nodded. "You're right," she said. "He wouldn't." She picked Melissa up and set her down in her lap. She squeezed her daughter in a bear hug. "You know that you can trust what Uncle Jack says because you trust Uncle Jack, right?"

Melissa smiled, nodded, and returned her mother's hug.

"Well, I want you to know the same thing is true of God, Melissa," Mom said. "You can trust him. He's a wonderful God, a God who loves you and would never do anything to hurt you."

Melissa closed her eyes and snuggled cozily in Mom's lap.

"And," Mom continued, "because you can trust God, you can trust his commands too. When God says to do something, or not to do something, you can believe that his command is good, because he is good. Do you understand?"

Mom waited for an answer from Melissa, but no answer came. She lifted her daughter's head and looked at her face. Melissa had fallen asleep. Mom kissed her and gently laid her on the bed. "Sleep tight," she whispered. "And dream of catching lots of fish!"

TO DO: Parents, tell your children a story from your experience (keep it short!) that illustrates why you trust God and his commands.

TO PRAY: "We know from experience that we can trust you, Lord. But sometimes we forget those past experiences. Remind us, Lord, that you are trustworthy."

14 Hide 'n' Peek

WE DON'T HAVE TO WONDER WHAT'S RIGHT OR WRONG; GOD HAS MADE BOTH CLEAR.

Bible Reading of the Day: Read Romans 12:14-16.
Verse of the Day: *"All of you, clothe yourselves with humility toward one another, because, 'God opposes the proud but gives grace to the humble'"* (1 Peter 5:5, NIV).

"Quick! Hide!" Lindsey pushed Tracy's head below the shelves of the music and video store and pulled Kara down to the floor by the arm.

"What's going on?" Kara whispered as she crouched behind the racks of CDs.

"Yeah," Tracy said in a loud voice, "would you please let go of my head?"

"Shh!" Lindsey said. "Be quiet and stay down."

"Why?" Tracy said, standing up straight, unconcerned with Lindsey's warnings.

"Will you please cut it out?" Lindsey hissed, pulling Tracy back down into a crouching position behind the rack. "She'll see you!"

"Who?" Tracy asked. She popped up again to look over the rack, forcing Lindsey to tackle her by the legs. The two girls hit the floor in a heap, laughing.

"Who are we hiding from?" Kara whispered as her two friends giggled on the floor.

"That's what I want to know," Tracy said, her voice still loud.

"Shh!" Lindsey repeated. "Andrea Peters," she answered at last, nodding toward the entrance to the store, which was hidden from their view. "That weird girl from church."

"Why are we hiding?" Tracy asked.

"Because," Lindsey answered, "if she sees us, she'll come over and talk!"

"So?" Tracy said and Kara echoed.

"Come on," Lindsey whined. "She's *weird*. I don't want to be seen with her."

Tracy shook her head. "How can you be that way, Lindsey?" she asked.

"How can *I* . . . ?" Lindsey glared at her friend. "I just don't want to hang around with Andrea Peters. There's nothing wrong with that!"

Tracy glared back. "Yes, there is!" she said. "It's called being conceited. You think you're too good for her. Well, maybe you're too good for her, but I'm not." Tracy jumped up from the floor, dusted off her jeans, and stomped away.

"Tracy, wait!" Lindsey hissed. She reached out an arm to stop her friend, but Tracy was already out of reach. She and Kara watched as Tracy walked up to Andrea and smiled without looking back at Lindsey and Kara.

Lindsey drew a big breath and sighed. It was too late to say anything to Andrea now, unless she swallowed her pride. She didn't want to do that, so she and Kara just watched as Tracy and Andrea left the store together.

TO DISCUSS: Was Lindsey right when she said, "I just don't want to hang around with Andrea Peters. There's nothing wrong with that"? Why or why not? What does being conceited mean? Do we have to decide whether being conceited is right or wrong? Why or why not?

TO PRAY: "Lord, help us remember that excusing our behavior never makes it right."

15 Dad's Secret

GOD COMMANDS US TO BE HUMBLE, NOT PROUD.

Bible Reading of the Day: Read Ephesians 4:1-3.

Verse of the Day: *"All of you, clothe yourselves with humility toward one another, because, 'God opposes the proud but gives grace to the humble'"* (1 Peter 5:5, NIV).

"My dad's better than your dad!" little Keith said. He sat on his tricycle in front of the neighbor's house. His friend Rachel blocked his way.

"Is not!" Rachel countered. "My dad can beat up your dad!"

"No he can't!" Keith said. "And your bike is old and ugly. Mine is better!"

"Is not!" Rachel repeated. "My bike can go faster than your bike!"

"Oh yeah?" Keith argued.

"Yeah!" Rachel said. Then, as if to prove her point, she turned her handlebars and headed down the sidewalk. "I can beat you to the corner."

"No fair!" Keith shouted without moving. "You had a head start!" Suddenly, he saw a shadow on the sidewalk. He turned and saw his dad standing beside him.

"What was that all about?" Dad asked.

"I was just telling Rachel that my dad's better than hers." Keith looked up, smiling.

Dad squatted beside Keith. "And what did Rachel say?"

Keith's smile disappeared. "She said her dad can beat you up."

Dad chuckled and placed a hand on Keith's shoulder. "Maybe he could," he said with a wink. "But that's not as important to me as what you said."

"You mean when I said you're better than her dad?"

Dad nodded. "And when you said your bike was better than hers. Do you know what you were doing when you said those things?"

"No," Keith said quietly.

"You were bragging, Son," Dad said. "And do you know what God thinks about bragging?" Keith shook his head. "He doesn't like it very much," Dad answered. "In fact, God says we should be humble. That means we shouldn't brag, and we shouldn't act like we're better or more important than someone else."

Keith looked up and saw Rachel racing back up the sidewalk toward him. "Do I have to tell Rachel I'm sorry?" he asked.

"I think you should," Dad said, smiling. He stood and stretched his back.

"OK," Keith said. "But I still think you're the best dad in the world."

Dad laughed and rubbed Keith's head. "I'm glad you feel that way," he said, "but we'll make that our secret, OK?"

"OK," Keith answered.

 TO DISCUSS: Do you know people who try to act as if they are more important than everyone else? How do you think that makes others feel? How do you think it makes God feel? Which is better, pride or humility? Why?

 TO PRAY: "Lord, forgive us for bragging and for trying to act important. We want to please you by our words and our actions."

16 Pop Go Dad's Knees!

GOD COMMANDS HUMILITY BECAUSE GOD VALUES HUMILITY.

Bible Reading of the Day: Read Isaiah 66:1-2.
Verse of the Day: *"This is what the Lord says . . . 'I will bless those who have humble and contrite hearts, who tremble at my word'" (Isaiah 66:1-2).*

"Amen!" Tad said as he lifted his head from his nightly prayers.

"Amen!" said Mom and Dad in unison as they knelt on either side of him.

"All right," Mom said. "Into bed."

Tad jumped up and scampered under the covers of his bed.

As Dad stood, the three of them looked at each other in surprise when his knees made a loud popping noise.

"Does that hurt, Daddy?" Tad asked.

Dad smiled. "No," he said. "It just means I'm getting old."

"That's OK, Daddy," Tad said in a voice of comfort. "You were already old, anyway."

Mom and Dad laughed together, and Dad held out a hand to help Mom get off her knees. As she stood with an exaggerated groan, Tad asked, "Mom, Dad—why do we kneel when we pray?"

"That's a good question, Son," Dad said. "We don't have to kneel to pray. We can pray when we're walking or lying down or even while we're driving a car."

"But we kneel whenever we can," Mom added, "because it's a way of showing our respect to God. It's a way of humbling ourselves before God."

"What? What does that mean?" Tad asked.

"To be humble means not to be proud," Mom explained. "It means to admit that you're not the greatest or most important person in the world."

"God is!" Tad said.

"That's right," Dad said, nodding. "That's why God says we should be humble, because when we're humble, we admit that he's greater than we are. And we admit that other people are important too."

"God likes it when we're humble," Mom said. "That's why he commands us to be humble, because humility is something God likes."

"So we kneel when we pray to show God that we're humble," Tad said.

Mom nodded. "We kneel before him because he's our King, and kneeling shows how important we think he is."

"And it shows how old Daddy's knees are too!" Tad added.

Dad chuckled. "Yes, it does," he admitted. "It sure does."

TO DO: Instead of praying while seated or standing today, kneel in a circle and hold hands as you humble yourselves before God and ask him to teach you humility. Be sure to listen for popping knees as you all stand up!

TO PRAY: "Lord God, we admit that we sometimes fail to act humbly. We sometimes forget that you are God and we are your creatures. Forgive us, Lord, and remove any hidden seeds of pride from our lives."

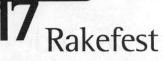17 Rakefest

GOD VALUES HUMILITY BECAUSE GOD IN CHRIST HUMBLED HIMSELF.

Bible Reading of the Day: Read Matthew 11:28-30.
Verse of the Day: *"Take my yoke upon you. Let me teach you, because I am humble and gentle, and you will find rest for your souls"* *(Matthew 11:29).*

"All right, gang," the youth director told the kids who had gathered for their church's annual Youth Group Rakefest, "remember that you not only represent our church, but you represent Jesus Christ, too. Be sure you do what Jesus would do, and act the way Jesus would act." He read Matthew 11:28-30, then prayed. When he said amen, the church youth group erupted in cheers.

"I love doing this," Amie told Martha as they piled into a station wagon with their rakes. "It's so much fun."

"I do too," Martha agreed. "I love seeing the looks on the old people's faces when we rake their yards for free."

Amie, Martha, and three other kids were driven by one of the kids' parents to a nearby neighborhood. They had orders to stop at a house, across the street from First Church, their church's rival, a church that always seemed to beat their church in volleyball and softball, and even Sunday school contests.

They spent over an hour raking the leaves for the elderly woman who lived across the street from the church, then went on to other yards. When they gathered together back at church, their youth leader asked them how it went.

"It was so much fun!" Amie said.

"Yeah," Martha agreed. Then she laughed and added, "After we got done raking the first yard, the lady who lived there invited us in for some cider."

"Yeah," Amie said. "And she kept thanking us and telling us how wonderful we were and how much she appreciated all us kids from First Church!"

"She thought you were from First Church?" the youth leader said. "What did she say when you told her you were from our church?"

Martha and Amie exchanged glances. "We didn't," they said, smiling.

"Why not?" the youth leader asked.

The girls shrugged. "You said to do what Jesus would do," Martha said.

"We decided that Jesus would have been humble enough to let First Church get the credit," said Amie. "So we didn't say anything!"

Amie and Martha grinned. The youth leader shook his head in amazement. "So," he said in a voice tinged with wonder, "you kids *do* listen to what I say."

"Sometimes!" Martha and Amie answered together, then laughed.

 TO DISCUSS: God values humility because he humbled himself in the person of Jesus Christ. Do you think what Amie and Martha did was good? Why or why not? How can you let Jesus teach you to be humble and gentle today?

 TO PRAY: "Lord, when we forget to be humble, remind us of Jesus' humble example."

18 The Dangers of Pride

PRIDE CLOSES YOUR HEART TO GOD; HUMILITY OPENS YOUR HEART TO GOD.

Bible Reading of the Day: Read Deuteronomy 8:6-14.

Verse of the Day: *"Do not become proud . . . and forget the Lord your God" (Deuteronomy 8:14).*

Pastor White locked the front doors of the church behind him as his family waited for him on the steps.

"That was a good sermon, Dad," Stephen said.

"Yeah!" his sister, Mary, agreed. "I liked the stories you told."

Dad chuckled. "Well, thank the Lord."

They walked slowly along the sidewalk between the church and their house.

"Why do you always say 'thank the Lord' when someone tells you they liked your sermon?" Stephen asked.

Dad looked at Stephen. "You've noticed that?" he asked. Dad leaned over and lifted Mary into his arms. "I do that for a very good reason," he said.

"When I was just a young man," Dad continued, "before either of you were even born, I went to school to become a preacher."

"That's where you met Mommy, isn't it?" Mary asked.

Dad nodded. "That's right. And when Mom and I arrived at our first church, I was determined to preach the best sermon those people had ever heard on my very first Sunday."

"Did you?" Mary asked.

"Well, I thought I did," Dad answered, smiling. "I was sure that I was preaching a sermon they would never forget, and I was pretty proud of the job I did."

He set Mary down on the porch of their house and opened the door for his wife and children. Then he followed them in.

"After I finished," Dad said, "I almost ran to the back of the church to shake people's hands and receive their congratulations for the wonderful job I did. The first person I met was an old woman—everybody in the church called her 'Grandma Andrews'—who said, 'Pastor, that was some mighty fine preaching.' I smiled and thanked her, and then she leaned real close and said, 'But God can use a humble preacher more than the best sermon in the world.'"

"Did she really say that?" Stephen asked.

Dad nodded. "She sure did. And that's why, ever since then, I try to please God instead of impressing people. And I try to give him the glory instead of taking it myself."

TO DISCUSS: What does today's Bible reading say is one of the dangers of comfort and pride? Can you think of other dangers? Which do you think God can use more, pride or humility? Which do you think draws you closer to God?

TO PRAY: "Guard us, Lord, against pride and other flaming arrows of the enemy."

19 Obstruction Site

PRIDE OBSTRUCTS THE FLOW OF GOD'S BLESSING TO US; HUMILITY OPENS WINDOWS OF PRAYER AND BLESSING.

Bible Reading of the Day: Read 2 Chronicles 7:11-14.

Verse of the Day: *"Then if my people who are called by my name will humble themselves and pray and seek my face and turn from their wicked ways, I will hear from heaven and will forgive their sins and heal their land" (2 Chronicles 7:14).*

"Are you girls all packed for the youth retreat?" Mom called to Dawn and Leslie.

The girls appeared, each lugging a duffel bag. "Yeah, we're ready," Dawn said.

"Don't forget your music," Mom said. Their church youth pastor had asked Dawn and Leslie to sing two duets during the weekend.

"Yeah, if we forgot it, Pastor might have to ask Belinda to sing!" Dawn said.

Leslie laughed. "That would be awful!"

Mom opened her mouth to speak but didn't. Then she pointed toward the family room. "Why don't you girls watch a little TV until it's time to leave?"

Dawn and Leslie dumped their duffel bags by the sliding glass doors and flopped onto the couch. They were soon engrossed in a TV program.

Suddenly Mom appeared with a vacuum cleaner and started vacuuming. The vacuum cleaner filled the room with noise and disturbed the image on the TV screen.

"Mom! Can't you wait till we leave to do that?"

Mom turned off the vacuum cleaner. "Is this bothering you?" she asked sweetly.

"Yeah," Dawn said. "It, like, messes up the picture, and we can't hear anything."

"I see," Mom said. She shrugged. "I guess TV is more important than your retreat."

"What?" Dawn said. "What are you talking about?"

Mom sat in a chair opposite the couch. "You're worried about the vacuum cleaner interfering with the television show you're watching," she said. "But you should be worried about your attitudes interfering with this weekend."

"Huh?" Dawn asked, looking puzzled. Leslie also looked puzzled.

Mom's voice was gentle. "I think it's great that Pastor asked you girls to sing this weekend. But make sure your pride about your musical talent doesn't interfere with what God wants to do for you this weekend. Pride can choke off the blessings God wants to pour out on you. But if you go to this retreat with a humble spirit, it will be much easier for God to speak to you and bless you."

"You're right, Mom," Dawn said. She looked at Leslie. "We don't want anything to mess up this weekend. I guess we were getting a little snotty." She turned off the TV. "You can go ahead and vacuum in here. We don't need to watch anything."

"Oh, that's OK," Mom said, smiling. "I just vacuumed in here yesterday anyway!"

 TO DISCUSS: What four things did God tell his people to do if they wanted him to forgive them and heal their land? Why do you think God blesses humble people? Do you need to humble yourself in any way?

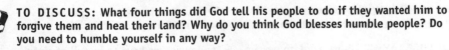 **TO PRAY:** "Lord, we want your blessing and healing on our nation. We want to persevere in humbling ourselves and seeking you."

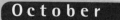

20 Quarterback Jack

PRIDE INVITES DESTRUCTION; HUMILITY LEADS TO WISDOM.

Bible Reading of the Day: Read Proverbs 11:2; 16:18-19.
Verse of the Day: *"Pride goes before destruction, and haughtiness before a fall" (Proverbs 16:18).*

"Come on, Coach!" Jack screamed from his seat on the bench. "Put me in! I'm a better quarterback than Glenn!"

The coach didn't seem to hear Jack's words, but the other players did.

"Give it up, Jack," said Jason. "Coach isn't gonna put you in, all right?"

"But I'm better than Glenn," Jack insisted. "He just won't give me a chance!"

Even Glenn, the team's starting quarterback, heard Jack from the sidelines. He threw an incomplete pass at third down and jogged off the field as the rest of the team stayed to punt the ball to the other team.

"You think you can do a better job?" Glenn asked Jack.

"Yeah, I do," Jack answered, jutting his chin out proudly.

A few moments later, Jack looked up from his seat on the bench and was surprised to see Coach standing in front of him.

"You want a chance?" he asked Jack. "Put your helmet on and warm up."

Jack jumped up from the bench and slid his helmet on over his head. He picked up a ball and asked Jason to toss with him. Jason shook his head. Jack asked several other guys on the bench to help him warm up, but they all said no.

Finally, the coach called his name and Jack raced onto the field. On his first play, rather than handing the ball to his running back, Jack tried to run it himself and was tackled without gaining a yard. On the next play, he tried to pass, but the ball fell to the ground before it reached the receiver. At third down, Jack threw the ball again. This time it was caught—by a member of the other team, who ran the ball past Jack across the goal line for a touchdown.

Jack stomped back to the sidelines after his unsuccessful stint as the quarterback. His coach came over after he dropped his helmet on the ground and sat on the bench.

"You made only one mistake out there, Jack," Coach said.

Jack looked at the man in disbelief. "Only one? I made a bunch of mistakes!"

"I know," Coach said. "But they were all related to your one mistake."

"Which was . . . ?" Jack asked.

"Thinking too much of yourself, and not enough of your teammates," Coach said. "A proud young man like you is a disaster just waiting to happen, Son. I hope the next time you get a chance, you'll remember that."

As Coach walked away, Jack sighed. "I will," he said seriously.

 TO DISCUSS: What was Jack's big mistake? Coach said, "A proud [person] . . . is a disaster just waiting to happen." Do you think that's true? If so, why?

TO PRAY: "Help us, Lord, to beware any tendencies we have to be full of sinful pride."

21 Nature Hike

THE HOLY SPIRIT LEADS US INTO ALL TRUTH.

Bible Reading of the Day: Read John 14:15-17.
Verse of the Day: *"I will ask the Father, and he will give you another Counselor, who will never leave you. He is the Holy Spirit, who leads into all truth" (John 14:16-17).*

Deanna sat down on a log by the trail.

"Come on," said her friend Joyce. "We're supposed to stay with the group."

"I know," Deanna answered. "I'm just going to rest for a minute. I can catch up."

"But our leader said we should never lose sight of him," Joyce protested.

Deanna waved a hand. "Don't worry," she said. "I can catch up."

Joyce shrugged, then jogged to catch up with the short line of nature hikers.

Deanna looked all around from her comfortable seat on the log. She knew that the hike leader had warned them to stay close together and close to him, but she liked doing things her own way and at her own pace. She liked sitting in the woods alone. Being surrounded by the sounds of the birds and the leaves blowing in the trees was so different from being in the city.

Suddenly Deanna jumped up. She could hear nothing but the sounds of the birds and the leaves blowing in the trees! The noise created by her friends and the hike leader had disappeared! She dashed up the path where she had seen Joyce go, and soon came to a fork in it. Three paths joined together. Though she peered carefully down each one, she couldn't tell which path her friends had taken.

"I wish I'd never sat down," she said. "I should have stayed close to the hike director, like I was supposed to." She panicked as she thought over which path to take. Finally, she made her choice and ran down the one to her right, hoping that it was the right choice. Soon the trees seemed to part in front of her, and she saw a gravel path. "Thank you, God!" she said. She recognized the path back to the camp. After a while, she found the rest of the kids and breathlessly fell into step behind Joyce.

"Deanna's back!" Joyce called to the hike leader.

The hike leader stopped everyone, then walked back to where Deanna stood blushing with relief and embarrassment. "Deanna," he asked, "where were you?"

"I . . . I kinda stopped back there, and then I couldn't see you anymore and I didn't know which way to go."

The hike director placed a gentle hand on Deanna's shoulder. "Always remember," he said, "that the best way to know which way to go is to stay with someone who knows the way. OK?"

Deanna smiled and nodded and silently vowed never to forget that.

TO DISCUSS: How is following the Holy Spirit like following a hike director on a hike? How can we stay close to the Holy Spirit?

TO PRAY: "Holy Spirit, keep us close to you. Guard us from wandering away on our own."

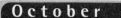

22 Love Notes

GOD'S COMMANDS ARE ONE OF THE WAYS HE EXPRESSES HIS LOVE FOR US.

Bible Reading of the Day: Read John 14:18-21.
Verse of the Day: *"Those who obey my commandments are the ones who love me" (John 14:21).*

Teddy opened his lunchbox and took out a sandwich, a plastic bag of cookies, an apple, and a juice box.

"What's that?" his friend Kyle, who sat next to him, asked. Kyle pointed at a yellow note stuck inside the lid of Teddy's lunchbox.

Teddy smiled. "Oh, that's just a note from my mom."

"Why?"

"She just likes to write notes," Teddy answered. He pulled the note off and showed it to Kyle. "It says, 'I love you.'"

"I know what it says," Kyle said. "I can read, you know."

Teddy and Kyle ate in silence for a few moments. Finally, Kyle spoke again.

"The only time my mom writes notes to me is when she wants me to remember something. She'll say, 'Wear your gloves home,' or, 'Feed the dog,' or stuff like that."

"My mom does that sometimes too," Teddy said.

"But my mom never writes 'I love you' notes like your mom does," Kyle said.

"Sure she does," Teddy suggested.

"No, she doesn't."

"Yes, she does. Like when her note says to wear your gloves home. She wants you to wear your gloves because she loves you, right?"

Kyle wrinkled his nose as if Teddy wasn't making sense. Teddy continued.

"If she didn't love you, she wouldn't much care if you wore your gloves or not," he explained. "But if you caught a cold, that would make her sad, because she loves you."

Kyle's nose wrinkled again.

"Sure," Teddy insisted. "It's just like what my mom says about God's commands. She says she tells me what to do or not do because she loves me, just like God gives us commands because he loves us. I bet your mom is the same way."

"Maybe," Kyle said.

"I've got an idea!" Teddy said.

"What?" Kyle asked.

"Why don't *you* write an 'I love you' note to your mom? Then maybe she'll write you one back!"

"Yeah," Kyle said. "That's a good idea."

 TO DO: God expresses his love to us in many ways. One of those ways is in the loving commands he gives to us. To demonstrate an expression of love, you could surprise other family members this week with love notes in surprising places (lunch boxes, briefcases, schoolbooks, the bathroom mirror, and so on).

 TO PRAY: "Thank you, Lord, for your immeasurable love. Help us to love others as you love us."

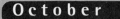

23 "Fewer than Five Day"

RIGHT CHOICES PAY OFF.

Bible Reading of the Day: Read Proverbs 9:9-12.
Verse of the Day: *"If you become wise, you will be the one to benefit. If you scorn wisdom, you will be the one to suffer"* (Proverbs 9:12).

"Hi, Pastor!" Joel called. He crossed the floor of the large fast-food restaurant and stood beside the table where Pastor Brown had just sat down with a tray on which stood a hamburger, fries, and soft drink.

"Hello, Joel," the pastor said. Surprise registered on his face, behind a broad smile. "What are you doing here in the middle of a school day?"

Joel's eyes sparkled. "Today's 'Fewer than Five Day,'" he said excitedly.

"'Fewer than Five Day'?" Pastor Brown echoed. "What's that?"

"Our school has a point system," Joel explained. He cast a glance behind him at his buddies, who were still waiting in a long line at the food counter. "If we get in trouble, we get a point; for some things—really bad things—we might get more than one point. Anyway, if we get too many points, we could be suspended or expelled."

"I see," the pastor said.

"But if we get fewer than five points in a semester," Joel continued, "we get a 'Fewer than Five Day.' Last spring, we got to watch a video . . . *during school hours!*"

Pastor Brown chuckled. "I see," he said. "And today you got to come to Hamburger Heaven because you had fewer than five points, right?"

"Yup," Joel said. He smiled proudly. "I don't have *any* points yet!"

"Well, congratulations," Pastor Brown said. "I'm glad to hear that, Joel. And you know what else? I want you to remember how much fun you're having right now."

"You do?" Joel said. "Why?"

"Because 'Fewer than Five Day' is just one of the ways that doing right, and behaving well, and being diligent pays off. It may not always have immediate rewards, but people who follow God and make wise choices usually enjoy a lot more good things than those who pursue evil and get themselves in trouble. That's something that will be true even after you finish school."

"Hey, Pastor," Joel said, glancing over his shoulder again at the line of his friends. He took a step or two away from the pastor's table and called back, "Maybe *you* should have a 'Fewer than Five Day!'"

Pastor lifted his hamburger to his mouth and prepared to take a large bite. "That's what I'm doing right now," he said with a wink.

TO DISCUSS: Who do you think has more fun: those who are always getting in trouble, or those who follow the rules? How does a person begin to be wise, according to today's Bible reading? Have you ever enjoyed any rewards for making right choices? Are you enjoying any rewards of right choices right now? If so, tell about them.

 TO PRAY: "Lord, thank you for the good things you bring to us when we make right choices."

24 Sticking to the Pattern

GOD'S CHARACTER IS THE PATTERN FOR EVERYTHING THAT IS GOOD AND RIGHT.

Bible Reading of the Day: Read Isaiah 46:3-5, 9-10.

Verse of the Day: *"Among the gods there is none like you, O Lord; no deeds can compare with yours" (Psalm 86:8, NIV).*

Even through the closed door of her sewing room, Mom could hear Becky shouting at her little brother.

Mom opened the door. "Becky!" she called. "Would you come here, please?" She heard Becky hurl a few final threats at her brother before stomping upstairs. Becky entered the sewing room and closed the door behind her.

"I need your help while I cut this pattern," Mom said softly. A large piece of fabric was spread on the carpet, and a dress pattern was pinned to the cloth.

Becky knelt by the pattern and held it as her mom started cutting.

"It sounds like you and your brother are having a little problem," Mom said.

"I knew you were going to talk to me about that," Becky answered. "I know I shouldn't yell at him like that, but he gets on my nerves! At least I'm not as bad as Fran," she said, referring to one of her friends. "She gets into fist fights with her brothers."

Mom cut around the pattern for a few moments without saying anything. Then she looked up at Becky with a smile. "I think this will make a nice winter coat for your father, don't you?"

Becky's gaze flitted from her mom's face to the pattern. "Mom," she said, "this is a *dress* pattern."

"Oh, I know. But I think I can make it into a nice coat."

"What are you talking about? You can't make a coat from this! It's the wrong pattern!"

"Mom locked her gaze onto her daughter and said, "If you can't make a coat from a dress pattern, what makes you think you *can* make right choices using the wrong pattern?"

"What?" Becky responded.

"You're trying to explain your behavior by saying at least you're not as bad as Fran; but Fran shouldn't be your pattern—God should be."

"Oh," Becky said, suddenly understanding. "I see what you mean. I shouldn't try to excuse my behavior by comparing it to Fran."

Mom nodded and smiled. "Because she's not your pattern for what's good and right—God is. *He's* the one you should compare your behavior to."

Becky smiled at her mom. "You didn't really need my help with this, did you?"

 TO DO: Copy the "Verse of the Day" onto an index card and place it in a prominent spot as a reminder that God is the standard for everything good and right.

 TO PRAY: "God, help us to remember that you are the only true pattern for what's good and right. Help us to compare our deeds to you and not try to excuse our behavior by comparing them to others."

25 That Thing You Do

LOVE IS RIGHT BECAUSE GOD IS LOVE.

Bible Reading of the Day: Read Psalm 145:8–13.

Verse of the Day: *"By this all men will know that you are my disciples, if you love one another" (John 13:35, NIV).*

"Hey," Joey said, "do that again!" Joey sat at Bridget's table in science class. Joey also lived two houses from Bridget's house and sometimes played with her brother.

"Do what again?" asked Bridget.

"You just did something with your mouth," Joey explained. "I've seen somebody else do that. Who is it?" he said, tapping his forehead as if he were trying to jar the memory loose from his brain.

"I don't know what you're talking about," Bridget said.

That evening at dinner, Bridget told her parents and brother about her conversation with Joey. As she talked, Mom and Dad exchanged smiles.

"What's so funny?" Bridget asked.

"We know exactly what Joey was talking about, don't we, dear?" Mom said to Dad.

Dad chuckled and nodded. "Joey's probably seen your brother do the same thing."

"What?" Bridget demanded. "Will somebody please tell me what you're talking about?"

"Actually, your father does it too," Mom added. "It's a little mannerism you got from your father. Sometimes when you chew or smile a certain way, your lip curls slightly; sort of an Elvis Presley kind of thing."

"No! Really?" Bridget said, laughing. "I do that too? I've seen Dad and Eli do it, but I didn't know I do it too."

Dad nodded. "I've had people tell me they knew you were my daughter because they saw you do that," he said.

"That reminds me of a Bible verse," Mom said.

"Oh, Mom," Eli complained. *"Everything* reminds you of a Bible verse."

Mom paid no attention to Eli's complaint, but turned to John 13:35. She read: "'By this all men will know that you are my disciples, if you love one another.' That's one trait I hope you'll both inherit from your Father—your *heavenly* Father."

"That's right," Dad said. "In fact, nothing would make your mom and me happier than to have you kids reflect God's nature the way your lip shows people that you're my kids!"

Bridget tried to stifle a giggle but couldn't. The others at the table pointed at her.

"See!" Dad said. "You're doing it again!"

 TO DO: On a sheet of paper, write the names of three or four people you see every day. Write beside each name at least one action you can take to show love to that person this week. Copy John 13:35 at the bottom and keep the paper in your pocket or purse as a reminder to love those people.

TO PRAY: "Lord, we want to show love for others in practical ways. Show us what to do this week."

26 Rat's Nest

TRUTH IS OF NO VALUE UNLESS IT IS OBEYED.

Bible Reading of the Day: Read James 1:19–25.
Verse of the Day: *"Be doers of the word, and not merely hearers who deceive themselves" (James 1:22, NRSV).*

Bronson was the last one in the family to arrive at the table for breakfast. As he entered the room, he saw that his two brothers and his parents were waiting for him. He sat down without saying a word, spread his paper napkin in his lap, and bowed his head to indicate that he was ready to pray.

"Bronson," Mom said, "did you even look at yourself in a mirror this morning?"

Bronson lifted his head and looked at Mom. "Yeah," he said, shrugging. "Why?"

Bronson's brothers started laughing.

"You must have still been asleep when you looked in the mirror," Dad suggested, "because your hair looks like a rat's nest." As Bronson reached up with a hand to smooth his hair down, Dad continued. "Son, why don't you make a trip to the bathroom, after we say grace, and apply a comb and a little water to your hair."

Bronson nodded. The family prayed, and when Bronson returned to the table, his appearance was much improved.

After they finished breakfast together, Dad reached for the Bible.

"I think I'll read some verses from the first chapter of James," he said, with a twinkle in his eye. He read James's words about God's commands. "'If you just listen and don't obey, it is like looking at your face in a mirror but doing nothing to improve your appearance.'"

Bronson smiled sheepishly as his father read, and his brothers elbowed each other and tried not to giggle. Dad smiled and continued reading. "'But if you keep looking steadily into God's perfect law—the law that sets you free—and if you do what it says and don't forget what you heard, then God will bless you for doing it.'" Dad closed the Bible. "Now," he said, looking around at his three sons, "what do those verses mean?"

"That we should comb our hair before coming to the breakfast table," Bronson's younger brother, Billy, said.

Dad smiled. "Not exactly," he said. "It says that it's not enough to *know* what God says to do; we must also *do* it. In other words, if we only learn God's commands and don't *obey* them, we're leaving the most important job undone."

Bronson smiled at his dad, eager to demonstrate that he was a good sport. "Like someone who looks in the mirror without combing his hair!"

 TO DO: Copy the verse of the day on several sheets of paper and tape a copy to every mirror in the house to remind everyone to learn God's commands *and* to obey them!

TO PRAY: "Give us a plan, Lord, that will help us be doers of the Word, and not hearers only."

27 Not by Might

WE CAN'T CONSISTENTLY MAKE RIGHT CHOICES IN OUR OWN STRENGTH.

Bible Reading of the Day: Read Psalm 44:1-8.
Verse of the Day: *"'Not by might nor by power, but by my Spirit,' says the Lord Almighty" (Zechariah 4:6, NIV).*

"Dad, can I run the buffer this time?" Erin asked. Erin's dad was the custodian at the school she attended. She often went with him on weekends to sweep and wax the floors.

"We'll see," he said. "But first we need to sweep and pick up." He and Erin walked around the room, picking up homework papers, candy wrappers, and other items the students had left behind. Erin picked up a multicolored hair "scrunchy." She walked toward the large plastic garbage can on wheels.

"You're not going to throw that away, are you?" Dad asked. "That should go in the lost-and-found box. Whoever owns it will want it back."

"I know who it belongs to," Erin said.

"Well, then, why don't you keep it and give it to her on Monday?"

"It belongs to Gabrielle," she said. "She's . . . well, she's just not very nice. I'll just put it in the lost-and-found box."

When the floor had been swept thoroughly, Dad mopped it and applied a coat of wax. After the wax dried, Erin begged her dad again to let her run the machine that buffed the floor to a brilliant shine. Dad plugged the machine in, and Erin held the handles. She wrestled the spinning base of the machine across the floor. After only a few moments, her arms were sore from her struggle against the machine.

Dad smiled when she stopped to take a break. "Pretty hard work, isn't it?"

Erin nodded. "I don't think I'm strong enough to do it," she said.

"You don't have to be strong," Dad said. "You just have to let the machine do the work. You're trying to steer the buffer by using your muscles. And you're right—you don't have the strength for that. But you can steer the buffer with one finger, if you don't try to 'muscle' it where you want to go." He demonstrated, lifting the handle gently when he wanted the buffer to move right, and lowering the handle when he wanted it to go left; the circular motion of the buffer's base did the work.

"You know, Erin," he said after his short demonstration, "it's not so different when there's someone who's unkind to you. You don't have the 'muscle' to love that person in your own strength." He pointed a finger at her chest. "As a Christian, you have God's Spirit living inside you. *He* can find ways to be kind to Gabrielle through you, if you're willing."

Erin nodded. "I guess I do wanna do the right thing," she said. "And I'm gonna need God's help to love Gabrielle—that's for sure!"

 TO DISCUSS: None of us is strong enough to make right choices all the time. That's why we need God's help. Do you have God's Spirit living inside you? How can you depend on God to make right choices through you?

 TO PRAY: "Lord, remind us that we can't do anything on our own. We need your Spirit."

28 No Trick to It

YOU CAN'T EXPECT TO MAGICALLY PULL RIGHT CHOICES OUT OF THIN AIR.

Bible Reading of the Day: Read Jude 20-21, 24-25.
Verse of the Day: *"But you, dear friends, must continue to build your lives on the foundation of your holy faith. And continue to pray as you are directed by the Holy Spirit" (Jude 20).*

"Why do I have to be grounded?" Chip asked his mom.

Mom smiled patiently. "Chip, honey, you got in trouble at school. You know what the consequences are when you make a wrong choice like that."

"I'm sorry," he said. He hung his head. "I know you want me to make right choices, but I just can't. I try, I really do, but I just can't."

Later, Chip went to play video games in the basement. After a while, Dad came down and pulled out an old trunk from the basement closet. Chip recognized the trunk; it housed Dad's collection of magic tricks. His dad was a gospel magician who performed "magic with a message."

"Dad," Chip said, "you've promised me for a long time that someday you would show me how you do some of your tricks, so maybe I can start doing gospel magic too. Can you show me some tricks now? Please?"

Dad smiled as he hung several colorful silk handkerchiefs on the lid of the trunk. "First, you need to understand that there's really no 'magic' to a 'magic trick.'"

"There isn't?" Chip asked.

"Nope," Dad answered. He pulled a collapsible silk hat from the trunk. "I could never take a rabbit out of this hat," he said, producing a stuffed rabbit from the trunk, "unless I first put the rabbit *in* the hat."

"But you show the empty hat before you pull the rabbit out!" Chip protested.

Dad smiled. "Right. But there's a little pocket inside the hat," he said, turning it so Chip could look inside.

Chip's face lit up as he inspected the hat. "Oh," he said, "It's a special hat!"

"Right," Dad said. "You know, Son, making right choices works pretty much the same way. You can't expect to pull right choices out of thin air, like magic. You have to 'put the rabbit in the hat,' so to speak."

"What's that supposed to mean?" Chip asked.

"Well, it means you have to do the preparation first, by praying and worshiping and reading your Bible every day. If you build your faith by putting those things into your life, God will help 'pull' right choices *out* of your life!"

Chip nodded. "You're right, Dad. Will you help me?"

"You bet I will."

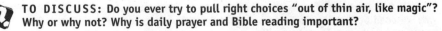

TO DISCUSS: Do you ever try to pull right choices "out of thin air, like magic"? Why or why not? Why is daily prayer and Bible reading important?

TO PRAY: "Lord, we know that mature faith doesn't come by magic. Help us to be faithful in praying and reading your Word."

29 Avoiding Temptation

MAKING RIGHT CHOICES BEGINS WITH AVOIDING TEMPTATION.

Bible Reading of the Day: Read Proverbs 4:14–15.

Verse of the Day: *"Run from all these evil things, and follow what is right and good" (1 Timothy 6:11).*

"Mommy," Alyssa said, "you look beautiful!"

Mom smiled; she had just gotten her hair done at the beauty parlor. "Thank you, Alyssa," she said. Mom took Alyssa's hand as they left the beauty parlor together.

"Where are we going now, Mommy?" she asked.

"Home," Mom answered.

"But our car's that way," Alyssa said, pointing her finger behind her.

"I know, sweetheart." Mom stopped at the crosswalk and waited for the light to change, then crossed the street and turned back down the street toward the car.

"Why are we walking on this side of the street, Mommy?"

Mom sighed and shook her head. "You're just full of questions today, aren't you?" she said, smiling. "You know Mommy's on a diet, don't you?"

Alyssa nodded.

"And sometimes I get tempted to eat things I shouldn't eat."

Again Alyssa nodded. Mom pointed to a building a few doors down from the beauty parlor. "Do you see that building?" she asked.

"The one with the picture of the donut on the window?" Alyssa asked.

"Yes, that's the one," Mom answered, chuckling. "Well, that's a bakery, and there's all sorts of delicious donuts and crullers and pastries in there." She licked her lips.

"Can we buy some?" Alyssa asked innocently.

"No!" Mom said. "That's why we're walking on this side of the street, Alyssa. I'm trying to avoid the temptation to walk in there and buy everything I see."

"Oh," Alyssa said. "But can't you just walk by the donut store?"

"Sometimes I can, but other times I smell those donuts and I can't resist."

"So you walk on this side of the street so you won't eat donuts?"

"Right," Mom said. "I'm trying to steer clear of the temptation. If I don't go near the donut store, I don't have to fight the temptation to go in!"

"Oh," Alyssa said again. "You're not tempted to eat all those good donuts in that store now, are you, Mommy?"

Mom shook her head in a gesture of hopelessness. "If you keep talking about donuts, you're going to make me march right over there and gobble them all up right now!" she said. "Can we talk about something else, *please?*"

 TO DISCUSS: An important step in making right choices is to avoid tempting circumstances. How did Mom avoid temptation in the story above? How did Alyssa make it hard for her? What are some temptations you face often? Can you avoid those things before you're even tempted? How?

 TO PRAY: "Lord, please help us avoid the things that tempt us to sin."

30 Darkness and Light

IF YOU WERE DOING THE RIGHT THING, YOU WOULDN'T HAVE TO HIDE.

Bible Reading of the Day: Read John 3:16-21.
Verse of the Day: *"Those who do what is right come to the light gladly, so everyone can see that they are doing what God wants"* (John 3:21).

"Hey," Larry said. "Close the door!"

Stan stepped into the bedroom he shared with his brother Larry and quickly shut the door behind him.

"What are you doing?" he asked Larry.

"Nothin'," Larry answered.

Stan walked slowly to the bed, where Larry was counting a stack of baseball cards.

"Where'd you get all those?" Stan asked.

Larry shrugged. "I found 'em."

"*Where* did you find them?" Stan's tone indicated that he didn't believe his brother.

"I just did, OK?" Larry glared at his brother. "I didn't do anything wrong. I just found a bunch of baseball cards, and I'm gonna sell some of them to Joey Whitacre, OK?"

"If you didn't do anything wrong, then you wouldn't mind me leaving the door open while I hang out, would you?" Stan stepped to the door and grabbed the doorknob.

"No!" Larry shouted. He leaned over the cards as if to hide them with his body. "No, I want the door closed."

Stan let go of the doorknob and faced his brother. "If you weren't doing anything wrong, you wouldn't care if the door were closed. If you were doing the right thing, you wouldn't have to hide."

Larry stared at Stan for a few moments. Finally he rolled his head slightly and sighed. "All right," he said. "I found them in Dad's trunk down in the basement."

"And you were just gonna sell them to Joey Whitacre without telling Dad?"

"Just the ones that are worth money," Larry said.

"Oh well," Stan said sarcastically. "*That's* not so bad."

The two brothers stared at each other for a long moment before Larry started laughing. "I see what you mean," he said. Stan laughed too. "OK," Larry said finally. "I'll put them back where I found them."

 TO DISCUSS: What was wrong with what Larry was planning to do? What should have helped him realize that what he was doing was wrong? Do you ever do things you don't want people to see or know about? If you're doing what God wants, would you probably try to hide it or not try to hide it? What can you learn from Larry's example?

 TO PRAY: "Lord, make our actions good and right so we will not try to hide in shame."

31 Trick or Treat

THE DEVIL TRIES TO TRICK US BY MAKING WRONG CHOICES LOOK GOOD AND
BY MAKING RIGHT CHOICES LOOK HARD.

Bible Reading of the Day: Read Hebrews 10:32-36.
Verse of the Day: *"Patient endurance is what you need now, so you
will continue to do God's will. Then you will receive all that he has
promised" (Hebrews 10:36).*

Sara couldn't believe her luck! She and her friend Chris were in the girls' locker room
the afternoon before a regional cheerleading competition.

"Look," Chris said. "That's Tammy's uniform!"

Sara looked in disbelief at the folded uniform on the locker room bench. She
pivoted her head from side to side and saw that she and Chris were alone.

"This is your chance!" Chris said.

Sara knew exactly what Chris meant. Tammy was the one who had started a fight
that had gotten Sara suspended from school—and grounded—right before the prom.
Sara had wanted to get even with her rival ever since then. This was the chance she'd
been waiting for.

"All you've got to do," Chris whispered, "is get out of here with Tammy's uniform.
If her uniform disappears, she's out of the competition!"

"It would serve her right for all she's done to me, wouldn't it?" Sara said. It was
so tempting. It would feel so good to get even with Tammy.

Chris said, "If you don't do this, you'll regret it forever."

Sara still hesitated. She knew hiding Tammy's uniform would be satisfying—at
least for a while. And if she didn't do it, she'd probably never get a chance like this
again. But there was another consideration; she also knew it would be wrong.

"I don't know," she said, shaking her head.

"Don't be stupid!" Chris said. "You know that Tammy would do it to you if she
had the chance. Come on!"

Sara reached for Tammy's uniform and picked it up. *It would feel so good to get
even with her,* she thought. But then she dropped the uniform as if it were on fire.

"I can't do it," she told Chris.

"How can you pass up a chance like this?" Chris pleaded.

Sara knew she had passed up a one-in-a-million chance to get even with a rival.
She knew Chris probably thought she was crazy. But even though getting even with
Tammy might feel good, she knew that it would be wrong. So she turned and walked
out of the locker room.

 TO DISCUSS: Do you think Sara made the right choice? If so, why? Sometimes the
wrong choice seems to be the one that would "feel good," and the right choice seems
to be the hard choice. Why do you think that is? If Sara had hidden Tammy's uniform,
what good or bad things might have happened to Sara? What good or bad things
might result from Sara's right choice?

 TO PRAY: "The thought of doing wrong seems so attractive sometimes, dear Lord.
We need your perspective and strength to say no to sin."

1 Photo Opportunity

OFTEN, RIGHT CHOICES ARE RIGHT FOR MORE THAN ONE REASON.

Bible Reading of the Day: Read Philippians 2:12-15.
Verse of the Day: *"God is working in you, giving you the desire to obey him and the power to do what pleases him"* (Philippians 2:13).

Emily looked over the page layout for the school yearbook with her friend Drew.

"When are we taking the yearbook staff picture?" she asked.

Drew gazed up at the ceiling. "How about tomorrow afternoon?"

"Tomorrow afternoon?" Emily said. "Why so sudden?"

Drew shrugged, but smiled mischievously. "Oh, I don't know," he said. "It might have something to do with the band trip."

Instantly, Emily knew what Drew was talking about. If they took the staff picture tomorrow afternoon, Lana wouldn't be in the picture. She was on a four-day trip with the concert band. Drew and Lana were not exactly enemies, but they had trouble getting along with each other, especially since Lana had been chosen as the yearbook editor and Drew had been made the assistant editor.

"Drew," Emily said in a scolding tone.

Drew lifted his hands in the air as if he were helpless to do anything. "I've already scheduled it," he said. "Everybody but Lana can make it."

"You can't do that, Drew," Emily said. "You know it's wrong."

"What's wrong with it?" Drew said. "It's just a stupid picture, Emily."

"What's wrong with it?" Emily repeated, holding her hand out with the index finger extended. "First, it's not fair. You wouldn't be doing this if it were anyone besides Lana." She held up two fingers. "Second, it's not kind. It's a mean and cruel thing to do, Drew, and you know it." She unfolded a third finger. "Plus, it's not loving. I know you and Lana have had your differences, Drew, but you're supposed to be a Christian, and what you're planning to do is wrong because it's not the loving thing to do!"

"All right," Drew said, lifting his hands in a gesture of surrender. "You win! It's not like it's a big deal. It's just a dumb yearbook picture."

Emily relaxed and shook her head. "It would be a big deal to Lana, wouldn't it?" she said, a slight smile appearing on her face.

Drew smiled back. "Yeah," he admitted. "You're right. I guess I just wasn't thinking."

She slapped him playfully on his shoulder. "You were thinking, all right—you just weren't thinking the right things!"

TO DISCUSS: What did Emily say was wrong with Drew's plan? Do you think a wrong choice can be wrong for more than one reason? Do you think a right choice can be right for more than one reason? If yes, think of some examples.

TO PRAY: "Lord, give us the strength to put right choices into action."

2 Virtues and Values

SOME PEOPLE SAY THERE IS NO RIGHT OR WRONG, BUT GOD SAYS, "DO GOOD," AND AVOID EVIL.

Bible Reading of the Day: Read Isaiah 64:4-5.
Verse of the Day: *"You welcome those who cheerfully do good, who follow godly ways" (Isaiah 64:5).*

Dad and Mandy sat together on the couch.

"I can't believe I get to watch television for *homework!*" Mandy said. She had been assigned to watch a television documentary and write a report on it. Her dad had suggested that they watch the show together, since it was on a music video channel that Mandy wasn't normally allowed to watch.

The show—*Virtues and Values*—featured short video clips of ordinary people and famous stars talking about their "values."

One man, whose nose ring was connected to his earring by a silver chain, said, "We all need to find our own values, you know? That's part of the fun of becoming!"

A woman dressed in a business suit said, "There's really no right or wrong anymore. Might makes right. Whoever wins the war writes the history books."

An older woman peered thoughtfully into the camera and said, "I've always taught my children that the major task of growing up is to form your own value system. . . . I never wanted to impose my ideas of right and wrong on them."

After the show ended. Dad clicked the remote to turn off the television.

"What are you thinking?" Dad asked.

"I don't know," Mandy answered. Her spiral notebook lay open on her lap.

"Did you agree with any of the things those people said?"

"I don't know," Mandy said. "Some of them sounded pretty smart."

Dad nodded. "Did you disagree with anything they said?"

Mandy nodded. "Yeah. I mean, none of them talked about God at all. It's like they're all talking about values and right and wrong and stuff, but they're acting like all that matters is what *they* think. They're acting like God never said 'do this,' and, 'don't do that.' It's like they never heard of the Ten Commandments!"

"Or they're trying to *ignore* what God has said," Dad suggested.

"Yeah," Mandy answered. "So basically, it's like, either they're wrong—or *God* is!"

Dad smiled. "So who are *you* going to believe?"

Mandy reacted as if she were surprised by the question. "Well, duh," she said. "I'm *obviously* going to listen to God."

"Good," Dad said. "Why don't you write that in your report?"

Mandy picked up her pen and started writing notes. "I think I will!" she answered.

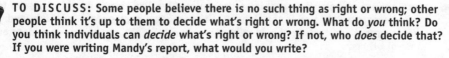

TO DISCUSS: Some people believe there is no such thing as right or wrong; other people think it's up to them to decide what's right or wrong. What do *you* think? Do you think individuals can *decide* what's right or wrong? If not, who *does* decide that? If you were writing Mandy's report, what would you write?

TO PRAY: "Lord, we believe that you set the standard for right and wrong. We choose to obey your commands."

3 The Wrong Measuring Cup

GOD IS THE STANDARD FOR DETERMINING WHAT IS RIGHT.

Bible Reading of the Day: Read Psalm 1.
Verse of the Day: *"For the Lord watches over the way of the righteous, but the way of the wicked will perish"* (Psalm 1:6, NIV).

Jermaine stirred the contents of the mixing bowl together while Mom greased the cookie sheets.

"I notice you've been getting phone calls from Tyree again," Mom said.

Jermaine flashed a quick look at his mom and then continued stirring. "Yes, ma'am," he said.

"What does he want?" Mom asked.

Jermaine shrugged. "He just wants to be friends, Mom, that's all. You know Ty."

"Mm hmm," Mom said. "I know Tyree all right. Is he still working for those men on the street corner?"

Jermaine stopped stirring and set the bowl on the counter. He sighed. "Mom, he just does things for them."

"You know those men are drug pushers," Mom said.

"But Ty never touches any drugs. He just, you know, runs to the store for a can of pop or mails letters for them. You know, stuff like that. He says there's nothing wrong with it because he doesn't even touch drugs or anything like that, and his family needs the money."

"That's what *Tyree* says," Mom said. She picked up one of the cups they had used to measure flour and sugar. "It sounds to me like Tyree is using the wrong cup."

"What do you mean, Mom?"

"Tyree says there's nothing wrong with what he's doing. But he's deciding that based on *what he thinks* . . . or on what those drug pushers are telling him. Either way, that's no way to decide right from wrong. That's like using an old shoe to measure how much sugar to put in a cookie recipe. What Tyree *should* be doing is basing his decisions on God and what God says. *God* is the standard for knowing good from evil, not what Tyree says or thinks or does. And God says, 'Blessed is the man who does not walk in the counsel of the wicked or stand in the way of sinners or sit in the seat of mockers.' Tyree should be listening to what God says, not to what those men on the corner say."

"I know that, Mom."

"I hope you do, child," Mom said. "I hope you do."

TO DO: Make an arrangement of measuring cups and spoons, along with a Bible, as a centerpiece on your dinner table or kitchen counter. Use this as an object lesson to remind everyone that God is the standard—the measurement—of what is right and what is wrong, and that we should rely on him and his Word, not on our own ideas or those of others.

TO PRAY: "Lord God, we acknowledge that your Word is the standard that we live by. Help us to make right choices based on your commands."

4 Baking Soda

RIGHT CHOICES MAY NOT HAVE IMMEDIATE BENEFITS, BUT GOD WILL USE THEM FOR OUR BENEFIT.

Bible Reading of the Day: Read Romans 8:28-30.
Verse of the Day: *"And we know that God causes everything to work together for the good of those who love God and are called according to his purpose for them" (Romans 8:28).*

Mom had been talking to Jermaine about his friend Tyree. Just then she pulled a cookie sheet filled with fragrant chocolate-chip cookies from the oven. "Don't those smell good?" she asked Jermaine. "Back to Tyree, he knows better than to ask you to run errands for those drug pushers on the corner, doesn't he?"

Jermaine scratched his head nervously. "That's why he's been calling me, Mom. He wants me to help him."

"Mm hmm," Mom said. "You told him no, didn't you?"

"Not yet."

"Not yet?" Mom barked. "Child, you get on that phone right now and tell Tyree you're not allowed anywhere near that corner."

"Mom," Jermaine said, his tone pleading, "he'll think I'm a little kid. And he'll start messin' with my reputation at school."

"Doing the right thing isn't always easy. But the Lord will work it all together for good."

"You're always saying that, Mom, and I don't even know what it means."

Jermaine was right; she used that Romans 8:28 phrase often, and she had always assumed that he knew what she meant. She picked up a teaspoon and dipped it into the small can of baking soda on the counter. Then she held the spoon up to Jermaine's mouth. "Here," she said, "taste this."

Jermaine immediately made a sour face. "Ugh!" he said. "That's nasty!"

"OK, then." She picked up a warm cookie from the tray on the counter. "Try this."

He chewed it. "That's better. Don't make me eat that nasty stuff again."

Mom nodded. "That's what Romans 8:28 means. The baking soda didn't taste very good, did it? But put it together with eggs and sugar and chocolate chips, and the result is real fine, isn't it? Well, right choices don't always have pleasant consequences. But God mixes them all together like a batch of cookie dough and blesses the right choices we make, even if they don't taste sweet by themselves."

Jermaine sighed as he walked across the kitchen and picked up the telephone receiver. Mom didn't have to ask what he was doing. She knew he was calling Tyree with the news that he would not help him run errands for the men on the street corner.

 TO DISCUSS: Do you think right choices sometimes have unpleasant consequences? What makes you think that? Do you think we should make right choices even if they have unpleasant consequences? Why or why not?

 TO PRAY: "Heavenly Father, your Word tells us that you cause everything to work together for the good of those who love you. Help us, Father, to believe that—even when we feel afraid or sad."

5 Jodie's Scream

TO BE SELF-CONTROLLED MEANS TO CONTROL YOUR ANGER INSTEAD OF LETTING YOUR ANGER CONTROL YOU.

Bible Reading of the Day: Read Ephesians 4:26-27, 31-32.
Verse of the Day: *"Don't sin by letting anger gain control over you. Think about it overnight and remain silent" (Psalm 4:4).*

"Ow!" Jodie cried. She gripped her left arm with her right hand and glared at her brother, who had just snapped her with a rubber band. Suddenly, she let out a bloodcurdling scream in the middle of the library.

Jodie's mom, who had recognized her scream, came running. "Jodie," she said, picking up her little daughter and holding her in her arms. "Are you hurt?"

Jodie screamed and cried, and Mom became frantic. She turned to her son Mark. "What happened?" she asked, trying to talk over Jodie's loud sobs.

Mark flashed his mom a guilty look. "I just hit her with a rubber band," he said.

Mom grabbed the rubber band out of Mark's hand, then took Jodie to the women's restroom. Once inside, she set Jodie on the sink.

"That's enough, young lady," Mom said in a quiet voice.

Jodie stopped screaming. Her face was red and streaked with tears. Mom held up the rubber band. "Did Mark snap you with the rubber band?" she asked.

Jodie nodded angrily and looked as if she wanted to scream again.

"Did that make you angry?"

Jodie pursed her lips and nodded her head.

"What Mark did was wrong," Mom said. "But what you did was wrong too."

Jodie looked confused. "It . . . it was?"

Mom nodded. "It's not always wrong to be angry. Sometimes you can't help it. But even if you get angry at someone, God still wants you to be self-controlled."

"What's that?" Jodie asked.

Mom nodded toward the library outside the restroom. "Out there," she said, "when you started screaming, you were letting your anger control you. That's not good. God wants *you* to learn to control your anger."

"But Mark snapped me!" Jodie said indignantly.

"I know," Mom answered. "And he was wrong to do that. But don't you think you could have done something else instead of screaming?"

Jodie nodded. "I could have told you."

Mom smiled. "That's right. If you had done that instead of screaming, you would have shown me that you're getting to be a big girl who can control her temper."

"I *am* a big girl," Jodie said.

"OK," Mom conceded, lifting Jodie off the sink. "You're a big girl."

TO DISCUSS: Today's Bible reading says not to let anger control you. Describe a time when you got angry. Did you let your anger control you, or did you control your anger? Which is better? Why?

TO PRAY: "Lord, it's so easy to let our anger get out of control. Remind us, Lord, that we can choose to control our anger, rather than letting it control us."

6 Wanting and Waiting

TO BE SELF-CONTROLLED MEANS TO CONTROL YOUR DESIRES AND APPETITES
INSTEAD OF LETTING THEM CONTROL YOU.

Bible Reading of the Day: Read 1 Peter 1:13-16.
Verse of the Day: *"Therefore, prepare your minds for action; be self-controlled; set your hope fully on the grace to be given you when Jesus Christ is revealed"* (1 Peter 1:13, NIV).

"Mom, please, please, *please!*" Enrique clasped his hands together as if he were praying and rocked in front of his mother in the discount store aisle.

"No, Enrique," she said. "Your birthday is still two weeks away."

"But I want the Super Graphics Game System *now!*" Enrique said. "Can't you just get it for me now?"

Mom shook her head.

"What difference does it make?" Enrique asked, an impatient edge entering his voice. "It won't make any difference if you buy it for me now or later."

"Maybe not," Mom said, shrugging. "But I think it could make a big difference."

"How?" Enrique asked.

"Well, Enrique," Mom said, "part of my job as your mother is to help you grow up to be a responsible young man. I want you to become a young man who knows how to control his desires and his appetites."

"What do you mean, appetites? I'm not even hungry! I just want a Super Graphics Game System!"

"I know, and you want it *now,* don't you?"

"Yes!"

"But if I get you a Super Graphics Game System now, I'm not helping you learn how to wait for the things you want, and how to learn self-control."

"Oh, come on, Mom, you're just trying to torture me!"

"No," Mom said, laughing. "I'm not trying to torture you; I'm trying to teach you self-control. I'm trying to teach you how to control your desires instead of letting them control you. That's a very important lesson to learn."

Enrique rolled his eyes. "Oh, man," he said. "What if I promise you I'll be really self-controlled from now on?"

Mom shrugged. "Well, then, maybe I'd get you a Super Graphics Game System."

"Really?"

Mom smiled mischievously. "For your birthday—in two weeks."

Enrique sighed and shook his head. "All right! You win. I'll wait."

TO DISCUSS: What are some of the things for which you, like Enrique, have a difficult time waiting? Do we always have to wait for the things we really want? Why or why not? What can we learn by waiting?

TO PRAY: "God, we know that you want us to be self-controlled. Help us to control our desires instead of letting our desires control us. And teach us to be holy because we know you are holy."

7 Beat the Thunder

TO BE SELF-CONTROLLED MEANS TO CONTROL YOUR WORRIES AND FEARS INSTEAD OF LETTING THEM CONTROL YOU.

Bible Reading of the Day: Read Mark 4:35-41.
Verse of the Day: *"When I am afraid, I will trust in you"*
(Psalm 56:3, NIV).

"Mommy!" Jeremy screamed. He tried to peer through the darkness. The soft yellow glow of his night light had disappeared; the bright red numbers on the clock beside his bed were gone too.

He could hear the wind blowing outside his bedroom window, and every once in a while lightning and thunder pierced the sky. He cried again but soon felt his mother's presence beside him. He stretched out his arms and wrapped them around his mother as she sat on the side of his bed. She held a flashlight in her hand.

"I'm scared, Mommy," he said.

"I know, sweetheart, but it's only a thunderstorm."

"Don't you ever get scared?"

"Everybody gets scared, sweetheart," Mom said. "But when I'm scared I pray about it and ask God to help me not be scared. Would you do that with me now?"

Jeremy nodded and closed his eyes tight while his mom prayed a short prayer. When he opened his eyes, Mom was already looking at him. "Do you feel any better?"

"A little," he answered.

"You know what else I do?" she asked. Jeremy shook his head. "I try to control my fear instead of letting my fear control me."

"How do you do that?"

"Well, by praying . . . and by doing something to help me forget my fear."

"Like what?"

"I've got an idea," Mom said. She handed the lighted flashlight to Jeremy. "Why don't we play a game? Every time you see a flash of lightning in the sky, you try to turn the flashlight off before you hear the thunder. Then when you hear the thunder, you turn the flashlight back on until you see the next flash of lightning! See how many times you can beat the thunder!"

"OK!" Jeremy said. He waited quietly for the next streak of lightning. When it came, he jumped a little before remembering to flip the flashlight off. A second or two later, he heard the thunder. "I won!" he said. He did it a few more times while Mom sat next to him. Finally, he turned to his mom. "Can I keep playing?" he asked.

Mom nodded. Then she stood and backed out of the room as Jeremy sat staring out his window, waiting anxiously for the next flash of lightning.

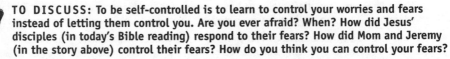

TO DISCUSS: To be self-controlled is to learn to control your worries and fears instead of letting them control you. Are you ever afraid? When? How did Jesus' disciples (in today's Bible reading) respond to their fears? How did Mom and Jeremy (in the story above) control their fears? How do you think you can control your fears?

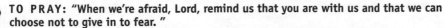

TO PRAY: "When we're afraid, Lord, remind us that you are with us and that we can choose not to give in to fear. "

8 Guarded Behavior

GOD COMMANDS SELF-CONTROL BECAUSE GOD VALUES SELF-CONTROL.

Bible Reading of the Day: Read 1 Peter 4:7-11.
Verse of the Day: *"The end of all things is near. Therefore be clear minded and self-controlled so that you can pray"* (1 Peter 4:7, NIV).

Dad stood in front of Buckingham Palace with his daughters, Patsy and Amy.

"Thanks for bringing us on this trip with you, Dad," Patsy said. "This is so cool."

Dad smiled. His company had asked him to travel to England for a four-day trip. He was glad he had been allowed to take his daughters with him. After all, the trip had been a "smashing success."

Now they watched in fascination as the palace guards marched stiffly to their posts and stood like stone sentinels at the gates. Every once in a while, a tourist would approach the gates and play the familiar game of trying to prompt one of the guards to smile or flinch.

"How do they stand so still?" Amy asked without taking her eyes off the guards.

Dad shrugged. "They're trained to stand at attention and to let nothing distract them from their duty."

They watched in silence for a few moments longer. The soldiers didn't even seem to blink.

Amy shook her head. "That's so cool," she said.

"I think so too," Dad said. "But tell me why you think so."

"Well, because," Amy said, "it's just cool that they can be so still and not crack up laughing when people make faces at them."

Dad nodded. "It is pretty admirable, isn't it? Do you know *why* it's admirable?"

"Well, because it's—" Patsy paused. "Because—oh, I don't know."

Dad laughed. "I think it's admirable because we admire self-control."

The girls were silent for a moment as they continued to study the palace guards. "Yeah," Amy said finally.

"And I think we admire self-control," Dad continued, "because we know it's a good thing."

"And because it's so hard," Patsy offered.

"For *some* of us," Amy said, teasing her sister.

"But as Christians," Dad continued, "we also know that God commands self-control. He commands it because he values it."

"So he must really like those guys," Patsy said, pointing to the stone-faced guards.

Dad chuckled. "Maybe so," he said.

 TO DISCUSS: Do you know anyone who shows a lot of self-control? If so, who? Do you admire (or value) self-control? Do you need to develop self-control in any areas of your life? If so, what areas? How can your family help you develop self-control? How can God help?

 TO PRAY: "God, you know us inside and out. You know the areas where we are weakest. Thank you for the fruit of the Spirit, which allows us to be self-controlled."

9 Ronnie and God

GOD VALUES SELF-CONTROL BECAUSE HE EXERCISES SELF-CONTROL.

Bible Reading of the Day: Read Ezekiel 20:13–17.

Verse of the Day: *"The Lord is slow to anger and rich in unfailing love, forgiving every kind of sin and rebellion"* (Numbers 14:18).

Dad picked up Veronica at school and held her hand as they crossed the street together. They started walking the three blocks to their house.

"I talked to your teacher today," Dad said.

"You did?" Veronica's eyes widened.

Dad nodded. "She told me you did something very good on the playground today."

"She *did?*" Veronica asked.

Dad smiled. They crossed another street. Neither said anything until they reached the opposite curb.

"It wasn't my fault, Daddy," she said. "Wesley pushed me down." She stopped and twisted her hand out of her father's grip. She held up both hands; her palms were badly skinned.

"I know that," Dad said. "But your teacher also told me what you did when you got up."

"He made me mad, Daddy."

Dad smiled and squeezed Veronica's hand in his again. They kept walking. "I'm sure he did. But your teacher said you didn't hit him or push him back."

Veronica shook her head. "I wanted to," she said.

"But you didn't. That's what's important, Ronnie," he said, using his pet name for his daughter. "You *controlled* your anger. I think that's really great."

"You do?"

Dad nodded. "And you know who else thinks it's great?" They crossed another street. "God thinks it's great, Ronnie, because when you decided to control your temper, you acted like God."

"I did?" Veronica asked. A tiny smile crept across her face.

"A long time ago, after God led his people out of Egypt and gave them the Ten Commandments, they disobeyed him and treated him even worse than Wesley treated you today. But God didn't destroy them, even though he was angry. He controlled his anger—just like you controlled your anger today."

"Neat," Veronica said, skipping lightly for a moment.

"I think so too," Dad said, skipping with her.

 TO DISCUSS: What makes self-control right? Why does God value self-control? Can you think of any other instances in which God exercised self-control? Do you think he sometimes exercises self-control with you? Why or why not?

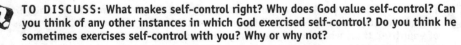 **TO PRAY:** Have a time of silent prayer to give everyone the opportunity of talking privately with God about areas where he or she lacks self-control. Then let someone close in prayer aloud.

10 Run for the Prize

SELF-CONTROL BRINGS SHORT-TERM AND LONG-TERM REWARDS.

Bible Reading of the Day: Read 1 Corinthians 9:24-27.

Verse of the Day: *"All athletes practice strict self-control. They do it to win a prize that will fade away, but we do it for an eternal prize"* (1 Corinthians 9:25).

"I never knew there were so many rules for a dumb track team!" Manny said as he and Billy left the orientation meeting for the school track team.

"Like what?" Billy asked.

"Like these!" Manny answered, pulling a crumpled pack of cigarettes out of his coat pocket. "The coach said if he saw us smoking, we'd be kicked off the team."

Billy smiled. "Yeah, well, that's the way it goes."

"That's easy for you to say. You don't smoke."

Billy shrugged. "Like Coach said, if you want to win, you won't be putting that stuff into your lungs." They stopped at Billy's locker; he pulled out his book bag and then slammed the locker shut. They headed for the front doors of the school.

Manny squinted at Billy as he asked, "You think it really makes a difference? You think I'll really run faster if I quit smoking?"

"Think about it," Billy said. "Do you think *breathing* has anything to do with running?"

"Yeah," Manny admitted, "I guess you're right. It's just gonna be so hard to quit."

"But if you want to win, you're going to have to show some self-control, and . . ."

"That's easy for you to say," Manny interrupted. "You're not the one who has to quit. You don't know what it's like."

"I don't?" Billy said. "You think it doesn't take self-control to say no when all your friends are pushing cigarettes and stuff on you? You think it doesn't take guts not to start in the first place? You think you're the only one who has to do something hard?"

"No, I didn't mean it like that," Manny said, holding his hands in the air as if Billy were holding him at gunpoint. "I meant that you already have self-control; you're already in shape for the track team. I've got to start getting in shape. Somehow."

"I'll help you," Billy said. "Give me your cigarettes."

"Now?" Manny asked.

"Yeah," Billy answered. "Like you said, you've got to start getting in shape."

Manny rolled his eyes and dug in his pocket. He drew out the pack of cigarettes and handed it to Billy.

TO DISCUSS: According to today's Bible reading, what two kinds of prizes might people get when they exercise self-control? Which kind of prize do you think Manny was trying for? Which kind of prize do you think Billy was trying for? Who are you most like: Manny or Billy? Why?

TO PRAY: "Lord, when it comes to self-control, sometimes we come in dead last. Help us to run toward the eternal prize that you promise."

11 Healthy Choices

SELF-CONTROL INCREASES HEALTH AND ENJOYMENT OF LIFE.

Bible Reading of the Day: Read Daniel 1:3-15.
Verse of the Day: *"A person without self-control is as defenseless as a city with broken-down walls" (Proverbs 25:28).*

"Daddy," Meghan said, as she watched him cut vegetables for dinner, "you're getting really skinny." She sat on a high stool as her dad stood at the kitchen counter.

"Why, thank you, Meghan," Dad said. "I *have* lost some weight."

"Is it hard to lose weight?"

Dad stopped cutting and cocked his head to one side. "Yes, it is, I guess. It does take self-control—that's for sure."

"What's self-control?"

"Well," Dad said thoughtfully, "it's being able to say no to some of the things you want so you can have other things you want more."

"Self-control isn't very fun, is it, Daddy?"

Dad stopped chopping and looked at Meghan. "Sometimes it's not," he said. "But sometimes it can make other things fun."

"Like what?"

Dad cleared his throat. Meghan's questions could be exasperating at times. He suddenly got an idea. He opened the refrigerator and pulled out a leftover hot dog in a plastic bag.

"Watch this," he said. He called Cody, the family dog, who lumbered into the kitchen and immediately smelled the hot dog in Dad's hands. Dad tossed the hot dog to the animal, who caught it in midair and swallowed it in one gigantic gulp. Then Dad turned to Meghan. "Do you think Cody enjoyed that hot dog?"

Meghan giggled. "He ate it without even chewing it!"

Dad nodded. "That's how I've been eating, Meghan." He chuckled too. "I've been gulping down food in a hurry, not even tasting it sometimes. But now that I've started to change my eating habits, I'm enjoying my food more. Because I chew it carefully now, I taste it more. And I'm eating healthier foods too, so just that little bit of self-control is making me happier *and* healthier."

Meghan climbed down from her stool and looked up at her dad. "Daddy, can we eat now? I'm getting hungry!"

Dad chuckled again. "Me too, Meghan. Me too!"

TO DO: Make a snack of vegetables and water as a reminder of Daniel's self-control. Discuss how his (and Meghan's dad's) self-control might have made him happier and healthier.

TO PRAY: "Lord, give us the strength we need to be self-controlled."

12 School Fair

SELF-CONTROL WINS THE ESTEEM AND RESPECT OF OTHERS.

Bible Reading of the Day: Read Titus 2:11-14.
Verse of the Day: *"We should live in this evil world with self-control, right conduct, and devotion to God" (Titus 2:12).*

Robbie and George had wandered around the school fair for a couple of hours. The halls and the classrooms were filled with noisy students playing games, getting their faces painted, drinking soda pop, and eating hamburgers, hot dogs, and baked goods.

"Look!" Robbie pointed to a booth with flashing lights and loud music. "I'm gonna play Mr. Thompson's game!"

George followed Robbie to Mr. Thompson's booth. Behind Mr. Thompson, they saw a row of painted coffee cans perched on a box. Robbie plopped down a dollar bill on the counter and asked for six balls to try to knock down the cans.

Mr. Thompson turned to George before he handed the balls to Robbie. "Would you like to play, George?" he asked.

George fingered the five-dollar bill in his pocket. "No, thanks," he said.

Robbie tossed the balls and knocked all but one of the cans off the box. Mr. Thompson handed him a plastic key chain as a prize.

Later that afternoon, the two boys sat on the brick wall in front of the school and waited for George's parents to pick them up.

"Do you have any money left?" Robbie asked.

George nodded. "I only spent a dollar on a hot dog and a soda. What about you?"

Robbie frowned as he shook his head. "No. I wish I did. I wanted to play that coin toss game one more time. How come you didn't play any games?"

George shrugged. "I wanted to, I guess. But I'm going to use this money for a *TurboJam* remote-controlled car. I've been saving for weeks to get it."

"Oh, man! I've wanted a *TurboJam* forever! You're so lucky."

"Why don't you save up like I did?"

Robbie shook his head and frowned. "I could never do that. I'm not as good at that kinda stuff as you are. I wish I were."

"I think you could do it if you really tried," George suggested.

"Think so?" Robbie asked. A dreamy look entered his eyes. "That would be so cool," he said. He pulled his new plastic key chain out of his pocket. "Better than a dumb key chain, that's for sure."

 TO DO: Start a family savings project for a practical application of controlling desires. Choose an amount of time for this project, such as one month. Have everyone save the money that might normally be spent on snacks (those outside the daily nutritional requirements) or entertainment. At the end of the allotted time period, pool all of your money and do something nice for the whole family.

 TO PRAY: "God, we know that self-control is right, and we know you can bless us when we obey you. Help us to live in this evil world with self-control, right conduct, and devotion to you."

13 Remote Controlled

SELF-CONTROL, LIKE ALL TRUE VIRTUES, COMES FROM GOD.

Bible Reading of the Day: Read Romans 8:5-14.
Verse of the Day: *"But you are not controlled by your sinful nature. You are controlled by the Spirit if you have the Spirit of God living in you"* *(Romans 8:9).*

George's dad called him in from the garage, where he had been playing for over an hour with his new remote-controlled car. "It's time to wash up for dinner," Dad said.

George reluctantly turned the battery-powered car off and set his new *TurboJam* set down by the garage door. A few moments later he sat down at the dinner table.

After the family said grace together, George talked about his new car. He told his parents about his friend Robbie's reaction to his purchase.

"Robbie says he wishes he could save money like I can," he said proudly. "He thinks I'm really cool because I can save up for things instead of spending all my money as soon as I get it like he does."

Dad said, "George, why don't you and I go play with your new car together?"

"Really?" George said, his voice tinged with excitement. "That would be cool!"

A few moments later, Dad held the controller to George's new car as George showed him how it worked. Finally, Dad nodded as if he understood. He put the controller on the tool shelf against the garage wall and knelt down beside the car. He turned on the switch beneath the car and set it on the garage floor. "Let's see what it can do," he said.

"You need the controller, Dad," George said, pointing to the shelf.

Dad shrugged. "I thought we'd try it without the controller."

George's forehead wrinkled in confusion. "It won't work without the controller, Dad. That's where everything comes from."

Dad didn't move toward the shelf, but instead fastened his eyes on George. He nodded. "That's what I thought," he said. He laid a hand on George's shoulder. "And it's the same way with you and me, Son." He stood. "I think it's great that you saved your money instead of spending it, and I'm not surprised that Robbie wishes he were more like you. But I want you to understand that true self-control is really 'remote control' . . . because it comes from the Spirit of God. That means he gives us the power to be *self*-controlled—"

"And we shouldn't think we did it all by ourselves, right, Dad?" George asked.

"Yeah," Dad said, smiling. "That was my point."

"OK," George said. "I'm sorry. You still want to play?"

"Absolutely!" Dad said as he reached for the remote control.

TO DISCUSS: Complete the following statement: "Today's Bible reading says you are controlled by the Spirit of God if_____." How can you let God's Spirit control you more and more?

TO PRAY: "Lord, thank you for enabling us to live Spirit-controlled lives."

14 Grabbing for Good

SEIZE EVERY OPPORTUNITY TO DO THE RIGHT THING.

Bible Reading of the Day: Read Ephesians 5:10-16.
Verse of the Day: *"Make the most of every opportunity for doing good"*
(Ephesians 5:16).

Toby sat on a horse by himself and listened to Grandpa, who sat on the horse next to Toby's. Grandpa balanced Callie, Toby's little sister, in front of him. Toby liked riding the merry-go-round, or "carousel," as his Grandpa called it, on the boardwalk of the seaside resort town where his grandparents lived.

"When I was your age," Grandpa said, "a carousel would usually have a shiny brass ring hanging on a ribbon from the roof. As we rode the horses 'round and 'round, we would try to snatch that ring off the ribbon." He described how they would wait until just the right moment and then try to grab the ring as their horse passed by it. "There were only so many chances to get that ring, so we grabbed when we got the chance, because whoever got the ring got a special prize!"

"What kind of prize?" Callie asked.

"Oh, nothing like the toys you kids have," Grandpa said, his eyes twinkling. "Just a little trinket; maybe a tin trumpet or a little wooden train. But in those days that was something special."

"I wish this merry-go-round had a ring," Toby said as the ride slowed and they prepared to get off. "I would *jump* up like this—" he pushed himself off the horse's back and stretched his arm high in the air— "and I'd get the prize for sure."

"I wouldn't be surprised if you did," Grandpa said, smiling.

As they left the carousel Grandpa spied a woman in a wheelchair. She was by herself and was wheeling herself to the steep ramp that led up to the boardwalk.

"Wait right here," Grandpa said.

Toby and Callie watched as Grandpa said hello to the woman; got behind her wheelchair; and pushed her up the ramp. She thanked him, and Grandpa turned and joined Toby and Callie again.

"Why did you do that, Grandpa?" Callie asked.

"I think I know!" Toby said. "It's like grabbing the ring, isn't it, Grandpa? You saw that she needed help, so you grabbed the chance to help her, didn't you?"

Grandpa smiled in amazement. "I reckon you're right," he said. "I never thought of it that way, but the Bible does tell us to do good to everyone as we have the opportunity. You're a bright young man, Toby."

"But Grandpa," Callie asked, "you don't get a prize for helping that lady, do you?"

"Oh, yes, I do," Grandpa said, "but I won't know what it is until I get to heaven!"

 TO DO: Make a pledge as a family to look for—and seize—opportunities for doing good during the next twenty-four hours. Report back tomorrow on how you made the most of those opportunities.

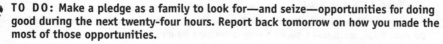 **TO PRAY:** "Father God, show us the opportunities we have for doing good to others."

15 New Specs

THE BIBLE HELPS US SEE RIGHT CHOICES MORE CLEARLY AND CHOOSE THEM
MORE OFTEN.

Bible Reading of the Day: Read Psalm 119:129-133.

Verse of the Day: *"Guide my steps by your word, so I will not be overcome by any evil" (Psalm 119:133).*

"What's that you're reading?" the doctor asked as he entered the examination room and saw Trisha with a book opened on her lap.

Trisha blushed slightly. "It's, uh, the Bible."

"Oh?" the doctor said, as he took a pair of eyeglasses out of a plastic bag. "I didn't know they made the Bible in paperback!"

"Oh, yeah," Trisha answered.

"Why do you read it?" the doctor asked. Then, before Trisha could answer, he continued. "I mean, with all the different kinds of books out there, I would think an old, outdated book like that would be pretty boring."

"Oh, no," Trisha said. "It's not like that at all. It really helps me . . . well, it's like . . . I don't know . . ." Trisha felt frustrated because she couldn't express what she was thinking.

The doctor raised the new pair of glasses he had taken out of the bag. Trisha removed her old glasses, and he placed the new pair on her face, checking behind her ears to see how the new glasses fit.

"Wow!" Trisha said immediately. "What a difference!"

The doctor smiled. "You didn't realize how much you were missing with your old pair of glasses, did you?"

"No," Trisha said, turning her head around to take in everything around her. "Everything is so sharp and clear now." Suddenly she had a thought. "Hey," she said. "That's why I read the Bible!"

The doctor didn't say anything, but a question showed in his expression.

"Reading the Bible gives me a pair of glasses," she said, "that I wouldn't have otherwise. It's like, when I read the Bible—and especially when I memorize verses—it helps me see more clearly. It helps me see what's right, and what's wrong, and it helps me find the power to choose the right thing too."

"Reading the Bible really does that?" the doctor asked.

Trisha nodded vigorously. "You really ought to try it," she told him.

He waved her old pair of glasses back and forth in his hand. "Maybe I'll do that," he said.

TO DISCUSS: Do you think reading the Bible can help you make right choices? If not, why not? If so, how? Can you give an example of a time when the Bible helped you make a right choice?

TO PRAY: "Lord Jesus, thank you for the Holy Spirit, who was sent to remind us of your Word. Help us to avoid being overcome by evil."

November

16 Cleaning Day

FORGIVENESS IS RIGHT BECAUSE GOD IS FORGIVING.

Bible Reading of the Day: Read Psalm 86:5-11.
Verse of the Day: *"Be even-tempered, content with second place, quick to forgive an offense. Forgive as quickly and completely as the Master forgave you"* (Colossians 3:13, The Message).

Mom dragged a fishing pole out of the hall closet. "Benito," she said, "why is this old thing still in here?"

Benito paused the video game he was playing and looked up. He shrugged when he saw the pole.

"Well, I'm throwing it away," Mom announced.

"No!" Benito called. He almost threw the video game controller on the floor as he jumped up and darted over to claim his pole. "I don't want you to throw it away."

"Why not?" Mom asked. "You never use it anymore."

"It's broken," Benito said with a frown. "Matt broke it last summer."

"Well, either fix it or get rid of it," Mom said.

"I *can't* fix it," Benito complained. "It's no good anymore. I still get mad whenever I think about it."

Mom shook her head. "It sounds to me like this pole isn't the only thing you need to get rid of."

"What do you mean?"

"Didn't Matt tell you he was sorry for breaking your pole?" Mom asked.

"Yeah," Benito said. "But it's still broken."

"And so is your attitude!" She propped her hands on her hips. "You've been holding on to an attitude of unforgiveness, just like you've been holding on to that old pole! And neither one of them is ever going to do you any good!"

Mom and Benito stared at each other for a few moments without speaking. Finally, Benito said, "What am I supposed to do?"

"You tell me," Mom said, smiling and crossing her arms on her chest.

Benito hung his head. "You're right," he said. "I was just so mad at him for breaking my pole."

"Well, I don't know about you, but I've done a lot worse in my lifetime, Benito, and God has forgiven me."

"I know," Benito said. "He's forgiven me too." He looked at the fishing pole in his hands. It seemed so silly to hold a grudge against his friend because of a broken fishing pole. He turned and tossed it back on the pile.

Mom smiled and wrapped her arms around him. "That's better, Benito," she said.

 TO DISCUSS: Why is it right to forgive others? Is there anyone *you* need to forgive? If so, why not do it now? Is there anyone you need to ask for forgiveness? If so, why not do it now?

 TO PRAY: "Lord, we need your courage and your love to forgive others. Help us to let go of any grudges we're holding on to."

321

17 The Reading Couch

RESPECT FOR GOD IS RIGHT.

Bible Reading of the Day: Read Ecclesiastes 12:1, 13-14.
Verse of the Day: *"Fear God and obey his commands, for this is the duty of every person" (Ecclesiastes 12:13).*

Cora and Alan sat in the "Reading Corner" of their classroom at their Christian school. Each of them had earned "quiet reading time" by helping the teacher pass out papers and clean up the classroom. Now they sat on opposite ends of an old soft couch, each reading the same book.

Suddenly Alan lowered the book and said *God* as if it were a cussword. Then he said, "You won't believe what happens in chapter six!"

Cora's mouth hung open for a moment. "I've already read chapter six," she said, then added, "and you shouldn't say that!"

"Say what?" Alan asked.

"You just said *God!*"

"So? You did too."

"Not like *you* said it. You said it like a cussword."

"Oh," Alan said, rolling his eyes, "what's wrong with that? *God* can't be a bad word!"

"It's the way you said it that was bad," Cora said.

"Why?" Alan asked defiantly. "What's wrong with what I said?"

"Well," Cora started, then stopped, unsure of what to say next.

"Do you mind if *I* answer that question?" Mrs. Evans, their teacher, had suddenly appeared behind the couch. She knelt on the floor and propped her forearms and chin against the padded back of the couch. She looked back and forth from Alan to Cora.

"Go ahead, Mrs. Evans," Cora said.

The teacher smiled. "I think you're right, Cora," she said. *"And* I think you're right too, Alan."

"How can we both be right?" Alan asked.

"Well," Mrs. Evans said, looking at Alan, "you're right that the word *God* is not a bad word. It's one of the names we use for our very good and holy God."

Alan looked at Cora, jutting his chin in her direction as if to say, "Take that!"

"But Cora is right too," the teacher added, without taking her eyes off Alan. "The way you used that word is not very respectful. The Bible tells us that we should always be respectful toward God."

Cora smiled. "That's what *I* would have said," she announced.

Mrs. Evans smiled and stood. "I thought so," she said.

TO DISCUSS: Are you respectful to God in the way you use his name? Are there other ways to show your respect for God? Name some. How can you show respect for God today?

TO PRAY: "Lord God, we're sorry about the times when we used your name in ways that are disrespectful. May your name be praised as you deserve."

18 Mom's Memory Game

RESPECT FOR YOUR PARENTS IS RIGHT.

Bible Reading of the Day: Read Ephesians 6:1-3.
Verse of the Day: *"You children must always obey your parents, for this is what pleases the Lord"* (Colossians 3:20).

Mom sat on the edge of Sean's bed and pulled the covers up to his chin.

"I'm not tired, Mommy," Sean complained.

"Maybe not, but it's your bedtime," Mom insisted.

"But I won't be able to sleep. Can't I please stay up for a little while?"

"No," she said softly as she stood. Then she paused and sat back down. "I have an idea," she said. "Why don't we play Mom's memory game?"

"How do you play it?"

"Well, I'll say a Bible verse that I remember, and then you say a Bible verse you remember. We'll take turns remembering as many Bible verses as we can. I bet by the time we've said all the Bible verses we know, you'll be ready to go to sleep."

"That's not fair," Sean said. "You know more than I do."

Mom smiled. "Don't be so sure," she said, winking at her son. "But just to make sure, I'll help you if you get stuck. OK?"

"OK. I go first. 'For God so loved the world that he gave his one and only Son, that who . . . whoever believes in him shall not perish but have eternal life.'"

"Very good!" Mom said, clapping her hands. "OK, my turn; 'Rejoice in the Lord always: again I say, Rejoice.'"

A disappointed look crossed Sean's face. "I was going to say that one!" he complained.

Mom smiled. "All right, I'll let you count that one as one of yours, then, and I'll say another one." She smiled again as Sean nodded with satisfaction. "OK, I've got one. 'Children, obey your parents because you belong to the Lord, for this is the right thing to do.'"

Sean's eyes narrowed. "No fair! You made that up!" he said accusingly.

Mom giggled at Sean's suspicious reaction. "No, really, Sean, it's in the Bible. You want me to show it to you? It's Ephesians 6:1."

Sean seemed to be searching his mother's face for any sign of deceit. Finally, his expression changed. "OK," he said at last. "I believe you."

Mom said, "It's in the Bible, Sean, because God wants us all to respect our parents. One way we show that we respect them is by obeying them."

Sean nodded through heavy eyelids. "OK, Mom, but can we finish the game tomorrow? I think I'm ready to go to sleep."

 TO DISCUSS: Why is it right to show respect for our parents? How do you show respect for your parents?

 TO PRAY: "God, help us to show respect for our parents, as well as other family members who have been like parents to us."

19 The Last Seat on the Bus

RESPECT FOR YOUR ELDERS IS RIGHT.

Bible Reading of the Day: Read 1 Timothy 5:1-2.
Verse of the Day: *"Show your fear of God by standing up in the presence of elderly people and showing respect for the aged" (Leviticus 19:32).*

Nadia sat next to her father on the bus, watching the buildings go by the bus windows. She noticed that more and more people got on the bus. Finally, every seat was taken.

When the bus stopped again to let more people on, Nadia leaned over and whispered to her dad, "Daddy, where are those people going to sit?"

Dad looked at Nadia, then looked down the aisle of the bus. He shrugged and leaned his mouth close to Nadia's ear. "They usually just stand and hold on to those railings," he said, pointing to the silver rails that hung from the ceiling of the bus.

As Dad and Nadia watched, a gray-haired woman stepped slowly toward the back of the bus. She turned her head from side to side as she walked, looking for an empty seat. Finally, she reached Dad and Nadia's row.

"Excuse me, ma'am," Dad said to the lady, "would you like to sit here?"

The woman looked blankly at Dad for a moment. "It's been a long time since a gentleman has offered me a seat," she said. "Thank you very much."

Some time later, Dad and Nadia reached their stop. Dad held his daughter's hand as they descended the steps of the bus and paused on the sidewalk while the bus pulled away.

"Daddy," she said as they started walking down the sidewalk, "why did you do that?"

"Do what?" he asked. Then, suddenly understanding what Nadia meant, he added, "You mean give my seat to that lady?"

Nadia nodded.

"Well, because she was older, and offering my seat was a way of showing respect to her."

"Did you know that lady?" Nadia asked.

"No," Dad said. "But we can respect people who are older than us even if we don't know them. In fact, the Bible says that respecting our elders is the right thing to do."

"The next time we ride the bus," Nadia said, "*I* want to give my seat to an old lady."

Dad laughed. "That would be nice," he said. "Just do me a favor, will you?"

"What?" Nadia asked.

"Don't tell the person you give your seat to that she's an old lady, OK?"

"OK," Nadia said.

TO DO: Brainstorm ways that you (as a family and as individuals) can show respect to your elders this week/this month/always.

TO PRAY: "Heavenly Father, help us remember to honor those who are older than we are. May your name be praised through our actions."

20 The Substitute

RESPECT FOR THOSE IN AUTHORITY IS RIGHT.

Bible Reading of the Day: Read Titus 3:1-2, 8.
Verse of the Day: *"Remind the people to be subject to rulers and authorities, to be obedient, to be ready to do whatever is good"* *(Titus 3:1, NIV).*

Tess breezed into the bedroom she shared with her older sister, Karen, and dropped her books onto her bed. Karen sat at the desk doing homework.

"How was school?" Karen said absently, without looking up from her work.

"It was great!" Tess plopped onto her bed, folded her hands behind her head, and leaned against the wall. "We had a substitute teacher today."

Karen looked up briefly, smiled, and then turned her attention back to the large textbook that lay open on her desk.

"We got away with all kinds of stuff today," Tess continued. "Marcy told her we only have to hand in our homework on Fridays and that our regular teacher lets us go to the drinking fountain anytime we want to. And Ben Watkins sat next to Jerry Miller all day, even though that wasn't his seat."

Karen lifted her head and looked at Tess, who continued to talk excitedly.

"And everyone laughed really hard when I called her Mrs. Hog! Her name's really Mrs. Hogue—get it?"

"You really did that?" Karen asked.

"Yeah, pretty cool, isn't it?" Tess answered.

"You think it's cool to be disrespectful?"

Tess stopped and answered slowly, "Well, she was just a substitute."

"Don't you think even a *substitute* teacher deserves respect?"

"Well . . . I guess so. I didn't really think it mattered that much."

Karen turned her face back toward her textbook, but her attention was still on her sister. "Well, God says it matters. The Bible says we should respect people who have authority over us, whether that's church leaders or government people or even substitute teachers, because God has put them in authority over us."

Tess thought about what her sister had said. Karen pretended to read her textbook while she waited for Tess's response.

Finally, Tess said, "I hope we have Mrs. Hogue tomorrow."

"Why?" Karen asked.

"So I can apologize," Tess said.

Karen smiled and went back to working on her homework.

 TO DISCUSS: Take turns naming as many people as you can who have authority over you. For example, teachers, police officers, pastors, elders, governors, and other civic leaders. Do you show respect to all of them? Name some ways to show respect to those in authority.

TO PRAY: "Lord, show us how to respect the people in authority over us."

21 Old Lady Marcum

RESPECT FOR OTHERS IS RIGHT REGARDLESS OF RACE, SEX, AGE, OR STATUS.

Bible Reading of the Day: Read 1 Peter 2:12-17.

Verse of the Day: *"Show proper respect to everyone"* (1 Peter 2:17, NIV).

Hannah opened the front door and let her friend Buffy in. They plopped down on opposite ends of the living room couch; Hannah switched on the TV.

"Guess who I saw on the way over here," Buffy whispered.

"Who?" Hannah asked.

"Old Lady Marcum," she answered. "She was walking that mean little dog of hers."

"Did she say anything?"

"Are you kidding?" Buffy answered. "What would she say to me?"

"She might have put a curse on you," Hannah suggested. "I heard her dog used to be a little kid who stepped on her grass!"

The two girls were laughing so hard they didn't notice Hannah's dad enter the room and sit on a footstool.

Dad waited for them to finish laughing. Then he asked, "Do you mind if I tell you a story? It won't take long," Dad promised.

"A few years ago, there was a boy in this neighborhood who had very few friends. One day," his tone became eerie, "that boy wandered into Old Lady Marcum's yard. He walked on her grass, and even sat on her porch, all by himself. Before long, the door opened, and there stood Old Lady Marcum. She smiled at the boy and invited him into her house—and, believe it or not, he went into that scary old house. When she had him all alone in the house, you know what she did to him?"

"What?" the two girls whispered at the same time.

Dad leaned back and his voice changed. It was no longer eerie. "She gave him milk and cookies and asked him to come back as often as he wanted to. And he did, about once a week for the next few years, until he went off to college."

"You're that little boy, aren't you, Dad?" Hannah asked.

Dad nodded.

"And you're saying we shouldn't say mean things about Old Lady Marcum," Buffy added.

Dad smiled. "I'm saying you shouldn't say mean things about anybody, whether they're old or young, white or black, or bald or fat. Even people who are different from you deserve your respect, because the Bible says to show proper respect to everyone."

"OK, Dad," Hannah said. "We're sorry."

"Good," Dad said. He stood to leave, but paused. "Oh, and by the way," he said. "She got that dog from the animal shelter. Just in case you were wondering."

 TO DO: Think of ways your family can learn more about a culture that is different from yours. Perhaps you might try a different type of cuisine or visit a museum that features exhibits on a specific culture.

 TO PRAY: "God, help us obey your command to show proper respect to everyone. Remind us especially to respect those who are different from us."

22 The Respect Game

RESPECTING YOURSELF IS RIGHT.

Bible Reading of the Day: Read 1 John 3:1-2.
Verse of the Day: *"See how very much our heavenly Father loves us, for he allows us to be called his children, and we really are!" (1 John 3:1).*

"What's wrong, Dad?" Kirsten asked. "You seem sad today."

Dad set his fork beside his dinner plate and sighed as he wiped his mouth with his napkin. "I guess I am a little sad, Kirsten," he said.

"Rough day at work?" Mom asked gently.

Dad nodded. "Lloyd came into my office today," he said, referring to his supervisor. "He launched into one of his temper tantrums. He told me he had lost all his respect for me because I had objected to a new company policy that I thought was wrong. So, I guess I'm feeling a little down."

"I still respect you, Daddy," Kirsten said.

"Me too, Daddy," her little sister, Kendra, added.

"Kids," Mom said, "why don't we play a round or two of our 'respect game'?"

"Can I start?" Kendra asked. Mom nodded, so Kendra looked at her dad. "I respect you because . . . because you're a good daddy!"

Dad started to say something but Kirsten interrupted him. "You know the rules, Dad; you can't talk until we're finished."

Dad nodded and moved his hand as if he were zipping his mouth shut.

"I respect you," Kirsten said, "because you work really hard."

Mom reached a hand over and touched the back of Dad's hand. "I respect you because you're a wonderful father to two wonderful children . . . and because you always do what you say you will do."

"No fair!" Kendra said. "You got to say two things."

Mom chuckled. "All right, Kendra, you can have two turns in a row then."

They continued for the next several minutes that way, telling Dad why they each respected him. Finally, they decided to stop.

Dad's eyes were rimmed with tears as he said, "Thank you, ladies. I sure needed that tonight."

"That's OK, Dad," Kirsten said as she stood from her chair, stepped next to her dad's chair, and wrapped her arms tightly around his neck. "You do the same thing for us when we need to remember to respect ourselves."

"I get a hug too!" Kendra called. She jumped up from her chair and hugged Dad from the other side.

TO DISCUSS: Do you think it's good to respect yourself? If so, why? What good reason does today's Bible reading give for respecting ourselves? How can you show respect for yourself more in the future? Do you think respecting yourself can help you respect others? If so, how?

TO PRAY: "Lord, sometimes we forget that we need to respect ourselves. Help us, Lord, to give ourselves and others respect."

23 Matchless Value

RESPECT IS RIGHT BECAUSE WE ARE ALL CREATED IN THE IMAGE OF GOD.

Bible Reading of the Day: Read Genesis 1:1, 26–27.
Verse of the Day: *"So God created people in his own image; God patterned them after himself; male and female he created them"* (Genesis 1:27).

Walt finally found his dad in the basement workshop. "I've been looking all over for you," he said. "You won't believe what happened to me in school today."

Dad looked up from his work. He was carefully removing the staples from matchbooks; he would then remove the matches and flatten the match cover on the table. Later, he would add the covers to his collection, which was kept in plastic sleeves in thick loose-leaf albums.

"We did square dancing in gym today," Walt continued, "and guess who my partner was—Belinda Ramsey!"

"Who's Belinda Ramsey?" Dad asked.

Walt rolled his eyes. "She's a retard, Dad!"

"Walt," Dad answered sternly, "that's not very nice."

"No, I mean it. I'm not calling her a name. She's really a retard. She's really slow up here," he said, tapping his temple with his forefinger.

Dad's face wore a serious expression. He cleared his throat. "Son, could you hand me those two matchbook covers?" he asked, pointing across the room. Walt located the matchbooks on a small table inside the workshop. He handed them to his father.

"Why do you collect those, anyway?" Walt asked. "Will they be worth a lot of money someday?"

Dad chuckled and shook his head. "Not likely," he said. But they're worth something to me." He turned the pages of one album and pointed. "That's from the inn where your mom and I spent the first two nights of our honeymoon. And this one—" he turned a few more pages—"is from Luxembourg, from a trip I took to Europe with my junior high school concert band." He shrugged. "They're valuable to me, even if they're not valuable to anyone else . . . sort of like Belinda."

"What's Belinda got to do with your matchbooks?"

Dad cleared his throat again. "Well, Son, even if she doesn't seem valuable to you, she's valuable to God. Whether she's handicapped or not, she's still made in the image of God. And as a unique child of God, she still deserves respect, just like everyone who's made in God's image."

"I never thought of it that way," Walt said.

"That's why I'm here," Dad said, winking. "To help you think!"

 TO DO: Place a matchbook in a prominent place today (such as your dinner table) to remind you of the matchless value of every human being.

TO PRAY: "Lord, thank you for the matchless value you place on each of us."

24 Respect and Relationships

RESPECT ENCOURAGES HEALTHY RELATIONSHIPS.

Bible Reading of the Day: Read Genesis 32:3-7; 33:1-4.
Verse of the Day: *"Love each other with genuine affection, and take delight in honoring each other" (Romans 12:10).*

Joni and Missy were playing together in the backyard when Mom called them in.

"Lunch is ready, girls," she called. Joni had asked if her friend Missy could stay for lunch, and Mom had agreed to prepare Missy's favorite meal—sloppy joes.

As the two girls approached the sliding door, Joni stepped aside and waved her hand. "You go first," she said.

At that exact moment, however, Missy had stepped away from the door and said, "You go first."

The two girls smiled at each other and went through the wide doorway side by side. After they had hung up their coats and washed their hands, they sat at the kitchen counter to eat their sloppy joes.

"Jessica doesn't like sloppy joes," Missy said as she lifted her sandwich to take a bite.

Mom, who was working in the kitchen while they ate, asked, "Missy, do you still play with Jessica? I haven't seen you two together for a while."

Missy and Joni exchanged glances with each other. "My mom says I need to 'take a break' from Jessica," Missy said.

"Oh?" Mom answered. "Why?"

Missy finished chewing a bite of sandwich. "Jessica does things that Mom says aren't very respectful," she said. "She calls me names sometimes and treats me like she's special and I'm not."

"I see," Mom said. "Does she treat you that way, Joni?"

Joni nodded. "She treats everybody that way."

"That's too bad," Mom said. "But it should teach you something."

"What?" the two girls said at the same time.

Mom waited for them to finish giggling before she continued. "It should remind you why treating other people with respect is good and treating them disrespectfully is bad. If Jessica treated people more respectfully, she'd probably have more friends— friends who would probably want to spend more time with her."

Missy nodded enthusiastically. "She could be fun if she treated people right."

"Like the way you two treat each other," Mom said. "I like that."

Joni and Missy smiled at each other. "We do too!" they said in unison.

TO DISCUSS: In today's Bible reading, how did Jacob show respect for his brother, Esau? Do you think that helped or hurt their relationship? Why? Do you think Jessica's attitudes and actions helped or hurt her friendships? Why? Do you think treating other people with respect encourages good relationships? If not, why not? If so, how?

TO PRAY: Take turns praying for the people you respect. Give thanks to God for each person.

25 The Right Call

RESPECT INVITES THE ADMIRATION AND APPRECIATION OF OTHERS.

Bible Reading of the Day: Read Romans 13:2-3.
Verse of the Day: *"Do what is good, and you will have praise"*
(Romans 13:3, NASB).

Bruce huddled with the rest of his team. Their church youth group had divided into two teams to play a game of touch football. Bruce was the captain of his team; their youth pastor, Pastor Paul, was the captain of the other team. Bruce's team was ahead by two touchdowns.

"I've got an idea," Dylan said as Bruce and the others formed a tight circle to plan their next football play. He smiled mischievously. "On this next play, Kevin and I are going to run straight for Pastor Paul . . . *and de-pants him!"*

Bruce lifted his head and scanned the large group of boys and girls who were playing and watching the game. "You can't do that!" Bruce said.

"Why not?" Dylan grinned wickedly. "Hope his underwear's clean!"

"No way," Bruce said, shaking his head. "It's not right."

"Oh, come on," Dylan said. "Loosen up. It's just a harmless prank."

"It wouldn't be right," Bruce repeated. "Look, Pastor Paul's a cool guy, and he's a lot of fun and all that, but he's still our youth pastor. I think it would be disrespectful."

"No, it wouldn't," Dylan said, but the other faces around the huddle wore expressions that seemed to agree with Bruce. "All right," he said, frowning. "Let's just play football."

The game continued. Although Pastor Paul's team staged a comeback and tied the game, Bruce's team won, scoring a touchdown on the final play of the game.

Later, after most of the youth group had left, Pastor Paul approached Bruce and clamped a hand on his shoulder.

"Hey, Bruce," he said, smiling, "I hear Dylan was plotting to *de-pants* me during the game."

"Yeah," Bruce said, nodding.

"I also hear you told him to forget it, that it would have been disrespectful."

"Yeah."

Pastor Paul released Bruce's shoulder and slapped him firmly on the back. "Thanks, *amigo,"* he said. He locked gazes with Bruce. "You made the right call, and I really appreciate it."

Pastor Paul walked away then, but his words left a warm feeling in Bruce's heart.

 TO DISCUSS: Do you think Bruce made the right call? Why or why not? How do you show respect for your church leaders and for others in authority? Why do you think Pastor Paul's words gave Bruce a warm feeling? Do you think those who are respectful usually receive more admiration and appreciation than those who are disrespectful? Why or why not?

TO PRAY: "Lord, open our eyes to the ways respect for others benefits *us."*

26 Ten Rules of Respect

RESPECT IS THE BEGINNING OF BASIC MORALITY.

Bible Reading of the Day: Read Exodus 20:3-17.
Verse of the Day: *"Show proper respect to everyone"* (1 Peter 2:17, NIV).

Stacy ran to the front door as soon as she heard her parents put their key in the lock. She and her preschool brother had stayed home with a baby-sitter while Mom and Dad went to Stacy's school to meet with her teacher.

"What did she say?" Stacy asked, before Mom and Dad had even taken their coats off. "Did she show you my artwork? Did you sit at my desk?"

Mom and Dad laughed at Stacy's excitement, but asked her to wait until they had hung up their coats and paid the baby-sitter. Once the baby-sitter left, Mom and Dad sat on the living room couch on either side of Stacy.

They started answering her questions, and Dad finally said, "We're very proud of you, Stacy. Your teacher said many good things about you. But do you know what we think is the best thing she said?" After Stacy shook her head, Dad continued, "She said you are her most respectful student."

Stacy smiled broadly as her mother added, "That's what we liked best out of all the good things your teacher said about you, because respect is so important . . . and so rare these days."

"I've got an idea!" Stacy announced. "Let's play the 'What If?' game!"

"All right," Mom said, shrugging and exchanging smiles with Dad. "What if everyone in the world treated others with respect?"

Stacy jumped up and down. "Nobody would . . ." she said, then started over. "Nobody would break the Ten Commandments."

"Where did that come from?" Mom asked, surprised at Stacy's unexpected answer. "What do you mean?"

"Wait a minute," Dad said, his eyes wide with realization. He looked at Stacy. "Stacy, you're absolutely right." He turned to his wife. "Think about it," he said. "One way to look at the Ten Commandments is that they're commandments to respect. The first commandment tells us to respect God. The second commandment says to respect God's uniqueness. And the third and fourth commandments say to respect God's name and God's Sabbath."

Mom looked from Dad to Stacy. "Respect your parents," she added. "Respect life. Respect marriage. Respect other people's property . . . you're right! If we truly respect others, we wouldn't break the Ten Commandments—just like Stacy said!"

Stacy beamed at both her parents. "Did I give a good answer?" she asked.

"You sure did," Mom and Dad said simultaneously.

TO DISCUSS: How do the Ten Commandments encourage respect? What other commandments can you think of that encourage respect for others?

TO PRAY: "Father God, help us to see how important respect is. Help us to see that respect for you and for others pleases you. And help us to see that respect for others will help us make other right choices."

27 Tommy's Tantrum

GOD'S COMMANDS AREN'T INTENDED TO MAKE US MISERABLE—THEY'RE INTENDED FOR OUR WELL-BEING.

Bible Reading of the Day: Read Deuteronomy 6:20-25.
Verse of the Day: *"The Lord our God commanded us to obey all these laws and to fear him for our own prosperity and well-being, as is now the case" (Deuteronomy 6:24).*

"I *hate* Coach Burns!" Tommy said as he met his parents at the car after football practice.

"Tommy!" Mom chided.

"Son, that's not a very kind thing to say," Dad added. "I hope you don't mean it."

Tommy opened the car door and tossed his helmet onto the seat, then slumped down beside it. "Well," he said, "I guess I don't *hate* him, but I think he's awful mean."

"Why?" Dad asked.

"Because!" Tommy whined. "He does things just to make us miserable."

"Like what?" Dad asked as he opened the passenger-side door for his wife.

"Like making us do 'two-a-days,'" he answered, referring to the two daily practices the coach called on Saturdays in preparation for the regional championship game.

Dad chuckled. "You think he calls 'two-a-days' just to be mean?"

"Yeah," Tommy answered sullenly.

"I know you're tired right now," Dad said, "but I think you know better than that. Coach Burns probably has a hundred other things he could be doing, rather than spending almost all day Saturday listening to you and your teammates complain about how mean he is. You know he makes you practice hard so you can play better."

"Humph," Tommy answered.

Mom turned around in her seat to face Tommy. "Did you have fun this season?" she asked.

Tommy nodded.

"Are you excited about going to the regional championships?"

He nodded again.

"And are you having fun playing?"

"Yeah," Tommy admitted.

"Then you should thank Coach Burns. If he didn't demand your best effort, your season would have ended a couple of weeks ago."

Tommy sat very still in the backseat and stared out the window. He hated it when his parents were right.

TO DISCUSS: Why do you think Tommy thought Coach Burns wanted to make him miserable? Do you think Tommy was right or wrong about Coach Burns? A lot of people think the same thing about God; they think he gave us commands in order to be mean or make us miserable. What does today's Bible reading say about why God gave his commands to us? Are they intended to do us good or to do us harm? Should we be upset at God or thankful to him for giving his commands to us?

TO PRAY: "Lord, you know how easily we fall into complaining. Thank you for bearing with us and for reminding us that your commands are for our good."

28 Trail of Balloons

GOD'S WORD AND HIS COMMANDS ARE INTENDED TO LEAD US TO A RELATIONSHIP WITH HIM.

Bible Reading of the Day: Read Isaiah 55:6-7.

Verse of the Day: *"Seek the Lord while you can find him. Call on him now while he is near" (Isaiah 55:6).*

"Can I carry some of the balloons, Daddy?" Valerie asked.

Dad carefully separated the strings that tied the bundle of balloons together and handed five to his daughter.

"Don't let go of them, OK?" he warned.

Valerie nodded and tightened her fist around the strings as they walked out the front door of their house and down the sidewalk. Valerie watched as Dad tied five balloons to the mailbox in front of their house. Then Dad took Valerie's free hand in his, and they turned down the sidewalk and walked toward the next intersection. At the end of the block, Dad tied his last five balloons to the street sign at the corner.

"Daddy," Valerie asked, "why do we have to leave the balloons here? Why can't we just keep them and play with them?"

Dad grunted from the effort of tying the strings high on the street sign. "Well, because the balloons will help people find our house. You don't want your new friends to get lost coming to your birthday party, do you?"

"How will they know how to get here?" Valerie asked, suddenly worried.

"Because when I told all their parents how to get to our new house, I told them to look for the balloons."

Valerie looked at the balloons in her hand. "What are these balloons for?" she asked.

Dad leaned over and touched her lightly on the nose. "Those are for you!"

That night, after a very successful—and tiring—birthday party, Dad read to Valerie from the book of Isaiah in the Bible. He read the words "Seek the Lord while you can find him. Call on him now while he is near."

As he finished reading, Valerie said, "Maybe God needs some of our balloons!"

"Why do you say that?" Dad asked.

"So people can find him, like they found my birthday party."

Dad thought for a few moments. Finally, he said, "You know what, Valerie? I think you're right. But I think God uses his Word instead of balloons. He gave commands to his people to show them how to find and follow him. That's why he wants us to read his Word and follow his commands—so we can find him and stay close to him."

"The Bible is like a trail of birthday balloons?" Valerie asked.

Dad nodded. "A little bit. If we follow it, we'll become closer and closer to God."

 TO DO: Tie or tape a balloon to your family Bible today to remind you to seek the Lord by reading and obeying his Word.

TO PRAY: "Lord, you tell us that if we seek you, you will be found by us. We want to seek you today and always."

29 A Downhill Slope

HUMILITY IS RIGHT BECAUSE GOD IN CHRIST HUMBLED HIMSELF.

Bible Reading of the Day: Read Philippians 2:3-11.

Verse of the Day: *"Pride goes before destruction, and haughtiness before a fall" (Proverbs 16:18).*

"I can ski better than you can!" Curtis boasted to his older sister, Amanda. He stood at the top of the intermediate slope. "I'll beat you to the bottom."

Amanda made a slight noise of disapproval and rolled her eyes at her brother. "Everything is not a competition, Curtis."

"Ha, ha!" Curtis cackled. "You know you're going to lose!"

"I can't lose," she answered, "because I'm not even racing."

"Ready?" Curtis said. "Go!"

Curtis took off down the slope. Even though Amanda hadn't intended to race him, she launched herself just a second after her brother said the word. As she started downhill, she became more and more determined to pass her brother and beat him to the bottom of the slope.

Amanda sped faster and faster and kept her eyes on Curtis, who turned every once in a while to see his sister skiing close behind. Soon, however, Amanda's eyes opened wide with apprehension. She saw two skiers ahead of Curtis who had stopped along the way to talk, and she knew immediately what was going to happen. She knew that Curtis would not give the stopped skiers the three to five-foot margin that was considered common courtesy. She watched in horror as Curtis skied too close to the pair.

Amanda arrived just a couple of seconds after Curtis had tumbled into the couple, sending all three of them to the ground in a heap. "Are you all right?" she asked. She was relieved to see that the strangers were laughing, but she still glared at her brother as she helped him back to his feet.

The other skiers helped each other up. "I sure saw that one coming," one said to his partner.

The other man turned to Curtis. "You need to be a little more careful on the slopes, Son."

Curtis nodded, his expression showing his embarrassment. He apologized to the men, and he and Amanda continued their descent down the slope . . . slowly.

"I sure made an impression on those guys," Curtis said sheepishly.

"Yeah . . . the *wrong* impression!" Amanda said.

"I'm sorry, Sis," Curtis said. "I guess I was a little cocky."

"A *little?*" Amanda teased. "And I guess Mount Everest is a little hill, right?"

TO DISCUSS: What was wrong with Curtis's behavior? Why is pride and boasting wrong, and humility right? (HINT: Check today's Bible reading.) Did Curtis's boasting have good or bad results? Do you ever act like Curtis? Why or why not?

TO PRAY: "Lord Jesus, thank you for humbling yourself to die for our sins. Help us to remember your example when we're tempted to be prideful."

30 Bicycle Bait

THE FOOLISH HEART DENIES AND DISOBEYS GOD.

Bible Reading of the Day: Read Psalm 14:1-5.

Verse of the Day: *"God is with those who obey him" (Psalm 14:5).*

Wendy could tell that Josh was up to no good. She saw him enter her backyard through the gate. He walked fast and looked around as he approached her.

"Hi, Josh," she said. She and Josh played together sometimes, and they had even built a crude clubhouse in the woods behind her house.

"Guess what," Josh said in a whisper. He continued without waiting for her to answer. "Somebody left a new mountain bike in the alley behind Papa's Pizza."

A new mountain bike sure sounded tempting. Wendy shrugged. "It's got to belong to somebody."

"Well, duh!" Josh answered. "But whoever left it there didn't lock it up."

"So?"

"So, we could go take it and keep it in our clubhouse. That way it could belong to both of us."

Wendy flashed Josh an exasperated look, as if she couldn't believe he would suggest such a thing. "Josh, that would be stealing!"

"Well, duh!" he said again. "But how do we know the person it belongs to didn't steal it too?"

Wendy's face wrinkled in an expression of confusion. "What difference does that make? Besides," she said, "God says not to steal."

It was Josh's turn to look confused. "Oh, come on, Wendy," he said. "I don't believe in all that God-and-Sunday-school stuff anyway. Are you going to help me or not?"

Wendy flashed Josh a disgusted look. *"Not!"* she said emphatically.

"Oh, you're such a wimp!" he said as he stomped away.

Wendy was glad to see Josh leave. She played by herself for a while, then walked around to the front yard when she heard dogs barking down the street. Her mouth dropped open as she saw a police car in front of Josh's house. A police officer walked Josh up the steps of his front porch.

She remembered her earlier conversation with Josh and instantly knew what had happened. She prayed without closing her eyes. "I'm sorry Josh is in trouble," she said, "but I'm really glad I obeyed you."

TO DISCUSS: Why was Wendy able to make the decision that she did? Have you ever faced a similar situation? What did you do?

TO PRAY: "Heavenly Father, please help us remember that it is foolish to deny you or disobey you. We need your help to make right choices, Father. Please help us choose right and stay away from evil, because we know that you are with all those who obey you."

1 Faith and Deeds

WE ARE SAVED BY GRACE THROUGH FAITH, BUT OUR FAITH SHOULD PRODUCE RIGHT CHOICES.

Bible Reading of the Day: Read James 2:14-20.

Verse of the Day: *"We continually remember before our God and Father your work produced by faith" (1 Thessalonians 1:3, NIV).*

"I don't understand something, Dad," Joel said. He and his dad were working together in the family orchard. Dad drove the tractor between the rows of trees while Joel stood behind him, balancing on the back of the tractor and holding on to Dad's shoulders. "You know how you and Mom grounded me for taking money out of Mom's purse to go to the store with Randy?"

"Uh-huh," Dad said, nodding. "What don't you understand?"

"Well, I don't understand what the big deal is. I mean, I know I shouldn't have done it, but you act like I'm not a Christian if I do something wrong."

Dad said nothing. He stopped the tractor in front of a barren orange tree and shut off the engine. He climbed down from the tractor and walked over to the tree.

"See this tree?" Dad asked. He pulled an ax from his belt.

Joel stood with his hands in the pockets of his blue jeans. "Yeah. Why?"

"I've been planning to cut it down," Dad said. "You think I should?"

Joel shrugged again. "Yeah," he said. "It's dead."

"How do you know?"

"Look at it! It's been dead since last season."

"You're right," Dad said. "It doesn't bear any fruit." He began chopping at the base of the tree. After a few minutes of strenuous work, he gave the tree a push, and it toppled toward the tractor. Joel helped him pick up the tree and toss it into the trailer behind the tractor.

As Dad climbed back into the seat of the tractor, Joel spoke again. "I think I get your point, Dad," he said. He was used to his dad's unique way of using object lessons to teach.

Dad turned around and smiled at his son. "You're right in thinking that doing good doesn't make you a Christian," he said. "Only God's grace can do that, just as only God can make an orange tree. But a Christian should try to make right choices and produce good things, not bad things—just as an orange tree should produce oranges. And if it doesn't produce those things, you know something's wrong." Dad turned the key and the tractor engine roared to life.

"I hate to admit it," Joel said over the noise of the tractor, "but you're right."

Dad reached behind without turning around and elbowed his son in the ribs. "You should be used to that by now," he joked.

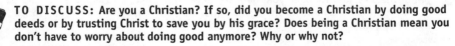

TO DISCUSS: Are you a Christian? If so, did you become a Christian by doing good deeds or by trusting Christ to save you by his grace? Does being a Christian mean you don't have to worry about doing good anymore? Why or why not?

TO PRAY: "Lord, your grace and only your grace saves us. Please help us respond to your grace with loving obedience."

2 Ellen's Pact

FAITHFULNESS IS RIGHT BECAUSE GOD IS FAITHFUL.

Bible Reading of the Day: Read Genesis 40:1-23.
Verse of the Day: *"The unfailing love of the Lord never ends! . . . Great is his faithfulness" (Lamentations 3:22-23).*

"Let's make a pact," Kelly suggested.

"A what?" her friend Ellen asked. They sat together on the benches outside the school gym, waiting for their names to be called. They were each trying out for parts in the school play.

"You know, where two people agree to something," Kelly said. "Let's make a pact that if one of us gets a part in the play and the other person doesn't, we'll still help each other learn our parts and stuff."

"OK," agreed Ellen with a shrug.

Kelly held her little finger up in the air. Ellen wrapped her pinkie finger around Kelly's finger, and they shook. "It's a deal?" Kelly said.

"Deal," Ellen said.

The following Monday, the play parts were posted on the gym doors.

"I can't bear to look," Kelly said. She covered her eyes with her hand. "Did I make it?"

Ellen didn't answer for a few moments. When she spoke, her voice was dull. "You got the part."

Kelly opened her eyes and screamed. She wrapped her arms around Ellen and danced up and down for a few moments. Then she let go. "What's wrong?" she asked Ellen, and immediately knew the answer. "You didn't make it?"

"No," Ellen said crossly. "If you must know."

"Are you sure?" Kelly stepped toward the gym door and peered at the list.

"Yes, I'm sure," Ellen answered. "I've got to go, OK?" She started walking away.

"OK," Kelly answered, catching up to her friend from behind. "I'll call you, OK? I'll get the script and we can . . . you know, work on my part together, OK? That could be kinda fun."

Ellen waved a hand carelessly at her friend. "I'll probably be too busy," she said. She didn't look at Kelly. "I don't think I can."

Kelly stopped then and watched her friend walk away down the long school hallway. She knew she'd have to find someone else to help her study her part . . . pact or no pact.

 TO DISCUSS: What was wrong with Ellen's behavior? How was it like the cupbearer's behavior in today's Bible reading? What makes faithfulness right and unfaithfulness wrong? Do you ever act like Ellen? Why or why not?

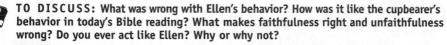 **TO PRAY:** "Lord, help us to be faithful in word and deed because we know you are faithful."

3 Footsteps

TO BE LIKE JESUS IS TO BE RIGHT.

Bible Reading of the Day: Read 1 Peter 2:21-25.
Verse of the Day: *"Direct my footsteps according to your word; let no sin rule over me" (Psalm 119:133, NIV).*

It was the first big snowstorm of the year. Grandpa put on his coat to go outside.

"Where are you going, Grandpa?" Sherrie asked.

Grandpa zipped the coat and pulled a wool cap over his ears. "I'm going out to the woodpile to get some wood for the stove," he said.

"Can I come?" Sherrie asked.

Grandpa seemed to think for a moment, then answered, "I reckon you can, little lady. I could use an extra pair of hands."

A few moments later, Sherrie wore a coat, hat, and boots just like her grandfather. Grandpa opened the side door of the house and stepped into the deep snow. He took a few steps, then turned around. Sherrie was still waiting just outside the door.

"The snow is too deep, Grandpa," she called.

"Just follow in my footsteps," Grandpa called back.

Sherrie studied the path Grandpa had made through the snow and bravely put her foot into the first footprint he had left. Then she put her other foot in the next footprint and had soon caught up with Grandpa as she walked in his footsteps. It became a sort of game to her as she stayed a few steps behind him to and from the woodpile.

Later that night, as the family gathered around the fireplace, Grandpa told the others how Sherrie had helped him that afternoon. Then he read from the Bible about following in the footsteps of Jesus.

"Jesus has shown us the way," he said afterward. "He has left his footprints in the snow for us, just as I did for Sherrie. If we follow in his footsteps, we can be sure we're going the right way, because the Bible says that Jesus 'did no sin, neither was guile found in his mouth.' If we follow in his steps, we'll never have to wander around, wondering what's right and what's wrong. We'll know what's right or wrong, because we know that to be like Jesus is to be right."

Sherrie climbed into her grandfather's lap. "Grandpa," she asked, "did you know Jesus when he was on earth?"

Grandpa joined the others in laughter. "No, little lady," he answered. "I *have* known him for many years, but I'm not quite that old!"

 TO DISCUSS: What does it mean to "follow in Jesus' footsteps"? What are some practical ways to do this?

 TO PRAY: "God, thank you for sending Jesus to live and die for our sake. Help us to follow his example and to be more and more like him every day in every choice we make."

4 Deceitful Ways

DISHONESTY IS WRONG—EVEN WHEN IT'S "NO BIG DEAL."

Bible Reading of the Day: Read Psalm 119:27-29.
Verse of the Day: *"Keep me from deceitful ways" (Psalm 119:29, NIV).*

Kristie showed Yolanda the new hair barrettes she'd bought at the mall.

"I love these!" Yolanda said. "They're so cool."

"Why don't you buy a set of your own when we go to the mall tonight?" Kristie suggested.

"How much do they cost?" Yolanda asked.

Yolanda's face dropped when Kristie told her. "I don't have enough," she said.

Kristie's face dropped too. "Maybe your parents would loan you the money."

Yolanda shook her head. "They don't let me borrow money," she explained. "Something about teaching me not to go in debt for the things I want."

The two girls exchanged mournful glances. After a few moments, Kristie's face brightened. "I have an idea," she said. "Why don't you tell your parents you need money for school . . . for . . . for new art supplies, or something like that."

"I can't do that." Yolanda answered.

"Let me finish," Kristie said. "You could get the money from them for art supplies, and we could go to the mall tonight and buy your barrettes. Then—when do you get your allowance?"

"Friday," Yolanda answered.

"OK," Kristie announced, as if that settled everything, "Friday, you get your allowance from your parents, and then explain to them that you didn't need the new art supplies after all. You give them your allowance, and everybody's happy!"

"It doesn't . . . it doesn't seem right."

"Look," Kristie explained patiently, "it's not going to hurt anybody. Your parents won't lose any money, and you'll be able to get the barrettes you want."

Yolanda's face wrinkled. She was tempted to follow her friend's advice.

"All you have to do—" Kristie said, but Yolanda interrupted her.

"All I have to do," Yolanda interrupted, "is lie to my parents and borrow money from them without them knowing."

"Yeah!" Kristie answered, then, "No! You wouldn't be lying."

"If it's not lying, what is it?"

"This is no big deal."

"Yes it is," Yolanda said. "I just realized why it doesn't seem right."

"Why?" Kristie asked.

"Because it's not!" Yolanda answered.

 TO DO: Dishonesty is wrong, even when it's "no big deal." Count how many hair barrettes or decorative combs you see people wearing today to remind you to be honest like Yolanda (just be careful not to stare!).

TO PRAY: "Keep us honest when we are tempted, Lord."

5 Lost and Found

GOD ALONE SAYS WHAT'S RIGHT OR WRONG.

Bible Reading of the Day: Read Joshua 6:20; 7:1, 19–21.
Verse of the Day: *"The honest person will live in safety, but the dishonest will be caught" (Proverbs 10:9, New Century Version).*

Donna paid for her new scarf and gloves and shoved the change into her coat pocket. Then she headed out of the store with her friend Jenny into a brisk wind.

"Brrr!" Jenny said, hunching her shoulders. "That wind is cold."

"I'm glad I wore this coat," Donna said, zipping up her warm winter coat.

Suddenly, Jenny nudged Donna with her elbow. She nodded toward a street vendor's cart at the curb. Steam rose from the cart, and crude cardboard signs advertised hot dogs, hot chestnuts, and hot chocolate for sale.

"Let's get some hot chocolate," Jenny suggested.

Donna looked longingly at the vendor's cart. "I can't," she said. "I don't have enough money." She thrust her hand into her coat pocket and pulled out the change the cashier had given her. "I've only got—wait a minute." Her eyebrows scrunched together as she counted the money in her palm. Then she looked up at her friend. "That lady gave me too much change."

"Great!" Jenny said, leaning over to count the money in Donna's hand. "That means you can buy us both some hot chocolate."

"What?" Donna said. "I can't keep this money. It would be like stealing."

"No, it wouldn't," Jenny pleaded. "It was her mistake, not yours."

"But it's not my money."

"I can think of a hundred reasons why you should keep the money," Jenny said.

"I can only think of one reason why I shouldn't," Donna said. "But it's the only reason that counts because God says not to take things that don't belong to you."

Jenny jumped up and down on the curb. "Come on, Donna," she begged. "I'm cold and I want some hot chocolate!"

Donna shook her head and gripped her friend's elbow. "Let's go," she said, dragging Jenny toward the store. Inside the store, Donna walked to the counter and found the cashier who had given her the wrong change. She explained what had happened and told her she'd come to return the money.

"I'm so glad you came back," the cashier said, reaching under the counter and pulling out a bag. "You forgot your purchase!"

Donna's mouth dropped open. She had paid for her scarf and gloves and then absentmindedly left the store without them! "Thank you so much," she said.

"Thank you," the cashier said, "for being honest."

TO DISCUSS: What would you have done if you were in Donna's situation? Why? How did Donna know which was the right thing to do? How do you think the story might have ended if she had listened to her friend?

TO PRAY: "Lord, the old saying Honesty is the best policy is true. It is true because you have shown us that honesty is right."

6 Playing Pretend

GOD COMMANDS HONESTY.

Bible Reading of the Day: Read Leviticus 19:1-2, 11.
   Verse of the Day: *"So put away all falsehood and 'tell your neighbor the truth'"* (Ephesians 4:25).

Tiffany was standing by the sliding glass door to the small patio, looking outside, when Mom came into the room.

Tiffany whirled around and faced Mom with a guilty look.

Alerted by Tiffany's behavior, Mom realized that the family dog wasn't around. "Where's Fluffles?" Mom asked.

"I don't know," Tiffany answered.

"Tiffany," Mom said slowly, "did you let Fluffles outside?"

Tiffany's voice was barely a whisper when she spoke. "No," she said.

Mom scooped Tiffany into her arms and sat down on one of the kitchen chairs, settling her daughter on her lap. She brushed a strand of Tiffany's hair out of her face. "Tiffany, do you remember yesterday afternoon when you and I were playing with your play kitchen set? You pretended to serve me lunch at your play table, and I pretended to eat? It was fun to play pretend, wasn't it?"

Tiffany nodded.

"But there's a difference between playing pretend and telling a lie. Do you know what the difference is?"

"Pretend is just for fun," Tiffany said. "But telling a lie is real."

Mom cocked her head to one side. "That's right," she said. "When you play pretend with someone, you both know it's pretend. But when you tell a lie, you're trying to fool someone and make the other person believe something that's not true." Mom brushed Tiffany's hair out of her face again. "There's nothing wrong with playing pretend, but God says not to tell lies. He says we should be honest and always tell the truth."

Tiffany turned her head and looked at the sliding door. "I didn't tell the truth, Mommy." Her eyes welled up with tears. "I opened the door and let Fluffles go outside."

"Thank you for finally telling me the truth," Mom answered. "I'll tell you what; you go get Fluffles's leash, and we'll go look for her together."

Tiffany started to turn away, but Mom gripped her gently by the arm. "Do you think you can remember to play pretend with someone only when the other person knows you're pretending, and tell the truth the rest of the time?"

"OK," Tiffany said. "Let's pretend Fluffles is a pig, and we're trying to catch a pig!"

Mom laughed. "All right," she said. "If Fluffles has gotten into the neighbors' garbage, we may not have to pretend!"

 TO DISCUSS: What's the difference between playing pretend and telling a lie? Is it OK to play pretend? Why or why not? Is it OK to tell a lie? Why or why not?

 **TO PRAY:** "Guard us, Lord, against giving in to the impulse to lie."

7 The Honesty Party

GOD COMMANDS HONESTY BECAUSE GOD VALUES HONESTY.

Bible Reading of the Day: Read Zechariah 8:14-17.

Verse of the Day: *"You must not cheat each other" (Leviticus 25:17, New Century Version).*

Keith tossed his book bag onto the overstuffed chair beside the front door and strode to the kitchen to grab an after-school snack. When he reached the doorway to the dining room, he stopped and stared. The room was decorated with balloons and streamers, and party hats sat on the table at each place setting.

Amber breezed into the room, and Keith nodded at the decorations. "What's this all about?" he asked his sister.

Amber shrugged. "Mom says it's a surprise."

That evening as the family gathered around the table for dinner, Keith and Amber were still curious about the decorations. After Dad prayed, he stood and put on his party hat. He nodded to the hats near everyone's plates.

"Put them on," he said, smiling.

"Why?" Keith asked. "What's going on?"

Mom suddenly reached into a drawer in the china cabinet and pulled out a large silver medal. The "medal" was actually a three-inch circle of cardboard wrapped in aluminum foil and attached to a thick red ribbon. She handed it to Dad.

"This is our family's first 'Honesty Party,'" Dad said. "We're having this party to celebrate an act of honesty that was done by someone in our family." Keith and Amber exchanged quizzical glances. "Keith, would you stand, please?" Dad asked. Keith stood, and Dad stepped over to his son and slipped the ribbon over his head.

"What's this for?" Keith asked, smiling.

"Dad and I met with your teachers this week," Mom said. "And Mr. Henson, your math teacher, told us that somebody tried to give you the answers to a quiz last week—"

"Yeah," Keith interrupted. "That was Jim Hooper."

"And Mr. Henson said you wouldn't take them. He said he saw everything in the school hallway. That's when we decided to do this," Mom said. "We wanted to honor you and tell you we're proud of you."

"And also because we want you to know," Dad added, "that we really value honesty in this family, because we serve a God who values honesty and hates dishonesty."

"Thanks," Keith said. He shrugged. "I never thought that much about it."

"Well, we do," Mom said. "And so does God."

TO DO: Plan an "honesty party" sometime soon to reward a family member for an act of honesty.

TO PRAY: "Lord, you command us to be honest, even if honesty doesn't bring us rewards here on earth. Help us to obey your commands."

8 Karee's Discovery

GOD VALUES HONESTY BECAUSE GOD IS A GOD OF TRUTH.

Bible Reading of the Day: Read Exodus 34:4-6.
Verse of the Day: *"The Lord, The Lord God, merciful and gracious, long-suffering, and abundant in goodness and truth"* *(Exodus 34:6, KJV).*

"Oh, no!" Karee said. She sat in the backseat of the car, next to her friend Lisa. Her father sat in the driver's seat, waiting for Mom to come out of the convenience store.

"What's wrong?" Lisa asked.

Karee pulled her hand out of her coat pocket. She held a set of tiny earphones in her hand. "I never gave these back to Gina," she moaned. "I haven't worn this coat for a long time, and I forgot all about borrowing Gina's headphones."

Lisa shrugged. "Forget it," she suggested. "If Gina hasn't mentioned it in all that time, she's probably forgotten about it."

"Yeah, but—"

"You're always looking for headphones," Lisa said. "Now you've got an extra pair."

"But they're not mine!" Karee said. "I have to give them back to her and apologize for keeping them this long."

When Mom finally came out of the convenience store, Dad dropped Lisa off at her house. As Dad pulled away from the curb, he looked in the rearview mirror.

"I couldn't help but overhear your conversation about the headphones," he told Karee. "I'm glad you recognize that keeping those headphones would be wrong. Do you know why it would be wrong?"

Karee thought for a moment, then met her father's gaze in the rearview mirror. "Because it would be like stealing."

Dad nodded. "But why is stealing wrong?"

Karee shrugged. "Because God says not to steal," she answered.

"But why does God say not to steal?"

Karee rolled her eyes. "I don't know," she said.

Dad smiled at her. "Because he values honesty. And do you know why he values honesty?"

"No, but I bet you're gonna tell me," she answered in a teasing tone.

Dad chuckled. "God values honesty because he is a God of truth. He is completely honest, completely true. *That's* why giving those headphones back to Gina is the right thing to do."

"Hey," Karee said, looking out the window. "You passed our house."

"I know," Dad said with a smile. "I'm going to Gina's house."

TO DISCUSS: Is honesty right? If so, why? How do God's commands (don't steal, don't lie, and don't cheat) reflect his character? What are some other words that mean *honest*? (For example, ethical, moral, honorable, truthful, true.) Is God all of those things? How do you know?

TO PRAY: "Lord, we want to be truthful, ethical, and honorable because you are."

9 Finders Keepers

HONESTY ENCOURAGES TRUST; DISHONESTY INVITES DISTRUST.

Bible Reading of the Day: Read Luke 16:10–12.

Verse of the Day: *"Kings take pleasure in honest lips; they value a man who speaks the truth"* (Proverbs 16:13, NIV).

"Look what I got!" Barry grinned at his friend Darrick as he jammed his hand into his book bag.

Darrick leaned against Barry's locker, his eyes opened wide. *"Street Slam?"* he said, referring to the video game cartridge in Barry's hand. "How'd you get that? I've been saving money for weeks and I'm not even close to having enough to buy *Street Slam.*"

Barry shrugged as he opened his locker. "I didn't even have to buy it," he said.

"How'd you get it?"

"It used to be Marvin Kyser's," he answered.

"He *gave* it to you?"

"Not exactly," Barry said. "He was showing it around at his lunch table, you know, showing off and stuff. Then he set it down on top of his books on the floor and forgot about it. I got Tyler to walk by his table and 'accidentally' give Marvin's books a good kick in my direction. The game landed almost right at my feet. It was sweet."

Darrick stared at Barry, his mouth hanging open. "So you stole it?"

"No, man, I just found it on the floor in the cafeteria."

Darrick's mouth remained open. He shook his head. "You can't do that," he said. "That's not your game, it's Marvin's. And if you keep it, you're stealing it."

"You can call it stealing if you want to. I call it 'finders keepers.'"

"It doesn't matter what you call it. All that matters is, it's wrong."

"What are you gonna do, tell on me?" Barry asked.

"That's not the question, Barry. The question is, what are *you* gonna do?"

Barry stared at his friend for a few moments in silence. Finally he turned and slammed his locker door shut. He flashed Darrick a sour look. "I guess I'll go find Marvin Kyser," he said.

Darrick nodded. "Good," he said. "I'll go with you."

Barry extended his hands and turned his palms outward. "What, don't you trust me?"

"Should I?" Darrick asked in response. "Should Marvin?"

Barry rolled his eyes. "All right," he said. "You made your point."

Darrick smiled and slapped Barry on the back. "I hope so," he said.

 TO DISCUSS: Whom would you trust more: Darrick or Barry? Why? Name some people you trust. Why do you trust them? Do you think your honesty in "small matters" makes people want to trust you with greater responsibilities?

 TO PRAY: "Heavenly Father, when we're tempted to excuse 'small matters' of dishonesty, remind us that no sin is 'small' in your sight. Keep us on the path to honesty."

10 The Dishonesty Trap

DISHONESTY IS A TRAP.

Bible Reading of the Day: Read Proverbs 11:1, 3, 5-6.
Verse of the Day: *"Good people are guided by their honesty; treacherous people are destroyed by their dishonesty" (Proverbs 11:3).*

Everyone had finished eating dinner except Joy.

"Joy, did you get into the cookie jar before dinner?" Mom asked.

"No," Joy answered, shaking her head solemnly.

"Please clean your plate," Mom said.

Once everyone else had gone, Mom cleared the table and started doing the dishes. While her mother had her back turned, Joy set her plate on the floor and let Whiskers, the family cat, eat the chicken and vegetables on her plate. When Mom returned to the table, Joy sat before an empty plate.

"Very good!" Mom said. "You sure took care of *that* dinner, didn't you?"

"It was good," Joy said, smacking her lips.

Just then, however, Whiskers began to make coughing and choking noises.

"What's wrong with Whiskers?" Mom asked.

"I don't know," Joy said quickly, though she knew it was another lie.

Mom knelt down by Whiskers. "Did you see him eat anything?" she asked.

"No," Joy answered.

Mom picked up Whiskers and carried him into the kitchen. "I feel so helpless," she said. "I don't know how to help the poor little fellow." She stood silently for a few moments, while Whiskers' choking and coughing got worse. Finally, a look of determination crossed her face. "We're going to have to take him to the vet," she said.

"No!" Joy cried. She knew the vet would tell her mom that Whiskers had swallowed a chicken bone, and Mom would figure out what had happened. Joy's eyes filled with tears. "I didn't eat my dinner," she confessed. "I gave it to Whiskers."

Mom balanced Whiskers in one hand and stretched her other arm around Joy.

"I'm sorry, Mom," Joy said. "I didn't mean to keep lying to you, but it was like once I lied about eating my dinner I had to keep telling lies to cover up the other lies, and . . . and . . ." She was sobbing now.

Mom hugged her daughter. "I know, Joy," she said. "That's what dishonesty does. It traps us into telling more and more lies, and bigger and bigger lies. That's why honesty is so much better. But I forgive you, and I hope you'll remember this the next time you're tempted to lie."

"Oh, I will," Joy said through her tears.

"Now let's help Whiskers," said Mom.

 TO DISCUSS: What was the first lie that started Joy's web of lies? How many lies did she have to tell to cover up that lie? Have you ever been trapped by your own dishonesty? If so, tell about it. Why is honesty better than dishonesty?

 TO PRAY: "Before we weave a web of lies, remind us, Lord, how much one lie hurts you and disrupts our fellowship with you."

11 Eddie's Reputation

HONESTY PROTECTS US FROM SHAME AND ESTABLISHES A GOOD REPUTATION.

Bible Reading of the Day: Read Ephesians 4:17-25, 28.
Verse of the Day: *"Choose a good reputation over great riches, for being held in high esteem is better than having silver or gold" (Proverbs 22:1).*

Wayne and Eddie walked into the convenience store on their way home from school. Wayne waved at the clerk behind the counter. He almost always stopped at the store on his long walk home from school, and he and Milt had gotten to know each other.

The two boys walked over to the candy counter and stood for a few moments discussing their options. While Eddie was trying to decide between a Boffo Bar and Chewy Sugar Hearts, Wayne glanced toward the cash register and noticed that the clerk watched them closely.

Wayne looked back and forth from the clerk to Eddie a couple of times, but couldn't seem to catch the clerk's eye. Finally, he tapped Eddie on the shoulder and said, "I'm going to get a soda pop instead of candy." He walked over to the large cooler and pulled out a plastic bottle of his favorite soft drink. When he turned around and looked toward the cash register, he saw that the clerk's eyes had not left the candy aisle—and Eddie.

After they had paid for their purchases and left the store, Wayne stopped around the corner from the store. "Did you see what happened in there?" he said.

"What?" Eddie asked.

"Milt was watching every move you made," Wayne said. "He never took his eyes off you for one second."

Eddie's face flushed red, and his gaze dropped to his tennis shoes.

"What?" Wayne asked, surprised by Eddie's reaction. "What's wrong?"

Eddie shrugged and kicked the toe of his tennis shoe in the dirt. "I—I, uh, tried to steal something from that store last year," he said. "It was just a dumb pack of bubble gum, but I got caught. My parents wouldn't even let me go near the store for a long time."

Wayne's mouth dropped open in surprise. "So you think Milt thinks—"

"He was there when I did it," Eddie said. "He probably thinks I'll do it again."

"Oh," Wayne said, finally putting all the pieces together. Eddie's stolen pack of gum had ruined his reputation with Milt; that's why Milt had watched him so closely.

"Promise you won't tell anybody," Eddie said. "It's bad enough that Milt thinks I'm a thief."

Wayne nodded. He had never realized how easy it could be to mess up your reputation. He knew he wouldn't ever want to be in Eddie's shoes. "I won't tell anybody," he said.

 TO DISCUSS: A reputation is what other people think about you. For example, they may think you're honest, or they may think you're dishonest. How did Eddie mess up his reputation? Would you rather have a good reputation or a bad reputation? How can being honest help your reputation?

 TO PRAY: "Lord, as humans, we sometimes do things to ruin our own lives. Remind us that obeying your commands will protect us *and* our reputations."

12 People and Pens

WE CAN'T MAKE THE WHOLE WORLD HONEST, BUT WE CAN TRY TO BE
HONEST OURSELVES.

Bible Reading of the Day: Read Leviticus 26:3-6, 9-12.
Verse of the Day: *"People with integrity have firm footing, but those who
follow crooked paths will slip and fall" (Proverbs 10:9).*

Jillian's feet moved fast as she tried to keep up with her father's long strides on the
shopping plaza corridor. She and Dad were spending the morning together as Dad ran
his weekly errands.

Next, Dad stopeped at the bank. Jillian walked beside her father to a high table.
He took a slip of paper out of a rack and began writing with a pen that was anchored
to the table with a small chain of silver beads.

Afterward, Jillian followed her dad to a long line that wove through a maze of
silver posts and thick red ropes. "Daddy," she said when they had joined the
slow-moving line, "why was that pen tied to that big desk?"

Dad cocked his head to one side, unsure at first what Jillian was talking about.
Then he realized she was talking about the bank pen he had used to fill out his deposit
slip. "Oh, that," he said. "The bank has to tie the pens to the table or people will take
them, I guess."

"You mean people *steal* here?" Jillian asked.

"Yes," Dad said, chuckling. "Some people might not mean to take them, and others
do, I suppose."

Jillian looked back at the table. "They shouldn't have to tie everything down."

"You're right," Dad said. "And if everyone were honest, they wouldn't have to."

"Are you playing the 'What If?' game, Daddy?" Jillian asked.

Dad chuckled again and crouched down to face his daughter better. "I guess I am,"
he said. "So . . . what if everyone in the world were honest?"

"Banks wouldn't have to tie their pens to the tables!" Jillian said.

Dad nodded. "What else?"

"Umm . . ." She looked around the bank. "They wouldn't have to put the money
in big, big safes!"

Dad glanced behind him and saw the massive safe door. "That's right. What else?"

Jillian's head rotated around and around. She pointed at a surveillance camera.
"They wouldn't need those cameras, would they, Daddy?"

"No," Dad said, "they wouldn't. They wouldn't have to watch everybody who
came into their bank."

"I wish everybody in the world really was honest," Jillian said. "That would be nice."

"Well," Dad answered, "let's make sure *we* are honest, OK? That's a good start."

TO DO: Play the 'What If?' game as a family, imagining how things would be
different if everyone in the world were honest.

TO PRAY: "Lord, keep us alert to the many blessings and advantages of honest
behavior."

13 The Only Way

JESUS IS THE WAY, THE TRUTH, AND THE LIFE.

Bible Reading of the Day: Read John 14:1-6.
Verse of the Day: *"Jesus told him, 'I am the way, the truth, and the life. No one can come to the Father except through me'"* (John 14:6).

"Honey, wake up," Mom said, nudging her husband, who reclined in the front passenger seat while she drove.

Dad rubbed his eyes, sat up, and raised the back of his seat. They had traveled many hours to get to his brother's new house in a distant city. Mom had driven the last hundred miles.

"We're almost there," she said. "John said to look for two stone pillars on the side of the street. Would you help me look on that side?"

"Yes," Dad said. He gazed out the windshield, looking for the pillars.

After a few moments, Dad yelled, "There it is!" and pointed to a pair of stone pillars flanking the entrance to a side street.

"Yea!" Randy cheered. "We're almost there! Is this Uncle John's street?"

Mom smiled. "Not yet. But Uncle John said there's only one way to get to his street, and that's through those stone pillars."

"There's only one way to get to heaven, too," Dad said. He turned in his seat to face the kids. "And you know what that way is, right?"

"Being good!" Randy answered.

"No," Dad answered. "None of us is ever good enough to get to heaven. The only way to heaven is by knowing Jesus and letting him make us good."

"But aren't we supposed to obey the Ten Commandments?" Marcia asked.

Dad nodded. "Yes, but only Jesus can get us to heaven. He said, 'I am the way, the truth, and the life. No one can come to the Father except through me.' When we love Jesus and put our faith in him, he helps us obey his commands. We're not Christians because we obey his commands. It's the other way around—we obey him because we're Christians."

Suddenly, Dad, Marcia, and Randy realized that Mom had stopped the car.

"We're finally here," she said, "and you three act like you want to stay in the car for another ten hours!"

"Not me!" Randy cried as he unbuckled his seat belt and opened the car door. "Me neither!" Marcia added.

TO DISCUSS: When we trust Christ for salvation, God's Holy Spirit actually enters our lives (Romans 8:9; 1 Corinthians 3:16). It is the Holy Spirit that claims and seals us for God, not the following of commandments (Ephesians 4:30; 2 Corinthians 1:21-22). Obedience is a result of our relationship with God, not the cause of it. Are you following the one who said, "I am the way, the truth, and the life"? How does knowing Jesus help you obey his commands?

TO PRAY: "Father God, thank you for sending your only Son to die in our place. Because of him, we can have eternal life."

14 Window Seat

FAIRNESS IS RIGHT BECAUSE GOD IS FAIR.

Bible Reading of the Day: Read Psalm 67:1-5.

Verse of the Day: *"Tell all the nations that the Lord is king. The world is firmly established and cannot be shaken. He will judge all peoples fairly"* (Psalm 96:10).

Aaron and Faith walked in front of Mom onto the huge plane. They were returning home from a short vacation with their grandmother. Mom struggled down the aisle behind them, carrying her large purse in front of her and an even larger bag of books, magazines, and cross-stitch supplies for the long flight home.

Aaron and Faith hurried ahead and found their seats. By the time Mom arrived at their row, Faith sat in the window seat while Aaron remained in the aisle.

"Mom, tell her to move!" Aaron whined.

"I don't have to move," Faith said.

Other passengers began lining up behind Mom and Aaron, who were blocking the aisle. Mom placed her purse in the overhead storage compartment and shoved her cross-stitch bag under the seat in front of hers.

"Just sit down for now," she told Aaron, who frowned as he plopped down.

After the passengers were all seated, Mom turned to her daughter. "Faith," she said, "who sat in the window seat on the way to Grandma's house?"

"I don't know," Faith said with a shrug.

"She's lying!" Aaron protested. "She knows that she sat in the window seat."

"So?" Faith countered loudly. "I got here first."

Mom placed a finger over her lips and talked in a low voice. "Faith," she said, "which do you think is right, fairness or unfairness?"

Faith answered without looking at her mother. "Fairness," she said.

"And do you know *why* fairness is right and unfairness is wrong?"

"No," came the answer.

"Because God is fair," Mom said. "Fairness is right because when we're being fair, we're showing others what God is like."

"But I was here first," Faith said.

"I know," Mom said. "And if you really think that sitting in the window seat on the way to Grandma's and on the way back is a fair way to treat your brother—well, then, I guess it's the right thing for you to do."

Faith looked from her mother to her brother. Finally, she reached down and unfastened her seat belt. "OK," she said. "You can sit next to the window, Aaron."

Mom smiled and reached for her cross-stitch pattern as her children traded seats.

TO DISCUSS: Have you ever acted like Faith? How would you act differently? Why is fairness right, and unfairness wrong? What does today's Bible reading say about God's fairness? Do you treat other people fairly? Give an example.

TO PRAY: "Lord, help us to treat others fairly, because you are completely fair and just."

15 Ernest's Prayer

RIGHT CHOICES ARE MUCH EASIER IF YOU PRAY THAT TEMPTATION WILL NOT OVERPOWER YOU.

Bible Reading of the Day: Read James 5:16-18.
Verse of the Day: *"Keep alert and pray. Otherwise temptation will overpower you" (Mark 14:38).*

Ernest got off the school bus and headed toward the school entrance. Suddenly, he stopped walking. Standing between his bus and the school entrance were Rick and Jason, two of his friends. They stood in a tight circle with some other kids, all of whom were smoking.

"Oh, man!" he said.

He stood frozen to the sidewalk, wondering what to do. He had become a Christian a few months ago and hadn't had a cigarette since then. He knew that his parents didn't want him to smoke, but until he became a Christian he'd just disobeyed his parents. But now he knew that if he was going to obey God and honor his parents, he shouldn't smoke.

He glanced quickly at the group; nobody had seen him yet. He knew if he went anywhere near that circle of kids, they'd try to get him to smoke. But if he kept standing where he was, they'd see him and wonder why he was just standing there. He suddenly veered off toward one corner of the school building, about fifteen yards away. There was no way to get into school on that side of the building, but it would give him time to think.

Ernest leaned his back against the brick wall. "God," he said, his breath making puffs of steam in the cool morning air, "I really need your help. I don't want to mess with cigarettes anymore, but if I go near Rick and Jason, I know they're going to offer me a 'smoke.' I might take it just to—you know—fit in."

He closed his eyes. "OK, God, I'm just gonna try to walk into school, right past Rick and Jason. Please help me not to give in if they offer me a cigarette. . . . Amen."

Ernest swallowed and sighed. Then he stepped away from the school building and headed toward the main entrance, keeping his eyes glued to the sidewalk beneath his feet.

Finally, he knew he was getting close to the circle of his friends, and he lifted his gaze in their direction—but they weren't there! He looked all around in amazement. Rick, Jason, and the others had disappeared.

They must have gone into school while I was praying, Ernest thought. He breathed a sigh of relief. "Thanks, God," he whispered.

TO DISCUSS: Do you think God answered Ernest's prayer? If so, how? Do you pray every day and ask God to help you make right choices? How can you develop a daily habit of praying in the morning and asking God to deliver you from temptation?

TO PRAY: "Lord, turn our hearts and minds toward you every day for help in resisting temptation."

16 Toy Room Disaster

MERCY IS RIGHT BECAUSE GOD IS MERCIFUL.

Bible Reading of the Day: Read Psalm 103:1-8.
Verse of the Day: *"Be merciful, just as your Father is merciful"*
(Luke 6:36, NIV).

Joey stomped down the basement stairs, walked into the toy room, and froze.

"Hi, Joey," said his little sister, Bailey. She sat cross-legged in the midst of several boxes. Joey looked closer at the boxes and saw that each box contained hundreds of plastic Lego interlocking pieces.

He swallowed hard before speaking. "W-what are you doing?" he asked his sister.

Bailey smiled proudly at her brother, whom she knew spent hours building things with his Lego pieces. He had built a working train out of the tiny plastic pieces, a train that ran through a Lego-made village. But Joey could see none of his elaborate creations. Instead he saw six boxes filled with the tiny pieces.

"I sorted your Lego for you, Joey," Bailey announced. She smiled broadly at her brother. She pointed at the boxes, starting with the box directly beneath her elbow. "I put all the red pieces in this box, all the green pieces in this box, all the white pieces in this box—"

"You—you took *all* my Legos apart and put them in those boxes?" Joey stammered.

Bailey nodded. "Uh-huh," she said. "Do you like it?"

Joey stared at his sister for a long moment. She had destroyed every train, every car, every building he had created. It would take weeks, maybe months, to put everything back together. *How could she do that?* he thought. He wanted to scream at her but didn't. "That's really great, Bailey," he said through gritted teeth. "That's really great."

He turned back toward the steps that led from the basement to the kitchen and ran into his mom. He started to open his mouth to complain to his mom, but she held her index finger up to her lips and led him up the stairs. When she had reached the top of the stairs and closed the door to the basement, she lowered her finger.

"I know," she said. "I know she destroyed your whole village. But she did it because she loves her big brother and wants so badly to please him."

"But—"

"And I want you to know how proud I am of you," Mom continued. "It would have been so easy for you to break a little girl's heart just then, but you didn't. You acted with mercy and compassion toward your little sister, and I'm so proud of you, I can't stand it!" She pulled Joey to her in a tight hug. He closed his eyes and sighed.

 TO DISCUSS: Why was Mom so proud of Joey? Do you think it's right to be merciful? If so, why? What does today's Bible reading say about the nature of God? How was Joey like that? How can you be more merciful toward your brothers and sisters? toward your parents or children? toward others?

 TO PRAY: "Lord, we want to be merciful as you are merciful."

17 Fast Forward

SELF-CONTROL IS RIGHT BECAUSE GOD IS ALWAYS IN CONTROL—OF HIMSELF
AND OF THE UNIVERSE HE HAS MADE.

Bible Reading of the Day: Read Genesis 25:29-34.
Verse of the Day: *"Follow God's example in everything you do, because you are his dear children" (Ephesians 5:1).*

Darcelle sat at the kitchen table and munched her breakfast cereal while Mom sipped a cup of black coffee.

"Why aren't you eating breakfast, Mom?" Darcelle asked. "Aren't you hungry?"

Mom blew lightly across the surface of her hot coffee. "I'm fasting today," she said. "Just for breakfast and lunch."

"What's fasting?" Darcelle asked, eating another mouthful of cereal.

"Fasting means going without food," Mom explained.

"But why?" Darcelle asked. "Why are you skipping breakfast and lunch?"

Mom shrugged. "Several reasons, honey," she answered. "I fast every once in a while to remind myself that I need to control my appetites instead of letting them control me. It's really an exercise in self-control." She took another sip of coffee. "And I also fast as a way of submitting to God, because I spend my mealtimes praying instead of eating."

"I don't see how you can do that," Darcelle said. "I'd get hungry."

"I don't think I'd want you to fast at your age, because it might not be good for you. But I've checked with my doctor and a short fast is actually good for me, even though I *do* get a little hungry. But that's the point—I want to build self-control."

"What's so great about self-control?"

Mom smiled and set her coffee mug on the table. "Well, first of all, God commands us to be self-controlled. His Word says we ought to be alert and self-controlled because our enemy, the devil, is like a roaring lion, prowling about looking for ways to devour us. It takes self-control to stay out of trouble. But God also commands self-control because he values it—and he values self-control because he is the ultimate example of self-control. He is always in control—of himself and of the universe he has made. He never loses control of his passions, his emotions, or his desires like we so often do. So self-control is right, Darcelle, because it's like God. And that's why I'm fasting today—to give God a better chance to make me like him."

"Cool," Darcelle said. She lifted her bowl off the table and kissed Mom on the cheek. "Thanks for the sermon, Mom," she said. "I gotta get to school."

Mom smiled as she watched her daughter leave the kitchen. Then she turned around and lifted her coffee to her lips. "Kids!" she said.

 TO DISCUSS: In today's Bible reading, do you think Esau showed self-control? Why or why not? Do you think self-control is important? Why or why not? What makes self-control right? Do you struggle to control your appetites and desires? your temper? your tongue? How can you become more self-controlled in those areas?

 TO PRAY: "Heavenly Father, we want to be self-controlled because you value self-control."

18 A Lasting Foundation

THE PERSON WHO PRAYS AND READS THE BIBLE EVERY DAY IS BUILDING A SOLID FOUNDATION.

Bible Reading of the Day: Read Matthew 7:24-27.
Verse of the Day: *"Disaster strikes like a cyclone, whirling the wicked away, but the godly have a lasting foundation" (Proverbs 10:25).*

"I don't see how Grandpa does it," Tyler told his dad.

They stood beside a great pile of logs and were preparing to stack the logs in a wooden frame Dad had built to shelter their woodpile.

"What do you mean?" Dad asked. He and Tyler had begun the first row of logs, placing them firmly side by side on the ground.

"Well, I don't know, it's like Grandpa has arthritis, and he has to take care of Grandma because she has 'Old-Timer's Disease.'" He handed his dad a couple of logs from the pile.

"That's 'Alzheimer's Disease,' Ty," Dad said.

"Whatever," Tyler answered. "It's just like he has all these problems, but he's still the best Christian there is." He handed his dad another log.

Dad nodded. "I see what you mean," he said. "You're right, your grandfather has been through a lot of hard times, especially since Grandma got Alzheimer's."

Tyler tossed a log on the ground in a haphazard way. "Wait a minute," Dad said. "Let's be more careful than that. See, if the bottom row is good and solid, then the rest of the woodpile won't fall down."

When Dad straightened again, he looked at the neat row of logs that formed the foundation of their woodpile. "Now that I think about it, Tyler, that's exactly how your grandfather survives all the storms he's been through."

"What do you mean?"

"Well, Grandpa's like this woodpile. He has a solid foundation, because he reads his Bible and prays every day. He obeys what he reads and lives what he prays. Jesus said a person like that is like a man who builds his house on a rock. Winds and storms may blow against the house, but it won't fall down because it has a firm foundation."

Tyler pointed to the woodpile. "Just like if that bottom row is straight, the stack won't fall over."

Dad nodded. "Right."

"I see what you mean, Dad."

"Do you?" Dad asked. "Because I think we could both do better at building that kind of foundation in our lives."

"You're right," Tyler said. "I'm gonna start as soon as we're done stacking wood."

 TO DISCUSS: Which of the two people described in today's Bible reading are you most like? Are you building a lasting foundation against life's storms and disasters? If not, why not? If so, how? How can you start building that kind of foundation in your life?

 TO PRAY: "Lord, we want to build a lasting foundation against life's storms and disasters. Draw us close to you through prayer and the reading of your Word."

19 Patience Is a Virtue

PATIENCE IS RIGHT BECAUSE GOD IS PATIENT.

> **Bible Reading of the Day: Read 1 Timothy 1:15–17.**
> **Verse of the Day:** *"Imitate those who through faith and patience inherit what has been promised" (Hebrews 6:12, NIV).*

"I can't wait for Christmas!" Noah said. He sat beside his mom and his sister on the bench waiting for the city bus.

"It seems so far away," Natalie complained. "I wish it would hurry up and get here."

"The first gift I'm going to open is going to be my *Five-Star Sound Studio,*" Noah said. His eyes sparkled with anticipation. "Wait 'til you see it, Nat!"

Natalie looked up curiously at her older brother. "How do you know you're getting a *Five-Star Sound Studio?*" she asked.

Mom, who had been looking for their bus, suddenly turned and looked at Noah. "Yes, Noah," she said, "how *do* you know you're getting a *Five-Star Sound Studio?*"

Noah's eyes got real big. "I . . . I . . . I don't," he said, laughing nervously.

"I think I know," Mom said. "You've been snooping around, haven't you? And you found one of your Christmas presents that I had hidden, didn't you?"

Noah swallowed hard. "I . . . I'm sorry, Mom," he said. "I just couldn't stand waiting anymore, so I thought if I just peeked, it would make it easier to wait."

"Did it?" Mom asked.

Noah lowered his chin onto his chest. "No," he said. "It's been even harder."

Mom nodded. "Well, patience is a virtue, Son."

"What's that mean?" Noah asked.

"It means patience is right. Because patience is something God values."

"Why?" Natalie asked.

"Because God is patient."

"He is?" Noah said.

"Oh, yes," Mom answered. "He waited twenty-nine years for your dad to trust Christ, and he had to wait almost as long for me!"

"I should have been more patient," Noah said. "Now I know what I'm getting for Christmas."

"It won't be as much fun for you or for us," Mom said.

"Why won't it be fun for you?" Noah asked.

"Because we won't get to surprise you," she answered. "So your impatience hasn't just made your Christmas less fun, it's made my Christmas less fun too."

"I'm sorry, Mom," Noah said. He looked earnestly into his mother's face. "I'll be more patient from now on, I promise."

 TO DISCUSS: Take turns answering the following questions: "Do you think God has been patient with you? If so, how do you know?" and "How can you be more patient?"

 TO PRAY: "Patience is a virtue that's difficult to develop. But Lord, we know you want us to be patient. Thank you for your patience with us as we seek to be patient with others."

20 Cover-Up

IT'S BETTER TO ADMIT WRONG CHOICES INSTEAD OF TRYING TO COVER THEM UP.

Bible Reading of the Day: Read Genesis 4:8-12.

Verse of the Day: *"People who cover over their sins will not prosper. But if they confess and forsake them, they will receive mercy"* (Proverbs 28:13).

Aiko loved to play in the bathroom sink. She plugged the drain and turned on the water. Then she rolled up her sleeves and placed her plastic toy boats in the churning water.

"Uh-oh!" she said, as one of the boats was drawn under the waterspout and capsized in the water. She grabbed the other boat and guided it toward the sinking boat. "Rescue! Rescue!" she said.

Suddenly, Aiko got an idea. She could make the water in the sink blue! All she needed was some blue food coloring from the kitchen cabinet, and the water in the sink would look like a real ocean! Aiko left her boats in the sink and dashed out of the bathroom. She tramped down the stairs and slid across the kitchen floor on her sock-covered feet. A few moments later, she had found the blue food coloring and headed back upstairs. As she approached the bathroom, however, her eyes opened wide with surprise.

A stream of water ran out of the bathroom toward the steps where she stood. She had left the faucets on, and the sink had overflowed! Aiko splashed to the bathroom and quickly turned off the faucets. She grabbed the towels off the towel rack behind her and tried to wipe up the mess, but there was too much water.

"Oh," she said out loud. "Oh, no!" She reached for the bathroom door and slammed it shut. *I'll take a bath and tell Mommy the water splashed out,* she decided.

She knew immediately, however, she couldn't do that. She opened the door, ran downstairs, and found her mom typing on the computer.

"Mommy, I was just playing, and now the water's all over the floor!" she said. She started to cry.

"Where?" Mom asked, standing up. "Show me where, Aiko."

Mom grabbed a mop, then Aiko led her upstairs to the bathroom. Mom quickly cleaned up the water. Then she sat down on the side of the bathtub and pulled Aiko onto her lap.

"Thank you for coming to tell me about the water, Aiko," she said. "If you hadn't told Mommy, the water might have leaked through the floor and into the room below. *That* would have made an even bigger mess!"

"I'm sorry I made a mess," Aiko said, her eyes still red from crying. "But I'm glad I told you, Mommy."

 TO DISCUSS: Do you think it's better to admit wrong choices instead of trying to cover them up? If not, why not? If so, why? Which do you usually do: confess your sins or cover them up? Why?

 TO PRAY: "God, give us the courage to confess our sins, rather than trying to hide them."

21 A Day at the Circus

GENEROSITY IS SIMPLY SHARING THE GOOD THINGS GOD HAS GIVEN YOU.

Bible Reading of the Day: Read Numbers 10:29-32.
Verse of the Day: *"Share with God's people who are in need"*
(Romans 12:13, NIV).

Sarina stood in line with her father at the circus ticket window. She couldn't wait to see the animals and clowns and performers.

As they waited, Sarina noticed that there was a large family ahead of them in line. She counted six children with their father. She watched them with interest for a few moments. She could tell by their clothes that they weren't a wealthy family. Yet all seven were going to the circus.

For the first time, Sarina looked up at the ticket prices painted on a large wooden board near the ticket window. She tried to figure out how much seven tickets would cost, but there were different prices for different ages, and she finally gave up. She could tell, though, that the children were very happy to be going to the circus.

Soon the children's father stepped to the ticket window. She saw him smile at his children as he passed his money to the cashier.

"How many tickets?" the teller said. The man told her. "I'm sorry, sir," the teller said. "I'm going to need ten dollars more."

Sarina watched as the expression on the man's face turned from happiness to disappointment and embarrassment. He obviously didn't have any more money.

Suddenly, however, Sarina saw her dad, who had been standing beside her the whole time, drop something on the ground. She looked down. It was a twenty-dollar bill. She started to bend to pick it up, but Dad put out a hand to stop her.

"Er, excuse me, sir," Dad said. The man in front of him turned around. Dad stooped, picked up the bill, and held it out to the man. "Did you drop this?" he asked the man. "It was lying on the ground right behind you and your children."

The man met Dad's gaze. He looked at his children. They hadn't seen what Sarina's dad had done. He smiled knowingly and gratefully. "Thank you," he said, taking the money from Dad's grip. Then he stretched out his other hand and shook hands with Dad. "Thank you," he repeated.

He smiled again, turned around, and handed the money to the cashier.

Sarina gazed at her dad with new admiration. "That was really cool," she said after the man and his children had left the ticket window.

Dad smiled. "It's a wonderful feeling to be able to share the good things God has given to us."

"It sure is!" Sarina said.

TO DISCUSS: In today's Bible reading, why do you think Moses promised to share with Hobab? Name some of the good things God has done for you or given to you. How can you share them with others?

TO PRAY: "Lord, you have blessed us so much. Help us to be generous with others."

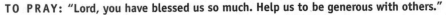

22 The Piñata

GREED IS WRONG, NO MATTER HOW WE MAY TRY TO EXPLAIN IT OR JUSTIFY IT.

Bible Reading of the Day: Read Ephesians 5:3-7.
Verse of the Day: *"Be on your guard against all kinds of greed; a man's life does not consist in the abundance of his possessions" (Luke 12:15, NIV).*

Lupe watched as her brother Mañuel stood under the brightly colored donkey-shaped piñata. Mañuel, who was celebrating his birthday, was blindfolded. He grasped a broomstick in both hands, and his father held the other end of the broomstick. Mañuel waited for the signal.

Finally, Father let go of the broomstick, and Mañuel swung it at the piñata, which he could not see. He turned around and around, swinging the broomstick wildly in all directions.

The children cheered each time Mañuel touched the piñata. Finally, Mañuel lifted the stick over his head and, with a mighty swing, broke the piñata open and sent pieces of candy spraying in all directions.

Lupe pounced on the candy that landed at her feet, then saw the piñata swaying by a thread from the ceiling. She picked up the broomstick her brother had dropped and touched the piñata, sending it tumbling to the floor at her feet. She scooped it up and shouted in excitement. It was still half filled with candy.

As she picked up her treasure, Lupe saw a little girl standing on the edge of the crowd, watching the children scrambling frantically after every piece of candy. Lupe noticed her tearful eyes and empty hands.

As she watched, two voices seemed to battle inside Lupe's mind.

Look at her, one voice said. *She doesn't have any candy and you have more than anyone else.*

But immediately another voice seemed to argue, *You don't have to give her your candy! You found every piece, fair and square.*

But she's so little, the first voice seemed to say, *and she's not getting any candy.*

That's her tough luck, said the second voice. *There's nothing wrong with keeping what's yours.*

In that moment, however, Lupe knew what she would do. She knew that hoarding all that candy to herself would be greedy, no matter how she tried to explain it to herself. And she knew that greed was wrong, not because she thought so, but because God thought so.

Lupe smiled as she walked over to the little girl. She crouched down in front of her and held out the piñata. "Take as much as you want," she said.

TO DISCUSS: What does it mean to be greedy or stingy? Why are they both wrong? Do you think Lupe did the right thing? Why or why not? How did Lupe know what was the right choice?

TO PRAY: "Lord, help us to share with others with an open hand, instead of trying to keep everything for ourselves."

23 Ride Sharing

GOD COMMANDS GENEROSITY.

Bible Reading of the Day: Read Deuteronomy 24:19–22.
Verse of the Day: *"Don't forget to do good and to share what you have with those in need, for such sacrifices are very pleasing to God"* *(Hebrews 13:16).*

"Do we have to pick up Marvin again?" Kelly whined as Dad backed the car out of their driveway. Marvin was an elderly man in their congregation.

"Yeah, Dad," her brother Adam agreed. "It takes forever to pick him up on our way to church!"

Dad opened his mouth to answer, but Kelly spoke again.

"It's like we go a half hour out of our way. Why do *we* have to take him to church?"

"Well," Dad said, "we *don't* have to."

"Good!" Adam said.

"But I know you would both want to choose to be obedient to God," Dad said, his voice soft and gentle.

"What's God got to do with picking up Marvin?" Kelly asked.

"Well, Kelly," Dad continued, "God commands us to be generous with other people, especially those who are in need. Now, you've been to Marvin's apartment. . . ."

"Yeah," Kelly said, nodding. Marvin lived in a poor section of the city, and his apartment barely had any furniture in it.

"You know that Marvin doesn't have much," Dad continued.

"Why don't we just take him a bag of groceries every once in a while instead of picking him up every Sunday for church?" Adam suggested.

"I've tried to do things like that," Dad answered, "but I haven't been able to get Marvin to accept any groceries or gifts. I think it embarrasses him."

Mom joined the conversation. "But he *will* let us take him to church every Sunday."

"So you're, like, helping him with your time and your car instead of with groceries or stuff," Kelly said.

Dad nodded. "Right. This is a way to be generous with Marvin in a way he'll accept." Dad paused and studied his two children in the rearview mirror. "But, if you insist, I guess I could tell him we can't pick him up anymore."

"N-no," Kelly said. "That's all right."

"Yeah," Adam agreed. "It's not *that* far out of our way."

Dad and Mom exchanged smiles. "Well, all right," he said, his eyes twinkling. "Have it your way."

TO DISCUSS: In today's Bible reading, why do you think God commanded the Israelites not to harvest all their crops? Does your family make a habit of being generous? Name some people you've been generous to in recent days. Can you think of new ways to be generous to others?

TO PRAY: "Lord, remind us that you command us to be generous. Help us use our resources to provide for those you send our way."

24 The Gifts of the Magi

GOD COMMANDS GENEROSITY BECAUSE GOD VALUES GENEROSITY.

Bible Reading of the Day: Read Matthew 2:1-2, 9-12.
Verse of the Day: *"Praise the Lord, the God of Israel, because he has visited his people and redeemed them" (Luke 1:68).*

The kids all gathered around Grandpa, who sat in his big chair with the high back. The family had just finished a big Christmas Eve meal, and it was time for the first reading of the Christmas story. For many years, a tradition in the family had been to read the story of Jesus' birth from Matthew's Gospel on Christmas Eve, and to read from Luke's Gospel on Christmas morning.

"Ohhhh," Grant moaned. He lay on his belly at Grandpa's feet. "I ate too much!"

"Me too," his cousin Scott groaned. He rubbed his stomach with his hand.

Grandpa chuckled as he opened his big, black Bible. The moaning and groaning subsided as Grandpa began reading from the Gospel of Matthew. He read about Mary becoming pregnant through the work of the Holy Spirit. He read about the angel's appearance to Joseph, Mary's fiancé, at that point. And he read about the visit of the wise men to Bethlehem. Finally, he closed the Bible.

"Now," Grandpa said, addressing the children in the room, "what was different about the gifts the wise men unwrapped that Christmas morning?"

"They were gold, and frankincense, and myrrh!" Scott said. "We'll get toys!"

"Yeah," Grant agreed. He glanced at the Christmas tree in the corner of the room. "And their gifts probably weren't wrapped with Garfield wrapping paper!"

Grandpa and the other adults in the room laughed. "What else?" he asked, looking at the children. Several of the other children said something, and then Grandpa leaned forward in his chair. "Let me ask you this: did the wise men give gifts *to each other?*"

Grant and Scott looked at Grandpa. They shook their heads.

"You're right," Grandpa said. "Think about that. The first Christmas gifts were given to Jesus . . . but all our Christmas gifts are addressed *to us, not to Jesus!*"

"I never thought about that before," Scott said.

"You see, kids," Grandpa continued, "it's so easy to get caught up in *getting* things at Christmas time; but Christmas isn't about getting, it's about *giving,* because God values generosity, not greed." Then Grandpa asked everyone in the room to join hands, and he prayed.

When Grandpa finished praying, Grant turned to his cousin, with excitement written on his face. "I know what we could give to Jesus tomorrow!" He whispered in Scott's ear.

"Yeah!" Scott answered. "That'll be fun!"

 TO DISCUSS: What does Christmas mean to you? Is it about *getting* or about *giving?* Can you think of a gift you could give to Jesus tomorrow?

 TO PRAY: "Lord, this time of year, we're reminded of how Jesus came to earth as a man. May our actions reflect your generosity."

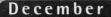

25 The Best Gift

GOD VALUES GENEROSITY BECAUSE GOD GENEROUSLY GIVES.

Bible Reading of the Day: Read Luke 2:1, 3-7.

Verse of the Day: *"For God so loved the world that he gave his only Son, so that everyone who believes in him will not perish but have eternal life" (John 3:16).*

Catherine drummed her fingers on her knee as she sat cross-legged in front of the Christmas tree, waiting for her parents to start passing out presents. She had already identified all the packages under the tree, and she knew which ones were for her.

Finally, Mom sat down on the couch and Dad put on his bright red wool hat with a white ball on the end, the signal that it was time to start unwrapping presents. He handed the first present to Cindy, Catherine's younger sister. Then he handed a brightly wrapped package to Catherine.

She ripped off the wrapping paper and tossed it onto the floor to reveal a Munching Molly doll! "Yea!" Catherine screamed. She jumped up and down, hugging the doll. Her celebration stopped, however, as her dad held out another gift. She quickly sat down and dropped Munching Molly on the floor beside her.

Less than a half hour later, Catherine was surrounded by a stack of presents, some big, some small. Wrapping paper covered the floor.

"I love my presents!" she announced. "I love them so much, I can't decide which one to play with first."

Suddenly, Mom pulled Cindy onto her lap and motioned to Catherine. Catherine sat beside her mom and snuggled against her arm.

"What was your favorite gift this Christmas?" Mom asked the girls.

"My play set!" Cindy answered, referring to a set of plastic kitchen appliances.

"Munching Molly," Catherine said. "But I like all my gifts."

"You know what my favorite gift is?" Mom asked. "My favorite gift is Jesus."

"Jesus?" Catherine asked.

Mom nodded. "I like all the gifts I unwrapped this morning," she explained, "but the best gift *ever* is the gift God gave when he sent his Son to be born and later become our Savior."

"Yeah, but God gave Jesus a long time ago," Catherine said.

"Jesus was born a long time ago," Mom said, "but God gives me the gift of Jesus every day. And that's the best, most generous, most loving gift I've ever gotten."

"Me too," Catherine said. "Jesus is my favorite gift too."

 TO DISCUSS: Have you received the gift of Jesus? Does Jesus live in your heart? If not, why not accept God's loving Christmas present and ask Jesus to forgive your sins? If you have received the gift of Jesus, take a few moments to thank God for his perfect gift!

TO PRAY: "Jesus, you are our favorite gift. Thank you for your willingness to take our sins on yourself. We love you."

26 Haleys' Cookies

GENEROSITY BRINGS BLESSING; GREED BRINGS DISAPPOINTMENT.

Bible Reading of the Day: Read Philemon 4-6.

Verse of the Day: *"Put your generosity to work, for in so doing you will come to an understanding of all the good things we can do for Christ"* (Philemon 6).

"You think we should do *what?*" Trixie said. She looked at her mom as though a sunflower stalk had just sprouted from the top of her mom's head.

"I think you should take a plate of Christmas cookies to the Haleys," Mom said.

Trixie and her brother, Will, exchanged confused expressions. "Mom," Will said, "the Haleys don't like us."

"They're always yelling at us to go away," Trixie added.

"They even called the police on us last summer when our trash cans blew into their flower bed, remember?" Will said.

Mom nodded. "I know," she said. "But look at it this way: a plate of cookies can't make things any worse, can it?"

"I don't know," Trixie said. "The Haleys might call the police on us for giving cookies away without a license!"

A few moments later, Trixie and Will each held a plate of cookies wrapped in clear plastic and tied with a fancy ribbon. They paused at the front door.

"If we're not back in twenty-four hours," Will said, "call the FBI!"

When Will and Trixie returned, Mom asked what the Haleys had said.

Trixie shrugged. "Mrs. Haley just said thanks. Then she closed the door."

"Well, the important thing is that you shared a little bit of your Christmas with them," Mom said.

Later that day, someone knocked on the door, and Mom answered. Mr. and Mrs. Haley stood on the porch, holding the plates Mom had sent earlier—only now they were stacked with chocolate-chip cookies!

"We were so surprised by your generosity," Mrs. Haley said. "We've lived here for ten years, and no one in this neighborhood has ever done anything like that for us!" Her eyes were rimmed with tears. "We baked these for you and your children."

Mom thanked the Haleys and invited them to come in. They refused, but as they turned to walk back to their house, they smiled.

"That was cool!" Trixie said.

"It sure was," Will agreed. "Maybe they're not so bad after all."

Mom smiled. "The Haleys are probably thinking the exact same thing about you and Trixie right now!" Trixie and Will looked surprised for a moment before all three of them started laughing.

 TO DISCUSS: Which is better, being stingy and greedy or being generous? Why? Have you ever made new friends by being generous? If so, talk about it.

TO PRAY: "Lord, ignite a flame of generosity within us. Help us to give to others in your name."

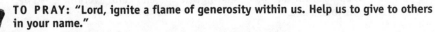

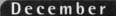

27 The Giveaway Box

GENEROSITY IS FULFILLING; GREED NEVER SATISFIES.

Bible Reading of the Day: Read Luke 6:30-31, 38.
Verse of the Day: *"Remember the words of the Lord Jesus: 'It is more blessed to give than to receive'" (Acts 20:35).*

Only a few days had passed since Christmas, but Chris and Chad had already played with their new toys so much they'd grown tired of them.

Mom carried a large, empty box into the bedroom the kids shared. She sat down on the bottom bunk bed and told Chris and Chad about some children at a nearby home for the handicapped. "Most of the children only received a piece of fruit, a pair of socks, and a small toy on Christmas Day," she said. "I bet we could fill this box with some of your new toys that those children would really love."

Chris and Chad sat silently for a few moments. Then Chad said. "I know! I could give away my old Dino-bot! I never play with it anymore." He scrambled over to the closet and pulled a motorized dinosaur out of a pile of old toys. It was missing a leg.

"Is that the kind of toy *you* would like to get?" Mom asked.

Chad looked at Mom with wide eyes. "You want us to give some of our *new* toys?"

Mom shrugged. "It's just a suggestion," she said. "I'm not saying you should give *all* your new toys away, but Jesus does say to do for others what you would like them to do for you." She stood then and left the room.

Chad and Chris sat in silence for a few moments after Mom left. Then Chris gripped one of his new toys. "I still have the box for this!" he said. He put the toy and carton in the big box.

"Hey," Chad said. "If you don't want that, give it to me!"

"It's not for you," he said. "It's for the kids at the handicap home."

Chad shrugged, then after a pause, added one of his favorite toys to the box. By the time Mom returned to the room, the box contained several new toys. On the following day, Mom, Chad, and Chris drove together to the home and delivered the toys to some of the children, who received them with overwhelming joy and appreciation. As they left the home, Chad turned to Mom.

"Can we do this every year, Mom?" he asked.

"Yeah, can we do it *before* Christmas next year, so the kids can open their gifts on Christmas Day?" Chris asked.

"I didn't think you boys were that excited about giving your toys away," Mom said.

"We weren't at first," Chad said, "but that was fun!"

"Yeah," Chris agreed. "That was a *lot* of fun!"

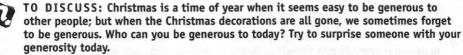 **TO DISCUSS:** Christmas is a time of year when it seems easy to be generous to other people; but when the Christmas decorations are all gone, we sometimes forget to be generous. Who can you be generous to today? Try to surprise someone with your generosity today.

 TO PRAY: "Thank you for the joy of sharing with others, Lord. Everything we do, we want to do in your name."

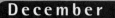
28 Cleanup Day

PURITY IS RIGHT BECAUSE GOD IS PURE.

Bible Reading of the Day: Read 2 Corinthians 6:16–7:1.

Verse of the Day: *"All of us who look forward to his Coming stay ready, with the glistening purity of Jesus' life as a model for our own"* (1 John 3:3, The Message).

Sarah ran the vacuum cleaner while Mom dusted the furniture. Dad dragged the Christmas tree outside while his other daughter, Rachel, carried boxes of Christmas ornaments up to the attic. Then Dad and Sarah went outside and worked together to take down the Christmas lights, while Rachel helped Mom carry bags and bags of trash out to the curb.

Their annual after-Christmas cleanup party was in full swing. When it was over, they all plopped in exhaustion onto the couch and chairs in the living room.

"I love Christmas," Sarah said, "and all the decorations we put up and everything, but I like it when we put everything back to normal too."

"Me too," Rachel agreed. "I'm glad I don't have to pick up any more pine needles out of the carpet!" Picking up the needles that fell from the tree was always Rachel's job.

"And I feel like I've been picking up wrapping paper for years!" Sarah added.

Mom smiled and looked around the room. "It is a nice feeling when everything's neat and clean again, isn't it?"

"Sure is," Rachel said.

"Clean is good," Sarah added, smiling.

They sat in silence for a few minutes, enjoying the quiet. Then Dad said, "You know, you're right. Clean *is* good. . . . Have any of you ever stopped to think *why* clean is good?"

"Because clean is healthier," Mom said.

"And prettier," Rachel added.

Sarah's expression was suddenly serious. "Because clean is like God," she said, acting as though her answer surprised even herself. "Right, Dad? Because God is perfect and pure—*that's* why clean feels so good and dirty seems so . . . well, so dirty!"

Dad nodded his head. "You're right, Sarah," he said. "You're absolutely right. And that's not just why a clean room is so nice; it's also why pure hearts and lives are right. Because the God who made us—and made everything around us—is pure."

"Yea, Sarah," Rachel muttered. Everyone looked at her. Her head bobbed forward until her chin touched her chest. Dad, Mom, and Sarah smiled at each other; Rachel had fallen asleep!

TO DO: Shave a bar of fragrant soap into tiny slivers (a potato peeler works well for this) and pour the slivers into a pretty teacup; place it on the kitchen windowsill or by a bathroom sink. Let the fresh, clean smell remind you that purity is right because God is pure.

TO PRAY: "May your purity rub off on us, O Lord."

29 Pop's Trade

WRONG CHOICES SOMETIMES OFFER IMMEDIATE REWARDS, BUT THE REWARDS
OF RIGHTEOUSNESS ARE GREATER.

Bible Reading of the Day: Read Romans 8:12-14, 17.
Verse of the Day: *"For our light and momentary troubles are achieving
for us an eternal glory that far outweighs them all"* (2 Corinthians
4:17, NIV).

Isaiah walked through the giant arena with his grandfather. Booth after booth was filled
with sports memorabilia and collectors' items. "Pop," Isaiah said, using the name he
had always called his grandfather, "can I buy some of that candy?"

Pop shrugged. "It's your money," he said. "I'll wait right here for you."

Isaiah walked over to a counter filled with all kinds of candy. Isaiah made his
purchase and counted his change as he walked away from the counter. The cashier
had given him too much change! He returned to the counter, explained what had
happened, and returned the overpayment to the cashier.

When Isaiah explained what had happened, Pop's eyes sparkled with pride. "You
did the right thing, Isaiah," he said. "I'm right proud of you."

Isaiah smiled. "I wish I could have kept it. I could've gotten a Wad-o-Gum too."

Pop nodded. "I suppose," he said. "Sometimes it's tempting to do wrong, because
the right choice doesn't seem to have as many benefits, at least not right away." He
suddenly spied a booth displaying an assortment of baseball cards. He led Isaiah over
to the booth. "You see those cards?" he asked. He pointed to cards bearing pictures of
Jackie Robinson, Willie Mays, and other great baseball players. "I had every one of
those cards when I was your age. Some of them are worth hundreds of dollars now."

"Why didn't you keep 'em, Pop?"

Pop peered intently into Isaiah's eyes. "I traded my whole card collection to
Tyrone Harris. He had two tickets to the fair, and I wanted to go so bad, nothing else
mattered to me. So my friend Sticks Benjamin and I went to the fair."

"Wow," Isaiah said. "Just think what your card collection would be worth now!"

Pop rested a hand on Isaiah's shoulder. "I was sorry almost as soon as I got home
from the fair, because I knew I'd given away something worth a lot more to me than
two fair tickets. It's the same way when we do wrong, Son. The wrong choice may
look real good right now, but in the long run, it's worth a lot more to do the right
thing. I hope you'll always remember that."

"I'll try, Pop," Isaiah said.

"Now, how 'bout I go buy you a Wad-o-Gum for being so honest?"

"All right!" Isaiah said.

**TO DISCUSS: Think of a time when you were tempted to do wrong. What
happened? If you didn't give in, how did you feel? If you did give in to temptation,
what do you know now that you wish you had known then?**

**TO PRAY: "Father God, sometimes the wrong choice does look good to us, which is
why we're so tempted at times. Help us always to remember that, in your own way and
in your own time, you will reward us for making right choices."**

30 Patty's Parties

FAITHFULNESS IS RIGHT BECAUSE GOD IS FAITHFUL.

Bible Reading of the Day: Read Psalm 89:1-2, 8.
Verse of the Day: *"O Lord God Almighty! Where is there anyone as mighty as you, Lord? Faithfulness is your very character" (Psalm 89:8).*

Patty was putting the finishing touches on a party she had planned for a friend who was moving away. "Naomi will be so surprised," she told her mom as she finished frosting the cake. "She doesn't have a clue about the party."

The phone rang. Mom answered it and handed the receiver to Patty. "It's for you."

Patty took the phone and continued to frost the cake. She said very little during the conversation. After she hung up, she looked gloomily at Mom. "That was Emily," she said. "She's not coming. She said she has to do something else."

The phone rang two more times in the next thirty minutes, each time with the news that a friend wouldn't be attending the party. Patty's frustration showed as she complained to her mom. "They claimed something better came up," she said. "I feel bad for Naomi now. It's like they think, 'She's moving away anyway, so why go to a party for her?'"

A couple of weeks later, Patty was invited to a party by someone she barely knew. She accepted the invitation, but a few hours later received another invitation. The second invitation was to another party scheduled for the same night. She knew all of her friends would be at this second party.

"I'm really sorry," she told the person who had invited her to the second party. "But I've already accepted an invitation for that night." She listened for a moment as the other person spoke. "No," she answered, "I can't cancel it. Sorry."

When she hung up the phone, she saw Mom standing behind her.

"I'm proud of you for being faithful and keeping your word," Mom said.

"I didn't want to," Patty answered. "I really wanted to go to the other party."

"I know," Mom said. "If it were easy to be faithful, everyone would do it."

"Yeah," Patty said. "And I know how it feels when somebody cancels on you and lets you down."

"You should also know that it pleases God when you're faithful, because *he's* faithful. That's why it's right to be faithful, and that's why you've made me a happy mom."

Patty smiled at her mom. "I guess I should look at the bright side," she said. "I got invited to two parties on the same day! That's pretty cool!"

"You're right," Mom said. "That is pretty cool."

 TO DISCUSS: Which is right: faithfulness or unfaithfulness? Why? Would you have done what Patty did? If so, why? If not, what would you have done differently? Have you broken a promise to anyone lately? Are you being faithful in all your relationships?

TO PRAY: "Lord, help us to be faithful, because we know you are faithful."

31 Bees and Apple Trees

SPEND YOUR TIME THINKING ABOUT THINGS THAT ARE TRUE, RIGHT, PURE, AND ADMIRABLE.

Bible Reading of the Day: Read Philippians 4:8-9.
Verse of the Day: *"Finally, brothers, whatever is true, whatever is noble, whatever is right, whatever is pure, whatever is lovely, whatever is admirable—if anything is excellent or praiseworthy—think about such things" (Philippians 4:8, NIV).*

Lydia walked with her Uncle Pete to the orchard. Uncle Pete and Aunt Mary lived on a farm. Everybody said their apple trees bore the best apples in the area.

"I wish I could be as smart as you, Uncle Pete," Lydia said.

"What makes you say that?" Uncle Pete asked. They walked side by side through the lines of apple trees toward a line of white boxes on the other side of the orchard.

"Well, it's like you know right and wrong better than anybody I know. You always know the right thing to say, or the right thing to do—stuff like that."

Uncle Pete nodded. "I see," he said. He stopped walking and knelt beside one of the white boxes and put his hand on the lid. "Lydia," he said, "do you know what this is?"

Lydia looked at the white box. She nodded. Inside was a beehive. Uncle Pete and Aunt Mary took care of the beehives, and the bees fertilized their apple trees.

"Do you know how these bees get the pollen that fertilizes all those apple trees?" he asked, waving his hand toward the orchard. Lydia shook her head. "They fly from flower to flower. And as they land on a flower, the pollen sticks to their hind legs. Now, if they just flitted around, touching a flower here and there, it wouldn't do my apple trees any good. But they *land* on the flower and stay there for a while, sucking nectar into their mouths. All the while, the hairs on their legs are collecting pollen."

"Cool!" Lydia said.

Uncle Pete smiled. "It's the same way with learning right from wrong, Lydia," he said. "Things stick to us kind of like they stick to bees. If we spend our time thinking about true and noble and right things, those things will stick with us and help us when we face a choice between right and wrong. But what do you think will happen if we just read our Bible on Sundays or think about God every once in a while?"

"It won't stick with us!" Lydia answered.

Uncle Pete nodded. "Or worse, if we spend our time watching violence or thinking impure thoughts, it will be those things that stick with us."

"I'd rather have good things stick to my hairy legs!" Lydia said.

Uncle Pete broke into uncontrollable laughter. "Now, don't go telling your Aunt Mary that I said you have hairy legs," he said. "I never said any such thing!"

TO DO: Go around the table and have everyone name something right, noble, pure, lovely, or admirable.

TO PRAY: "Lord God, turn our thoughts often to you and your nature, and help us to dwell on good thoughts and right actions."

Suggested Prayer Plan for Your Family

For each day of the month, pray that the blessing, virtue, or fruit listed by that day will be shown in your children now and in the future.

1. salvation
2. growth in grace
3. love
4. honesty and integrity
5. self-control
6. love for God's Word
7. justice
8. mercy
9. respect (for self, others, authority)
10. strong, biblical self-esteem
11. faithfulness
12. courage
13. purity
14. kindness
15. generosity
16. peace
17. joy
18. perseverance
19. humility
20. compassion
21. responsibility
22. contentment
23. faith
24. servant hearts
25. hope
26. willingness and ability to work hard
27. passion for God
28. self-discipline
29. prayerfulness
30. gratitude
31. hearts for missions

Index of Bible Readings of the Day

Index of Verses of the Day

Passing On the Truth to Our Next Generation

The Right From Wrong message, available in numerous formats, provides a blueprint for countering the culture and rebuilding the crumbling foundations of our families.

The Right from Wrong Book for Adults

Right from Wrong: What You Need to Know to Help Youth Make Right Choices
by Josh McDowell and Bob Hostetler

Our youth no longer live in a culture that teaches an objective standard of right and wrong. Truth has become a matter of taste. Morality has been replaced by individual preference. And today's youth have been affected. Fifty-seven percent of our churched youth cannot state that an objective standard of right and wrong even exists!

As the centerpiece of the Right From Wrong Campaign, this life-changing book provides you with a biblical, yet practical, blueprint for passing on core Christian values to the next generation.

Right from Wrong, Trade Paper Book
ISBN 0-8499-3604-7

The Truth Slayers Book for Youth

Truth Slayers: The Battle of Right from Wrong
by Josh McDowell and Bob Hostetler

This book, directed to youth, is written in the popular NovelPlus format. It combines the fascinating story of Brittney Marsh, Philip Milford, Jason Withers, and the consequences of their wrong choices with Josh McDowell's insights for young adults in sections called "The Inside Story."

Truth Slayers conveys the critical Right From Wrong message that challenges you to rely on God's Word as the absolute standard of truth in making right choices.

Truth Slayers, Trade Paper Book
ISBN 0-8499-3662-4

103 Questions Book for Children

103 Questions Children Ask about Right from Wrong
Introduction by Josh McDowell

"How does a person really know what is right or wrong?" "How does God decide what's wrong?" "If lying is wrong, why did God let some people in the Bible tell lies?" "What is a conscience and where does it come from?" These and 99 other questions are what kids ages 6 to 10 are asking. The 103 Questions book equips parents to answer the tough questions kids ask about right from wrong. It also provides an easy-to-understand book that a child will read and enjoy.

103 Questions, Trade Paper Book
ISBN 0-8423-4595-7

The Topsy-Turvy Kingdom Picture Book

The Topsy-Turvy Kingdom
by Dottie and Josh McDowell, with David Weiss

This fascinating story from a faraway land is written in delightful rhyme. It enables adults to teach children the importance of believing in and obeying an absolute standard of truth.

The Topsy-Turvy Kingdom, Hardcover Book for Children
ISBN 0-8423-7218-0

The Josh McDowell Family and Youth Devotionals

Josh McDowell's One Year Book of Family Devotions by Bob Hostetler
Josh McDowell's One Year Book of Youth Devotions by Bob Hostetler

These two devotionals may be used alone or together. Youth from ages 10 through 16 will enjoy the youth devotionals on their own. And they'll be able to participate in the family devotionals with their parents and siblings. Both devotionals are packed with fun-filled and inspiring readings. They will challenge you to think—and live—as "children of God without fault in a wicked and depraved generation, in which you shine like stars in the universe" (Philippians 2:15, NIV).

Josh McDowell's One Year Book of Family Devotions
ISBN 0-8423-4302-4
Josh McDowell's One Year Book of Youth Devotions
ISBN 0-8423-4301-6

Truth Matters,
Adult Video Series
ISBN 0-8499-8587-0

Setting Youth Free to Make Right
Choices, Youth Video Series
ISBN 0-8499-8585-4

Video Series for Adults and Youth

Truth Matters for You and Tomorrow's Generation Five-part Adult Video Series featuring Josh McDowell
Setting Youth Free to Make Right Choices Five-part Youth Video Series featuring Josh McDowell

These two interactive video series go beyond declaring what is right and wrong. They teach how to make right moral choices based on God's absolute standard of truth.

The adult series includes five video sessions, a comprehensive Leader's Guide with samplers from the five *Right from Wrong* workbooks, the *Right from Wrong* book, the *Truth Slayers* book, and an eight-minute promotional tape that will motivate adults to go through the series.

The youth series contains five video sessions, a Leader's Guide with reproducible handouts that include samplers from the *Right from Wrong* workbooks, and the *Truth Slayers* book.

The Right from Wrong Musicals for Youth

The Truth Works musical by Dennis and Nan Allen
The Truth Slayers musical by Steven V. Taylor and Matt Tullos

The Truth Slayers musical for junior high and high school students is based on the *Truth Slayers* book. *The Truth Works* musical for children is based on the *Truth Works* workbooks. As youth and children perform these musicals for their peers and families, they have a unique opportunity to tell of the life-changing message of Right from Wrong.

Each musical includes complete leader's instructions, a songbook of all music used, dramatic script, and accompanying soundtrack on cassette or compact disc.

Workbook for Adults

Truth Matters for You and Tomorrow's Generation
Workbook and Leader's Guide
by Josh McDowell

    The Truth Matters workbook includes 35 daily activities that help you to instill within your children and youth such biblical values as honesty, love, and sexual purity. By taking just 25 to 30 minutes each day, you will discover a fresh and effective way to teach your family how to make right choices—even in tough situations.
    The Truth Matters workbook is designed to be used in 8 adult group sessions that encourage interaction and support building. The 5 daily activities between each group meeting will help you and your family to make right choices a habit.

Truth Matters,
Member's Workbook
ISBN 0-8054-9834-6
Truth Matters, Leader's Guide
ISBN 0-8054-9833-8

Workbook for College Students

Out of the Moral Maze, Workbook with Leader's Instructions
by Josh McDowell

Students entering college face a culture that has lost its belief in absolutes. In today's society, truth is a matter of taste; morality, a matter of individual preference. *Out of the Moral Maze* will provide any truth-seeking collegiate with a sound moral guidance system based on God and his Word as the determining factor for making right moral choices.

Out of the Moral Maze
Member's Workbook and Leader's Instructions
ISBN 0-8054-9832-X

Workbook for Junior High and High School Students

Setting You Free to Make Right Choices
Workbook and Leader's Guide
by Josh McDowell

With a Bible-based emphasis, this workbook creatively and systematically teaches your students how to determine right from wrong in their everyday lives—specifically applying the decision-making process to moral questions about lying, cheating, getting even, and premarital sex.

Through 8 youth group meetings, followed each week with 5 daily exercises of 20 to 25 minutes per day, your teenagers will be challenged to develop a lifelong habit of making right moral choices.

Setting You Free to Make Right Choices,
Member's Workbook ISBN 0-8054-9828-1
Setting You Free to Make Right Choices,
Leader's Guide ISBN 0-8054-9829-X

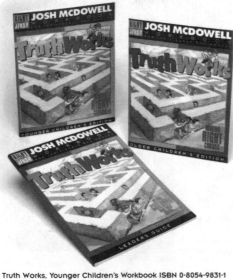

Workbooks for Children

Truth Works: Making Right Choices
Workbooks and Leader's Guide
by Josh McDowell

To pass on the truth and reclaim a generation, we must teach God's truth when our children's minds and hearts are young and pliable. Creatively developed, *Truth Works* includes two workbooks, one directed to younger children in Grades 1 to 3, the other to older children in Grades 4 to 6.

In 8 fun-filled group sessions, your children will discover why such truths as honesty, justice, love, purity, self-control, mercy, and respect work to their best interests. They see how 4 simple steps will help them to make right moral choices an everyday habit.

Truth Works, Younger Children's Workbook ISBN 0-8054-9831-1
Truth Works, Older Children's Workbook ISBN 0-8054-9830-3
Truth Works, Leader's Guide ISBN 0-8054-9827-3

Contact your Christian supplier to help you obtain these Right From Wrong resources and begin to make it right in your home, your church, and your community.